The W. B. and George Yeats Library:
A Short Title Catalog

Wayne K. Chapman

W. B. Yeats in New York City, 1920, posing with one of three volumes of *The Works of William Blake: Poetic, Symbolic, and Critical*, edited by Edwin Ellis and W. B. Yeats (1893). The volume in hand bears the printed label of the London Library, St. James Square. Source: George Grantham Bain Collection, Library of Congress.

The W. B. and George Yeats Library:
A Short Title Catalog

Undertaken at Dalkey and Dublin, Ireland, 1986-2006

Wayne K. Chapman

CLEMSON
UNIVERSITY
PRESS

© 2019 Clemson University Press
All rights reserved

Third Edition, revised

ISBN: 978-1-949979-21-3 (hardcover)
ISBN: 978-1-949979-22-0 (paper)

For information about Clemson University Press,
please visit our website at www.clemson.edu/press.

Typeset in Minion Pro by Charis Chapman.
Printed and bound in the USA by Ingram/Lightning Source.

Cover portrait: W. B. Yeats, 1920—see frontispiece
(George Grantham Bain Collection, Library of Congress)

Contents

List of Illustrations	v
Introduction	vii
List of Supplemental Works	xvi
Other Abbreviations	xvii
Works in the Collection	1
Appendices	
On the W. B. Yeats Library in 1904	274
Related Collections and Resources	279
Index	281

List of Illustrations

Figure 1. Hand-colored Sephiroth in 23. Heinrich Cornelius Agrippa von Nettesheim, *Opera* (c. 1620 or 1630)   4

Figure 2. Annotations and marginal drawings by Edwin Ellis in 211. William Blake, *The Marriage of Heaven and Hell* (1790–93), Plate 4   23

Figure 3. Drawings in pencil by J. B. Yeats on advertisement page in 305. Robert Browning, *The Poetical Works* (1865)   33

Figure 4. Frontispiece and title page of 921. J. M. Hone and M. M. Rossi, *Bishop Berkeley: His Life, Writings, and Philosophy* (1931)   98

Figure 5. Frontispiece and title page of 1157. Cesare Lombroso, *After Death—What?* (1909)   122

Figure 6. Front cover of 2048. Emanuel Swedenborg, *Angelic Wisdom Concerning the Divine Love and Concerning the Divine Wisdom* (1883)   211

Figure 7. Front cover of 2371. W. B. Yeats, *Four Plays for Dancers* (1921; Wade 130)   246

Figure 8. Front cover of 2377. W. B. Yeats, *The Green Helmet and Other Poems* (1912; Wade 101)   248

Figure 9. Front cover of 2467. W. B. Yeats, *A Vision* (1937; Wade 191)   263

Figure 10. Front cover of 2473. W. B. Yeats, *Where There Is Nothing* (1902; Wade 42)   264

Figure 11. A partial view of the poetry section of the library in 1997, in the home of Anne Yeats, "Avalon," Dalkey, Ireland   272

Figure 12. Yeats and his books, Woburn Buildings, London, from *The Tatler*, no. 157 (29 June 1904)   274

Introduction

This catalog of bibliographic citations accounts for every publication identified as part of the W. B. Yeats Library, which, since the death of Anne Yeats in 2001, has become a distinct part of the National Library of Ireland (NLI). In effect, the alphabetical list constitutes a census of the items that define the Yeats Library as a body, not counting publications that were sold or otherwise dispersed by the poet or his wife, George Yeats, in their lifetimes, or by members of their family up to 1971, when the late Glenn O'Malley of Arizona State University made an inventory that became the foundation for SUNY Professor Edward O'Shea's *A Descriptive Catalog of the W. B. Yeats Library*, Volume 470 of the Garland Reference Library of the Humanities (New York: Garland Publishing, 1985). Although that volume is difficult to locate today beyond the libraries that acquired copies before the book went out of print, it was the decision of the NLI to maintain O'Shea's alphabetical arrangement and numbering system instead of the subject order used by Yeats and his wife and as reconstructed in the shelving arrangements that Anne Yeats and Yeats scholars found to be convenient when the library occupied her study at "Avalon," Dalkey, Co. Dublin.[1] (See Figure 11, p. 272, below.) As I've said elsewhere, most of the books at that time, "save those of W. B. Yeats and oversized, multivolume sets such as the three Cambridge history series (ancient, medieval, and modern periods)," were "in one room although at no time when Yeats was alive did he have a 'library' as such. The books he owned were distributed throughout his various residences in Dublin. Anne Yeats shelved her library from floor to ceiling and arranged the collection by row (or column) according to subjects her father and mother used when filling available space about their homes with the volumes of a 'working library'" (*ibid.*). There were 14 rows of shelves in Anne's library, the first two (immediately around the left doorjamb going in) contained her mother's books, which were generally not included in the O'Shea bibliography although many other books belonging to her were distributed about the library according to subject. O'Shea writes in his "Introduction" that the decision was his to depart from "the unique organization of Yeats's library as Anne Yeats remember[ed] it was arranged in his lifetime and as it has been reconstituted by Glenn O'Malley according to broad subject categories: poetry; drama; religion and myth; history; classical literatures; fiction; philosophy; theosophy, magic, astrology; Irish materials; and art (including Blake)" (xv–xvi).

The decision to depart from the Yeatses' subject order and its many inconsistencies was probably the right one from the standpoint of the printed volume in the Garland Reference Library, given the introduction of a subject index and an "Index of Autographs (Including Owners, Presenters, and Annotators, but not WBY)." In the online edition of the *Short-title Catalog*, first published in 2006 and still available on an open-access basis, an index was and is not necessary because the technology allows that contents (in PDF and HTML) are fully searchable in either format. After renovation of the Clemson University website in 2017, the *Short-title Catalog* was reissued only in PDF without embedded hyperlinks, which had been made obsolete by coding changes in the platform. In any case, O'Shea's autograph index was more a service to the descriptions given to annotated items in his bibliography than to either of my online editions. However, the new print edition of the *Short-title Catalog* is necessarily indexed by author and subject to assist readers. To cite yet another distinction, O'Shea's numbering system emulates the procedures of Allan Wade's *A Bibliography of the Writings of W. B. Yeats* (3rd edition, 1968), which, unfortunately, considering the system's incapacity to account for lost as well as recovered items, is a weakness of the O'Shea numbering system that the NLI uses to catalogue this collection. Consequently, the *Short-title Catalog* has had to adapt the system while assigning unique numbers for all volumes currently present in the NLI collection.

As the *Report of the Council of Trustees of the National Library of Ireland 2002* states (pp. 56–59), the Garland book describes only "for the main part" the contents of the Yeats Library. When unpacking the

82 crates that the NLI received in June 2002, "it became evident," as Assistant Keeper Gerard Long writes, "that the collection, as received, did not fully match the O'Shea catalogue; some items listed by O'Shea were not present, and, by way of compensation, some items were present which are not listed in the published catalogue." Some of the compensating additions came about when the NLI incorporated the two rows of George Yeats's personal copies that had been isolated in Anne Yeats's library. In part of its online conspectus, the NLI rightly calls the entire acquisition "The Library of W. B. Yeats and George Yeats" (see below). Many of the other additions to *YL* (as O'Shea's catalogue is frequently abbreviated) are noted in my work for *Yeats Annual*, particularly "Additional Books in the Library, 1989, and Other Problems," Part II of the illustrated piece "Notes on the Yeats Library, 1904 and 1989."[2] (See the first appendix, below, and Figure 12.) Without systematically checking every volume in the library, Anne Yeats and I recovered 20 titles not listed in *YL* and probably missed by O'Malley in his 1971 inventory. Anne and I were not counting her mother's books in rows 1–2. There were "also various Bibles, missals, and apocrypha" as well as (in Anne's words) "the hospital shelf," which carried partial and damaged works and ephemera, as well as a small shelf over the hall entry way laden with books associated with childhood—an old copy of *A Day in a Child's Life*, illustrated by Kate Greenway, for example. It took some time to determine that this book, like two others that I had reported as "Other Problems," was actually listed in *YL* but misattributed, necessitating some movement of *YL* items in relation to the NLI materials in the present collation.

Hence, the 2,492 entries in *YL* have now received a long overdue, systematic review and have been reconciled with the NLI's inventory of the Yeats family's 2002 Heritage Donation. In make-shift fashion, the NLI assigned shelf numbers beyond those found in *YL* (starting with the number 3001) for "Books in the Yeats Library [published during Yeats's lifetime] but not in the O'Shea *Catalog*." Some 86 such entries were introduced in this way, and they are listed below as NLI 3001–3075, with letters annexed to numbers to indicate duplicates.

The same procedure has been followed in re-numbering *only* those items confirmed in the NLI collections since the acquisition of 2002. If an item is missing, it has received an "x" in place of a number. *The W. B. and George Yeats Library: A Short-title Catalog* is thus intended to help scholars determine what materials they may need to see without having to locate a copy of *YL*. My collation incorporates notes on relevant addenda, errata, and missing items, as well as inserted and other associated matter. Library administration once entertained the possibility that, in the future, a scanned copy of *YL* might be linked to the NLI website, thus solving the problem of its unavailability but not the problem of collating it against the Yeats Library's actual stock, although that solution seems increasingly unlikely with every passing year.

To illustrate the problem, one might cite an extensive set of photocopies made after 1972 by Roger Nyle Parisious and Anne Yeats when she set about the task of putting her parents' library in order. Classified today as "Manuscript Material from the Library of W. B. Yeats and George Yeats / Photocopies of annotations, markings, bookmarks etc. made in publications; catalogues and lists; prints" (MSS 40,568–40,597 / Accession No. 6194), these backup copies are valuable to fill in some of the gaps. Referred to in the *Short-title Catalog*, in a separate set of brackets after the *YL* number is given (if applicable), I provide a manuscript and folder number thus: "NLI 40,568/17" (for example)—followed by the number of sheets in the folder as well as the NLI envelope number. As a frequent user of the library before it came to the National Library, I can advise here that bookmarks laid into some of the volumes are not by Yeats.[3] Still, that caveat aside, it is good to have available all of those photocopies. Certainly of service to one laboring at descriptive bibliography, the *Short-title Catalog* was created as a necessary first step toward a longer work in progress on Yeats's annotations, with the approval of the W. B. Yeats Estate, Michael Yeats and A. P. Watt Ltd. This comprehensive book of annotations, tentatively called *"Something that I read in a book": A Volume of Annotations by W. B. Yeats as Compiled from His Books in the National Library of Ireland*, is a work in progress that has propagated Shorter Notes for

Yeats Annual, exhibits for my introduction to an online edition of the Ellis-Yeats *Works of William Blake*, and materials reproduced in W. B. Yeats, *Rewriting* The Hour-Glass: *A Play Written in Prose and Verse Versions* (2016). Under the circumstances, incorporating notes on the NLI's photocopied materials and their extent seems entirely appropriate for the present aid, especially for the printed, library edition.

Parallel matter not specifically noted here, although reflected in the asterisks ("*") that O'Shea placed beside some of his numbers, is the card catalogue that someone (neither Yeats nor his wife) compiled in the 1920s in anticipation of moving or traveling.[4] The books listed in the card file that are also listed in *YL* receive the asterisk. Out of the 1,159 entries, O'Shea reported 521 missing (the NLI gives the number as "some 300") and published the list of AWOL items shortly after the appearance of *YL*.[5] Incorporating all of George Yeats's books with the collection into one Yeats library seems to have been one way to amend the early bookkeeping on its contents at that time. Apart from good luck, there are few means of learning where the other missing books from that era have gone. O'Shea writes: "Anne Yeats speculates that whole cartons of books may have been lost in frequent removals. Other items were lent out by the poet, a largesse that Mrs Yeats discouraged but apparently never stopped completely" (*ibid.*, p. 279). Looking for patterns in the list of books O'Shea did not locate by comparing O'Malley's foundational list against the 1920s card file, O'Shea supposed "certain kinds of books may have been intentionally 'weeded out'": for example, popular novels (despite Yeats's penchant for detective and cowboy fiction, as Anne Yeats reported), various occult writings, and "faded enthusiasms" such as Wordsworth, Katharine Tynan Hinkson, and G. R. S. Mead. One of the Meads that I reported finding in the library in 1989, *Orpheus* (London: Theosophical Publishing Society, 1896), had been returned by Kathleen Raine in September 1975, after finding it in John Watkins' Bookshop. I also reported as many as six volumes of poetry by Laurence Binyon that were *not* missing from the library as faded enthusiasms but sitting precisely where they were supposed to be by subject.

A poet's working library, like almost anyone's, is subject to change. In times of need, Yeats himself is known to have thinned his collection by selling copies of books he thought no longer necessary to have around. A "List of Books Sold to [the] National Literary Society, London, 9 Jan. 1894" (NLI 30,684) is a case in point, a receipt from James Duffy & Co. Ltd., Publishers, Printers, Bookbinders and Booksellers, recording the exact shillings and pence the young poet made by parting with some 46 books, fewer than half of which were of Irish interest. Editions of poets such as Gerald Griffins, Clarence Mangan, and Thomas Moore; speeches and political tractates by Grattan, Burke, and Swift; histories and anthologies such as *Patriot Parliament, Concise History of Ireland,* Gardiner's *History of England, Songs of Ireland, A Book of Irish Ballads, Young Ireland, Lays of the Western Gael,* and Yeats's own *Irish Fairy and Folk Tales* were only slightly outnumbered by "classic" works such as Dante in translation, Pope's translations of Homer's *The Iliad* and *The Odyssey*, Dryden's *Virgil*, Plutarch's *Lives*, a Globe Shakespeare, Bacon's *Essays*, Macauley's *Essays*, a 2-volume Walter Scott besides Thoreau's *Walden*, the novels *Ivanhoe, King Arthur, Robinson Crusoe, David Copperfield*, and selections from the poems of Wordsworth and Robert Browning. These books were all disposed of well before the Yeats library inventories of c. 1920 and 1971.

Every now and again, something appears that will have once been a part of the W. B. and George Yeats library. Ronald Schuchard ran across the listing of item "[58]" in a Maggs Bros. Ltd. sale catalogue (Cat. 1122), about a copy of *The Pre-Raphaelite Movement* (London: Reeves & Turner; Birmingham: William Downing, 1889) by [W.] Kineton Parkes. As a presentation copy to Yeats, the book drew this comment from the auctioneer: "Books from Yeats' library are rarely seen on the market and the bulk is believed to remain with his family." (I do not have a date on the catalogue.) Acquisitions at Emory University and elsewhere have occurred through the Yeats family over the years. The annotated copy of *Responsibilities* (Cuala Press, 1914) studied in an issue of *The South Carolina Review* is an instance (see Shelley Sharp Dirst on revisions to *The Hour-Glass* and Yeats's jottings on the dance sequence of *At the Hawk's Well*; *SCR* 36.2 [Spring 2004]: 120–34). And even more to the point, in 1993, I reported in a special issue of *Yeats Annual*, called *Yeats and Women* (No. 9, ed. Deirdre Toomey), the addition of 31 books to the Yeats Collection at the University of Kansas (Spencer Library) obtained in one of two major purchases from P. S. O'Hegarty. These books, of course, have not been listed in the *Short-title Catalog*, but they include, among others, 9 by Yeats, 2 more by Mead, and an exceedingly rare copy of the Edwin Ellis/W. B. Yeats edition of Blake's *Works* carrying (in volume 1) a letter of inscription from Yeats to Maud Gonne and notations by O'Hegarty on marginalia in the hand of Ellis. How O'Hegarty, the father of Graínne Yeats, came into possession of these books was explained in detail in an article that James Helyar and I published in 1993.[6] A book collector by avocation, O'Hegarty was practically a neighbor of the Yeatses when they lived in Rathfarnam. Books, for instance, that J. B. Yeats had decorated with drawings also came into O'Hegarty's possession by keeping "alert to rummaging through the stock of used books at Hodges Figgis and Greene's *precisely* when Mrs Yeats set about weeding the libraries of her sisters-in-law, and her own, in 1940 and 1949." The NLI has issued separate lists regarding *YL* "Numbered" and "Unnumbered" inserts and books listed in *YL* "but not received with the Yeats Library." Most of the books in List 1 were clean duplicate copies—certainly in the case of the 70 or so by W. B. Yeats—or of interest to the family, it seems (e.g., *YL* 2313, Susan Mary Yeats's *The Order of the Burial of the Dead* [London, nd], and essays by J. B. Yeats and obituaries, all duplicates [*YL* 704a, 705a, 706a, 707a, 708c]; but the missing inserts, unless photocopied by Parisious and therefore backed up in NLI 40,568–40,597, are unfortunately lost). The NLI Appendices, as well as the entire online conspectus pieced around the out-of-print *YL*, are cited as aids to *The Short-title Catalog*, in the second appendix, entitled "Related Collections and Online Resources."

In sum, information from several parts of the National Library of Ireland's online database on the Yeats Library has been sorted and incorporated, where appropriate, in *The Short-title Catalog*, including my own observations about lost and found items. I believe I have taken up generally, in this Preface, all materials in the NLI database, except for "Correspondence" and "Post 1941 publications received as part of the Yeats Library," which are outside the objective of the catalog but interesting to view as a testament to the industry of Yeats scholarship and criticism over a sixty-year period. In his "Editorial Miscellany" for *Yeats Annual* No. 4 (1986), Warwick Gould made one lengthy correction to a conjectural reading of George Yeats's inscription in *YL* 1649, regarding that correction to be a "modest contribution to the sort of work Professor O'Shea's standard work will now inaugurate" (269). My own response to *YL* has been more frequent and more extensive, but I hope no less polite. Professors O'Malley and O'Shea and their assistants, Mary Jo O'Shea and Professor Christina Hunt Mahony among others who came before I began to work in the Yeats Library in Dalkey, in 1986, have provided a valuable service by generally outlining the intellectual habitat of a great writer. Obviously, much more needs to be done—for instance, to bring this work to completion in a Marginalia, or book of annotations, to describe only Yeats's reading notes, significant inscriptions, drafts of poems, and copy text volumes in the library without having to make an account of the library as a whole. I must thank Catherine Fahy (NLI Keeper—Special Programmes) for locating scores of Cuala Press volumes that are linked as a supplement to the *Short-title Catalog* on the Clemson University Press website at the address given in the list of "Related Collections and Online Resources" at the end of this edition. Similarly, I'd be pleased to hear from anyone with information on books that may have a W. B. Yeats provenance—especially marked copies—and subsequently were dispersed by booksellers, auctioners, or private parties to libraries and collections accessible to scholars. I may be reached by email at cwayne@clemson.edu.

Acknowledgments

Finally, I am grateful to Clemson University for enabling this monograph with a sabbatical from teaching during spring semester 2006, to my family and my colleagues in the English Department and in the College of Architecture, Arts and Humanities, and to my daughter, Charis Chapman, who assisted in the production and indexing of this new (and revised) print edition of *The W. B. and George Yeats Library: A Short-title Catalog*. This book is also indebted to several resources that were helpful in verifying titles and publication data. Chief among those on the internet are COPAC (a free service providing access to the combined online catalogs of 24 major British and Irish university libraries, including the British Library and that of Trinity College, Dublin) and WorldCat (which provides subscription-based access, through Clemson University Libraries, to the combined catalogs of thousands of libraries from all over the world). Google and Project Gutenberg also proved useful on occasion. I am extremely grateful for the generosity of Michael and Anne Yeats, Yeats's literary agent A. P. Watt Ltd. (now United Agents LLP), especially for the assistance of Linda Shaughnessy (ret.). And thanks, as ever, too, to the dedicated staff of the National Library of Ireland, and to John Morgenstern and Alison Mero at Clemson University Press.

Wayne K. Chapman
Dublin, June 2006; Portland (Oregon), March 2019

Notes to the Introduction

1. On Anne Yeats's shelf order and the subject arrangement, see Wayne K. Chapman, "W. B. and George Yeats: The Writing, Editing, and Dating of Yeats's Poems of the Mid-1920s and 1930s with a Chronology of the Composition of the Poems," *Yeats's Collaborations: Yeats Annual No. 15: A Special Number*, ed. Wayne K. Chapman and Warwick Gould (London: Palgrave Macmillan, 2002), note 12.
2. *Yeats Annual* No. 8, ed. Warwick Gould (London: Macmillan Press, 1991): 199–202 and Plate 5.

3. See Wayne K. Chapman, "A Descriptive Catalog of W. B. Yeats's Library: Notes Supplementary," *Yeats Annual* No. 6, ed. Warwick Gould (London: Macmillan Press, 1988): 237.
4. The card file was probably made for the same reason inventories of manuscripts were made for steel "Drawer II of file" and "Drawer No. III of file," which were locked in a room "the key to be left with Mr Keller during the absence of Mr W. B. Yeats abroad." Yeats lectured in America and took his wife with him in 1920 and 1932. Mr Keller was their solicitor. See the article cited in note 1 above.
5. Edward O'Shea, "The 1920s Catalogue of W. B. Yeats's Library," *Yeats Annual* No. 4 (1986): 279–90. O'Shea notes that the card file "(excluding some of Mrs Yeats's books)" reflects the state of the Yeats library "as it existed in the year 1920 or shortly thereafter."
6. Wayne K. Chapman and James Helyar, "P. S. O'Hegarty and the Yeats Collection at the University of Kansas," *Yeats Annual* No. 10, ed. Warwick Gould (London: Macmillan Press, 1993): 221–38. This account is recommended as its authority derives from members of the Yeats and O'Hegarty families, who were interviewed and who generously contributed images featured in the illustrative plates accompanying the article.

List of Supplemental Works, Cited in the *Catalog* as "Chapman, YA…"
(followed by corresponding issue number, date, and pages)

Chapman, Wayne K. "Authors in Eternity: Some Sources for W. B. Yeats's Creative Mysticism." *Yeats's Collaborations: Yeats Annual No. 15: A Special Number*. Ed. Wayne K. Chapman and Warwick Gould. London: Palgrave Macmillan, 2002. 288–312.

———. "A Descriptive Catalog of W. B. Yeats's Library: Notes Supplementary." *Yeats Annual* No. 6. Ed. Warwick Gould. London: Macmillan Press, 1988. 234–45.

———. "George Yeats, *The Countess Cathleen* and P. S. O'Hegarty: Notes from the Libraries." *Yeats and Women: Yeats Annual* No. 9. Ed. Deirdre Toomey. London: Macmillan Press, 1992. 271–94.

———. "Notes on the Yeats Library, 1904 and 1989." *Yeats Annual* No. 8. Ed. Warwick Gould. London: Macmillan Press, 1991. 199–202 + plate 5. See Appendices, below, "On the W. B. Yeats Library in 1904.

Other Abbreviations

Bp	=	Bookplate(s)
GY	=	George Yeats (Mrs W. B. Yeats)
NLI	=	National Library of Ireland; also the NLI's MS. 3001+ series denoting materials not in *YL*
Wade	=	Allan Wade, *A Bibliography of the Writings of W. B. Yeats*, 3rd ed., rev. Russell K. Alspach (London, 1968)
WBY	=	W. B. Yeats
YA	=	*Yeats Annual*
YL	=	Edward O'Shea, *A Descriptive Catalog of the W. B. Yeats Library* (New York, 1985)

Works in the Collection

1.   [*YL* 1].
A., OE. *The Hazel Wand*. London: Grant Richards, 1925.

2.   [*YL* 2].
The Abbey Row. Not Edited by W. B. Yeats. [By P. L. Dickinson. With a cover and portraits of J. M. Synge and W. B. Yeats by R. C. Orpen and other illustrations by Sir William Orpen and the author]. Dublin: Maunsel, 1907.

3.   [*YL* 3].
[Abbey Theatre program], 23 February 1907. Lady Gregory's *The White Cockade* and *The Jackdaw*.

3a–d.   [*YL* 3a–d].
Four more copies inserted in *YL* 58a–d.

4.   [Not listed in *YL* and assigned NLI Number 3001].
[Abbey Theatre program]. *Abbey Theatre Special Programme. | British Association Visit | September 1908*. Dublin, 1908.

5.   [*YL* 4].
[Abbey Theatre program], 27 December 1925. Twenty-first anniversary performance.

5a–f.   [*YL* 4a–g]. [NLI missing one copy].
Seven more copies, of which five remain.

6.   [*YL* 5].
[Abbey Theatre program], 17 November 1930. First production of Yeats's *The Words Upon the Window Pane*.

x   [*YL* 6]. [NLI missing this copy].
[Abbey Theatre program], 25 June 1931. For the bicentenary of the Royal Dublin Society.

x   [*YL* 6a–g]. [NLI missing all copies].
Seven more copies.

x   [*YL* 7]. [NLI missing this copy].
[Abbey Theatre program], 10 August 1938. On first performance of Yeats's *Purgatory*.

x   [*YL* 8]. [NLI missing this copy].
[Abbey Theatre Dramatic Festival Souvenir], 6–20 August 1938.

7.   [*YL* 9].
Abdul-Ali, Sijil. "An Interpretation of Alchemy in Relation to Modern Scientific Thought." *The Journal of the Alchemical Society* 1 (March 1913): 34–48.

8.   [*YL* *10].
Abercrombie, Lascelles. *Mary and the Bramble*. Much Marcle, Herefordshire: Published by the Author, 1910.

9.   [*YL* 11].
——. *The Poems of Lascelles Abercrombie*. London: Oxford University Press, 1930.

10.   [*YL* 12].
Abercrombie, Patrick, Sydney Kelly, and Arthur Kelly. *Dublin of the Future*. London: Hodder and Stoughton, [1923].

11.   [*YL* 13].
The Acorn: An Illustrated Quarterly Magazine Devoted to Literature and Art 1 (Oct. 1905). London: Caradoc Press, 1905. Bp: GY

12.   [*YL* 14].
Acton, Lord [John Emerich Edward Dalberg]. *The Cambridge Modern History*. Ed. A. W. Ward, etc. 13 vols. Cambridge: The University Press, 1902–11.

13.   [Erroneously listed, under editors A. W. Ward et al., as *YL* 2225]. [See Chapman, *YA* 8 (1991): 201–202. The atlas stood beside the 13-vol. set (*YL* 14) when the library was in Anne Yeats's home in Dalkey].
——. *The Cambridge Modern History Atlas*. Ed. A. W. Ward et al. 2nd ed. Cambridge: University Press, 1924.

14.   [*YL* 15].
Adam, C. G. M. *Fresh Sidelights on Astrology*. London: Modern Astrology Office, 1916. Bp: WBY

15.   [*YL* 16].
Adams, Henry. *The Degradation of the Democratic Dogma*. New York: Macmillan, 1920. Bp: WBY

16.   [*YL* 17]. [Inserted review of *The Decline of the West*, see 688].
——. *The Education of Henry Adams: An Autobiography*. Boston: Houghton Mifflin, 1918. Bp: WBY

17.   [*YL* 18].
——. *The Education of Henry Adams: An Autobiography*. London: Constable, 1928.

18.   [*YL* 19].
——. *Mont-Saint-Michel and Chartres*. Boston: Houghton Mifflin, 1913. Bp: WBY

19.   [*YL* *20].
Adams, Morley. *In the Footsteps of Borrow and Fitzgerald*. London: Jarrold, [1914]. Bp: WBY

20.   [*YL* 21]. [NLI 40,568/1; 2 sheets; envelope 477].
Aeschylus. *The Agamemnon of Aeschylus*. Trans. Louis MacNeice. London: Faber and Faber. 1936.

21.   [*YL* 22].
Aeschylus. *The House of Atreus: Being the Agamemnon, Libation-bearers and Furies*. Trans. E. D. A. Morshead. London: Macmillan, 1901.

22.   [*YL* 23].
Agnelli, Giuseppe. *Ferrara e Pomposa*. Bergamo: Instituto Italiano d'Arti Grafiche, 1906. [Illustrated].

23.   [*YL* 24]. [NLI 40,568/2; 69 sheets; envelope 1234].
Agrippa von Nettesheim, Heinrich Cornelius. *Opera....* 2 vols. Lugduni: Per Beringos Fratres, n.d. [According to the Houghton Library, Harvard University, the publisher is actually Eberhard Zetner of Strasbourg, and the date should be 1620 or 1630]. [Only one volume].

24.   [*YL* *25]. [NLI 40,568/3; 16 sheets; envelope 1236].
Aksakoff, Alexandre. *Animisme et spiritisme: Essai d'un examen critique des phénomè mediumniques*. Trans. from Russian by Berthold Sandow. 5th ed. Paris: Librairie des Sciences Psychiques, 1906. Signed: WBY

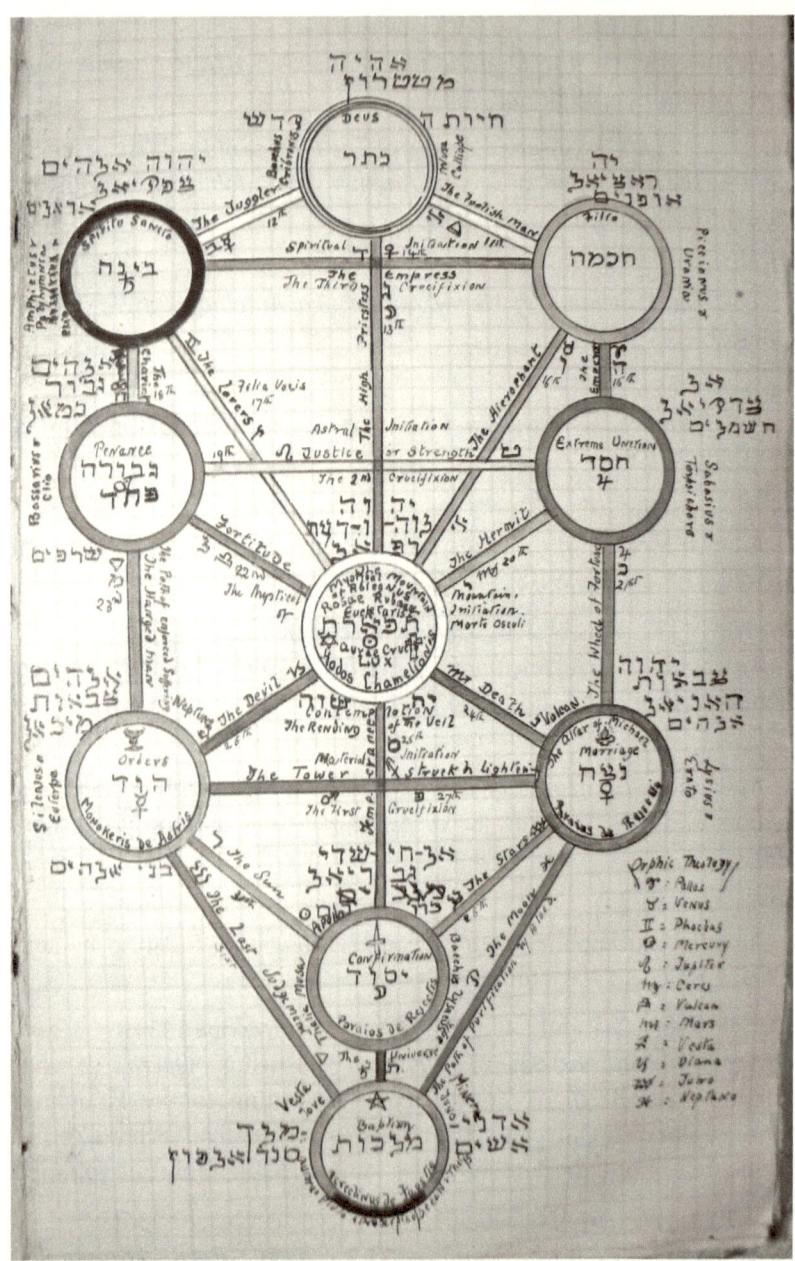

Figure 1. Hand-colored Sephiroth in 23. Heinrich Cornelius Agrippa von Nettesheim, *Opera* (c. 1620 or 1630)

25. [*YL* 26].
Aksakoff, Serghei. *A Russian Gentleman*. Trans. from Russian by J. D. Duff. Oxford: Oxford University Press, 1934.

26. [*YL* 27].
———. *A Russian Schoolboy*. Trans. from Russian by J. D. Duff. Oxford: Oxford University Press, 1924.

27. [*YL* 28].
Aldington, Richard. *Images, 1910–1915*. London: The Poetry Bookshop, [1915].

28. [*YL* 29].
———, trans. *Medallions from Anyte of Tegea, Meleager of Gadara, the Anacreontea, Latin Poets of the Renaissance*. London: Chatto and Windus, 1930.

29. [*YL* 30].
[Alfieri, Dino and Luigi Freddi]. *Exhibition of the Fascist Revolution: First Decennial of the March on Rome* [Mostra della rivoluzione fascista]. Rome: National Fascist Party, 1933. [Illustrated].

30. [*YL* 31].
Aliotta, Prof. Antonio. *The Idealistic Reaction Against Science*. Trans. Agnes McCaskill. London: Macmillan, 1914.

31. [*YL* *32].
Allingham, Hugh. *Captain Cuellar's Adventures in Connacht and Ulster, A.D. 1588*. London: Elliot Stock, 1897.

32. [*YL* *33].
Allingham, William. *Evil May-Day*. London: Longmans, [1883].

33. [*YL* *34].
———. *Flower Pieces*. London: Longmans, Green, 1893.

34. [*YL* *35].
———. *Life and Phantasy*. London: Reeves and Turner, 1889.

35. [*YL* *36].
———. *Thought and Word, and Ashby Manor, a Play in Two Acts*. London: Reeves and Turner, 1890.

36.   [*YL* 37].
[Alt, Phyllis Innocent]. *Rapallo Past and Present*. 6th ed. Milan: Modernissima, 1926. [Illustrated].

37.   [*YL* 38].
[Altdorfer, Albrecht]. *Albrecht Altdorfer*. Introduction by T. Sturge Moore. London: At the Sign of the Unicorn, 1902. [Illustrated].

38.   [*YL* 39].
Anderson, Maxwell. *Winterset*. Washington: Anderson House, 1935.

39.   [*YL* 40]. [NLI 40,568/4; 6 sheets; envelope 1389].
The Annals of Psychical Science: A Monthly Journal Devoted to Critical and Experimental Research in the Phenomena of Spiritism 2 (July–December 1905).

40.   [*YL* 41].
—— 3 (January–June 1906).

41.   [*YL* 42].
—— 4 (July–December 1906).

42.   [*YL* 43]. [NLI 40,568/5; 17 sheets; envelope 1392].
—— 5 (January–June 1907).

43.   [*YL* 44].
—— 6 (July–December 1907).

44.   [*YL* 45]. [NLI 40,568/6; 11 sheets; envelope 1394].
—— 7 (January–December 1908).

45.   [*YL* 46].
—— 8 (January–March 1909).

46.   [Not listed in *YL* and assigned NLI Number 3002].
Apocrypha. [Lacks publication details]. On fly leaf: "Sir J. Slater [?] | July 19 1781[?].

47.   [*YL* 47].
Apuleius. *The Golden Asse of Lucius Apuleius*. Trans. William Adlington. 1566. Reprint. London: Simpkin, Marshall, Hamilton, Kent, [1925].

48.   [*YL* *48].
Archer, William, ed. *Eminent Actors*. 3 vols. in 1. London: Kegan Paul, Trench, Trubner, 1890–91. Vol. 1: *William Charles MacReady*, by

William Archer; Vol. 2: *Thomas Betterton*, by Robert W. Lowe; Vol. 3: *Charles Macklin*, by Edward Abbott Parry.

49.   [*YL* 49].
Ardill, Rev. John Roche. *St. Patrick*. London: John Murray; Dublin: Hodges, Figgis, [1931].

50.   [*YL* 50].
Aristophanes. *Lysistrata*. Trans. Jack Lindsay. Illustrations by Norman Lindsay. London: Fanfrolico Press, 1926.

51.   [*YL* *51].
Armitage, Ella S[ophia]. *The Early Norman Castles of the British Isles*. With plans by D. H. Montgomerie. London: John Murray, 1912. Bp: WBY.

52.   [*YL* 52].
Arnold, Matthew. *Letters of Matthew Arnold, 1848–1888*. Ed. George W. E. Russell. 2 vols. London: Macmillan, 1895.

53.   [*YL* 53].
———. *On Translating Homer*. London: Longman, Green, Longman, and Roberts, 1862.

54.   [*YL* 54].
———. *Poetical Works*. London: Macmillan, 1892. Signed: WBY

55.   [*YL* 55]. [NLI 40,568/7; 9 sheets; envelope 1560].
———. *The Study of Celtic Literature*. London: Smith, Elder, 1891.

56.   [*YL* 56].
The Arrow, Ed. W. B. Yeats, 1 (20 October 1906).

57.   [*YL* 57].
——— 2 (24 November 1906).

57a.   [*YL* 57a].
Another copy.

58.   [*YL* 58].
——— 3 (23 February 1907).

58a–d.   [*YL* 58a–f]. [Inserted Abbey Theatre Programs in two copies; NLI missing two copies].
Six other copies, of which four remain.

59.   [*YL* 59].
—— 5 (25 August 1909).

60.   [*YL* 60].
The Arts (Brooklyn, NY). Ed. Hamilton Easter Field, (May 1921).

61.   [*YL* 61].
Ashton, Leigh. *An Introduction to the Study of Chinese Sculpture.* London: Ernest Benn, 1924. [Illustrated]. Bp: WBY

62.   [*YL* 62]. [Inserted in *YL* 2441a].
[*Athenaeum*]. Review of *A Book of Irish Verse* (1895) ed. W. B. Yeats, [6 Apr. 1895]: 434–35.

63.   [*YL* *63].
Atlas of Ancient and Classical Geography. London: J. M. Dent, 1910. [With maps].

64.   [*YL* 64].
Auden, W[ystan]. H[ugh]. *Look, Stranger!* London: Faber and Faber, 1936.

65.   [*YL* 65].
——. *The Orators.* London: Faber and Faber, 1932.

66.   [*YL* 66].
——. *Poems.* 2nd ed. London: Faber and Faber, 1933.

67.   [*YL* 67].
—— and Christopher Isherwood. *The Dog Beneath the Skin.* London: Faber and Faber, 1935. Signed: WBY.

68.   [*YL* *68]. [NLI 40,568/8; 3 sheets; envelope 1485].
Augustine, Saint. *The Confessions.* Ed. Arthur Symons. London: Walter Scott, [1898].

69.   [*YL* 69].
Austen, Jane. *The Novels of Jane Austen.* 2nd ed. Ed. R. W. Chapman. Vol. 2: *Pride and Prejudice.* Oxford: Clarendon Press, 1926.

70.   [*YL* 70].
Author's and Writer's Who's Who. Ed. Edward Martell. London: Shaw Publishing, 1934.

71.   [*YL 71*].
Aventinus, Johannes. *Des hochgelehrten weit berümbten beyerischen Geschichtschreibers Chronik...*[Bavarian Chronicle]. Frankfurt am Mann: Ben Georg Raben [et al.], 1566. Bp: GY

72.   [*YL 72*].
Baedeker, Karl. *Italy from the Alps to Naples*. 3rd ed. rev. Leipzig: Karl Baedeker, 1928. [With maps and figures].

73.   [*YL 73*]. [NLI 40,568/9; 10 sheets; envelope 1485].
——. *Southern Italy and Sicily*. With excursions to Sardinia, Malta, and Corfu. 16th ed. rev. Leipzig: Karl Baedeker, 1912. [With maps and figures].

74.   [*YL 74*].
Ball, F[rancis]. Elrington. *Swift's Verse*. London: John Murray, 1929.

75.   [*YL 75*].
Ballantyne, R[obert]. M[ichael]. *Man on the Ocean. A Book about Boats and Ships. A Book for Boys*. London: T. Nelson and Sons, 1874.

76.   [*YL 76*].
Balzac, Honoré de. *Comédie humaine*. Temple ed. Ed. George Saintsbury. 40 vols. New York: Macmillan, 1901. Vol. 1: *About Catherine de Medici*. Trans. Clara Bell. Bp: WBY

77.   [*YL 77*].
——. Vol. 2: *At the Sign of the Cat and Racket*. Trans. Clara Bell.

78.   [*YL 78*].
——. Vol. 3: *The Atheist's Mass*. Trans. Clara Bell. Bp: WBY

79.   [*YL 79*].
——. Vol. 4: *A Bachelor's Establishment*. Trans. Clara Bell. Bp: WBY

80.   [*YL 80*].
——. Vol. 5: *Beatrix*. Trans. James Waring. Bp: WBY

81.   [*YL 81*]. [NLI 40,568/9/A; 3 sheets; envelope 1121].
——. Vol. 6: *The Chouans*. Trans. Ellen Marriage. Bp: WBY

82.   [*YL 82*].
——. Vol. 8 [vol. 7 is missing]: *The Country Parson*. Trans. Ellen Marriage. Bp: WBY

83. [*YL* 83].
——. Vol. 9: *Cousin Betty*. Trans. James Waring. Bp: WBY

84. [*YL* 84].
——. Vol. 10: *Cousin Pons*. Trans. Ellen Marriage. Bp: WBY

85. [*YL* 85].
——. Vol. 11: *A Daughter of Eve and Letters of Two Brides*. Trans. R. S. Scott. Bp: WBY

86. [*YL* 86].
——. Vol. 12: *A Distinguished Provincial at Paris*. Trans. Ellen Marriage. Bp: WBY

87. [*YL* 87].
——. Vol. 13: *Eugene Grandet*. Trans. Ellen Marrriage. Bp: WBY

88. [*YL* 88].
——. Vol. 14: *A Father's Curse*. Trans. James Waring. Bp: WBY

89. [*YL* 89].
——. Vol. 15. *A Gondreville Mystery*. Trans. Ellen Marriage. Bp: WBY

90. [*YL* 90].
——. Vols. 17, 18 [vol. 16 is missing]: *A Harlot's Progress*. Trans. James Waring. Bp: WBY

91. [*YL* 91].
——. Vol. 19: *The Jealousies of a Country Town*. Trans. Ellen Marriage. Bp:WBY

92. [*YL* 92].
——. Vol. 20: *The Lily of the Valley*. Trans. James Waring. Bp: WBY

93. [*YL* 93].
——. Vol. 21: *Lost Illusions*. Trans. Ellen Marriage. Bp: WBY

94. [*YL* 94].
——. Vol. 22: *A Marriage Settlement*. Trans. Clara Bell. Bp: WBY

95. [*YL* 95].
——. Vol. 23: *The Member for Arcis*. Trans. Clara Bell. Bp: WBY

96. [*YL* 96].
——. Vol. 24: *The Middle Classes*. Trans. Clara Bell. Bp: WBY

97. [*YL 97*].
———. Vol. 25: *Modeste Mignon*. Trans. Clara Bell. Bp: WBY

98. [*YL 98*].
———. Vol. 26: *Old Goriot*. Trans. Ellen Marriage. Bp: WBY

99. [*YL 99*].
———. Vol. 27: *Parisians in the Country*. Trans. James Waring. Bp: WBY

100. [*YL 100*].
———. Vol. 28: *The Peasantry*. Trans. Ellen Marriage. Bp: WBY

101. [*YL 101*].
———. Vol. 29: *Pierette and the Abbe Birotteau*. Trans. Clara Bell. Bp: WBY

102. [*YL 102*].
———. Vol. 30: *A Princess's Secrets*. Trans. Ellen Marriage. Bp: WBY

103. [*YL 103*].
———. Vol. 31: *The Quest of the Absolute*. Trans. Ellen Marriage. Bp: WBY

104. [*YL 104*].
———. Vol. 32: *The Rise and Fall of Cesar Birotteau*. Trans. Ellen Marriage. Bp: WBY

105. [*YL 105*].
———. Vol. 33: *The Seamy Side of History*. Trans. Clara Bell. Bp: WBY

106. [*YL 106*].
———. Vol. 34: *Seraphita*. Trans. Clara Bell. Bp: WBY

107. [*YL 107*].
———. Vol. 35: *The Thirteen*. Trans. Ellen Marriage. Bp: WBY

108. [*YL 108*].
———. Vol. 36: *The Unconscious Mummers*. Trans. Ellen Marriage. Bp: WBY

109. [*YL 109*].
———. Vol. 37: *The Unknown Masterpiece*. Trans. Ellen Marriage. Bp: WBY

110.   [YL 110].
———. Vol. 38: *Ursule Mirouët*. Trans. Clara Bell. Bp: WBY

111.   [YL 111].
———. Vol. 39: *The Wild Ass's Skin*. Trans. Ellen Marriage. Bp: WBY

112.   [YL 112].
———. *Droll Stories, Collected from the Abbeys of Touraine*. Trans. [George R. Sims]. Illustrated by Gustave Dore. London: Camden Hotten, [1874]. [Illustrated].

113.   [YL 113].
Baring-Gould, S[abine]. *The Life of Napoleon Bonaparte*. London: Methuen, 1897.

114.   [YL 114].
Barker, Ernest. *Greek Political Theory*. London: Methuen, 1918.

115.   [YL 115].
Barker, George. *Calamiterror*. London: Faber and Faber, 1937.

116.   [YL 116].
———. *Poems*. London: Faber and Faber, 1935.

117.   [YL 117].
———. *Thirty Preliminary Poems*. London: David Archer, The Parton Press, 1933.

118.   [YL 118].
Barnes, Major J[ames]. S[trachey]. *Fascism*. Home University Library. London: Thornton Butterworth, 1931.

119.   [YL 119].
Barrett, Sir William F. *On the Threshold of the Unseen*. An examination of the phenomena of spiritualism and of the evidence for survival after death. London: Kegan Paul, Trench, Trubner, 1917. Bp: WBY

120.   [YL 120].
Barrington, Sir Jonah. *Recollections of Jonah Barrington*. Dublin: The Talbot Press; London: T. Fisher Unwin, [1918]. Signed: GY

121.   [YL *121].
Bartholomew, J[ohn]. G[eorge]. *A Literary and Historical Atlas of America*. London: J. M. Dent, [1911]. [With maps].

122.   [*YL* 122].

——, ed. *The Times Survey Atlas of the World*. London: The Times, 1922. [With maps; lacks general index].

123.   [*YL* *123]. [Though reported in *YL*, did not come to NLI with slip of paper at p. 219].

Barton, Sir D[unbar]. Plunket. *Links Between Ireland and Shakespeare*. Dublin and London: Maunsel, 1919.

124.   [*YL* *124]. [NLI 40,568/10; 39; envelope 1377].

Basilius Valentinus. [*The Last Will and Testament of Basil Valentine*] *with his treatise concerning the microcosme...man's body...with two treatises, the first declareth his manual operations....The second discovereth things natural and supernatural...*.London: Edward Brewster, 1670. Bp: WBY

125.   [*YL* 125].

——. *The Triumphal Chariot of Antimony. With the commentary of Theodore Kerckringius. Being the Latin version published at Amsterdam in the year 1685 translated into English with a biographical preface* [*by Arthur E. Waite*]. London: James Elliott, 1893.

126.   [*YL* 126].

Basnage, Mr. [Jacques]. *The History of the Jews, from Jesus Christ to the Present Time: Containing Their Antiquities, Their Religion, Their Rites, the Dispersion of the Ten Tribes in the East and the Persecution This Nation Has Suffer'd in the West; Being a Supplement and Continuation of the History of Josephus*. Trans. Thomas Taylor. London: J. Beaver and B. Lintot, 1708. Bp: WBY

127.   [*YL* 127].

Bastide, Charles. *The Anglo-French Entente in the Seventeenth Century*. London: John Lane, 1914.

128.   [*YL* *128].

Bate, Percy H. *The English Pre-Raphaelite Painters*. London: George Bell, 1899. [Illustrated].

129.   [*YL* 129].

Baudelaire, Charles. *Les fleurs du mal*. Bibliotheca Mundi. Leipzig: Insel-Verlag, n.d.

130.   [*YL* *130].
———. *Poems in Prose*. Trans. Arthur Symons. London: Elkin Mathews, 1905.

131.   [*YL* 131].
Baudouin, Charles. *Suggestion and Autosuggestion: A Psychological and Pedagogical Study Based upon the Investigations Made by the New Nancy School*. Trans. Eden and Cedar Paul. London: George Allen and Unwin, 1922.

132.   [*YL* *132].
Bayley, Harold. *A New Light on the Renaissance, Displayed in Contemporary Emblems*. London: J. M. Dent, 1909. [Illustrated].

133.   [*YL* 133].
Beardsley, Aubrey. *Under the Hill and Other Essays in Prose and Verse*. London and New York: John Lane, 1904. [Illustrated].

134.   [*YL* 134].
Beauclerk, Helen. *The Green Lacquer Pavilion*. Illustrated by Edmund Dulac. London: W. Collins Sons, 1926. [Illustrated].

135.   [*YL* *135].
Beaumont, Francis, and John Fletcher. *The Works of Francis Beaumont and John Fletcher*. 10 vols. Cambridge: The University Press, 1905-1912. Vol. 1: *The Maid's Tragedy and Other Plays*. Ed. Arnold Glover.

136.   [*YL* *136]. [NLI 40,568/11; 3 sheets; envelope 844].
———. Vol. 2: *The Elder Brother and Other Plays*. Ed. Arnold Glover and A. R. Waller.

137.   [*YL* *137].
———. Vol. 3: *The Mad Lover and Other Plays*. Ed. A. R. Waller.

138.   [*YL* 138]. [NLI 40,568/12; 117 sheets; envelope 1240]. [Though reported in *YL*, did not come to NLI with sheet of paper folded quarto, watermark of the Sussex Society" with headings and page nos. in Ezra Pound's hand].
Beaumont, John. *An Historical, Physiological and Theological Treatise of Spirits, Apparitions, Witchcrafts, and Other Magical Practices: Containing an Account of the Genii or Familiar Spirits, Both Good and Bad, That Are Said to Attend Men in This Life, and What Sensible*

Perceptions Some Persons Have Had of Them (Particularly the Author's Own Experience for Many Years). Also of Appearances of Spirits after Death, Divine Dreams, Divinations, Second Sighted Persons, &c; Likewise the Power of Witches and the Reality of Other Magical Operations, Clearly Asserted. With Refutation of Dr. Bekker's World Bewitch'd; and Other Authors That Have Opposed the Belief of Them. London: Printed for D. Browne, J. Taylor, R. Smith, F. Coggan, T. Browne, 1705. Bp: WBY.

139.   [*YL* *139].
Beckford, William. *The Episodes of Vathek.* Trans. Sir Frank T. Marzials. London: Stephen Swift, 1912. Bp: WBY.

140.   [*YL* *140].
——. *The History of the Caliph Vathek; and European Travels.* London: Ward, Lock, 1891. Bp: WBY.

141.   [Not listed in *YL* and assigned NLI Number 3003].
Bedell, William. *Leabhair an tSean Tiomna: ar na dtarruing on teanguidh ughdarach go Gaidhlig tré chúram agur sáothar.* Dublin: G. & A. Grierson & M. Keene [for the British and Foreign Bible Society], 1827.

142.   [*YL* 141].
Beedham, R. John. *Wood Engraving.* With introduction and appendix by Eric Gill. 4th ed. Hassocks, Sussex: Pepler and Sewell, 1935.

143.   [*YL* 142].
Beerbohm, Max. *The Happy Hypocrite.* New York: John Lane, 1906.

144.   [*YL* *143].
——. *The Poet's Corner.* London: William Heineman, 1904. [Illustrated].

145.   [*YL* *144].
[Bellini, Giovanni]. *Giovanni Bellini.* Introduction by Everard Meynell. London: George Newnes, [1906]. [Illustrated].

146.   [*YL* 145].
Belloc, Hilaire. *The Chanty of the Nona.* The Ariel Poems, no. 9. London: Faber and Gwyer, [1928].

146a.   [Not listed in *YL* and assigned NLI Number 3004].
Another copy.

147.   [YL 146].
Beltaine, [ed. W. B. Yeats], 1 (May 1899). Signed: Lily Yeats

147a.   [YL 146a].
Another copy.

147b.   [YL 146b].
Another copy.

148.   [YL 147].
——. 2 (February 1900).

148a.   [YL 147a].
Another copy.

149.   [YL 148]. [NLI 40,567/1; 10 sheets; Wade 226].
——. Bound vol., 1899–1900.

150.   [YL 149].
Benavente, Jacinto. *Plays*. Second series. Trans. John Garrett Underhill. New York: Charles Scribners, 1923.

151.   [YL 150].
Benda, Julien. *The Great Betrayal* [La trahison des clercs]. Trans. Richard Aldington. London: George Routledge, 1928.

152.   [YL 151].
Benson, E[dward]. F[rederic]. *Charlotte Bronte*. London: Longmans, Green, 1932. Signed: WBY

153.   [YL 152].
Benson, Stella. *Kwan-Yin*. San Francisco: Edwin Grabhorn 1922.

154.   [YL 153].
Berdyaev, Nicholas. *The Bourgeois Mind and Other Essays*. Trans. Countess Bennigsen and Donald Attwater. London: Sheed and Ward, 1934.

155.   [YL 154].
——. *The End of Our Time, Together with an Essay on the General Line of Soviet Philosophy*. Trans. Donald Atwater [sic]. London: Sheed and Ward, 1933.

156.   [YL *155].
Berger, P[ierre]. *William Blake, Poet and Mystic*. Trans. Daniel H. Conner. London: Chapman and Hall, 1914. Bp: WBY

157.   [*YL* 156]. [NLI 40,568/13; 88 sheets; envelope 1171].
Bergson, Henri. *Creative Evolution.* Trans. Arthur Mitchell. London: Macmillan, 1922.

158.   [*YL* 157]. [NLI 40,568/14; 118 sheets; envelope 1170].
——. *Matter and Memory.* Trans. Nancy Margaret Paul and W. Scott Palmer. London: Allen and Unwin, 1919.

159.   [*YL* 158].
Beritens, Germán. *Aberraciones del Greco científficamente consideradas: Nueva teoría que explica las anomalías de las obras de este artista.* Madrid: Librería de Fernando Fé, 1913.

160.   [*YL* 159].
Berkeley, George. *Berkeley's Commonplace Book.* Ed. G. A. Johnston. London: Faber and Faber, 1930.

160a.   [*YL* 159a].
Another copy.

161.   [*YL* 160]. [NLI 40,568/15; 20 sheets; envelope 1172].
——. *The Works of George Berkeley.* 2 vols. Dublin: John Exshaw, 1784. Bp: WBY

162.   [*YL* 161].
Bevan, Edwyn. *Stoics and Sceptics.* [Four lectures…for the Common University fund]. Oxford: Clarendon Press, 1913. Signed: WBY

163.   [*YL* *162].
Bhattâchâryya, Shiva Chandra Vidyârnava. *Principles of Tantra.* Ed. Arthur Avalon. 2 vols. London: Luzac, 1914-16.

164.   [Not listed in *YL* and assigned NLI Number 3005]. [See Chapman, *YA* 8 (1991): 201-202].
Biagi, Guido. *The Last Days of Percy Bysshe Shelley: New Details from Unpublished Documents.* London: T. Fisher Unwin, 1898. [Illustrated]. Signed: An Craoibhin Aoibhinn '99.

165.   [*YL* *163].
The Bibelot: A Reprint of Poetry and Prose for Book Lovers, Chosen in Part from Scarce Editions and Sources Not Generally Known (Portland, Maine), ed. Thomas B. Mosher, 1 (September 1895). "Hand and Soul" by Dante Gabriel Rossetti.

166. [*YL* *164].
—— 4 (January 1898). "St. Agnes of Intercession" by Dante Gabriel Rossetti.

167. [*YL* *165].
—— 5 (July 1899). "Translations from the French of Villon" by Algernon Charles Swinburne.

168. [*YL* *166].
—— 8 (March 1902). "The Story of the Unknown Church and Lindenborg Pool" by William Morris.

169. [*YL* *167].
—— 9 (February 1903). "Chrysanthema (concluded) and a Little Cycle of Greek Lyrics."

170. [*YL* *168].
—— 9 (March 1903). "Stéphane Mallarmé" by Arthur Symons.

171. [*YL* *169].
—— 9 (April 1903). "Lyrics" by Arthur Symons.

172. [*YL* *170].
—— 9 (May 1903). "The Madness of King Goll" by W. B. Yeats.

173. [*YL* *171].
—— 9 (October 1903). "Lyrics" by W. E. Henley.

174. [*YL* *172]. [NLI 40,567/2; 12 sheets; Wade 12].
—— 9 (June 1903). "The Land of Heart's Desire" by W. B. Yeats.

174a–b. [*YL* *172a–e]. [Three copies missing from NLI].
Five more copies, of which two remain.

174c. [*YL* *172f].
Another copy. Bound in greyish-blue boards; no advertising at end.

175. [*YL* *173].
—— 10 (March 1904). "Poems" by Lionel Johnson.

176. [*YL* *174].
—— 10 (May 1904). "Lyrics" by Rosamund Marriott Watson.

177. [*YL* *175].
—— 10 (June 1904). "Poems in Prose" by Oscar Wilde.

177a.   [*YL* *176].
　Another copy.

178.   [*YL* *177].
　—— 10 (October 1904). "Ballades" by William Ernest Henley.

179.   [*YL* *178].
　—— 11 (March 1905). "For Those Who Love Music and Raffaella" by Axel Munthe.

180.   [*YL* *179].
　—— 11 (July 1905). "Lecture on the English Renaissance and Rose Leaf and Apple Leaf: L'Envoi" by Oscar Wilde.

181.   [*YL* *180].
　—— 11 (October 1905). "Death's Disguises and Other Sonnets" by Frank T. Marzials.

182.   [*YL* *181].
　—— 11 (November 1905). "Vision and Memory" by Edward McCurdy.

183.   [*YL* *182].
　—— 12 (March 1906). "Lyrics" by Margaret L. Woods.

184.   [*YL* *183].
　—— 12 (April 1906). "Two Songs of the Springtides: I. Thalassius. II. On the Cliffs" by Algernon Charles Swinburne.

185.   [*YL* *184].
　—— 12 (June 1906). "Poems" by Thomas William Parsons.

186.   [*YL* *185].
　—— 12 (July 1906). "Charles Lamb: An Appreciation" by Walter Pater.

187.   [*YL* *186].
　—— 12 (October 1906). "Giordano Bruno" by Walter Pater. "Four Sonnets on Bruno" by Algernon Charles Swinburne.

188.   [*YL* 187].
　—— 19 (July 1913). "Riders to the Sea" by John M. Synge.

189.   [*YL* 188].
　—— 19 (August 1913). "In the Shadow of the Glen" by John M. Synge.

190.   [*YL* 189].
Bickley, Francis. *J. M. Synge and the Irish Dramatic Movement.* London: Constable, 1912.

191.   [*YL* *190].
Billson, Charles J. *The Popular Poetry of the Finns.* Popular Studies in Mythology, Romance and Folklore, no. 5. London: David Nutt, 1900.

192.   [Not listed in *YL* and assigned NLI Number 3006]. [See Chapman, *YA* 8 (1991): 201–202].
Binyon, Laurence. *Collected Poems of Laurence Binyon—London Visions, Narrative Poems, Translations.* London: Macmillan, 1931.

192a.   [Not listed in *YL* and assigned NLI Number 3006a]. Another copy.

193.   [Not listed in *YL*]. [See Chapman, *YA* 8 (1991): 201–202].
——. *Collected Poems: Lyrical Poems.* London: Macmillan, 1931.

194.   [*YL* 191].
——. *The Court Painters of the Grand Moguls.* London: Oxford University Press, 1921.

195.   [Not listed in *YL* and assigned NLI Number 3007]. [See Chapman, *YA* 8 (1991): 201–202].
——. *The Death of Adam and Other Poems.* London: Methuen, 1904. Signed onflyleaf: "To Frau Olga Julia Wegener with cordial regards | Lawrence Binyon | Dec 1909."

196.   [*YL* 192].
——. *The Drawings and Engravings of William Blake.* Ed. Geoffrey Holme. London: The Studio, 1922. [Illustrated].

197.   [Not listed in *YL* and assigned NLI Number 3008]. [See Chapman, *YA* 8 (1991): 201–202].
——. *First Book of London Visions.* London: Elkin Mathews, 1896.

198.   [Not listed in *YL* and assigned NLI Number 3009]. [See Chapman, *YA* 8 (1991): 201–202].
——. *Laurence Binyon.* The Augustan Books of Modern Poetry. London: Ernest Benn, n.d. [1925 or 1926?].

199. [*YL* 193].
———. "Mogul and Rajput Schools: Rock Temples of Ajanta." *The Times*, 17 Nov. 1921: xiv.

200. [Not listed in *YL* and given NLI number 3010]. [See Chapman, *YA* 8 (1991): 201–202]. [NLI 40,568/16; 12 sheets; envelope 218].
———. *Odes*. [London: Unicorn Press, 1901]. Author's presentation copy to Yeats, with annotations in "The Death of Tristram," pp. 29–47.

201. [*YL* *194].
———. *Painting in the Far East: An Introduction to the History of Pictorial Art in Asia, Especially China and Japan*. 2nd ed. London: Edward Arnold, 1913. Bp: WBY

202. [*YL* *195].
Bisson, Juliette Alexandre. *Les phénomènes dits de matérialisation: étude expérimentale*. Paris: Librairie Felix Alcan, 1914. [Illustrated].

203. [*YL* 196].
Bithell, Jethro. *W. B. Yeats*. Translated [into French] by Franz Hellens. Paris: Editions du Masque, [1913?].

204. [*YL* *197].
Bjørnson, Bjørnstjerne. *Pastor Sang: Being the Norwegian Drama Over ævne*. Trans. William Wilson. Frontispiece by Aubrey Beardsley. London: Longmans, Green, 1893.

205. [*YL* 198].
Blake, William. *The Book of Ahania*. Lambeth: William Blake, 1795; facsimile ed. London: Quaritch, [1892].

206. [*YL* 199].
———. *Facsimile of the Original Outlines before Colouring of the Songs of Innocence and of Experience, Executed by William Blake*. Ed. Edwin Ellis. London: B. Quaritch, 1893. [Illustrated].

207. [*YL* 200]. [NLI has title page and 7 of the 21 plates, which have been removed from the frames].
———. *Illustrations of the Book of Job*. London: William Blake, 1825. [Illustrated].

208.   [YL 201].

———. *Illustrations of the Book of Job*. London: William Blake and John Linnell, 1826; facsimile ed., London: J. M. Dent, 1902; New York: J. P. Putnam's, 1902. [Illustrated]. Bp: WBY

209.   [YL 202].

———. *Illustrations to the Divine Comedy of Dante*. London: The National Art-Collections Fund, 1922. [Illustrated].

210.   [YL *203].

———. *The Letters of William Blake, Together with a Life by Frederick Tatham*. Ed. Archibald G. B. Russell. London: Methuen, 1906. [Illustrated].

211.   [YL 204]. [NLI 40,568/17; 32 sheets; envelope 1886].

———. *The Marriage of Heaven and Hell*. London: William Blake, [c. 1790–93]; facsimile ed., London: J. C. Hotten, 1868. [Illustrated].

212.   [YL 205]. [NLI 40,568/18; 2 sheets; envelope 1894].

———. *The Marriage of Heaven and Hell [and] The Book of Los*. Offprints bound in one vol. from *Century Guild Hobby Horse* 2 (1887): 137–57 and 5 (1890): 82–89. Includes an introductory note to *The Book of Los* by F. York Powell.

213.   [YL 206]. [NLI 40,568/19; 14 sheets; envelope 1909C].

———. *Milton, A Poem in 2 Books*. Facsimilied…by William Muir, J. D. Watts, H. T. Muir, and E. Druitt. London: Bernard Quaritch, 1886. [Illustrated].

214.   [YL *207].

———. *The Poems of William Blake Comprising Songs of Innocence and Experience Together with Poetical Sketches and Some Copyright Poems Not in Any Other Collection*. New ed. [Ed. R. H. Shepherd]. London: Pickering and Chatto, 1887.

215.   [YL *208]. [Wade 219].

———. *The Poems of William Blake*. Ed. W. B. Yeats. The Muses' Library. London: Lawrence and Bullen, 1893.

216.   [YL 209]. [NLI 40,567/3; 11 sheets; Wade 220].

———. *The Poems of William Blake*. Ed. W. B. Yeats. Large paper ed. London: Lawrence and Bullen, 1893.

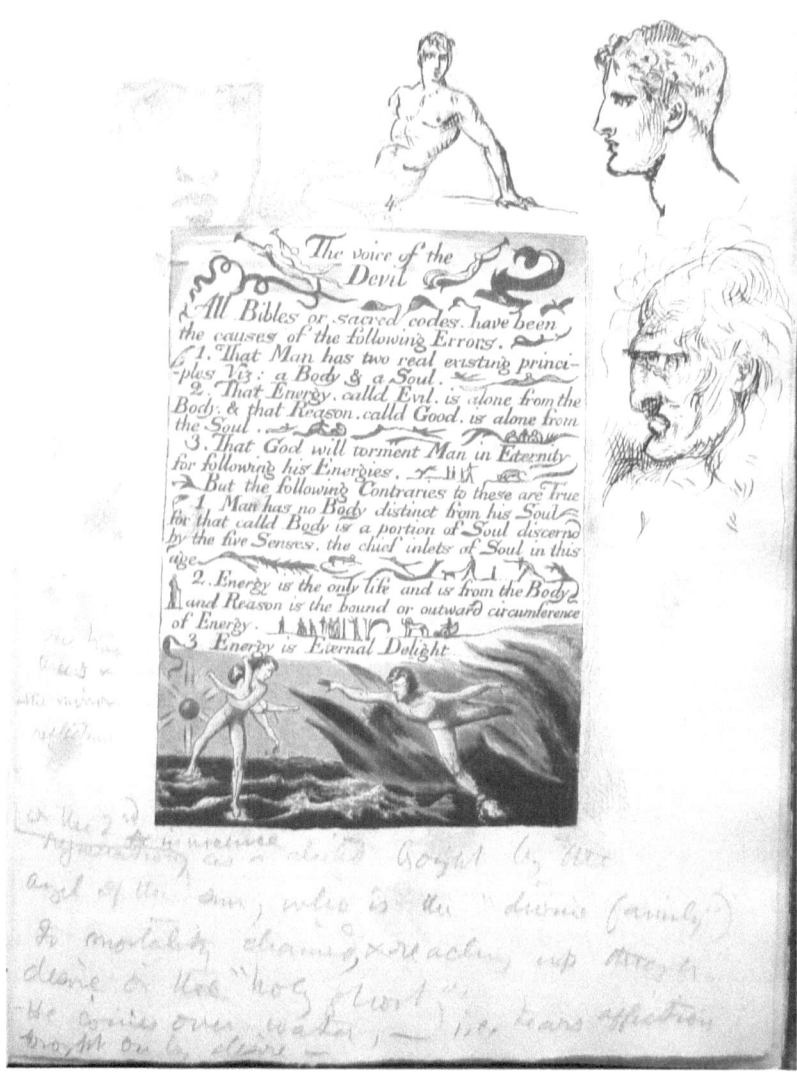

Figure 2. Annotations and marginal drawings by Edwin Ellis in 211. William Blake, *The Marriage of Heaven and Hell* (1790–93), Plate 4

217.   [*YL* 210]. [Wade 221].
——. *Poems of William Blake.* Ed. W. B. Yeats. Books that Marked Epochs, no. 2. London: George Routledge, 1910.

218.   [*YL* *211].
——. *The Poetical Works of William Blake.* Edited and annotated by Edwin J. Ellis. 2 vols. London: Chatto and Windus, 1906.

219.   [*YL* 212]. [NLI 40,568/20; 61 sheets; envelope 1183].
——. *The Poetical Works of William Blake, Lyrical and Miscellaneous.* Ed. William Michael Rossetti. The Aldine Edition of the English Poets. London: George Bell, 1890.

220.   [*YL* *213]. [NLI 40,568/21; 4 sheets; envelope 1884].
——. *The Poetical Works of William Blake.* Ed. John Sampson. London: Oxford University Press, 1914.

221.   [*YL* *214].
——. *The Prophetic Books of William Blake: Jerusalem.* Ed. E. R. D. Maclagan and A. G. B. Russell. London: A. H. Bullen, 1904.

222.   [*YL* 215].
——. *The Prophetic Books of William Blake: Milton.* Ed. E. R. D. Maclagan and A. G. B. Russell. London: A. H. Bullen, 1907.

223.   [*YL* 216].
——. *The Prophetic Writings of William Blake.* 2 vols. Ed. D. J. Sloss and J. P. R. Wallis. Oxford: The Clarendon Press, 1926.

224.   [*YL* 217]. [NLI 40,568/22; 3 sheets; envelope 1891].
——. *Selections from the Writings of William Blake.* With an introductory essay by Laurence Housman. London: Kegan Paul, Trench, Trubner, 1893. Signed: W B Y

225.   [*YL* 218].
——. *William Blake: Being All His Woodcuts Photographically Reproduced in Facsimile with an Introduction by Laurence Binyon.* Little Engravings, Classical and Contemporary, no. 2. Ed. T. Sturge Moore. London: At the Sign of the Unicorn, 1902. [Illustrated].

226.   [*YL* 219].
——. *William Blake's Designs for Gray's Poems: Reproduced Full-Size in Monochrome or Colour from the Unique Copy Belonging to His*

Grace the Duke of Hamilton. London: Oxford University Press, 1922. [Illustrated].

227.   [*YL* 220]. [NLI 40,567/4/1–3; 20, 29, and 5 sheets per vol.; Wade 218].
———. *The Works of William Blake*. 3 vols. Ed. Edwin Ellis and W. B. Yeats. London: Bernard Quaritch, 1893.

227a.   [*YL* 220a]. [NLI 40,568/23; 6 sheets; envelope 1887A]. [Though reported in *YL*, did not come to NLI with a sheet of stationary headed "18 Woburn Buildings, | W. C."].
———. [A black-and-white facsimile of *Jerusalem* bound and entitled on spine: *The Song of Jerusalem*. No preliminary matter. Reproduction compares with same size in *Jerusalem*, vol. 3 of the Ellis and Yeats edition of Blake's *Works* (*YL* 220).].

228.   [*YL* 221].
———. *The Writings of William Blake*. 3 vols. Ed. Geoffrey Keynes. London: The Nonesuch Press, 1925.

229.   [*YL* 222].
Blum, Etta. *Poems*. New York: Golden Eagle Editions, 1937.

230.   [*YL* 223].
Blunden, Edmund. *Edmund Blunden*. The Augustan Books of Modern Poetry. First series. London: Ernest Benn, [1925].

231.   [*YL* 224].
———. *The Poems of Edmund Blunden, 1914–30*. London: Cobden-Sanderson, 1930.

232.   [*YL* 225].
———. *The Waggoner and Other Poems*. London: Sidgwick and Jackson, 1920.

233.   [*YL* 226].
———. *Winter Nights, A Reminiscence*. The Ariel poems, no. 17. London: Faber and Gwyer, [1928].

234.   [*YL* *227].
Blunt, Wilfrid Scawen. *The Bride of the Nile: A Political Extravaganza in Three Acts of Rhymed Verse*. N.p.: Privately printed, 1907.

235.   [*YL* 228].
———. *Fand of the Fair Cheek: A Three-Act Tragedy in Rhymed Verse.* Written for the Irish National Theatre Society. Privately printed, 1904.

235a.   [*YL* 228a].
Another copy. Signed: WBY

235b–d. [*YL* 228b–e]. [NLI missing one copy].
Four other copies, of which three remain.

236.   [*YL* 229].
[Blunt, Wilfrid Scawen]. "Proteus." *Sonnets and Songs.* London: John Murray, 1875.

237.   [*YL* 230].
Boas, George. *The Adventures of Human Thought: The Major Traditions of European Philosophy.* New York and London: Harper, 1929.

238.   [*YL* *231].
Boccaccio, [Giovanni]. *The Decameron of Giovanni Boccaccio.* Trans. J. M. Rigg. Illustrated by Louis Chalon. 2 vols. London: A. H. Bullen, 1903. [Illustrated].

238a.   [*YL* *231a].
———. *Decameron.* [A folder of eight illustrations by Louis Chalon to the *Decameron*].

239.   [*YL* 232].
———. *Life of Dante.* Trans. Philip Henry Wicksteed. San Francisco: Printed by John Henry Nash for his friends, 1922.

240.   [*YL* 233].
Bodkin, Thomas. *Hugh Lane and His Pictures.* Verona: The Pegasus Press for the Government of the Irish Free State, 1932. [Illustrated].

241.   [Not listed in *YL* and assigned NLI Number 3011].
Another ed. Dublin: Browne and Nolan, 1934.

242.   [*YL* 234]. [See Chapman, *YA* 15 (2002): 288–312].
Boehme, Jacob. *The Aurora.* Ed. C. J. B[arker]. and D. S. H[ehner]. Trans. John Sparrow. London: John M. Watkins, 1914. Bp: WBY

243.   [*YL* 235]. [See Chapman, *YA* 15 (2002): 288–312].
———. *Concerning the Three Principles of the Divine Essence.* Trans. John Sparrow. London: John M. Watkins, 1910. Bp: WBY

244.   [*YL* 236]. [NLI 40,568/24; 20 sheets; envelope 1244]. [See Chapman, *YA* 15 (2002): 288–312].

——. *The Forty Questions of the Soul and the Clavis*. Trans. John Sparrow. Emendated by D. S. Hehner. London: John Watkins, 1911. Bp: WBY

245.   [*YL* 237]. [NLI 40,568/25; 12 sheets; envelope 1242]. [See Chapman, *YA* 15 (2002): 288–312].

——. *The High and Deep Searching Out of the Threefold Life of Man through, or According to, the Three Principles*. Trans. John Sparrow. London: 1650; reprint ed. by C. J. B[arker]. London: John M. Watkins, 1909. Bp: WBY

246.   [*YL* 238]. [See Chapman, *YA* 15 (2002): 288–312].

——. *Mysterium Magnum, or An Exposition of the First Book of Moses Called Genesis*. Ed. C. J. B[arker]. Trans. John Sparrow. 2 vols. London: John M. Watkins, 1924.

247.   [*YL* 239]. [NLI 40,568/26; 31 sheets; envelope 1238]. [See Chapman, *YA* 15 (2002): 288–312].

——. *The Works of Jacob Behmen, the Teutonic Theosopher…to Which is Prefixed, the Life of the Author; With Figures, Illustrating His Principles, Left by the Rev. William Law*. [Contains *The Threefold Life of Man, The Answers to Forty Questions Concerning the Soul, The Treatise of the Incarnation, The Clavis*, corresponding to the contents of vol. 2 of a 4-vol. set of the same title]. London: Joseph Richardson, 1763. [Illustrated].

248.   [*YL* 240]. [NLI 40,568/27; 7 sheets; envelope 1226].

Bolton, L[yndon]. *An Introduction to the Theory of Relativity*. London: Methuen, 1921. [With figures].

249.   [*YL* 241].

Bond, C[harles]. J[ohn]. *Some Causes of Racial Decay: An Inquiry into the Distribution of Natural Capacity in the Population; The Need for a National Stock-taking*. The Galton Lecture, Feb. 16, 1928. London: The Eugenics Society, [1928].

250.   [*YL* 242].

The Bookman: An Illustrated Monthly Journal 5 (Oct. 1893).

251.   [*YL* 243].

—— 5 (Feb. 1894).

252.   [*YL* 244].
—— 6 (June 1894).

253.   [*YL* 245].
—— 6 (Aug. 1894).

254.   [*YL* 246].
—— 11 (March 1897).

255.   [*YL* 247].
—— 12 (Sept. 1897)

256.   [*YL* 248].
—— 27 (Jan. 1905).

256a.   [*YL* 248a].
Another copy.

x   [*YL* 249]. [NLI missing this copy].
The Book of Common Prayer. Oxford: The University Press, [1935?].

257.   [*YL* 250].
The Book of the Rhymer's Club. London: Elkin Mathews, 1892.

258.   [*YL* 251].
The Book of the Thousand Nights and One Night: Rendered from the Literal and Complete Version of Dr. J. C. Mardrus and Collated with Other Sources by E. Powys Mathers. 4 vols. London: The Casanova Society, 1923. [Illustrated].

259.   [*YL* 252].
Borthwick, Norma, ed. *Ceachta beaga Gaedhilge = Irish Reading Lessons*. Vol. 2. Illustrated by Jack B. Yeats. Dublin: The Irish Book Co., 1914. [Illustrated].

260.   [*YL* 253].
——. *Ceachta beaga Gaedhilge = Irish Reading Lessons*. Vol. 3. Illustrated by Jack B. Yeats. Dublin: Irish Book Co., [191?]. [Illustrated].

261.   [*YL* 254]. [NLI 40,568/28; 27 sheets; envelope 1147].
Bosanquet, Bernard. *The Meeting of Extremes in Contemporary Philosophy*. London: Macmillan, 1924.

262.   [*YL* 255].
Bosis, Lauro de. *The Story of My Death*. [With biographical note and original French text]. Trans. Ruth Draper. London: Faber and Faber, 1933.

263.   [*YL* *256].
Boswell, James. *Boswell's Life of Johnson*. Ed. Augustine Birrell. 6 vols. London: The Times Book Club, 1912.

264.   [*YL* *257].
Bottomley, Gordon. *Chambers of Imagery*. Second series. London: Elkin Mathews, 1912.

265.   [*YL* *258].
———. *The Gate of Smaragdus*. London: At the Sign of the Unicorn, 1904.

266.   [*YL* 259]. [NLI 40,568/29; 2 sheets; envelope 910]. [Though reported in *YL*, did not come to NLI with a letter of presentation from Bottomly].
———. *Gruach and Britain's Daughter: Two Plays*. London: Constable, 1921.

267.   [*YL* *260].
———. *King Lear's Wife, The Crier by Night, The Riding to Lithend, Midsummer Eve, Laodice and Danae*. London: Constable, 1920.

267a.   [*YL* 260a].
Another copy.

268.   [*YL* 261].
———. *Lyric Plays*. London: Constable, 1932.

269.   [*YL* *262].
———. *Midsummer Eve*. Illustrated by James Guthrie. Harting, Petersfield, Hampshire: Pear Tree Press, 1905. [Illustrated].

270.   [*YL* 263].
———. *Scenes and Plays*. London: Constable, 1929.

271.   [*YL* 264].
Boucicault, Dion. *The Colleen Bawn, or The Brides of Garry Owen*. London: Samuel French, [1860?].

272.   [*YL* *265].
Boyd, Ernest A[ugustus]. *The Contemporary Drama of Ireland*. Boston: Little, Brown, 1917.

273.   [YL *266].
Boyle, William. *The Mineral Workers: A Play in Four Acts*. Dublin: M. H. Gill, 1910.

274.   [YL 267].
Brabazon, Elizabeth Jane. *Outlines of the History of Ireland for Schools and Families*. Dublin: Printed by J. S. Folds, 1844.

275.   [YL 268].
Bradby, G[odfrey]. F[ox]. *Short Studies in Shakespeare*. London: John Murray, 1929.

276.   [YL 269].
Bradley, F[rancis]. H[erbert]. *Appearance and Reality: A Metaphysical Essay*. London: George Allen and Unwin, 1925.

277.   [YL *270].
Bradley, John W[illiam]. *Illuminated Manuscripts*. Little Books on Art. London: Methuen, 1905.

278.   [YL 271].
Brereton, Austin. *Henry Irving: A Biographical Sketch*. New York: Scribner and Welford, 1884. [Illustrated].

279.   [YL *272].
Breton, Nicholas, George Wither, and William Browne. *Nicholas Breton. Pastoral Poems | George Wither. Selected Poetry | William Browne, of Tavistock. Pastoral Poetry*. The Pembroke Booklets, first series, no. 3. Hull: J. R. Tutin, 1906.

280.   [YL *273].
Brewer, R[obert]. Frederick. *Orthometry: The Art of Versification and the Technicalities of Poetry; With a New and Complete Rhyming Dictionary*. Edinburgh: John Grant, 1912.

281.   [YL *274].
Bridges, Robert. *Achilles in Scyros*. London: George Bell, 1892.

282.   [YL *275].
———. *Eight Plays*. Vol. 4: *The Christian Captives*. London: Edward Bumpus, 1890.

283.   [YL *276].
———. *Eros and Psyche*. London: George Bell, 1894. 170 pp.

284.   [YL 277].
———. *New Verse Written in 1921: With the Other Poems Written in That Year and a Few Earlier Pieces*. Oxford: Clarendon Press, 1925.

285.   [YL 278].
———. *Ode, For the Bicentary Commemoration of Henry Purcell*. London: Elkin Mathews, 1896.

286.   [YL *279].
———. *Poems Written in the Year MCMIII*. Chelsea: Printed by St. John Hornby at the Ashendene Press, 1914.

287.   [YL *280].
———. *The Shorter Poems*. London: George Bell, 1890.

288.   [YL 281].
———. *The Testament of Beauty*. Oxford: Clarendon Press, 1929.

289.   [YL 282].
———, ed. *The Chilswell Book of English Poetry*. London: Longmans, Green, 1924.

290.   [YL *283].
———, ed. *The Spirit of Man, An Anthology*. London: Longmans, Green, 1916.

291.   [Not listed in *YL* and assigned NLI Number 3017]. [See Chapman, *YA* 8 (1991): 201–202].
British Museum. *Examples of Indian Sculpture at the British Museum*. London: The India Society, 1910.

292.   [YL *284].
British Museum, Dept. of Egyptian and Assyrian Antiquities. *A Guide to the First and Second Egyptian Rooms: Predynastic Antiquities, Mummies, Mummy-cases, and Other Objects Connected with the Funeral Rites of the Ancient Egyptians*. [By E. A. Wallis Budge]. 2nd ed. London: By order of the trustees, 1904. [Illustrated].

293.   [YL *285].
———. Dept. of Manuscripts. *Reproductions from Illuminated Manuscripts*. Second series. London: Longmans, 1907.

294.   [*YL* 286].
[Brodie-Innes, J. W.]. Sub Spe., Th. A. M., Former Imperator of Amen Ra. *Concerning the Revisal of the Constitution and Rules of the Order.* R. R. and A. C. [1901].

295.   [*YL* 287].
Brodzky, Horace. *Henri Gaudier-Brzeska, 1891–1915.* London: Faber and Faber, 1933.

296.   [*YL* *288].
Brooke, Rupert. *Poems.* London: Sidgwick and Jackson, 1911. Bp: WBY

297.   [*YL* *289].
Browne, Sir Thomas. *Religio Medici, and Urn Burial.* [Ed. Israel Gollancz]. The Temple Classics. London: J. M. Dent, 1896.

298.   [*YL* 290]. [NLI 40,568/30; 46 sheets; envelope 866].
———. *Religio Medici, Urn Burial, Christian Morals, and Other Essays.* Edited with an intro. by John Addington Symonds. London: Walter Scott, 1886.

299.   [*YL* 291].
Another ed. Ed. C. J. Holmes, Decorated by C. S. Ricketts. London: The Ballantyne Press, 1902. Bp: WBY

300.   [*YL* *292].
Brownell, W[illiam]. C[rary]. *French Art: Classic and Contemporary Painting and Sculpture.* Westminster: Archibald Constable, 1902.

301.   [*YL* 293]. [NLI 40,568/31; 8 sheets; envelope 250].
Browning, Elizabeth Barrett. *Poems.* 3 vols. 5th ed. London: Chapman and Hall, 1862.

302.   [*YL* *294].
———. *Prometheus Bound and Other Poems.* London: Ward, Lock and Bowden, 1896.

303.   [*YL* *295].
———. *A Selection from the Poetry.* Leipzig: Bernhard Tauchnitz, 1872.

304.   [*YL* *296]. [NLI 40,568/32; 45 sheets; envelope 246].
Browning, Robert. *The Poetical Works.* 4th ed. Vol. 2: *Tragedies and Other Plays.* London: Chapman and Hall, 1865.

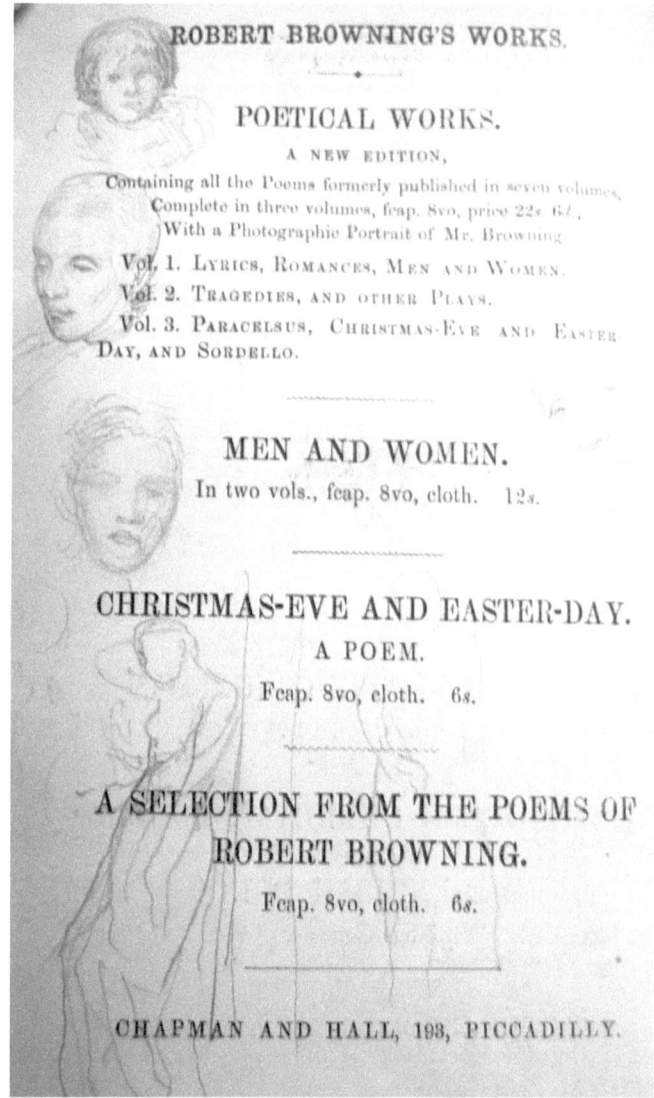

Figure 3. Drawings in pencil by J. B. Yeats on advertisement page in 305. Robert Browning, *The Poetical Works* (1865)

305.   [YL *297]. [NLI 40,568/33; 82 sheets; envelope 247].
——. Vol. 3: *Paracelsus, Christmas-Eve and Easter-Day, Sordello*. London: Chapman and Hall, 1865.

306.   [YL 298].
——. *The Poetical Works of Robert Browning*. [Ed. Augustine Birrell and Sir Frederic G. Kenyon]. 2 vols. London: John Murray, 1919. Bp: WBY

307.   [YL 299].
Bruck, Arthur Moeller van den. *Germany's Third Empire*. Condensed by D. C. Lorimer. London: George Allen and Unwin, 1934.

308.   [YL 300].
Bryan's Dictionary of Painters and Engravers. New edition, revised and enlarged under the supervision of George C. Williamson. 5 vols. London: G. Bell, 1919–21.

309.   [YL 301].
Bunting, Basil. *Redimiculum matellarum*. Milan: Grafica Moderna, 1930.

309a–d. [YL 301a–d].
Four more copies.

310.   [YL 302].
Bunyan, John. *The Pilgrim's Progress*. London: The Religious Tract Society, [1820?].

311.   [YL *303].
Burdy, Samuel. *The Life of Philip Skelton*. Dublin: William Jones, 1792; reprint ed., Oxford: Clarendon Press, 1914. Bp: WBY

312.   [YL *304].
Burghclere, Lady (Winifred Gardner). *The Life of James First Duke of Ormonde, 1610–1688*. 2 vols. London: John Murray, 1912. Bp: WBY

313.   [YL 305].
Burke, Edmund. *Selections. With essays by Hazlitt, Arnold and Others*. Oxford: Clarendon Press, 1928.

314.   [YL 306]. [NLI 40,568/34/1–5; 10, 5, 24, 6, 4 sheets, respectively, from vols. 1, 2, 3, 5, and 6; envelope 1599].
——. *The Works of the Right Honourable Edmund Burke*. 8 vols. Bohn's Standard Library. London: George Bell, 1877–83.

315. [*YL* 307]. [NLI 40,568/35; copy of letter from F. C. Burkitt to WBY (8 June 1933); 3 sheets; envelope 1540]. [Though reported in *YL*, did not come to NLI with said letter from Burkitt].

Burkitt, F[rancis]. C[rawford]. Offprint. Review of *St. Patrick—A.D. 180* by the Rev. John Roche Ardill. *The Journal of Theological Studies* 33 [July 1932].

316. [*YL* 308]. [NLI 40,568/36; 32 sheets; envelope 1154]. [See Chapman, *YA* 15 (2002): 288–312].

Burnet, John. *Early Greek Philosophy*. London and Edinburgh: Adam and Charles Black, 1892. Bp: WBY

317. [*YL* 309].

[Burney, Fanny]. *Camilla: Or, A Picture of Youth*. 3 vols. Dublin: Printed by William Porter, 1796.

318. [*YL* *310].

The Poetry of Robert Burns. Ed. William Ernest Henley and Thomas F. Henderson. 4 vols. The Centenary Burns. London: T. C. and E. C. Jack, [1896–97].

319. [*YL* *311]. [NLI 40,568/37; 18 sheets; envelope 872]. [See Chapman, *YA* 6 (1988): 234–45].

Burton, Robert. *The Anatomy of Melancholy*. Ed. Rev. A. R. Shilleto. 3 vols. Bohn's Libraries. London: G. Bell, 1912. Bp: WBY

320. [*YL* 312].

Bury, J[ohn]. B[agnell], S. A. Cook, and F. A. Adcock, eds. *The Cambridge Ancient History*. 13 vols. Cambridge: The University Press, 1923–36.

321. [*YL* 313].

———. *The Cambridge Ancient History: Volume of Plates I[–V]*. Prepared by C[harles]. T[heodore]. Seltman. [5 vols.?]. Cambridge: The University Press, 1927[–39].

322. [*YL* 314]. [Inserted reader's slip signed M. B. Yeats].

———. *The Cambridge Medieval History*. Ed. H. M. Gwatkin and J. P. Whitney. 8 vols. Cambridge: The University Press, 1911–1936.

323. [*YL* 315].

Busch, Julius Herrmann Moritz. *Bismarck: Some Secret Pages of His History; Being a Diary Kept by Dr. Moritz Busch During 25 Years'*

Official and Private Intercourse with the Great Chancellor. Condensed ed. London: Macmillan, 1899.

324.   [*YL* 316].
Bushell, Stephen W[ooton]. *Chinese Art.* 2 vols. London: Victoria and Albert Museum, 1921.

325.   [*YL* 317].
Butler, Samuel. *The Poetical Works of Samuel Butler.* With biography, annotations, critical dissertation by Rev. George Gilfillan. 2 vols. Edinburgh: James Nichol, 1854.

326.   [*YL* 318].
Butt, Isaac. *The History of Italy from the Abdication of Napoleon I.* 2 vols. London: Chapman and Hall, 1860.

327.   [*YL* *319].
The Butterfly Quarterly (Philadelphia) 5 (Winter 1908–1909).

328.   [*YL* *320].
——— 6 (Spring 1909).

329.   [*YL* *321].
Butterworth, Adeline M. *William Blake, Mystic: A Study; Together with Young's Night Thoughts: Nights I and II.* [Includes illustrations by William Blake and frontispiece *Death's Door*, from Blair's "The Grave."] Liverpool: The Liverpool Booksellers, 1911. Bp: WBY

330.   [*YL* 322].
Bynner, Witter. *The New World.* San Francisco: John Henry Nash, 1919.

331.   [*YL* 323].
Byron, George Gordon, Lord. *The Letters and Journals of Lord Byron, Selected.* Camelot Classics. London: Walter Scott, 1886.

332.   [*YL* 324].
———. *Lord Byron's Correspondence, Chiefly with Lady Melbourne, Mr. Hobhouse, The Hon. Douglas Kinnaird, and P. B. Shelley.* Ed. John Murray. 2 vols. London: John Murray, 1922.

333.   [*YL* 325].
———. *Poetical Works of George Lord Byron.* London: T. Noble, 1853.

334.   [*YL* *326].
——. *The Poetical Works of Lord Byron*. Reprinted from the original editions. [Annotated]. London: Frederick Warne, [1889].

335.   [*YL* 327].
Byron, Robert and David Talbot Rice. *The Birth of Western Painting: A History of Color, Form, and Iconography, Illustrated from the Paintings of Mistra and Mount Athos of Giotto and Fuccio, and of El Greco*. London: George Routledge, 1930. [Illustrated]. Bp: WBY

[*YL* 328 moved to 609].

336.   [*YL* 329]. [NLI 40,568/38; copy of letter inserted from Evie Hone to GY (6 Sept. n.y.); 2 sheets; envelope 156]. [Though reported in *YL*, did not come to NLI with said letter from Eve Hone].
C[otton]., S[ophia]. A[nne]. *Ancient Devotions for Holy Communion from Eastern and Western Liturgical Sources*. London: Burnes Oates and Washbourne, 1923.

337.   [*YL* 330].
Cabell, James Branch. *Ballades from the Hidden Way*. New York: Crosby Gaige, 1928.

338.   [*YL* 331]. [NLI 40,568/39; 23 sheets; envelope 1429A].
Cafferata, Canon Henry Taylor. *The Catechism Simply Explained*. New revised and enlarged edition. London: Burns Oates and Washbourne, [1932].

339.   [*YL* 332].
Caffin, Charles H[enry]. *American Masters of Painting. Being Brief Appreciations of Some American Painters*. New York: Doubleday, Page, 1903.

340.   [*YL* 333].
Calvert, Edward. *Ten Spiritual Designs: Enlarged from Proofs of the Originals on Copper, Wood, and Stone, 1827–1831*. Portland, Maine: Thomas Bird Mosher, 1913. [Illustrated]. Bp: WBY

341.   [*YL* 334].
Calvert, Samuel. *A Memoir of Edward Calvert, Artist*. London: Sampson Low, Marston, 1893. [Illustrated]. Signed: Samuel Calvert

342. [YL *335].
Campbell, John Gregerson. *The Fions: Or, Stories, Poems, and Traditions of Fionn and his Warrior Band*. Collected entirely from oral sources. With intro. and notes by Alfred Nutt. Waifs and Strays of Celtic Tradition. Argyllshire Series, no. 4. London: David Nutt, 1891.

343. [YL *336]. [NLI 40,568/40; 68 sheets; envelope 1251].
——. *Superstitions of the Highlands and Islands of Scotland*. Collected entirely from oral sources. Glasgow: James MacLehose, 1900.

344. [YL 337].
Campbell, Roy. *Adamastor: Poems*. London: Faber and Faber, 1932.

345. [YL 338].
——. *The Flaming Terrapin: Poems*. London: Jonathan Cape, 1924.

346. [YL 339].
Canfield, Curtis, ed. *Plays of Changing Ireland*. New York: Macmillan, 1936.

347. [YL 340].
Čapek, Karel, *The Macropulos Secret: A Comedy*. Trans. Paul Selver. London: Robert Holden, 1927.

348. [YL 341].
——. *R. U. R. (Rossum's Universal Robots): A Play in Three Acts and an Epilogue*. Trans. P[aul]. Selver and adapted for the English stage by Nigel Playfair. London: Oxford University Press, 1923.

349. [YL 342].
Caran d'Ache [pseud. for Emmanuel Poiré]. *Album* [*Album troisième*]. Paris: E. Plon, Nourrit, n.d. [Illustrated]. Signed: Lolly Yeats

350. [YL 343].
Carleton, William. *Art Maguire, or The Broken Pledge*. Dublin: James Duffy, [188?].

351. [YL 344].
——. *The Black Prophet: A Tale of Irish Famine*. Illustrated by J. B. Yeats. London: Lawrence and Bullen, 1899. [Illustrated].

352. [YL 345].
——. *Redmond Count O'Hanlon: The Irish Rapparee*. Dublin: James Duffy, 1886.

353. [YL 346].

———. *Rody the Rover, or The Ribbonman*. Dublin: James Duffy, [188?].

354. [YL *347].

———. *Traits and Stories of the Irish Peasantry*. Ed. D. J. O'Donoghue. 4 vols. London: J. M. Dent, 1896.

355. [YL 348]. [NLI 40,568/41; 18 sheets; envelope 1187].

Carr, H[erbert]. Wildon. *The Philosophy of Benedetto Croce; The Problem of Art and History*. London: Macmillan, 1917.

356. [YL 349].

Carrà, Carlo. *André Derain*. Rome: Valori Plastici, 1921. [Illustrated].

357. [YL 350].

Carroll, Lewis. *Through the Looking-Glass and What Alice Found There*. Illustrated by John Tenniel. London: Macmillan, 1872. [Illustrated].

358. [YL 351].

Castiglione, Baldassare. *The Book of the Courtier*. Trans. Sir Thomas Hoby. The Tudor Translations. London: David Nutt, 1900. Bp: WBY

359. [Not listed in *YL* and assigned NLI Number 3012].

Catalogue of Important Pictures by Old Masters Collected by the Late L. H. Bischoffsheim. London: Messrs. Christie, Manson &Woods, May 7th, 1926.

360. [YL *352].

Catalogue of the Celebrated Collection of Greek, Roman, and Egyptian Sculpture and Ancient Greek Vases. Being a portion of the Hope Heirlooms...which will be sold by Auction...on Monday, July 23, 1917... by Messrs. Christie, Manson, and Woods. London: Printed by William Clowes, 1917.

361. [YL 353].

Cattell, Raymond B[ernard]. *The Fight for Our National Intelligence*. London: P. S. King, 1937.

362. [YL 354].

Caulfield, James, ed. *The History of the Gun-Powder Plot*. London: Vernor and Hood, 1804.

363.   [*YL* 355]. [NLI 40,568/42; 4 sheets; envelope 84].
Cavalcanti, Guido. *Rime*. [With introduction and bibliographic material by Emilio Cecchi]. Lanciano: R. Carabba, 1910.

364.   [Not listed in *YL* and assigned NLI Number 3013]. [See Chapman, *YA* 8 (1991): 201–202].
———. *Rime*. Ed. Ezra Pound. Genoa: Edizioni Marsano, 1931. Inscribed "To George. | anno | XII | E[zra]. P[ound]."

365.   [*YL* 356].
———. *Sonnets and Ballate of Guido Cavalcanti*. Trans. Ezra Pound. London: Stephen Swift, 1912.

365a.   [*YL* 356a]. [NLI 40,568/43; 4 sheets; envelope 32].
Another copy.

366.   [*YL* 357].
Cecil, David. *The Stricken Deer, or The Life of Cowper*. London: Constable, 1930. Signed: GY

367.   [*YL* 358].
Cellini, Benvenuto. *The Life of Benvenuto Cellini*. Trans. John Addington Symonds. London: Macmillan, 1923.

368.   [*YL* 359].
A Celtic Christmas. Christmas Number of *The Irish Homestead* (Dec. 1902).

369.   [*YL* 360].
———. (Dec. 1903).

370.   [*YL* 361].
———. (Dec. 1904).

370a.   [*YL* 361a].
Another copy.

371.   [*YL* 362].
———. (Dec. 1905).

372.   [*YL* *363].
Cerfberr, Anatole and Jules Christophe. *Répertoire de la comédie humaine de H. de Balzac*. Paris: Callman Lévy, 1893. Bp: WBY

373. [*YL* 364].
Chadwick, Hugh Brailsford. *Safety Green: Selected Poems and Verses*. Poole: The Wessex Press, 1935.

374. [*YL* 365].
Chambers's Biographical Dictionary. Ed. David Patrick and Francis Hindes Groome. London: W. and R. Chambers, 1911.

375. [*YL* *366].
Chambers's Cyclopaedia of English Literature. New edition by David Patrick. 3 vols. London: W. and R. Chambers, 1903.

376. [*YL* *367].
Chambers's English Dictionary. Ed. Thomas Davidson. London: W. and R. Chambers, [1914].

377. [*YL* 368].
Chapman, George. *The Comedies and Tragedies of George Chapman*. 3 vols. London: John Pearson, 1873.

378. [*YL* *369]. [NLI 40,568/44; 19 sheets; envelope 846]. [See Chapman, *YA* 6 (1988): 234–45].
———. *The Works of George Chapman*. Vol. 1: *Plays*. Ed. Richard Herne Shepherd. New ed. London: Chatto and Windus, 1889.

379. [*YL* *370].
———. *The Works of George Chapman*. Vol. 2: *Poems and Minor Translations*. With an intro. by Algernon Charles Swinburne. New ed. London: Chatto and Windus, 1904.

380. [*YL* 371]. [NLI 40,568/45; 26 sheets; envelope 287].
Charpentier, John. *Coleridge, the Sublime Somnambulist*. Trans. M. V. Nugent. London: Constable, 1929.

381. [*YL* 372].
Charubel [pseud.]. *The Degrees of the Zodiac Symbolised*. [To which is added *The Theoretical Value of the Degrees of the Zodiac* by H. S. Green]. London: Nichols, 1898. Bp: GY

382. [*YL* *373]. [NLI 40,568/46; 15 sheets; envelope 1255].
Chatelain, Heli, ed. *Folk-Tales of Angola: Fifty Tales, with Ki-Mbundu Text, Literal English Translation, Introduction, and Notes*. Boston and New York: Published for the American Folk-lore Society by Houghton, Mifflin, 1894.

383.   [YL 374].
Chatterton, Thomas. *The Rowley Poems*. Ed. Robert Steele. Decorated by Charles Ricketts. 2 vols. London: Hacon and Ricketts, 1898. Bp: WBY

384.   [YL 375].
Chattopadhyaya, Harindranath. *Cross-Roads*. [Poems]. Madras: Shama'a Publishing House, 1934.

385.   [YL *376].
Chaucer, Geoffrey. *The Poetical Works, from the Text of Prof. Skeat*. 3 vols. The World's Classics. London: Grant Richards, [1903]. Vol. 3: London: Oxford University Press, [1906].

386.   [Erroneously listed as YL *2102 without attributing author]. [See Chapman, YA 8 (1991): 201–202].
———. *The Tale of Gamelyn, from the Harleian MS. No. 7334, Collated with Six Other MSS*. Ed. Walter W. Skeat. Clarendon Press Series. Oxford: Clarendon Press, 1884. Cf. YL *2102.

387.   [YL 377].
———. *The Works of Geoffrey Chaucer*. Ed. F[rederick]. S[tartridge]. Ellis. Illustrated by Sir Edward Burne-Jones. Printed by William Morris. Hammersmith: The Kelmscott Press, 1896. [Illustrated].

388.   [YL *378].
———. *The Works of Geoffrey Chaucer*. Ed. Alfred W. Pollard etc. The Globe Edition. London: Macmillan, 1908.

389.   [YL 379].
Chekhov, Anton. *The Cherry Orchard and Other Plays*. Trans. Constance Garnett. London: Chatto and Windus, 1925.

390.   [YL *380].
———. *The Seagull*. Trans. Julius West. London: Hendersons, 1915.

391.   [YL 381].
Cheney, Sheldon. *The New Movement in the Theatre*. New York: Mitchell Kennerley, 1914.

392.   [YL 382].
Chettur, Govinda Krishna. *Sounds and Images*. London: Erskine Macdonald, [1922].

393. [*YL* 383].
Choiseul-Meuse, Félicité, Comtesse de. *The Return of the Fairies.* Dublin: John Cummings, [1824].

394. [*YL* 384].
Church, Richard. *The Glance Backward: New Poems.* London: J. M. Dent, 1930.

395. [*YL* 385]. [Though reported in *YL*, did not come to NLI with an envelope bearing a note from Church to WBY dated "7.2.36"].
——. *Twelve Noon: Poems.* London: J. M. Dent, 1936.

396. [*YL* *386].
[Cibot, Pierre Martial]. *Lettre sur les caracteres chinois par Le Reverend Pere* **** [Cibot], *de la compagnie de Jesus.* [Bound with this]: *Lettre de Pékin, sur le génie de la langue chinoise, et la nature de leur ècriture symbolique, comparée avec celle des anciens ègyptiens; en réponse à celle de la Société royale des sciences de Londres, sur le même sujet: on y a joint l'extrait de deux ouvrages nouveaux de Mr. de Guignes...relatifs aux mêmes matieres.* Bruxelles: J. L. De Boubers, 1773. [Illustrated].

397. [*YL* 387]. [NLI 40,568/47; 11 sheets; envelope 1155].
Cicero, Marcus Tullius and Pythagoras. *Somnium Scipionis, translated into English, with an essay "The Vision of Scipio Considered As a Fragment of the Mysteries," by L. O; The Golden Verses of Pythagoras [trans. with notes] by A. E. A.; The Symbols of Pythagoras [Trans. with Notes] by S[apere]. A[ude].* Vol. 5 of *Collectanea hermetica,* ed. W. Wynn Westcott. London: Theosophical Publishing Society, 1894.

398. [*YL* 388].
The Citizen's Manual, Being a Simple Guide through the New [Irish] Constitution by a Member of the Bar. Dublin: James Duffy, 1938.

399. [*YL* 389].
Clarke, Austin. *Pilgrimage and Other Poems.* London: George Allen and Unwin, 1929.

400. [*YL* *390].
——. *The Vengeance of Fionn.* Dublin and London: Maunsel, 1917.

401.   [*YL* 391].
Clark, Barrett H[arper]. *The Blush of Shame: A Few Considerations on Verbal Obscenity in the Theater*. New York: Gotham Book Mart, 1932.

402.   [*YL* 392].
——. *The British and American Drama of To-Day*. NewYork: Henry Holt, 1915.

403.   [*YL* 393].
Claudel, Paul. *L'annonce faite à Marie: mystère en quatre actes*. Paris: Nouvelle Revue Française, 1913.

404.   [*YL* 394].
——. *Corona benignitatis anni Dei*. 4th ed. Paris: Nouvelle Revue Française, 1915.

405.   [*YL* 395].
Clifton, Harry. *Dielma and Other Poems*. London: Duckworth, 1932.

406.   [*YL* 396]. [NLI 40,568/48; copy of letter and postcard from H. Clifton to WBY inserted; 1 sheet; envelope 278].
——. *Flight: Poems*. London: Duckworth, 1934.

407.   [*YL* 397].
Clodd, Edward. *Memories*. London: Watts, 1926.

408.   [*YL* 398].
Cocteau, Jean. *Orphée: Tragedie en un acte et un intervalle*. Paris: Librairie Stock, 1927. Signed: GY

409.   [*YL* *399].
Coleridge, Mary E[lizabeth]. *Poems*. London: Elkin Mathews, 1909.

410.   [*YL* 400].
Coleridge, Samuel Taylor. *Biographia epistolaris: Being the Biographical Supplement of Coleridge's Biographia literaria, with Additional Letters, Etc. by A. Turnbull*. 2 vols. London: G. Bell, 1911.

411.   [Not listed in *YL*]. [NLI 40,568/49; 27 sheets; envelope --].
——. *Biographia literaria, or Biographical Sketches of My Literary Life and Opinions*. London: [Rest Fenner?], 1817.

412.   [*YL* 401]. [NLI 40,568/50; 25 sheets; envelope 282].
———. *Biographia literaria...and Two Lay Sermons: I. The Statesman's Manual; II. Blessed are Ye That Sow beside All Waters.* New ed. London: George Bell, 1876.

413.   [*YL* 402]. [NLI 40,568/51; 7 sheets; envelope 283].
———. *The Friend: A Series of Essays.* London: George Bell, 1875.

413A.   [*YL* 402A]. [NLI 40,568/52; 14 sheets; 14 sheets; envelope 284].
Another ed. Bohn's Standard Library. London: George Bell, 1906.

414.   [*YL* *403].
———. *Poems.* Selected and arranged with an intro. and notes by Arthur Symons. London: Methuen, 1905.

415.   [*YL* 404].
———. *The Poetical Works of Samuel Taylor Coleridge.* Ed. James Dykes Campbell. London: Macmillan, 1925. A reprint of the 1893 ed. Signed: GY

416.   [*YL* 405].
———. *Select Poetry and Prose.* Ed. Stephen Potter. London: Nonesuch Press, 1933. Signed: WBY

417.   [*YL* 406].
———. *Table Talk, and the Rime of the Ancient Mariner, Christabel, Etc.* London: George Routledge, [1884].

418.   [*YL* 407].
Coleridge, Sara. *Memoir and Letters of Sara Coleridge.* Ed. Edith Coleridge. 4th ed., abridged. London: Henry S. King, 1875.

419.   [*YL* *408].
Collins, Clifton W[ilbraham]. *Sophocles.* Ancient Classics for English Readers. Edinburgh and London: William Blackwood, 1897.

420.   [*YL* 409].
Collins Foreign Dictionaries. Italian. Italian-English/English-Italian. London and Glasgow: Collins, n.d.

421.   [*YL* 410].
Colum, Padraic. *Creatures.* New York: Macmillan, 1927.

422. [*YL* 411].
——. *Poems*. London: Macmillan, 1932.

423. [*YL* 412].
——. *Wild Earth: A Book of Verse*. Dublin: Maunsel, 1907.

423A. [*YL* *412A].
Another ed. Dublin: Maunsel, 1916.

424. [*YL* 413].
The Columban (Dublin) [the College of St. Columba's school journal] 59 (April 1938).

425. [*YL* *414]. [NLI 40,568/53; 2 sheets; envelope 450].
Colvin, Sidney. *Landor*. English Men of Letters. London: Macmillan, 1902. Bp: WBY

426. [*YL* 415].
Common Conditions. Ed. Tucker Brooke. Elizabethan Club Reprints, no. 1. New Haven: Yale University Press, 1915.

427. [*YL* *416].
Concordance to the Canonical Books of the Old and New Testaments, to Which Are Added a Concordance to the Books Called Apocrypha and a Concordance to the Psalter. London: Society for Promoting Christian Knowledge, [1859].

428. [*YL* *417].
Congreve, William. *The Comedies*. Ed. William E. Henley. 2 vols. English Classics. London: Methuen, 1895.

429. [*YL* 418].
Connolly, James B[rendan]. *Head Winds*. Charles Scribners, 1916.

430. [*YL* 419].
——. *Out of Gloucester*. Charles Scribners, 1902.

431. [*YL* 420].
Conrad, Joseph. *The Sisters*. New York: Crosby Gaige, 1928.

432. [*YL* 421].
——. *Well Done!* London: Privately printed by Clement Shorter, 1918.

433.   [Not listed in *YL* and given NLI number 3014]. [NLI 30,596; 13 sheets; see Wade 181 and *YL* 2369-2369e].
Convegno di lettere 8-14 Ottobre 1934—XII: Tema: Il teatro drammatico. Roma: Reale Academia d'Italia, 1935.

434.   [*YL* *422].
Copleston, Reginald S[tephen]. *Aeschylus*. Ancient Classics for English Readers. Edinburgh and London: William Blackwood, 1870. Signed: WBY

434A.   [*YL* 422A].
Another edition, 1897.

435.   [*YL* 423].
Coppard, A[lfred]. E[dgar]. *The Collected Poems*. London: Jonathan Cape, 1928.

436.   [*YL* 424].
Cornford, Frances. *Different Days*. [Poems]. London: The Hogarth Press, 1928.

437.   [*YL* 425].
——. *Mountains and Molehills*. [Poems]. Cambridge: The University Press, 1935.

438.   [*YL* *426].
Coryate, Thomas. *Coryat's Crudities*. London: 1611; reprint ed., 2 vols. Glasgow: James MacLehose, 1905. Bp: GY

439.   [*YL* 427].
Cotterill, H[enry]. B[ernard]. *A History of Art*. 2 vols. London: George G. Harrap, 1922-24.

x   [*YL* 428]. [NLI missing this copy].
The Courier (London) [newspaper], 18 January 1815.

440.   [*YL* 429].
Cousens, Henry. *The Architectural Antiquities of Western India*. London: The India Society, 1926. [Illustrated].

441.   [*YL* *430].
Cousins, James H[enry]. *Straight and Crooked*. [Poems]. London: Grant Richards, 1915.

442.   [*YL* 431].
Cousturier, Lucie. *Seurat.* Éditions des "Cahiers D'Aujourd'hui." Paris: Georges Crès, 1921. [Illustrated].

443.   [*YL* 432].
Craig, Edward Gordon. *Books and Theatres.* London and Toronto: J. M. Dent, 1925.

444.   [*YL* 433].
———. Review of *Diderot's Writings on the Theatre* edited by F. C. Green and *An Actor Prepares* by Constantin Stanislavsky. *The Sunday Times,* 20 June 1937, p. [9].

445.   [*YL* *434].
———. *Towards a New Theatre.* Forty Designs for Stage Scenes with Critical Notes by the Inventor. London: J. M. Dent, 1913.

446.   [*YL* 435].
[Crane, Walter]. *Walter Crane's Toy Books.* [Eight short children's books bound in one volume—*The Frog Prince, Goody Two Shoes, Beauty and the Beast, The Alphabet of Old Friends, The Yellow Dwarf, Aladdin or The Wonderful Lamp, The Hind in the Wood, Princess Belle Etoile*]. London and New York: George Routledge, [1874?].

447.   [*YL* 436]. [NLI 40,568/54; 15 sheets; envelope 1151].
Crespi, Angelo. *Contemporary Thought of Italy.* London: Williams and Norgate, 1926.

448.   [*YL* 437].
The Criterion (London) 2 (July 1924).

449.   [*YL* 438].
——— 14 (July 1935).

450.   [*YL* 439].
——— 14 (Oct. 1934–July 1935). Index. [Items indexed are by or about Yeats].

451.   [*YL* 440]. [NLI 40,568/55; 33 sheets; envelope 1181].
Croce, Benedetto. *Aesthetic as Science of Expression and General Linguistic.* Trans. Douglas Ainslie. 2nd ed. London: Macmillan, 1922.

452.   [*YL* 441].
——. *Ariosto, Shakespeare and Corneille*. Trans. Douglas Ainslie. London: George Allen and Unwin, [1921].

453.   [*YL* 442].
——. *An Autobiography*. Trans. R. G. Collingwood. Oxford: The Clarendon Press, 1927. Bp: WBY

454.   [*YL* 443]. [NLI 40,568/56; 19 sheets; envelope 1184].
——. *Historical Materialism and the Economics of Karl Marx*. Trans. C. M. Meredith. London: George Allen and Unwin, 1922.

455.   [*YL* 444]. [NLI 40,568/57; 245 sheets; envelope 1180].
——. *Logic as the Science of the Pure Concept*. Trans. Douglas Ainslie. London: Macmillan, 1917.

456.   [*YL* 445]. [NLI 40,568/58; 29 sheets; envelope 1183].
——. *The Philosophy of Giambattista Vico*. Trans. R. G. Collingwood. London: Howard Latimer, 1913.

457.   [*YL* 446]. [NLI 40,568/59; 121 sheets; envelope 1179].
——. *Philosophy of the Practical: Economic and Ethic*. Trans. Douglas Ainslie. London: Macmillan, 1913.

458.   [*YL* 447].
——. *The Poetry of Dante*. Trans. Douglas Ainslie. London: George Allen and Unwin, 1922.

459.   [*YL* 448].
——. *What Is Living and What Is Dead of the Philosophy of Hegel*. Trans. Douglas Ainslie. London: Macmillan, 1915. Signed: WBY

460.   [*YL* 449].
Crookes, William. *Researches in the Phenomena of Spiritualism*. Reprint from *The Quarterly Journal of Science*. London: J. Burns, [1874]. Bp: Annie M. Cooke

461.   [*YL* 450].
Cuala Industries. *Memorandum and Articles of Association of Cuala Industries, Limited*. Incorporated 6 Oct. 1938.

462.   [*YL* 451].
Cuala Press. *Complete List of Books Printed and Published by Cuala Press, Formerly Named Dun Emer Press, 1903–1926*, n.d.

463.   [*YL* 452].

——. *List of Books*. Cuala Press. Churchtown, [1914].

464.   [*YL* *453]. [NLI 40,568/60; 29 sheets; envelope 2039]. [See Chapman, *YA* 6 (1988): 234–45].

Cudworth, R[alph]. *The True Intellectual System of the Universe: The First Part; Wherein, All the Reason and Philosophy of Atheism is Confuted, and Its Impossibility Demonstrated*. London: Richard Royston, 1678.

465.   [*YL* 454]. [NLI 40,568/61/1–2; 2 and 19 sheets, respectively, in vols. 1 and 2; envelope 1256].

Another edition. 3 vols. London: Thomas Tegg, 1845. Bps : WBY

466.   [*YL* 455]. [NLI 40,568/62; 13 sheets; envelope 139].

Cumont, Franz. *Astrology and Religion among the Greeks and Romans*. New York and London: G. P. Putnam's, 1912. Bp: GY

467.   [*YL* 456]. [NLI 40,568/63; 12 sheets; envelope 1565]. [At plate XV, p. 16: a torn envelope inserted, adressed to WBY in London, 3 Aug. 1933].

Ćurčin, M[ilan]. *Ivan Meštrović: A Monograph*. London: Williams and Norgate, 1919. [Illustrated].

468.   [*YL* *457].

Curry, S[amuel]. S[ilas]. *Imagination and Dramatic Instinct: Some Practical Steps for Their Development*. Boston: The Expression Co., 1896.

469.   [*YL* *458].

——. *The Province of Expression: A Search for Principles Underlying Adequate Methods of Developing Dramatic and Oratoric Delivery*. Boston: School of Expression, 1891.

470.   [*YL* *459].

Curtin, Jeremiah, ed. *Hero-Tales of Ireland*. London: Macmillan, 1894.

471.   [*YL* *460].

Däath, Henrich. *Medical Astrology*. Astrological Manuals, no. 9. London: Sold by L. N. Fowler, n.d.

472.   [*YL* 461]. [A stamp inserted].
Dalton, O[rmonde]. M[addock]. *Byzantine Art and Archaeology.* Oxford: Clarendon Press, 1911. Bp: WBY

473.   [*YL* 462].
Daly, James. *The Guilty Sun.* [Pittsburgh]: Folio Press, 1926.

474.   [*YL* 463].
Damon, S[amuel]. Foster. *William Blake, His Philosophy and Symbols.* London: Constable, 1924.

475.   [*YL* *464].
Dampier, Captain William. *Dampier's Voyages.* Ed. John Masefield. 2 vols. London: Grant Richards, 1906.

476.   [*YL* 465].
Dan, Professor Inō, ed. *The Year Book of Japanese Art 1927.* Tokyo: National committee on intellectual co-operation of the League of Nations, 1928. [Illustrated].

477.   [*YL* *466].
Dante Alighieri. *Il Convito: The Banquet of Dante Alighieri.* Trans. Elizabeth Price Sayer. London: George Routledge, 1887. Signed: A. Senier

478.   [*YL* 467]. [NLI 40,568/64; 33 sheets; envelope 78].
———. *The Convivio of Dante Alighieri.* [Trans. Philip H. Wicksteed]. The Temple Classics. London: J. M. Dent, 1909. Bp: GY. Signed: Georgie Hyde Lees

479.   [*YL* 468].
———. *Dante's Inferno.* Trans. Laurence Binyon. London: Macmillan, 1933. Bp: WBY

480.   [*YL* 469].
———. *Dante's Purgatorio.* Trans. Laurence Binyon. London: Macmillan, 1938.

481.   [*YL* *470]. [NLI 40,568/65; 25 sheets; envelope 80].
———. *The Inferno of Dante Alighieri.* Trans. John Aitken Carlyle. Temple Classics. London: J. M. Dent, 1912.

482. [*YL* 471]. [NLI 40,568/66; 65 sheets; envelope 82].
——. *The Paradiso of Dante Alighieri*. Trans. P. H. Wicksteed. Temple Classics. London: J. M. Dent, 1910.

483. [*YL* *472]. [NLI 40,568/67; 29 sheets; envelope 81].
——. *The Purgatorio of Dante Alighieri*. Trans. T[homas]. O[key]. Temple Classics. London: J. M. Dent, 1906.

484. [*YL* 473].
——. *The Purgatory of Dante Alighieri: An Experiment in Literal Verse Translation*. Part I [Cantos 1–32]. Trans. Charles Lancelot Shadwell. Introduction by Walter Pater. London: Macmillan, 1892. Bp: WBY

485. [*YL* 474].
——. *The Purgatory of Dante Alighieri: An Experiment in Literal Verse Translation*. Part II [Cantos 28–33 ("The Earthly Paradise")]. Trans. Charles Lancelot Shadwell. London: Macmillan, 1899. Bp: WBY

486. [*YL* 475]. [NLI 40,568/68; 23 sheets; envelope 79].
——. *A Translation of the Latin Works of Dante Alighieri*. Trans. A. G. Ferrers Howell and Philip H. Wicksteed. Temple Classics. London: J. M. Dent, 1904.

487. [*YL* 476].
——. *The Vision: Or Hell, Purgatory, and Paradise of Dante Alighieri*. Trans. H. F. Cary. The Chandos Classics. London and New York: Frederick Warne, 1890.

488. [*YL* *477]. [NLI 40,568/69; 3 sheets; envelope 83].
——. *The Vita Nuova of Dante*. Ed. Ralph Radcliffe-Whitehead. London: The Chiswick Press, 1892.

489. [*YL* *478].
D'Annunzio, Gabriele. *Francesca da Rimini*. Trans. Arthur Symons. London: William Heinemann, 1902. Signed: WBY

490. [*YL* 479]. [NLI 40,568/70; 23 sheets; envelope 1067].
D'Arcy, Charles F[rederick]. *The Christian Outlook in the Modern World*. London: Hodder and Stoughton, [1929].

491. [*YL* *480].
[Daryush, Elizabeth (Elizabeth Bridges)]. Χαριτεσσι (*Charitessi*). [Poems]. Cambridge: Bowes and Bowes, 1912. Bp: WBY [All online catalog entries give the title as "*Charitessi, 1911*."]

491a.   [YL 480a].
Another copy.

492.   [YL 481].
——. *The Last Man and Other Verses.* London: Oxford University Press, 1936.

493.   [YL 482].
——. *Sonnets from Hafez and Other Verses.* London: Oxford University Press, 1921.

494.   [YL *483].
——. *Verses.* Oxford: B. H. Blackwell, 1916.

495.   [YL 484].
——. *Verses.* London: Oxford University Press, 1930.

496.   [YL 485].
——. *Verses, Second Book.* London: Oxford University Press,1932.

497.   [YL 486]. [Though reported in *YL*, did not come to NLI with a letter of presentation from David to WBY].
David, Villiers. *Poems.* London: The Unicorn Press, 1936.

498.   [YL *487].
Davidson, John. *In a Music-Hall and Other Poems.* London: Ward and Downey, 1891.

499.   [YL 488].
Davies, Rev. James. *Hesiod and Theognis.* Ancient Classics for English Readers. Edinburgh and London: William Blackwood, 1873. Signed: Arthur Graves [?].

500.   [YL *489]. [NLI 40,568/71; copy of letter inserted, James Guthrie to WBY (9 Oct. 1909); 2 sheets; envelope 312]. [Though reported in *YL*, did not come to NLI with said letter from Guthrie].
Davies, Oliver. *Between-Time Poems.* London: John Lane, 1909. Signed: Oliver Davies

501.   [YL 490].
Davies, W[illiam]. H[enry]. *Ambition and Other Poems.* London: Jonathan Cape, 1929.

502.   [YL *491].
——. *Collected Poems.* London: A. C. Fifield, 1916.

503.   [YL 492].
——. *Love Poems*. London: Jonathan Cape, 1935.

504.   [YL 493].
——. *Moss and Feather*. The Ariel Poems, no. 10. London: Faber and Gwyer, 1928.

505.   [YL *494].
——. *Nature Poems and Others*. London: A. C. Fifield, 1908.

506.   [YL 495].
——. *The Poems of W. H. Davies*. London: Jonathan Cape, 1934.

507.   [YL 496].
Davis, B[ernard]. E[ustace]. C[uthbert]. *Edmund Spenser: A Critical Study*. Cambridge: The University Press, 1933.

508.   [YL 497].
Davis, Thomas. *Essays Literary and Historical*. Preface by D. J. O'Donoghue and essay by John Mitchel. Dundalk: Dundalgan Press, 1914.

509.   [YL *498].
——. *Prose Writings*. Ed. T. W. Rolleston. The Camelot Series. London: Walter Scott, [1890]. Signed: WBY

509a.   [YL 498a].
Another copy.

510.   [YL 499].
[Day, John (attrib.)]. *The Return from Parnassus, or The Scourge of Simony*. Ed. Oliphant Smeaton. London: J. M. Dent, 1905.

511.   [Author erroneously attributed to composer and listed as YL 692, under "Foster, Miles B."]. [See Chapman, *YA* 8 (1991): 201–202].
A Day in a Child's Life. Illustrated by Kate Greenway. Music by Myles B[irket]. Foster. London: Routledge, n.d. [possibly 1882]. [Illustrated]. Cf. *YL* 692.

512.   [YL 500].
De Blacam, Aodh. *Old Wine: Verses from the Irish, Spanish, and Latin Done Chiefly in Irish Metres*. Dublin: At the sign of the three candles, [1936?].

513.   [*YL* 501]. [NLI 40,568/72; 18 sheets; envelope 2041].
Dee, Dr. John. *A True and Faithful Relation of What Passed for Many Yeers* [sic] *between Dr. John Dee…and Some Spirits.…Out of the original copy,…kept in the library of Thomas Cotton*. Ed. with preface by Meric Casaubon. London: Printed by D. Maxwell for T. Garthwait, 1659. [Illustrated]. Bp: WBY

514.   [*YL* 502].
Dekker, Thomas. *The Gull's Hornbook*. Ed. R. B. McKerrow. London: The De La More Press, 1904.

515.   [*YL* *503].
——. *Thomas Dekker*. The Mermaid Series. Ed. Ernest Rhys. London: T. Fisher Unwin, [1894].

516.   [*YL* 504].
De la Mare, Walter. *Alone*. The Ariel Poems, no. 4. London: Faber and Gwyer, [1927].

517.   [*YL* 505].
——. *At First Sight: A Novel*. New York: Crosby Gaige, 1928. Signed: Walter de la Mare

518.   [*YL* 506].
——. *Ding Dong Bell*. London: Selwyn and Blount, 1924.

519.   [*YL* *507].
——. *The Listeners and Other Poems*. London: Constable, 1916.

520.   [*YL* *508].
——. *Peacock Pie, A Book of Rhymes*. London: Constable, 1913.

521.   [*YL* 509].
——. *Poems, 1901 to 1918*. 2 vols. London: Constable, 1932.

522.   [*YL* 510].
——. *Self to Self*. The Ariel Poems, no. 11. London: Faber and Gwyer, [1928].

523.   [*YL* 511].
——. *A Snowdrop*. The Ariel Poems, no. 20. London: Faber and Faber, [1929].

524.   [*YL* 512].
——. *The Veil and Other Poems*. London: Constable, 1928.

525.   [*YL* *513]. [NLI 40,568/73; 4 sheets; envelope 1260].
Delanne, Gabriel. *Les apparitions matérialisées des vivants et des morts.* Vol. 2 [only vol. here]. Paris: Librairie Spirite, 1911.

526.   [*YL* 514].
Dempsey, Rev. T[homas]. *The Delphic Oracle: Its Early History, Influence and Fall.* Oxford: B. H. Blackwell, 1918.

527.   [*YL* 515].
Dennis, J[onas]. *Subversion of Materialism, by Credible Attestation of Supernatural Occurrences.* Bath: Upham, Collings, and Binns, 1826.

528.   [*YL* 516].
De Quincey, Thomas. *Confessions of an English Opium-Eater.* With intro. by William Sharp. London: Walter Scott, 1886. Signed: WBY. 1887

x   [*YL* 517]. [NLI is missing this copy, as well as *YL* 1972, into which it was inserted].
De Selincourt, Basil. Review of *The Oxford Book of Modern Verse* edited by WBY. *The Observer*, 22 Nov. 1936: 5. Inserted in *YL* 1972.

529.   [*YL* 518].
Deussen, Paul. *Outline of the Vedanta System of Philosophy According to Shankara.* Trans. J. H. Woods and C. B. Runkle. 2nd ed. Cambridge: Harvard University Press, 1927.

530.   [*YL* *519].
De Vere, Sir Aubrey. *Julian the Apostate and the Duke of Mercia: Historical Dramas.* London: Basil Pickering, 1858.

531.   [*YL* *520]. [NLI 40,568/74; 19 sheets; envelope 1263].
Devine, Rev. Arthur. *A Manual of Mystical Theology.* London: R. and T. Washbourne, 1903.

532.   [*YL* 521]. [NLI 40,568/75; 10 sheets; envelope 1939A].
Day, Sri Mukul Chandra. *My Pilgrimages to Ajanta and Bagh.* Intro. by Laurence Binyon. London: Thornton Butterworth, 1925. [Illustrated].

533.   [*YL* 522].
The Dial 76 (March 1924).

534.   [*YL* *523].
Diogenes Laërtius. *The Lives and Opinions of Eminent Philosophers.* Trans. C. D. Yonge. Bohn's Classical Library. London: George Bell, 1909.

535.   [Not listed in *YL* and assigned NLI Number 3015]. [See Chapman, *YA* 8 (1991): 201–202].
[Disraeli, Benjamin]. Lord Beaconsfield. *Tancred.* London: Longmans, Green, n.d. Bookplate: Anne Butler Yeats (1934).

536.   [*YL* 524].
Dobell, Sydney. *The Poems of Sydney Dobell.* London: Walter Scott, 1887.

537.   [*YL* 525].
Dodgson, Campbell. *A Catalogue of Etchings by Augustus John, 1901–1914.* London: Charles Chenil, 1920. Bp: Bethel and Gertrude Solomons

538.   [*YL* 526].
The Dome (London) 3 (Michaelmas Day, 1897).

539.   [*YL* *527].
———, n.s., 5 (Nov. 1899–Jan. 1900).

540.   [*YL* *528].
———, n.s., 6 (Feb.–April 1900).

541.   [*YL* 529].
Donaghy, John Lyle. *Primordia caeca.* Dublin: Eason, 1927.

542.   [*YL* 530].
Donne, John. *Complete Poetry and Selected Prose.* Ed. John Hayward. New York: The Nonesuch Press, 1929. Bp: WBY

543.   [*YL* *531].
———. *The Poems of John Donne.* Ed. Herbert J. C. Grierson. 2 vols. Oxford: Clarendon Press, 1912.

544.   [*YL* *532].
Donne William Bodham. *Euripides.* Ancient Classics for English Readers. Edinburgh and London: William Blackwood, 1872.

544a.   [*YL* 532a].
Another printing, 1898.

545.   [*YL* 533]. [NLI 40,568/76; 13 sheets; envelope 1264].
Donnelly, John J. *Subjective Concepts of Humans: Source of Spiritistic Manifestations*. New York: The International Press, 1922.

546.   [*YL* 534].
[Doolittle, Hilda] H. D. [pseud.] *Hymen: Poems*. London: The Egoist Press, 1921.

547.   [*YL* *535].
———. *Sea Garden: Poems*. London: Constable, 1916.

548.   [*YL* 536].
Doro, Edward. *Alms for Oblivion: Poems*. Paris: Casa Editorial Franco-Ibero-Americana, 1932.

549.   [*YL* *537].
Doughty, Charles M[ontagu]. *Adam Cast Forth: Sacred Drama in Five Songs*. London: Duckworth, 1908.

550.   [*YL* 538].
———. *Travels in Arabia Deserta*. 2 vols. London: Jonathan Cape and the Medici Society, 1923. Bp: WBY

551.   [*YL* *539].
———. *Wanderings in Arabia*. [Abridgement of *Travels in Arabia Deserta*]. Ed. Edward Garnett. 2 vols. London: Duckworth, 1908. Bp: WBY

552.   [*YL* 540].
Douglas, Norman. *In the Beginning*. London: Chatto and Windus, 1929.

553.   [*YL* 541].
Dowden, John. *The Saints in the Calendar and the Irish Synod: A Sermon Preached in St. Stephen's, Dublin, on Sunday, June 22, 1873*. Dublin: Edward Ponsonby, 1873.

554.   [*YL* *542].
Dowson, Ernest. *Decorations: In Verse and Prose*. London: Leonard Smithers, 1899.

555.   [YL *543].

———. *The Poems of Ernest Dowson.* Memoir by Arthur Symons. Illustrated by Aubrey Beardsley. Portrait by William Rothenstein. London: John Lane, 1909. [Illustrated]. Bp: WBY

556.   [YL 544].

———. *The Poetical Works.* Ed. Desmond Flower. London: Cassell, 1934.

557.   [YL *545].

———. *Verses.* London: Leonard Smithers, 1896.

558.   [YL 546].

Drayton, Michael. *Nimphidia, the Court of Fayrie.* Stratford-upon-Avon: The Shakespeare Head Press, 1921.

559.   [YL 547].

The Dream of Ravan: A Mystery. Reprinted from *The Dublin University Magazine.* London: The Theosophical Publishing Society, 1895.

560.   [YL *548].

Drinkwater, John. *Cophetua: A Play in One Act.* London: David Nutt, 1911.

561.   [YL *549].

———. *Lyrical and Other Poems.* Cranleigh: The Samurai Press, 1908.

562.   [YL 550].

———. *Persephone.* New York: William Edwin Rudge, 1926. Signed: John Drinkwater

563.   [YL *551].

———. *Poems of Love and Earth.* London: David Nutt, 1912.

564.   [YL *552].

———. *Poems of Men and Hours.* London: David Nutt, 1911.

565.   [YL *553].

———. *Rebellion: A Play in Three Acts.* London: David Nutt, 1914.

566.   [YL 554].

———. *Rupert Brooke: An Essay.* London: Printed for the author at the Chiswick Press, 1916.

567.   [YL *555].
——. *The Storm: A Play in One Act.* [Birmingham]: Published by the author at the Birmingham Repertory Theatre, 1915.

568.   [YL 556].
——. *Summer Harvest: Poems, 1924–1933.* London: Sidgwick and Jackson, 1933.

568a.   [YL 556a].
Another copy with presentation from Drinkwater to Yeats, dated November 1933.

569.   [YL *557].
Drummond, Sir William. *The Oedipus Judaicus.* London: Reeves and Turner, 1866.

570.   [YL *558].
Drummond of Hawthornden, William. *A Cypress Grove.* Stratford-on-Avon: The Shakespeare Head Press, 1907.

571.   [YL *559].
Dryden, John. *John Dryden: Plays.* Ed. George Saintsbury. 2 vols. The Mermaid Series. London: T. Fisher Unwin, [1904].

571a.   [YL *559a].
Another copy, vol. 2 only. Signed: GY

572.   [YL *560].
——. *The Poetical Works.* Ed. W. D. Christie. London: Macmillan, 1908.

573.   [YL 561].
Dublin Figaro: The Topical Journal of Ireland, n.s., 1 (18 June 1892).

574.   [YL 562].
The Dublin Magazine 2 (January 1924).

575.   [YL 563].
—— 6 (Oct.–Dec. 1931).

576.   [YL 564].
—— 7 (Jan.–March 1932).

577.   [YL 565].
—— 7 (Apr.–June 1932).

578.   [*YL* 566].
—— 8 (Oct.–Dec. 1933).

579.   [*YL* 567].
—— 9 (Apr.–June 1934).

580.   [*YL* 568].
—— 11 (Apr.–June 1936).

581.   [*YL* 569].
—— 13 (Apr.–June 1938).

582.   [*YL* 570]. [A greeting card inserted].
[*Dublin*] *Municipal Gallery of Modern Art: Illustrated Catalogue, with Biographical and Critical Notes*. Dublin: Dollard, 1908. [Illustrated].

583.   [*YL* 571].
[*Dublin*] *Municipal Gallery of Modern Art and Civic Museum*. [Book of plates on collections]. Dublin: Browne and Nolan, 1933.

583a.   [*YL* 571a].
Another copy.

584.   [*YL* 572].
[*Dublin University Magazine*]. Review of *Memoirs of Joseph Holt* as edited by T. Crofton Croker. [*Dublin University Magazine*] 12 (July 1838): 72–74.

584A.   [*YL* 572A].
Dublin University Review 1 (March 1885).

585.   [*YL* 573].
—— 1 (April 1885).

586.   [*YL* 574].
—— 1 (May 1885).

587.   [*YL* 575].
—— 1 (Aug.–Dec. 1885). Bound volume.

588.   [*YL* 576].
—— 1 (Sept. 1885).

588a.   [*YL* 576a].
Another copy.

589.   [*YL* 577].
—— 1 (Oct. 1885).

589a.   [*YL* 577a].
Another copy.

590.   [*YL* 578].
—— 2 (Feb. 1886).

591.   [*YL* 579].
—— 2 (March 1886).

591a.   [*YL* 579a–b]. [NLI missing one copy].
Two other copies, of which one remains.

592.   [*YL* 580].
—— 2 (April 1886).

593.   [*YL* 581].
—— 2 (Oct. 1886).

594.   [*YL* 582].
—— 2 (Nov. 1886).

595.   [*YL* 583]. [Though reported in *YL*, did not come to NLI with printed letter critical of WBY's essay on Ferguson].
—— 2 (Dec. 1886).

596.   [*YL* *584].
Du Chaillu, Paul B[elloni]. *The Viking Age: The Early History, Manners, and Customs of the Ancestors of the English-Speaking Nations.* 2 vols. London: John Murray, 1889.

597.   [*YL* 585]. [NLI 40,568/77; 17 and 5 sheets; envelope 1573].
Duffy, The Honorable Charles Gavan, ed. "*The Ballad Poetry of Ireland*" 40th Ed. and "*The National and Historical Ballads, Songs and Poems of Thomas Davis.*" Dublin: James Duffy, 1874.

598.   [*YL* *586].
——. *Short Life of Thomas Davis, 1840–1846* [sic]. London: T. Fisher Unwin, 1895.

599.   [*YL* *587].
——. *Young Ireland: A Fragment of Irish History, 1840–5.* London: T. Fisher Unwin, 1896.

600.   [*YL* 588].
Dunne, J[ohn]. W[illiam]. *An Experiment with Time*. London: A. and C. Black, 1929.

601.   [*YL* 589].
Dunsany, Lord [Edward John Moreton Drax Plunkett]. *The Old Folk of the Centuries: A Play*. London: Elkin Mathews and Marrot, 1930.

602.   [*YL* *590].
——. *The Sword of Welleran and Other Stories*. London: George Allen, 1908. Bp: Anne Butler Yeats | 1934

603.   [*YL* 591].
——. *The Travel Tales of Mr. Joseph Jorkens*. London and New York: G. P. Putnam's, 1931.

604.   [*YL* *592]. [NLI missing vol. 2].
Düntzer, Heinrich. *Life of Goethe*. Trans. Thomas W. Lyster. 2 vols. London: Macmillan, 1883.

604A.   [*YL* *592A].
Popular edition. London: T. Fisher Unwin, 1908.

605.   [*YL* 593].
Du Prel, Carl. *The Philosophy of Mysticism*. Trans. C.C. Massey. 2 vols. London: George Redway, 1889. Bp: WBY.

606.   [*YL* 594].
Durer, Albert. *The Little Passion of Albert Durer*. London: George Bell, 1894. [Illustrated].

607.   [*YL* *595].
Dutt, Romesh Chunder. *The Literature of Bengal: A Biographical and Critical History from the Earliest Times Closing with a Review of Intellectual Progress under the British Rule in India*. Calcutta: Thacker Spink, 1895.

608.   [*YL* 596].
Dutt, Toru. *Life and Letters of Toru Dutt*. [Ed.] Harihar Das. London: Oxford University Press, 1921. Bp: WBY

609.   [*YL* 328].
E., A. L. O. [pseud., Charlotte M. Tucker]. *My Neighbour's Shoes; or, Feeling for Others*. London: T. Nelson, 1875. [Illustrated].

610. [*YL* 597].
Easdale, Joan Adeney. *Clemence and Clare*. Hogarth Living Poets, no. 19. London: The Hogarth Press, 1932.

611. [*YL* 598].
——. *A Collection of Poems*. London: The Hogarth Press, 1931.

612. [*YL* 599].
The Eastern Buddhist (Otani University Library, Kyoto, Japan) 1 (July 1921).

612a–l. [*YL* 599a–l].
Twelve more consecutive numbers, from vol. 1 (Aug. 1921) to vol. 4 (July–Aug.–Sept. 1927).

613. [*YL* *600].
Eastlake, Allan. *The Oneida Community: A Record of an Attempt to Carry out the Principles of Christian Unselfishness and Scientific Race-Improvement*. London: George Redway, 1900. Stamped on half-title p.: Sent for review.

614. [Not listed in *YL* and assigned NLI Number 3016].
Ecclesiastes: Or the Preacher and the Song of Solomon. Vol. 1. [Lacks publication details]. On front cover: "File Copy | Not to be taken away."

615. [*YL* *601].
Eckartshausen, The Councillor Von [Karl von]. *The Cloud upon the Sanctuary*. Trans. Isabel de Steiger. Intro. by Arthur Edward Waite. London: Philip Wellby, 1903.

616. [*YL* 602].
Edel, Fritz. *German Labour Service*. Terramare Publications, no. 6. Berlin: Terramare Office, 1937.

617. [*YL* 603].
Eglinton, John [pseud., William Kirkpatrick Magee]. *Bards and Saints*. The Tower Press Booklets, no. 5. Dublin: Maunsel, 1906.

618. [*YL* 604].
——. *Irish Literary Portraits*. London: Macmillan, 1935.

619. [*YL* 605].
——. *Two Essays on the Remnant*. Dublin: Whaley, 1894. [bound with] *Pebbles from a Brook*. Kilkenny: Standish O'Crady, 1901.

620. [*YL* 606].

———, W. B. Yeats, AE [pseud., George Russell], and W[illiam]. Larminie. *Literary Ideals in Ireland*. London: T. Fisher Unwin, 1899; Dublin: Daily Express Office, 1899.

620a. [*YL* 606a].
Another copy.

621. [*YL* 607].
Einstein, Albert. *The Meaning of Relativity: Four Lectures Delivered at Princeton University, May, 1921*. Trans. Edwin Plimpton Adams. London: Methuen, 1922.

622. [*YL* 608].
The Election: A Comedy of Three Acts. London: n.p., 1749 and James Thomson [after Shakespeare etc.]. *Coriolanus: A Tragedy*. Dublin: G. and A. Ewing, J. Hoey, A. Bradley, J. Exshaw, W. Brien, and J. Esdall, 1749 [bound with] Thomas Otway [after Molière] *The Cheats of Scapin: A Farce*. Dublin: James Hoey, 1733 and P[aul]. H[iffernan], M. D. *The Self-Enamour'd or The Ladies Doctor: A Comedy*. Dublin: Augustus Long, 1750.

623. [*YL* 609].
Eliot, John. *The Parlement of Pratlers: A Series of Elizabethan Dialogues and Monologues Illustrating Daily Life and the Conduct of a Gentleman on the Grand Tour Extracted from "Ortho-epia gallica," a Book on the Corect Pronunciation of the French Language Written by Iohn Eliot, and Published in the Year 1593*. Ed. Jack Lindsay. London: The Fanfrolico Press, 1928. [Illustrated]. Signed.: Hall Collins [illustrator] and Jack Lindsay.

624. [*YL* 610].
Eliot, T[homas]. S[tearns]. *After Strange Gods: A Primer of Modern Heresy*. London: Faber and Faber, 1934.

625. [*YL* 611].
———. *Collected Poems, 1909–1935*. London: Faber and Faber, 1936.

626. [*YL* 612].
———. *Dante*. London: Faber and Faber, 1929.

627. [YL *613].
———. *Ezra Pound: His Metric and Poetry*. New York: Alfred A. Knopf, 1917.

628. [YL 614].
———. *Homage to John Dryden: Three Essays on the Poetry of the Seventeenth Century*. London: The Hogarth Press, 1924. Signed: WBY

629. [YL 615].
———. *Journey of the Magi*. The Ariel Poems, no. 8. London: Faber and Gwyer, [1927].

630. [YL 616].
———. *Murder in the Cathedral*. London: Faber and Faber, 1935.

631. [YL 617].
———. *Poems, 1909–1925*. London: Faber and Faber, 1932. Signed: GY

631a. [YL 617a].
Another printing, 1933.

632. [YL *618].
———. *Prufrock and Other Observations*. London: The Egoist, 1917.

633. [YL 619].
Another copy.

634. [YL 620].
———. *The Rock: A Pageant*. London: Faber and Faber, 1934. Signed: GY

635. [YL 621].
———. *The Sacred Wood: Essays on Poetry and Criticism*. London: Methuen, 1920. Signed: GY

636. [YL 622].
———. *A Song for Simeon*. The Ariel Poems, no. 16. London: Faber and Gwyer, [1928].

637. [YL 623].
———. *Sweeney Agonistes*. London: Faber and Faber, 1932.

638. [YL 624].
———. *The Use of Poetry and the Use of Criticism*. London: Faber and Faber, 1937. Signed: GY

639. [*YL* 625].
———. *The Waste Land*. London: The Hogarth Press, 1923.

639a. [*YL* 625a].
Another copy.

640. [*YL* *626].
Ellis, Edwin J[ohn]. *Sancan the Bard*. London: Ward and Downey, 1895.

641. [*YL* *627].
———. *Seen in Three Days*. Illustrated by the author. London: Bernard Quaritch, 1893. [Illustrated].

642. [*YL* *628].
Ellis, F[rederick]. S[tartridge]. *A Lexical Concordance to the Poetical Works of Percy Bysshe Shelley*. London: Bernard Quaritch, 1892.

643. [*YL* 629].
The Encyclopaedia Brittanica. 11th ed. 29 vols. New York, 1910.

644. [*YL* 630].
———. The New Volumes, constituting, in combination with the 29 vols. of the 11th ed., the 12th ed. 3 vols. London, 1922.

645. [*YL* 631].
The Enemy: A Review of Art and Literature (London), ed. Wyndham Lewis, 1 (Jan. 1927).

646. [*YL* 632].
——— 1 (Sept. 1927).

647. [*YL* 633].
——— 1 (First Quarter, 1929).

648. [*YL* 634].
The English Prayer Book: Together with the Psalter or Psalms of David. London: Society of SS. Peter and Paul, 1915.

649. [*YL* 635].
The English Review 117 (Aug. 1918).

650. [*YL* *636]. [NLI 40,568/79; vol. 1, 7 sheets; envelope 1268C].
Ennemoser, Joseph. *The History of Magic*. Trans. William Howitt. With appended "stories of apparitions, dreams, second sight, somnambulism, predictions, divination, witchcraft, vampires, fairies,

table-turning, and spirit-rapping" selected by Mary Howittt. 2 vols. London: H. G. Bohn, 1854. Bp: George R. Alexander.

651.   [*YL* 637].
The Erasmian (magazine of the [Erasmus Smith] High School, Dublin), n.s., 28 (Apr. 1937).

651a.   [*YL* 637a].
Another copy.

652.   [*YL* 638]. [NLI 40,568/80; 19 sheets, envelope 1145].
Erdmann, Johann Eduard. *A History of Philosophy*. English translation ed. Williston S. Hough. Vol. 2: *Modern Philosophy*. London: Allen and Unwin, 1924.

653.   [*YL* *639].
Ernst, Otto. *Master Flachsmann (Flachsmann als Erzieher): A Comedy in Three Acts*. Trans. H. M. Beatty. London: T. Fisher Unwin, 1909.

654.   [*YL* 640].
Esson, Luis. *Dead Timber and Other Plays*. London: Hendersons, 1920.

655.   [*YL* 641]. [NLI 40,568/81; 40 sheets; envelope 132].
Estens, John Locke. *The Paraclete and Mahdi; or, The Exact Testimony of Science to Revelation and Exposition of the Most Ancient Mysteries and Cults....* Sydney: John Sands, 1912. [Illustrated]. Bp: GY

656.   [*YL* 642].
[Eugen, Napoleon Nicolaus, Prince of Sweden]. *Prins Eugen: 60 reproduktioner i tontryck efter fotografier af originale*. [Monograph on the Swedish artist]. Sma Konstböcker, no. 15. Lund: Gleerupska Universitets-Bokhandeln, [1912?]. [Illustrated].

657.   [*YL* 643].
The Eugenics Review (London) 28 (Oct. 1936).

658.   [*YL* 644].
Euripides. *The Alcestis [of Euripides]: The Oxford Text with English Verse Translation by Sixth Form Boys of Bradfield College, 1904*. Oxford: James Parker, 1904.

659.   [*YL* *645].
———. *The Electra*. Trans. Gilbert Murray. London: George Allen, 1906.

659a.   [*YL* 645a].
Another copy, paper covers.

660.   [*YL* *646].
———. *The Hippolytus*. Trans. Gilbert Murray. London: George Allen, 1904.

661.   [*YL* *647].
———. *The Iphigenia in Tauris*. Trans. Gilbert Murray. London: George Allen, 1912.

662.   [*YL* *648].
———. *The Plays of Euripides in English*. 2 vols. Trans. Shelley, Dean Milman, Potter and Woodhull. Everyman's Library. London: J. M. Dent, [1906].

663.   [*YL* *649].
Everyman. With other Interludes, including eight miracle plays. London: J. M. Dent, 1910; New York: E. P. Dutton, 1910. Signed: GY

x   [*YL* 650]. [NLI missing this copy].
The Evening World (New York), 6 Sept. 1917: 1–2

664.   [*YL* 651].
Ewing, Juliana Horatia. *A Flat Iron for a Farthing*. London: George Bell, 1899. Signed: George Hyde-Lees.

665.   [*YL* 652].
The Exile 1 (Spring 1927). Ed. Ezra Pound.

665a.   [*YL* 652a].
Another copy.

666.   [*YL* 653].
——— 4 (Autumn 1928).

667.   [*YL* 654].
Exposition d'art irlandais. [Paris]: Galéries Barbazages, 109 Rue Du Faubourg-Saint-Honoré, 109. Ouverte du 28 Janvier au 25 Février 1922.

667a.   [*YL* 654a].
Another copy.

668.   [*YL* 655].
Exposition of the Malta Question, with Documents…February 1929–June 1930. [Translation]. Vatican: Vatican Polyglot Press, 1930.

669.   [*YL* 656].
Eyre, Thomas S[tephen]. *Our Days and Hours: What They Tell; A Method of Astro-philosophy*. Hull: The St. Stephen Press, 1907.

670.   [*YL* *657].
Fairfax, Edward. *Daemonologia: A Discourse on Witchcraft as It Was Acted in the Family of Mr. Edward Fairfax, of Fuyston, in the County of York, in the year 1621; Along with the Only Two Eclogues of the Same Author Known to Be in Existence*. Notes and biographical intro. by William Grainge. Harrogate: R. Ackrill, 1882.

671.   [*YL* 658].
Faraday, L[ucy]. Winifred. *The Edda: The Divine Mythology of the North*. Popular Studies in Mythology, Romance and Folklore, no. 12. London: David Nutt, 1902.

672.   [*YL* 659].
Farnell, Lewis Richard. *Greek Hero Cults and Ideas of Immortality*. The Gifford Lectures, delivered in the University of St. Andrews in the year 1920. Oxford: Clarendon Press, 1921.

673.   [*YL* *660].
Farquhar, George. *George Farquhar*. Ed. William Archer. The Mermaid Series. London: T. Fisher Unwin, [1906].

674.   [*YL* 661].
[Farr, Florence]. Advertisement for *Chanting and Speaking to the Music of the Psaltery* by Florence Farr.

675.   [*YL* 662].
———. Advertisement for *The Chorus of Classical Plays to the Music of the Psaltery* by Florence Farr.

675a–c.   [*YL* 662a–c].
Three more copies; inserted in *YL* 663.

675A. [*YL* 662A].

——— S[apientia]. S[apienti]. D[ono]. D[ata]. *Egyptian Magic*. Collectanea Hermetica, vol. 8. London: Theosophical Publishing Society, 1896.

676. [*YL* *663].

——— and Olivia Shakespear. *The Beloved of Hathor and The Shrine of the Golden Hawk*. [Lacks publication details].

677. [*YL* 664].

Faure, Elie. *History of Art*. Trans. Walter Pach. 4 vols. London: John Lane, 1921–24; New York: Harper, 1921–24.

678. [*YL* 665]. [NLI 40,568/82; 28 sheets; envelope 1271]. [See Chapman, *YA* 15 (2002): 288–312].

Fechner, Theodor. *On Life after Death*. Trans. Hugo Wernekke. 3rd ed. Chicago and London: Open Court Publishing, 1914.

679. [*YL* 666].

Ferguson, Sir Samuel. *Hibernian Nights' Entertainments*. First series. Dublin: Sealy, Bryers and Walker, 1887.

680. [*YL* 667].

———. *Hibernian Nights' Entertainments*. Third series: *The Rebellion of Silken Thomas*. Dublin: Sealy, Bryers and Walker, 1887.

681. [*YL* *668].

———. *Lays of the Red Branch*. London: T. Fisher Unwin, 1897.

682. [*YL* *669].

Festive Songs for Christmas. The Shakespeare Head Press Booklets, no. 2. Stratford: The Shakespeare Head Press, 1906.

683. [*YL* 670].

Field, Michael. *A Selection from the Poems*. Preface by T. Sturge Moore. London: The Poetry Bookshop, 1923.

684. [*YL* 671].

———. *Wild Honey, from Various Thyme*. London: T. Fisher Unwin, 1908.

685. [*YL* *672].

Fielding, Henry. *The Works of Henry Fielding, Esq.* Ed. James P. Browne. 11 vols. London: Bickers, 1902. Bp: WBY

686.   [YL 673].
Figgis, Darrell. *The Paintings of William Blake*. London: Ernest Benn, 1925. [Illustrated].

687.   [YL 674].
Fischer, E[duard]. W[ilhelm]. *Études sur Flaubert inédit*. Leipzig: Julius Zeitler, 1908.

688.   [YL 675]. [NLI 40,568/83; 2 sheets; envelope 1056].
Fisher, Right Hon. H[erbert]. A[lbert]. L[aurens]. Review of *The Decline of the West*, by Oswald Spengler. *The Observer*, 27 January 1929.

689.   [YL 676].
Five Favourite Tales from the Arabian Nights in Words of One Syllable. Ed. A. and A. E. Warner. London: H. K. Lewis, 1871. Bp: Elizabeth Corbet Yeats

690.   [YL 677].
Flambart, Paul. *Étude nouvelle sur l'hérédité: Accompagnée d'un recueil de nombreux exemples avec dessins de l'auteur*. Paris: Bibliothèque Chacornac, 1903.

691.   [YL 678].
Flammarion, Camille. *Death and Its Mystery before Death: Proofs of the Existence of the Soul*. Trans. E. S. Brooks [vol. 1] and Latrobe Carroll [vols. 2-3]. 3 vols. London: T. Fisher Unwin, 1921-23.

692.   [YL 679].
Flaubert, Gustave. *Bouvard and Pécuchet*. Trans. D. F. Hannigan. London: H. S. Nichols, 1896.

693.   [YL 680].
——. *The First Temptation of Saint Anthony*. Trans. Rene Francis from the 1849-56 manuscripts ed. Louis Bertrand. London: Duckworth, 1910.

694.   [YL 681].
——. *Sentimental Education: A Young Man's History*. Trans. D. F. Hannigan. 2 vols. London: H. S. Nichols, 1898. Signed: WBY

695.   [YL 682].
——. *The Temptation of Saint Antony*. Trans. D. F. Hannigan. London: H. S. Nichols, 1895.

696.   [YL *683].
Flecker, James Elroy. *The Collected Poems*. Ed. J. C. Squire. London: Martin Secker, 1916.

697.   [YL 684].
Fletcher, Phineas. *Venus and Anchises (Brittain's Ida) and Other Poems*. Ed. Ethel Seaton. London: Oxford University Press, 1926.

698.   [YL *685].
Flint, F[rank]. S[tewart]. *Cadences*. London: The Poetry Bookshop, [1915].

699.   [YL *686]. [A Christmas madrigal inserted].
Florilegio di canti toscani: Folk Songs of the Tuscan Hills. Trans. Grace Warrack. London: Alexander Moring, the de la More Press, 1914.

700.   [YL 687].
Form: A Quarterly of the Arts (London) 1 (April 1916). Ed. Austin O. Spare and Francis Marsden.

701.   [YL 688].
Formes: An International Review of Plastic Art, Appearing Ten Times a Year in Two Editions, French and English (Paris) 9 (Nov. 1930). English ed.

702.   [YL 689].
Forster, E[dward]. M[organ]. *What I Believe*. London: The Hogarth Press, 1939.

703.   [YL *690]. [NLI 40,568/84/1-2; 11 and 32 sheets in vols. 1 and 2, respectively; envelope 449/1-2].
Forster, John. *Walter Savage Landor, a Biography*. 2 vols. London: Chapman and Hall, 1869. Bp: WBY

704.   [YL 691].
Fortescue, [Winifred]. Lady. *Sunset House, More Perfume from Provence* [Reminiscences of Provence]. Edinburgh and London: Blackwood, 1937.

[YL 692, moved to *A Day in a Child's Life*].

705.   [YL *693].
Foucher, A[lfred]. *The Beginnings of Buddhist Art and Other Essays in Indian and Central Asian Archaeology*. Rev. by the author. Trans. L.

A. Thomas and F. W. Thomas. For the members of the India Society, 1917. London: Humphrey Milford, 1917.

706.   [Not listed in *YL* and assigned NLI Number 3018].

The Four Gospels of the Lord Jesus Christ According to the Authorised Version of King James I. Illustrated by Eric Gill. Berkshire: Golden Cockrell Press, 1931. [Illustrated]. Flyleaf: "W. B. Yeats from George Yeats | 1936." Back flyleaf: "This book was printed by Robert and Moira Gibbings at the Golden Cockrell Press at Walthan Saint Lawrence in Berkshire. Begun on the 20th of February, 1931, it was completed on the 28th of October in the same year. Compositors: F. Young and A. H. Gibbs. Pressman: A. C. Cooper. 500 copies have been printed, of which numbers 1–12 are on vellum. This is no. 16." In slipcase.

707.   [*YL* 694].

Franklin, Benjamin. *Autobiography*. Everyman's Library. London: J. M. Dent, 1937.

708.   [*YL* 695].

Frazer, J[ames]. G[eorge]. *The Belief in Immortality and the Worship of the Dead*. The Gifford Lectures, St. Andrews, 1911–12. London: Macmillan, 1913.

709.   [*YL* 696].

———. *Folk-Lore in the Old Testament: Studies in Comparative Religion, Legend and Law*. Abridged ed. London: Macmillan, 1923.

710.   [*YL* 697].

———. *The Golden Bough: A Study in Magic and Religion*. 3rd ed. Vols. 1 and 2: *The Magic Art and the Evolution of Kings*. London: Macmillan, 1911. Bp: WBY

711.   [*YL* 698].

———. Vol. 3: *Taboo and the Perils of the Soul*. London: Macmillan, 1911. Bp: WBY

712.   [*YL* 699].

———. Vol. 4: *The Dying God*. London: Macmillan, 1911. Bp: WBY

713.   [*YL* 700].

———. Vol. 5: *Adonis, Attis, Osiris*. 2nd ed., rev. and enlarged. London: Macmillan, 1907. Bp: WBY

714.   [*YL* 701].
——. Vols. 6 and 7: *Spirits of the Corn and of the Wild*. London: Macmillan, 1912. Bp: WBY [Vol. 8, *The Scapegoat*, is missing]

715.   [*YL* 702].
——. Vols. 9 and 10: *Balder the Beautiful. The Fire-Festivals of Europe and the Doctrine of the External Soul*. London: Macmillan, 1913. Bp: WBY

716.   [*YL* 703].
——. Vol. 12: *Bibliography and General Index*. London: Macmillan, 1915. Bp: WBY

717.   [*YL* 704].
The Freeman (New York). 3 (24 Aug. 1921).

x   [*YL* 704a]. [NLI missing this copy].
Another copy, consisting only of John Butler Yeats's essay "A Dialogue in Heaven"; in envelope labeled: "Articles in 'Freeman' U.S.A. | by JBY."

718.   [*YL* 705].
—— 4 (4 Jan. 1922).

x   [*YL* 705a]. [NLI missing this copy].
Another copy of John Butler Yeats's essay only, "A Painter of Pictures"; in envelope as above.

719.   [*YL* 706].
—— 4 (15 Feb. 1922).

x   [*YL* 706a]. [NLI missing this copy].
Another copy of John Butler Yeats's essay only, "The Soul of Dublin"; in envelope as above.

720.   [*YL* 707].
—— 4 (22 Feb. 1922).

x   [*YL* 707a]. [NLI missing this copy].
Another copy of the obituary notice of John Butler Yeats by E. A. Boyd; in envelope as above.

721.   [*YL* 708].
—— 4 (1 March 1922)]. "A Reviewer's Notebook," a remembrance of John Butler Yeats, pp. 598–99.

721a–b. [*YL* 708a–c]. [NLI missing one copy].
Three more copies, of which two remain, of the remembrance of John Butler Yeats only. At top: Van Wyck [Brooks] [in envelope as above].

722.   [*YL* 709].
[*The Freeman's Journal*]. Review of the Irish Literary Theatre's first performance of Hyde's *The Twisting of the Rope* and Yeats's and Moore's *Diarmuid and Grainne*, [22 Oct. 1901].

x   [*YL* 710]. [NLI missing this copy].
The Free State (Dublin) (19 Aug. 1922). War Special.

x   [*YL* 711]. [NLI missing this copy].
—— (30 Aug. 1922). Michael Collins Memorial Number.

723.   [*YL* 712]. [NLI 40,568/85; 2 letters inserted from C. French to WBY (27 June {1927}, 23 July 1923); 4 sheets; envelope 377].
French, Cecil. *Between Sun and Moon: Poems and Woodcuts.* London: The Favil Press, 1922. [Illustrated].

723a.   [Not listed in *YL* and assigned NLI number 3019].
Another copy.

724.   [*YL* 713].
——. *With the Years.* London: The Richards Press, 1927. Signed: Cecil French

725.   [*YL* 714].
Frercks, Rudolf. *German Population Policy.* Berlin: Terramare Office, 1937.

726.   [*YL* 715]. [NLI 40,568/86; 23 sheets; envelope 1069].
Frobenius, Leo. *Paideuma: Umrisse einer Kultur- und Seelenlehre.* München: C. Y. Beck'sche Verlagsbuchhandlung, 1921. Signed: D. Yard

727.   [*YL* 716].
From the Upanishads. [Trans.] Charles Johnston. Portland, ME: Thomas B. Mosher, 1913.

728.   [*YL* 717].
Il frontespizio (Florence) 6 (June 1938).

729.   [YL 718].
Fry, Roger. *Vision and Design*. The Phoenix Library. London: Chatto and Windus, 1928.

730.   [YL 719].
Fukui, Kikusaburo. *Japanese Ceramic Art and National Characteristics*. [Tokyo: K. Ohashi, 1927]. [Illustrated].

731.   [YL 720].
Fuller, Capt. J[ohn]. F[rederick]. C[harles]. *The Star in the West: A Critical Essay upon the Works of Aleister Crowley*. London: Walter Scott, 1907.

732.   [YL 721].
The Gael (New York) 21 (Dec. 1902).

733.   [YL 722].
——, n.s., 22 (Feb. 1903).

x   [YL 723]. [NLI missing this copy].
The Gaelic American (New York), 5 March 1904.

x   [YL 724]. [NLI missing this copy; inserted in *YL* 1837].
Gaiety Theatre (Dublin). *Performances by the Royal Carl Rosa Opera Company*. 24 Oct. 1921–4 Nov. 1921.

734.   [YL 725].
Galassi, Giuseppe. *Roma o Bisanzio: I musaici di Ravenna e le origini dell'arte italiana*. Roma: La Libreria dello Stato, 1930. [Illustrated].

735.   [YL 726].
Gardner, Arthur, ed. *French Sculpture of the Thirteenth Century: Seventy-Eight Examples of Masterpieces of Medieval Art Illustrating the Works at Reims and Showing Their Place in the History of Sculpture*. Intro. and notes by Arthur Gardner. The Medici Portfolios, no. 1. London: Philip Lee Warner, 1915. [Illustrated].

736.   [YL *727].
Gardner, Charles. *William Blake, the Man*. London: J. M. Dent, 1919. Bp: WBY

737.   [YL *728].
Gardner, Edmund G[arratt]. *Dukes and Poets in Ferrara: A Study in the Poetry, Religion and Politics of the Fifteenth and Early Sixteenth Centuries.* London: Archibald Constable, 1904.

738.   [YL *729]. [Though reported in YL, did not come to NLI with postcard showing "Casa di Ludovico Ariosto"].
——. *The King of the Court Poets: A Study of the Work, Life and Times of Lodovico Ariosto.* London: Archibald Constable, 1906.

739.   [YL *730]. [NLI 40,568/87; copy of letter inserted from Gardner to WBY (29 Sept. 1903); 2 sheets; envelope 1283]. [Though reported in YL, did not come to NLI with a letter from the author to WBY].
Gardner, F[rederick]. Leigh. *A Catalogue Raisonné of Works on the Occult Sciences.* Vol. 1: *Rosicrucian Books.* Intro. by Dr. William Wynn Westcott. London: Privately printed, 1903. Signed: F. Leigh Gardner

740.   [YL *731]. [NLI 40,568/88; 10 sheets; envelope 1284].
Garnett, Lucy M[ary]. J[ane]. *Greek Folk Poesy: Annotated Translations, from the Whole Cycle of Romaic and Folk-Verse and Folk-Prose.* Ed. with essays [etc.] by J. S. Stuart-Glennie. New Folklore Researches, vol. 2. London: David Nutt, 1896.

741.   [YL 732].
Garnett, Richard, trans. *A Chaplet from the Greek Anthology.* Cameo series. London: T. Fisher Unwin, 1892. Signed: WBY

742.   [YL 733].
—— and Edmund Gosse. *English Literature: An Illustrated Record.* 4 vols. London: William Heinemann, 1903.

743.   [YL *734].
Gascoigne, George [and Francis Kinwelmersh]. *Supposes and Jocasta: Two Plays Translated from the Italian, the First by Geo. Gascoigne, the Second by Geo. Gascoigne and F. Kinwelmersh.* Ed. John W. Cunliffe. Boston and London: D. C. Heath, 1906.

744.   [YL 735].
Gasparri, Peter Cardinal. *The Catholic Catechism.* Trans. the Dominican Fathers. London: Sheed and Ward, 1934.

745.   [YL 736].
Gaunt, W[illiam]. *Bandits in a Landscape: A Study of Romantic Painting from Caraveggio to Delacroix.* London: The Studio Limited, 1937.

746.   [YL *737].
Gayley, Charles Mills. *Plays of Our Forefathers, and Some of the Traditions upon Which the Plays Were Founded.* London: Chatto and Windus, 1908.

747.   [YL 738].
The Geeta: The Gospel of the Lord Shri Krishna. Trans. Shri Purohit Swami. London: Faber and Faber, 1935. Signed: Shri Purohit Swāmi

747a.   [YL 738a].
Another copy.

747b–d. [YL 738b–d].
Three more copies.

748.   [Not listed in *YL* and assigned NLI number 3020].
Another copy. Flyleaf: "To W. B. Yeats | from | Purohit Swami."

749.   [YL 739]. [NLI 40,568/89; 10 sheets; envelope 1285].
Geley, Gustave. *From the Unconscious to the Conscious.* Trans. Stanley de Brath. London: William Collins, 1921. [Illustrated].

750.   [YL 740].
Gentile, Giovanni. *La nuova scuola media.* Firenze: Vallecchi Editore, 1925.

751.   [YL 741].
——. *The Reform of Education.* Trans. Dino Bigongiari. With an intro. by Benedetto Croce. London: Macmillan, 1922.

752.   [YL 742]. [NLI 40,568/90; 37 sheets; envelope 1189].
——. *The Theory of Mind As Pure Act.* Trans. from the third ed. by H. Wildon Carr. London: Macmillan, 1922.

753.   [YL *743].
Gesta Romanorum. Trans. the Rev. Charles Swan. Revised and corrected by Wynnard Hooper. London: George Bell, 1905.

754. [YL *744].
Ghose, Manmohan. *Love-Songs and Elegies*. London: Elkin Mathews, 1898.

755. [YL *745].
Gibbon, Edward. *The Autobiographies of Edward Gibbon*. Ed. John Murray. London: John Murray, 1896.

756. [YL *746].
——. *The History of the Decline and Fall of the Roman Empire*. Ed. J. B. Bury. 7 vols. London: Methuen, 1909–14.

757. [YL 747].
Gibbon, Monk. *The Branch of Hawthorn Tree*. London: The Grayhound Press, 1927. Bp: Lily Yeats

758. [YL 748].
Gide, André. *Back from the U.S.S.R.* Trans. Dorothy Bussy. London: Martin Secker and Warburg, 1937. Signed: WBY

759. [YL 749].
Gill, Eric. *An Essay on Typography*. London: Sheed and Ward, 1936.

760. [YL *750]. [NLI 40,568/91; 22 sheets; envelope 1286]. [See Chapman, YA 6 (1988): 234–45].
Glanvil, Joseph. *Sadducismus triumphatus; or, A Full and Plain Evidence, Concerning Witches and Apparitions. In Two Parts. The First Treating of Their Possibility. The Second of Their Real Existence....*Trans. with additions by Dr. Horneck. 4th ed. London: Printed for A. Bettesworth and J. Batley...; W. Mears, and J. Hooke, 1726. Bp: WBY

761. [YL 751].
Goblet d'Alviella, Eugène Félicien Albert, Compte. *The Migration of Symbols*. [Trans.?] Sir George Birdwood. Westminster: Archibald Constable, 1894.

762. [YL 752].
Goddard, E. H. and P[hilip]. A[rnold]. *Civilisation or Civilisations: An Essay in the Spenglerian Philosophy of History*. London: Constable, 1926.

763.   [YL 753].
Goethe, Johann Wolfgag Von. *The First Part of the Tragedy of Faust*. Trans. Thomas E. Webb. New ed. [with the "Death of Faust"]. London: Longmans, Green, 1898.

764.   [YL 754].
Gogarty, Oliver St. John. *As I Was Going down Sackville St: A Phantasy in Fact*. London: Rich and Cowan, 1937.

765.   [YL 755]. [NLI 40,568/92; 6 sheets; envelope 1631; Wade 274].
———. *An Offering of Swans and Other Poems*. London: Eyre and Spottiswoode, [1924].

765a.   [YL 755a].
Another copy.

765b.   [YL 755b].
Another copy.

766.   [YL 756]. [NLI 40,568/93; 2 sheets; envelope 1633].
———. *Selected Poems*. New York: Macmillan, 1933.

767.   [YL 757].
Goldsmith, Oliver. *The Vicar of Wakefield*. London: Walker and Edwards, 1817.

768.   [YL 758].
Gore-Booth, Eva. *Poems*. Complete edition…with biographical introduction by Esther Roper. London: Longmans, Green, 1929. Bp: WBY

769.   [YL *759].
Gosse, Edmund. *On Viol and Flute: Poems*. London: William Heinemann, 1896.

770.   [YL 760].
[Gowans, Adam Luke, ed.]. *Some Moths and Butterflies and Their Eggs: Sixty Photographs from Nature by A. E. Tonge*. Gowans's Nature Books, no. 15. London: Gowans and Gray, 1907.

771.   [YL *761].
Gower, John. *Confessio Amantis*. Ed. Dr. Reinhold Pauli. 3 vols. London: Bell and Daldy, 1857. Bp: WBY

772. [YL 762].
Grant, Sir Francis J[ames], ed. *The Manual of Heraldry: A Concise Description of the Several Terms Used, and Containing a Dictionary of Every Designation in the Science.* New and rev. ed. Edinburgh: John Grant, 1937.

773. [YL 763].
Granville-Barker, Harley. *On Poetry in Drama.* The Romanes Lecture delivered in the Taylor Institution, 4 June 1937. London: Sidgwick and Jackson, 1937.

774. [YL 764].
Grattan, Henry. *The Select Speeches of the Right Hon. Henry Grattan: To Which is Added His Letter on the Union, with a Commentary on His Career and Character by Daniel Owen Madden.* Dublin: James Duffy, 1845.

775. [YL *765].
——. *Speeches of the Right Honorable Henry Grattan.* Vol. 1. Dublin: H. Fitzpatrick, 1811. Bp: George Pollexfen [?]

[YL 766 erroneously gives series title in place of title of work; moved to 779].

776. [YL 767].
Graves, Robert. *Poems, 1914–26.* London: William Heinemann, 1928.

777. [YL 768].
——. *Poems, 1926–1930.* London: William Heinemann, 1931.

778. [YL 769].
——. *Poems, 1930–1933.* London: Arthur Barker, 1933.

779. [YL 766].
——. *Robert Graves.* The Augustan Books of Modern Poetry. London: Ernest Benn, [1933?].

780. [YL *770].
Gray, John. *Spiritual Poems.* Frontispiece and border designed by Charles Ricketts. London: Hacon and Ricketts, 1896.

781.   [*YL* 771].
[Great Britain]. Laws, Statutes etc. *An Act for Incorporating a Company for the Improvement of Waste Lands in Ireland, 4th July 1836.* 6 and 7 William 4, ch. 97.

782.   [*YL* 772].
——. *An Act for Regulating and Improving the Town of Galway in the County of the Same Town, 4th July 1836.* 6 and 8 William 4, ch. 117.

783.   [*YL* 773].
——. *Patents, Designs, Copyright and Trade Marks Emergency Act, 1939.* 2 and 3 George 6, ch. 107.

784.   [*YL* 774].
Green, H. S. *Directions and Directing.* Foreword by Alan Leo. Astrological Manuals, no. 5. London: "Modern Astrology," 1905. Bp: GY

785.   [Not listed in *YL* and assigned NLI number 3021].
Another copy.

786.   [*YL* *775]. [NLI 40,568/94; sheets 20 and 4 sheets, respectively, in vols. 1 and 2; envelope 288A].
Green, Joseph Henry. *Spiritual Philosophy: Founded on the Teaching of the Late Samuel Taylor Coleridge.* Ed. with a memoir by John Simon. 2 vols. London and Cambridge: Macmillan, 1865. Bp: WBY

787.   [*YL* *776].
Greene, George A[rthur]. *Songs of the Open Air.* London: Elkin Mathews, 1912.

788.   [*YL* *777].
The Green Sheaf (London) 1 (1903). Ed. Pamela Colman Smith.

x   [*YL* 777a]. [NLI missing this copy].
Another copy.

789.   [*YL* *778].
—— 2 (1903).

790.   [*YL* *779].
—— 3 (1903).

x   [*YL* 779a]. [NLI missing this copy].
Another copy. Insertion as above.

791.   [*YL* *780].
    —— 4 (1903).

792.   [*YL* *781].
    —— 5 (1903).

x   [*YL* 781a]. [NLI missing this copy].
    Another copy.

793.   [*YL* *782].
    —— 6 (1903).

x   [*YL* 782a]. [NLI missing this copy].
    Another copy.

794.   [*YL* 783].
    —— 7 (1903).

795.   [*YL* 784].
    —— 8 (1903).

796.   [*YL* 785].
    —— 9 (1904).

797.   [*YL* 786].
    —— 11 (1904).

798.   [*YL* 787].
    —— 12 (1904)

799.   [*YL* 788].
    —— 13 (1904).

800.   [*YL* 789].
    Greenwood, Alice Drayton. *Horace Walpole's World: A Sketch of Whig Society under George III*. London: G. Bell, 1913.

801.   [*YL* *790].
    Gregory, Isabella Augusta, Lady. *A Book of Saints and Wonders*. London: John Murray, 1907. Bp: WBY

802.   [*YL* 791].
    ——. *Case for the Return of Sir Hugh Lane's Pictures to Dublin*. Dublin: The Talbot Press, 1926.

802a.   [*YL* 791a].
    Another copy.

803. [*YL* *792]. [NLI 40,567/5; 14 sheets; Wade 256].
———. *Cuchulain of Muirthemne: The Story of the Men of the Red Branch of Ulster*. Arranged and trans. Lady Gregory. With preface by W. B. Yeats. 3rd ed. London: John Murray, 1907. Bp: WBY. Signed: WBY.

804. [*YL* *793].
———. *The Full Moon: A Comedy in One Act*. [Dublin]: Published by the author at the Abbey Theatre, 1911.

805. [*YL* 794].
———. *The Gaol Gate*. Dublin: The Talbot Press, [1918].

806. [*YL* *795]. [NLI 40,567/6; 24 sheets; Wade 258].
———. *Gods and Fighting Men: The Story of the Tuatha de Danaan and of the Fianna of Ireland*. Arranged and trans. Lady Gregory. With a preface by W. B. Yeats. London: John Murray, 1904. Bp: WBY.

807. [*YL* *796].
———. *Hugh Lane's Life and Achievement, with Some Account of the Dublin Galleries*. London: John Murray, 1921.

808. [*YL* 797].
———. *The Image and Other Plays*. London: G. P. Putnam's, 1922.

809. [*YL* *798].
———. *Irish Folk-History Plays*. First series: *The Tragedies: Crania, Kincora, Dervorgilla*. New York and London: G. P. Putnam's, 1912. Signed: GY

809a. [*YL* 798a].
Another copy.

810. [*YL* *799].
———. *Irish Folk-History Plays*. Second series: *The Tragic-Comedies: The Canavans, The White Cockade, The Deliverer*. New York and London: G. P. Putnam's, 1912.

810a. [*YL* 799a].
Another copy.

811. [*YL* *800].
———. *The Kiltartan History Book*. Illustrated by Robert Gregory. Dublin: Maunsel, 1909. [Illustrated].

812.   [*YL* 801].
——. Another ed. London: T. Fisher Unwin, 1926.

813.   [*YL* 802].
——. *The Kiltartan Wonder Book*. Illustrated by Margaret Gregory. Dublin: Maunsel, [1910]. [Illustrated].

814.   [*YL* *803].
——. *Kincora: A Play in Three Acts*. Abbey Theatre Series, vol. 2. Dublin: The Abbey Theatre, 1905.

815.   [*YL* 804].
——. *Mirandolina: A Comedy Translated and Adapted from La Locandiera of Goldoni*. London and New York: G. P. Putnam's, 1924.

816.   [*YL* 805].
——. *My First Play*. London: Elkin Mathews and Marrot, 1930. Signed: A Gregory

817.   [*YL* *806].
——. *Our Irish Theatre: A Chapter of Autobiography*. New York and London: G. P. Putnam's, 1913. Bp: WBY

818.   [*YL* *807]. [NLI 40,568/95; 11 sheets; envelope 1640].
——. *Poets and Dreamers: Studies and Translations from the Irish*. Dublin: Hodges, Figgis, 1903.

819.   [*YL* 808].
——. *The Story Brought by Brigit: A Passion Play in Three Acts*. London and New York: G. P. Putnam's, 1924.

820.   [*YL* 809].
——. *Three Last Plays*. London and New York: G. P. Putnam's, 1928.

x   [*YL* 810]. [NLI missing this copy; removed to Anne Yeats Personal Library].
——. *Three Wonder Plays*. London and New York: G. P. Putnam's, [1923].

821.   [*YL* *811]. [NLI 40,567/7; 5 sheets; Wade 312].
——. *Visions and Beliefs in the West of Ireland*. Collected and arranged by Lady Gregory. With two essays and notes by W. B. Yeats. 2 vols. New York and London: G. P. Putnam's, 1920.

822.   [*YL* *812].
———, ed. *Mr. Gregory's Letter-Box, 1813–1830*. London: Smith, Elder, 1898.

823.   [*YL* 813].
———, ed. *Sir William Gregory, K.C.M.G., Formerly Member of Parliament and Sometime Governor of Ceylon: An Autobiography*. London: John Murray, 1894.

824.   [*YL* 814].
Greville, Charles C[avendish]. F[ulke]. *A Journal of the Reigns of King George IV and King William IV*. Ed. Henry Reeve. The Greville Memoirs. 3rd ed. 3 vols. London: Longmans, Green, 1875.

825.   [*YL* 815].
Grierson, Francis. *Modern Mysticism and Other Essays*. London: George Allen, 1899.

826.   [*YL* 816].
Grierson, Herbert J[ohn]. C[lifford]. *Metaphysical Lyrics and Poems of the Seventeenth Century: Donne to Butler*. Oxford: Clarendon Press, 1921.

827.   [*YL* 817].
Griffith, Arthur. *The Resurrection of Hungary: A Parallel for Ireland*. With appendices on Pitt's policy and Sinn Fein. 3rd ed. Dublin: Whelan, 1918.

828.   [*YL* 818].
Grose, S[idney]. W[illiam]. *Catalogue of the McClean Collection of Greek Coins*. 2 vols. Cambridge: University Press, 1923 and 1926. Signed: WBY

829.   [*YL* 819].
Gubernatis, Angelo de. *Zoological Mythology, or The Legends of Animals*. 2 vols. London: Trübner, 1872.

830.   [*YL* 820].
Guedala, Philip. *Bonnet and Shawl: An Album*. [Essays on 19th-century women]. New York: Crosby Gaige, 1928. [Illustrated]. Signed: Philip Guedala

831.   [*YL* *821].
Guiney, Louise Imogen. *Robert Emmet: A Survey of His Rebellion and of His Romance*. London: David Nutt, 1904.

832.   [*YL* 822].
Gwynn, Stephen. *Irish Literature and Drama in the English Language: A Short History*. London: Thomas Nelson, 1936.

833.   [*YL* 823].
———. *The Life and Friendships of Dean Swift*. London: Thornton Butterworth, 1933.

834.   [*YL* *824].
The Gypsy (London) 1 (May 1915).

x   [*YL* 825]. [NLI missing this copy].
Hackett, Francis. Review of *Poems and Translations* by John M. Synge. *The Chicago Evening Post*, Friday Literary Supplement, 2 July 1909: 1.

835.   [*YL* 826].
Hâfiz, Shirazi. *Selections from the Rubaiyât and Odes of Hâfiz, the Great Mystic and Lyric Poet of Persia*. Trans. "a member of the Persia Society of London" [Frank Montagu Rundall?]. With an account of Sûfi Mysticism. London: John M. Watkins, 1920.

836.   [*YL* 827].
Haldane, [Richard Burdon], Viscount. *Human Experience: A Study of Its Structure*. London: John Murray, 1926.

837.   [*YL* *828]. [NLI 40,568/96; 8 sheets; envelope 1216].
Halévy, Daniel. *The Life of Friedrich Nietzsche*. Trans. J. M. Hone. London: T. Fisher Unwin, 1911.

838.   [*YL* *829].
Hall, H[arry]. R[eginald]. *Aegean Archaeology*. London: Philip Lee Warner, 1915.

839.   [*YL* *830].
Hallam, Arthur Henry. *The Poems of Arthur Henry Hallam: Together with His Essay on the Lyrical Poems of Alfred Tennyson*. Ed. Richard Le Gallienne. London: Elkin Mathews, 1893.

840. [YL 831].
Hamer, John. *Selections of American Humour in Prose and Verse*. London: Cassell, [1883?].

841. [YL *832].
Hammer[-Purgstall], Joseph, trans. *Ancient Alphabets and Heiroglyphic Characters Explained: With an Account of the Egyptian Priests, Their Classes, Initiation, and Sacrifices, in the Arabic Language by Ahmad bin Abubekr bin Wahshih and in English by Joseph Hammer*. London: G. and W. Nicholl, 1806.

842. [YL 833].
Hannay, James Ballantyne. *The Rise, Decline, and Fall of the Roman Religion*. London: Privately printed for the Religious Evolution Research Society, 1925.

843. [YL *834].
Hardy, Thomas. *The Dynasts: An Epic-Drama of the War with Napoleon*. London: Macmillan, 1910.

844. [YL 835].
———. *Late Lyrics and Earlier*, with many other verses. London: Macmillan, 1922.

845. [YL 836].
———. *The Wessex Novels*. Macmillan's Pocket Hardy. 18 vols. London: Macmillan, 1906–. Vol. 2 [Vol. 1 missing]: *Far from the Madding Crowd*, 1906. Signed: Georgie Hyde-Lees. | Jan. 1909

846. [YL 837].
———. Vol. 3: *The Life and Death of the Mayor of Casterbridge*, 1916.

847. [YL 838].
———. Vol. 4: *Jude the Obscure*, 1910.

848. [YL 839].
———. Vol. 5: *The Return of the Native*, 1907. Signed: Georgie Hyde-Lees | October, 1909

849. [YL 840].
———.Vol. 6: *A Pair of Blue Eyes*, 1906. Signed: Georgie Hyde-Lees | Oct. 16, 1908

850.   [YL 841].

———.Vol. 7: *Two on a Tower*, 1906. Signed: Georgie Hyde-Lees, | Xmas 1907

851.   [YL 842].

———.Vol. 8: *The Woodlanders*, 1906. Signed: Georgie Hyde-Lees. | Xmas 1907

852.   [YL 843].

———. Vol. 9: *The Trumpet-Major and Robert His Brother*. Signed: Georgie Hyde-Lees | October 1907

853.   [YL 844].

———. Vol. 10: *The Hand of Ethelberta*, 1907. Signed: Georgie Hyde-Lees | February 1909

854.   [YL 845].

———. Vol. 12 [vol. 11 missing]: *Desperate Remedies*, 1907. Signed: Georgie Hyde-Lees, | February, 1909

855.   [YL 846].

———. Vol. 13: *Wessex Tales*, 1907. Signed: Georgie Hyde-Lees | Jan., 1909

856.   [YL 847].

———. Vol. 14 [vol. 15 missing]: *Life's Little Ironies: A Set of Tales, with Some Colloquial Sketches Entitled "A Few Crusted Characters,"* 1907. Signed: Georgie Hyde-Lees.

857.   [YL 848].

———. Vol. 16: *Under the Greenwood Tree*, 1907. Signed: Georgie Hyde Lees | Xmas 1907

858.   [YL 849].

———. Vol. 17 [vol. 18 missing]: *The Well-Beloved*, 1907.

859.   [YL 850].

Harrison, Henry. *Parnell Vindicated: The Lifting of the Veil*. London: Constable, 1931.

860.   [YL *851].

Hartland, Edwin Sidney, ed. *English Fairy and Other Folk Tales*. London: Walter Scott, [1890]. Signed: W B Yeats | June, 1890

861.   [*YL* 852]. [NLI 40,568/97; 2 sheets; envelope 1465].
Mythology and Folktales: Their Relations and Interpretation. Popular Studies in Mythology, Romance and Folklore, no. 7. London: David Nutt, 1900.

862.   [*YL* 853]. [NLI 40,568/98; 87 sheets; envelope 1248].
Hartmann, Franz. *The Life and Doctrines of Jacob Boehme, the God-Taught Philosopher: An Introduction to the Study of His Works*. London: Kegan Paul, Trench, Trubner, 1891. Signed: WBY

863.   [*YL* *854].
——, ed. and trans. *The Life of Philippus Theophrastus Bombast of Hohenheim Known by the Name of Paracelsus, and the Substance of His Teachings Concerning Cosmology, Anthropology, Pneumatology; Extracted and Translated from His Rare and Extensive Works and from Some Unpublished Manuscripts*. 2nd ed. London: Kegan Paul, Trench, Trubner, [1896]. Bp: WBY

864.   [*YL* 855]. [NLI 40,568/99; 7, 3, and 10 sheets from vols. 1, 11, and 12; envelope 2054].
Hastings, James, and John A[lexander]. Selbie et al., *Encyclopaedia of Religion and Ethics*. 12 vols. Edinburgh: T. and C. Clark, 1908–21.

865.   [*YL* 856].
Hauptmann, Gerhart. *The Dramatic Works*. Ed. Ludwig Lewisohn. 7 vols. London: Martin Secker, 1912–14. Vol. 3: *Domestic Dramas*, 1914.

866.   [*YL* 857].
——. *The Sunken Bell: A Fairy Play in Five Acts*. Trans. Charles Henry Meltzer. New York: R. H. Russell, 1899.

867.   [*YL* 858].
——. *The Weavers: A Drama of the Forties*. Trans. Mary Morison. New York: B. W. Huebsch, 1911.

868.   [*YL* 859].
Havell, E[rnest]. B[infield]. *A Handbook of Indian Art*. London: John Murray, 1920.

869.   [*YL* 860].
Hayes, Edward, ed. *The Ballads of Ireland*. 2 vols. London, Edinburgh, and Dublin: A Fullarton, 1855.

870.   [*YL* 861].
Hazlemere, Robert. *Starry Earth: A Book of Poems and Lyrics*. Toronto: McClelland and Stewart, 1929.

871.   [*YL* 862].
Head, Barclay V[incent]. *Synopsis of the Contents of the British Museum, Department of Coins and Medals: A Guide to the Principal Gold and Silver Coins of the Ancients*. 2nd ed. London: Longmans, 1881. [Illustrated]. Bp: The Right Hon. W.H. Gregory. K.C.M.G. | Coole Park, | Gort, | Ireland

872.   [*YL* 863].
Heard, Gerald. *The Ascent of Humanity: An Essay on the Evolution of Civilization from Group Consciousness through Individuality to Super-Consciousness*. London: Jonathan Cape, 1929.

873.   [*YL* 864].
Heath, Lionel, ed. *Examples of Indian Art at the British Empire Exhibition, 1924*. With an introductory and critical note by Lionel Heath. London: The India Society, 1925.

874.   [*YL* 865].
Heath, Thomas. *The Twentieth Century Atlas of Popular Astronomy: Comprising in Sixteen Plates a Series of Illustrations of the Heavenly Bodies*. 3rd ed. Edinburgh: W. and A. K. Johnston, [1922?]. [Illustrated].

875.   [*YL* 866].
Heathcote, Sir Henry. *Treatise on Stay-Sails, for the Purpose of Intercepting Wind between the Square-sails of Ships and Other Square-rigged Vessels…Mathematically Demonstrating the Defects of Those Now in Use and the Eminent Superiority of the Improved Patent Stay-sails Recently Invented by Sir Henry Heathcote*….London: Baldwin, Cradock, and Joy, 1824. [Illustrated].

876.   [*YL* 867].
Hedin, Sven. *Trans-Himalaya: Discoveries and Adventures in Tibet*. 3 vols. London: Macmillan, 1910–13. Bp: GY

x   [*YL* 868]. [NLI 40,568/100; copy of newsclipping inserted of review; 4 sheets; envelope 1195]. [NLI missing this copy].

Hegel, G[eorg]. W[ilhelm]. F[riedrich]. *Hegel's Logic of World and Idea: A Translation of the Second and Third Parts of the Subjective Logic*.

[Trans.] Henry S. Macran. Oxford: The Clarendon Press, 1929. Signed: WBY

877. [*YL* 869]. [NLI 40,568/101; 39 sheets; envelope 1194].

———. *The Logic of Hegel, Translated from "The Encyclopaedia of the Philosophical Sciences."* Trans. William Wallace. 2nd ed. Oxford: The Clarendon Press, 1892. Signed: WBY

878. [*YL* 870].

Heitland, W[illiam]. E[merton]. *The Roman Fate: An Essay in Interpretation.* Cambridge: The University Press, 1922.

879. [*YL* *871].

Henderson, T[homas]. F[inlayson]. *Scottish Vernacular Literature: A Succinct History.* 3rd ed. Edinburgh: John Grant, 1910. Bp: WBY

880. [*YL* *872].

Henley, W[illiam]. E[rnest]. *Burns: Life, Genius, Achievement.* Reprinted from *The Centenary Burns.* Edinburgh: T. C. and E. C. Jack, 1898.

881. [*YL* *873].

———. *Essays.* London: Macmillan, 1920.

882. [*YL* *874].

———. *Poems.* London: Macmillan, 1921.

883. [*YL* *875].

———. *Views and Reviews: Essays in Appreciation.* London: Macmillan, 1921.

884. [*YL* *876].

———, ed. *Lyra heroica: A Book of Verse for Boys.* London: Macmillan, 1921.

885. [*YL* *877].

——— and Robert Louis Stevenson. *Plays.* London: Macmillan, 1921.

886. [*YL* *878]. [See Chapman, *YA* 6 (1988): 234–45].

Herbert, Edward. *The Autobiography of Edward, Lord Herbert of Cherbury.* With intro. [etc.] by Sidney Lee. 2nd ed. London: George Routledge, [1906]. Bp: WBY

887.   [*YL* 879].
Herbert, George. *The English Poems of George Herbert: Together with His Collection of Proverbs Entitled "Jacula Prudentum."* London: Longmans, Green, 1902.

888.   [*YL* *880].
——. *The Works of George Herbert.* The Chandos Classics. London and New York: Frederick Warne, [1885?].

889.   [*YL* 881]. [NLI 40,568/102; 59 sheets; envelope 1295].
Hermes Trismegistus. *Hermetica: The Ancient Greek and Latin Writings Which Contain Religious or Philosophic Teachings Ascribed to Hermes Trismegistus.* Ed. with trans. and notes by Walter Scott. 3 vols. Oxford: The Clarendon Press, 1924.

890.   [*YL* 882]. [NLI 40,568/103; 6 sheets; envelope 128].
—— [Ermete Trimegisto]. *Il Pimandro, ossia, l'intelligenza suprema che si rivela e parla ed altri scritti ermetici.* Trans. [from Greek to Italian] by Dr. Giovanni Bonanni. Todi: Casa editrice "Atanòr," 1913.

891.   [*YL* 883]. [NLI 40,568/104; 52 sheets; envelope 1293].
——. *The Pymander of Hermes.* Ed. with preface by W. Wynn Westcott, Supreme Magus of the Rosicrucian Society. Collectanea Hermetica, vol. 2. London: Theosophical Publishing Society, 1894. Signed: Jas Stephens

892.   [*YL* *884].
——. [Hermès Trismégiste]. *Hermès Trismégiste: traduction complète, précédée d'une étude sur l'origine des livres hermétiques par Louis Ménard.* 2nd ed. Paris: Didier, 1867.

893.   [Not listed in *YL*]. [NLI 40,581; 25 sheets; at head of first photocopy: "orange book"].
Hermetic Students of the Golden Dawn. *Ritual J. Obligation.* [Golden Dawn ritual manual]. Signed: "Geo. Pollexfen, 31 Oct. 95."

894.   [*YL* *885]. [NLI 40,568/105; 138 sheets; envelope 178].
Herodotus. *Herodotus.* Trans. the Rev. Henry Cary. Bohn's Classical Library. London: G. Bell, 1912. Bp: WBY

895.   [*YL* *886].
Herrick, Robert. *The Complete Poems.* Ed. Alexander B. Grosart. 3 vols. London: Chatto and Windus, 1876.

896. [YL 887].
———. *Delighted Earth: A Selection from Herrick's "Hesperides."* Ed. Peter Meadows. Illustrated by Lionel Ellis. London: The Fanfrolico Press, [1927]. [Illustrated].

897. [YL *888].
———. *The Poems of Robert Herrick.* Ed. John Masefield. London: E. Grant Richards, 1906.

898. [YL *889].
———. *Poems Selected from the Hesperides.* Typographic designs by H. M. O'Kane. New Rochelle, New York: Printed and sold by Clarke Conwell at the Elston Press, 1903.

899. [YL 890].
Hessen, Prof. B[oris]. *The Social and Economic Roots of Newton's "Principia."* Papers read to the Second International Congress of the History of Science and Technology, by the delegates of the U.S.S.R. London: June 29th to July 3rd, 1931. London: Kniga, 1931.

900. [YL *891]. [NLI 40,568/106; 6 sheets; envelope 821].
Hettinger, Franz. *Dante's "Divina commedia": Its Scope and Value.* Ed. [and trans.?] Henry Sebastian Bowden. 2nd ed. London: Burns and Oates, 1894.

901. [YL *892].
[Heywood, Thomas]. *Thomas Heywood.* [Five plays]. Ed. A. Wilson Verity. Introduction by J. Addington Symonds. The Mermaid Series. London: T. Fisher Unwin, [1903].

901a. [YL 892a]. [Though reported in *YL*, did not come to NLI with a leaf torn from a magazine with a poem by Higgins on one side].
Another copy.

902. [YL 893]. [NLI 40,568/107; 4 sheets; envelope 1665].
Higgins, F[rederick]. R[obert]. *The Dark Breed: A Book of Poems.* London: Macmillan, 1927.

903. [YL 894].
———. *Island Blood.* With a foreword by AE [pseud., George Russell]. London: John Lane, 1925.

903a. [YL 894a].
Another copy.

904. [YL 895].
——. *Salt Air. Poems.* Decorated by W. Victor Brown. Dublin: Irish Bookshop, 1923.

904a. [YL 895a].
Another copy.

905. [YL 896].
The High History of the Holy Graal. Translated from the old French by Sebastian Evans. London: J. M. Dent, [1910].

x [YL 897]. [NLI missing this copy].
The History of the Theatre Royal, Dublin. From its foundation in 1821 to the present time. Reprinted with additions from Saunders' News-letter. Dublin: Edward Ponsonby, 1870.

906. [YL *898].
Hofmannsthal, Hugo von. *Electra: A Tragedy in One Act.* Trans. Arthur Symons. New York: Brentano's, 1908. Bp: WBY. Bp: Beatrice Stella Campbell

907. [YL 899].
Hogg, Thomas Jefferson et al. *The Life of Percy Bysshe Shelley, as comprised in "The Life of Shelley" by Thomas Jefferson Hogg, "The Recollections of Shelley and Byron" by Edward John Trelawny, "Memoirs of Shelley" by Thomas Love Peacock.* Ed. with an intro. by Humbert Wolfe. Illustrated by G. E. Chambers. 2 vols. London and Toronto: J. M. Dent, 1933. [Illustrated].

908. [YL 900].
[Hokusai, Katsushika]. *Owari tohekido 20 hangafusho tehon mokuroka.* [A vol. of a catalog of comic pictures by Hokusai]. Copied by Sirakuya Toshiro. [Lacks publication details].

909. [YL 901].
Holberg, Ludvig. *Three Comedies.* Trans. from Danish by Lieut. Colonel H. W. L. Hime. London: Longmans, Green, 1912.

910. [YL 902].
Holmes, Edmond. *The Silence of Love.* [Poems]. London and New York: John Lane, 1899.

911.   [*YL* 903]. [NLI 40,568/108; 32 sheets; envelope 1048].
Holmes, William Gordon. *The Age of Justinian and Theodora: A History of the Sixth Century A.D.* 2nd ed. 2 vols. London: G. Bell, 1912.

912.   [*YL* 904].
Holt, Joseph. *Memoirs of Joseph Holt, General of the Irish Rebels, in 1798.* Ed. T. Crofton Croker. 2 vols. London: Henry Colburn, 1838.

913.   [Not listed in *YL* and assigned NLI Number 3022].
The Holy Bible, Containing the Old and New Testament. Glasgow: William Collins, Sons, 1886.

914.   [*YL* 905].
Homer. *The Iliad.* Trans. with notes by Theodore Alois Buckley. London: Bell and Daldy, 1870.

915.   [*YL* 906].
Another ed. Trans. Andrew Lang, Walter Leaf, and Ernest Myers. Rev. ed. London: Macmillan, 1930. Signed: WBY

916.   [*YL* *907].
——. *The Odysseys of Homer.* Trans. George Chapman. London: J. M. Dent, 1906. 2 vols. Signed, Vol. 2: Georgie Hyde Lees | 1914

917.   [*YL* 908].
Hone, J[oseph]. M[aunsell]. *Ireland Since 1922.* Criterion Miscellany, no. 39. London: Faber and Faber, 1932.

917a.   [*YL* 908a].
Another copy.

918.   [*YL* 909].
——. *The Life of George Moore.* London: Victor Gollancz, 1936. Signed: GY

919.   [Not listed in *YL*]. [NLI 40,567/94; 52 sheets; Wade 331].
——. *W. B. Yeats 1865–1939.* London: Macmillan, 1942.

920.   [*YL* *910].
——. *William Butler Yeats: The Poet in Contemporary Ireland.* Irishmen of To-day. Dublin and London: Maunsel, [1915]. Bp: WBY

Figure 4. Frontispiece and title page of 921. J. M. Hone and M. M. Rossi, *Bishop Berkeley: His Life, Writings, and Philosophy* (1931).

921.   [*YL* 911]. [NLI 40,567/8; 7 sheets; Wade 280].
—— and M[ario]. M[anlio]. Rossi. *Bishop Berkeley: His Life, Writings, and Philosophy*. With an intro. by W. B. Yeats. London: Faber and Faber, 1931. Bp: WBY.

921a.   [*YL* 911a].
Another copy.

921b.   [Not listed in *YL* and assigned NLI number 3023].
Another copy.

922.   [*YL* 912]. [NLI 40,568/109; 7 sheets; envelope 1815].
Hone, Nathaniel, and John Butler Yeats. *A Loan Collection of Pictures by Nathaniel Hone, R.H.A. and John Butler Yeats, R.H.A.* On view at 6 St. Stephen's Green [Royal Society of Antiquaries], October 21st [1901] to November 3rd [1901].

923.   [*YL* *913].
Hopkins, Gerard Manley. *Poems*. Ed. with notes by Robert Bridges. London: Humphrey Milford, 1918.

924. [*YL* 914].
——. *Poems of Gerard Manley Hopkins*. Ed. with notes by Robert Bridges. With additional poems [etc.] by Charles Williams. 2nd ed. London: Oxford University Press, 1930.

925. [*YL* 915].
Hopper [Chesson], Nora. *Under Quicken Boughs*. [Poems]. London: John Lane, 1896.

925a. [*YL* *915a].
Another copy. Bp: W. H. Smith and Son's Subscription Library. Signed: Nora Hopper | 1899

926. [*YL* *916].
Horne, Herbert P[ercy]. *Diversi colores: Poems*. London: Published by the Author at the Chiswick Press, 1891.

927. [*YL* *917].
Horrwitz, E[rnest]. P[hilip]. *The Indian Theatre: A Brief Survey of the Sanskrit Drama*. London: Blackie, 1912. Signed: WBY

928. [*YL* *918]. [Wade 255].
Horton, W[illiam]. T[homas]. *A Book of Images*. Drawn by W. T. Horton. Introduction by W. B. Yeats. London: The Unicorn Press, 1898.

929. [*YL* *919].
——. *The Grig's Book*. [A children's book]. London: Moffatt and Paige, 1900.

930. [*YL* *920].
——. *The Way of the Soul: A Legend in Line and Verse*. London: William Rider, [1910].

931. [*YL* 921].
Housman, A[lfred]. E[dward]. *Last Poems*. London: The Richards Press, 1934.

932. [*YL* 922].
——. *R. L. S.* [a single sheet folded quarto]. An uncollected poem. Reprinted from *The Academy* of 22 December, 1894 in a limited edition of fifty copies, for the friends of Vincent Starrett and Edwin B. Hill.

933.   [YL *923].
——. *A Shropshire Lad.* London: Grant Richards, 1903. Signed: Olivia Shakespear

934.   [YL 924].
Howell, John Cyril, ed. *The Priest's English Ritual for Private Ministrations in the Provinces of Canterbury and York.* 2nd ed. London: The Society of SS. Peter and Paul, 1920.

935.   [YL 925].
Hsiung, S[hih]. I. *Mencius Was a Bad Boy: A Play.* London: Privately Printed, [1934].

936.   [YL 926].
Hubbell, Jay B[roadus]. and John O[wen]. Beaty. *An Introduction to Drama.* New York: Macmillan, 1927.

937.   [YL 927].
Huc, R[évérend]. P[ère]. [Évariste Régis]. *Souvenirs d'un voyage dans la Tartarie le Thibet et la Chine.* Paris: Plon Nourrit, 1926.

937a.   [YL 927a].
Another copy.

938.   [YL *928].
Hueffer [Ford], Ford Madox. *Songs from London.* London: Elkin Mathews, 1910.

939.   [YL 929].
Hügel, Baron Friedrich von. *The Mystical Element of Religion as Studied in Saint Catherine of Genoa and Her Friends.* 2 vols. London: J. M. Dent, 1927. Bp: WBY

940.   [YL 930].
Hughes, Richard. *Confessio juvenis: Collected Poems.* London: Chatto and Windus, 1926.

940A.   [YL 930A].
Another ed. The Phoenix Library. London: Chatto and Windus, 1934.

941.   [YL *931].
Hughes, Rev. S[amuel]. C[arlyle]. *The Pre-Victorian Drama in Dublin.* Dublin: Hodges, Figgis, 1904.

941a. [YL 931a].
Another copy.

942. [YL *932].
Hugo, Victor. *Dramas*. 2 vols. [4 vols in 2]. The Sterling Ed. Boston and New York: University Press, [189?]. [Illustrated]. Signed: Coraleen M. Paige | 1894.

943. [YL 933].
——. *Le roi s'amuse. Lucrece Borgia*. Paris: Nelson, Editeurs, [1912?]. Signed: Lennox Robinson

944. [YL 934].
——. *Translations from the Poems of Victor Hugo*. Trans. Henry Carrington. London: Walter Scott, 1885.

945. [YL 935].
Hulme, T[homas]. E[rnest]. *Speculations: Essays on Humanism and the Philosophy of Art*. Ed. Herbert Read. London: Kegan Paul, Trench, Trubner, 1924.

946. [YL 936].
Hume, David. *Essays and Treatises on Several Subjects*. 2 vols. New ed. Edinburgh: Bell and Bradfute and William Blackwood; and T. Cadell and W. Davies, 1809. [Lacks vol. 1]. Vol. 2: *An Inquiry Concerning Human Understanding, a Dissertation on the Passions; an Inquiry Concerning the Principles of Morals; and the Natural History of Religion*. Bp: Robert Corbet

947. [YL 937].
Husserl, Edmund. *Ideas: General Introduction to Pure Phenomenology*. Trans. W. R. Boyce Gibson. London: George Allen and Unwin, 1931.

948. [YL *938].
Hutchinson, Francis D. D. *An Historical Essay Concerning Witchcraft: With Observations upon Matters of Fact; Tending to Clear the Texts of the Sacred Scriptures, and Confute the Vulgar Errors about That Point ; And Also with Two Sermons, One in Proof of the Christian Religion, the Other Concerning Good and Evil Angels*. 2nd ed. with additions. London: R. Knaplock and D. Midwinter, 1720. Bp: WBY

949.   [YL 939].
Hüttemann, Gerta. *Wesen der Dichtung und Aufgabe des Dichters bei William Butler Yeats*. Inaugural-Dissertation, Friedrich-Wilhelms-Universität, Bonn, 1929.

950.   [YL 940].
Huxley, Aldous. *Point Counter Point*. London: Chatto and Windus, 1930.

951.   [YL *941]. [NLI 40,568/110; 3 sheets; envelope 1577].
Hyde, Douglas. *A Literary History of Ireland*. London: T. Fisher Unwin, 1899.

952.   [YL 942].
———, ed. *Giolla an fhiugha, or The Lad of the Ferule; Eachtra cloinne righ na h-Ioruaidhe, or Adventures of the Children of the King of Norway*. With translations, notes, and glossary. Irish Texts Society, vol. 1. London: The Irish Texts Society, 1899.

953.   [YL 943].
Hymns to the Goddess. Trans. from Sanskrit by Arthur and Ellen Avalon. London: Luzac, 1913.

954.   [YL 944].
Hyslop, James H[ervey]. *Life after Death: Problems of the Future Life and Its Nature*. New York: E. P. Dutton, 1919.

955.   [YL *945].
Iamblichus. *Iamblichus on the Mysteries of the Egyptians, Chaldeans, and Assyrians*. Trans. Thomas Taylor. 2nd ed. London: Theosophical Publishing Society, 1895.

956.   [YL 946].
Ibsen, Henrik. *Ghosts and Two Other Plays*. Trans. R. Farquharson Sharp. Everyman's Library. London: J. M. Dent, 1914.

957.   [YL 947].
———. "*Lady Inger of Ostrat*," "*The Vikings at Helgeland*," and "*The Pretenders*." Ed. William Archer. Trans. Charles and William Archer. London: Walter Scott, [1890].

958.   [*YL* 948].
———. "*Lady Inger of Ostraat*," "*Love's Comedy*," and "*The League of Youth*." Trans. R. Farquharson Sharp. Everyman's Library. London and Toronto: J. M. Dent, [1917?].

959.   [*YL* 949].
———. *Peer Gynt*. Trans. William and Charles Archer. London: Walter Scott, [1892?]. Signed: Bryan Cooper

960.   [*YL* 950].
———. *The Pillars of Society and Other Plays*. Ed. Havelock Ellis. London: Walter Scott, 1888.

961.   [*YL* 951].
Ilin, M. [Il'ya Yakovlevich Marshak]. *Moscow Has a Plan: A Soviet Primer*. Trans. G. S. Counts and N. P. Lodge. London: Jonathan Cape, 1931. Signed: GY [erased]

962.   [*YL* 952].
L'Illustration (Paris) 4579 (6 Décembre 1930).

963.   [*YL* 953].
Inchbald, Elizabeth, ed. *The British Theatre, or A Collection of Plays Which Are Acted at the Theatres Royal, Drury Lane, Covent Garden, and Haymarket*. 25 vols. London: Longman, Hurst, Rees, and Orme, 1800–17. Vol. 22: *The Castle of Andalusia* by John O'Keefe, *Fontainbleau* by John O'Keefe, *Wild Oats* by John O'Keefe, *The Heiress* by General Burgoyne, *The Earl of Essex* by Henry Jones.

964.   [*YL* *954]. [NLI 40,568/111; vol. 1, 6 sheets; envelope 1301].
Inge, William Ralph. *The Philosophy of Plotinus*. The Gifford Lectures at St. Andrews, 1917–18. 2 vols. London: Longmans, Green, 1918. Signed, both vols.: George Yeats | February 1919

965.   [*YL* 955].
———. *The Platonic Tradition in English Religious Thought*. The Hulsean Lectures at Cambridge, 1925–26. New York: Longmans, Green, 1926.

966.   [*YL* 956].
Ingoldsby, Thomas [Richard Harris Barham]. *The Jackdaw of Rheims*. Illustrated by Ernest M. Jessop. London: Eyre and Spottiswoode, [1889?]. [Illustrated].

967.   [*YL* 957].
Ireland To-Day (Dublin) 2 (January 1937).

968.   [*YL* 958].
Ireland (?-1922). National Museum of Science and Art. *General Guide to the Art Collections. Part IX—Glass. Chapter II—Irish Glass*, by M. S. D. Westropp. Dublin: His Majesty's Stationery Office, 1913. [Illustrated].

969.   [*YL* 959].
———. *General Guide to the Natural History Collection: A List of Irish Birds, Showing the Species Contained in the National Collection.* By Richard Ussher. Dublin: His Majesty's Stationery Office, 1908.

970.   [*YL* 960].
———. *Guide to the Collection of Irish Antiquities.* Part 5: *Irish Ethnographical Collection.* By Thomas J. Westropp. Dublin: His Majesty's Stationery Office, 1911.

971.   [*YL* 961].
———. *Short Guide to the Collections.* 52nd ed. Dublin: Dept. of Agriculture and Technical Instruction for Ireland, 1916.

972.   [*YL* 962].
———. *Description of the Raised Map of Ireland, Showing the Relation between the Geological Structure and the Surface Features of the Country.* By Grenville A. J. Cole. Dublin: His Majesty's Stationery Office, 1909. [Illustrated].

973.   [*YL* 963]. [Wade 317].
Irish Free State (1922–49). *Coinage of Saorstát Éireann 1928.* Dublin: The Stationery Office, 1928.

973a.   [*YL* 963a].
Another copy. Two words entirely canceled on flyleaf.

973b.   [*YL* 963b].
Another copy.

974.   [*YL* 964].
———. Coimisiún na Gaeltachta. *Map No. 1: A General Map of Ireland, Showing in Respect of the 1911 Census Percentage of Irish Speakers in Each Electoral Division.* 1926.

974a. [YL 964a].

———. *Map No. 2: Showing in Respect of the 1925 Special Enumeration for the Counties of Donegal, Mayo etc., Percentage of Irish Speakers in District Electoral Division.* 1926.

975. [YL 965].

———. Laws, Statutes etc. *Censorship of Publications Act.* Number 21 of 1929.

976. [YL 966].

———. *Industrial and Commercial Property (Protection) Act.* Number 16 of 1927.

976a. [YL 966a].

Another copy.

977. [YL 967].

———. National Gallery of Ireland. *Catalogue of Oil Pictures in the General Collection.* Dublin: The Stationery Office, 1932.

978. [YL 968].

———. *Catalogue of Pictures and Other Works of Art in the National Gallery of Ireland and the National Portrait Gallery.* Dublin: Stationery Office, 1928.

979. [YL 969].

———. *Official Handbook of Sáorstat Éireann. Ordnance Survey Map.* Dublin: Ordnance Survey Office, 1931.

980. [YL 970].

———. Seanad Eireann. *Parliamentary Debates: Official Report,* vols. 1–8 (11 December 1922–20 May 1927).

981. [YL 971].

———. *Standing Orders.* Vol. 1: *Public Business (1923).* Signed: WBY

982. [YL 972].

Irish Industries. *Illustrated Souvenir of the Irish Industries Pageant Held in Dublin St. Patrick's Eve 1909.* Dublin: Maunsel, 1909.

983. [YL 973].

[Irish Literary Theatre program]. First performances of *The Countess Cathleen* and *The Heather Field,* Dublin, 8–9 May 1899.

984.   [Not listed in *YL* and assigned NLI Number 3024; inserted interview with WBY from *The Observer*, Sunday, 19 June 1910].
The Irish National Theatre: Its Work and Its Needs. London: W. T. Haycock, 1909.

985.   [*YL* 974].
Irish Pleasantry and Fun: A Selection of the Best Humorous Tales by Carleton, Lover, Lever and Other Popular Writers. Illustrated by J. F. O'Hea. New Ed. Dublin: M. H. Gill, 1885.

986.   [*YL* 975].
The Irish Review (Dublin) 2 (December 1912).

987.   [*YL* 976].
[Irish scenes. Print]. *Antiquities in Ireland*. Four illustrations: *Round Tower at Kildare*; *Ruins of a Convent at Kildare*; *A Tumulus near Tipperary*; *An Ancient Brass Sword*. From *London Magazine* (September 1778).

988.   [*YL* 977].
———. *Cashel Cathedral, Tipperary*. Engraved by J. Walker from an original drawing by G. Holmes. London: J. Walker, 1800.

989.   [*YL* 978].
———. *Castle Connell in the County of Limerick*. By Eastgate. London: Alexander Hogg, n.d.

990.   [*YL* 979].
———. *Galway (from the Claddagh)*. Engraved by C. Cousen after W. H. Bartlett. London: George Virtus, n.d.

991.   [*YL* 980].
———. *Glenmore Castle*, the seat of Francis Synge, Esq., by J. Carr. London: R. Phillips, 1806.

992.   [*YL* 981].
———. *Lower Lake of Killarney, Ross Castle and Island*. By W. Westall. Engraved by E. Francis. [Lacks publication details].

993.   [*YL* 982].
———. *The Salmon Leap, at Ballyshannon, in Ireland*. [Lacks publication details].

994. [YL 983].
——. *Street in Galway*. By W. H. Bartlett. Engraved by T. Higham. [Lacks publication details].

995. [YL 984].
The Irish Statesman 1 (23 August 1919).

996. [YL 985].
—— 1 (30 August 1919).

997. [YL 986].
—— 1 (8 November 1919).

997a–b. [YL 986a–b].
Two more copies.

998. [YL 987].
—— 1 (10 January 1920).

999. [YL 988].
—— 2 (31 January 1920).

999a. [YL 988a].
Another copy.

1000. [YL 989].
—— 2 (21 February 1920).

1001. [YL 990].
—— 2 (3 April 1920).

1002. [YL 991].
—— 2 (17 April 1920).

1003. [YL 992].
—— 2 (24 April 1920).

1004. [YL 993].
—— 2 (1 May 1920).

1005. [YL *994].
—— 2 (January–June 1920).

1006. [YL 995].
—— 3 (8 November 1924).

1007. [YL 996].
——. "The Dublin of Berkeley (1703–1710)" (7 Sept. 1929).

1008. [YL *997].
The Irish Theosophist (Dublin) 3 (15 August 1895).

1008a–b. [YL *997a–b].
Two more copies.

1009. [YL * 998].
—— 3 (15 September 1895).

1010. [YL * 999].
—— 4 (15 October 1895).

1011. [YL *1000].
—— 4 (15 November 1895).

1011a. [YL *1000a].
Another copy.

1012. [YL *1001].
—— 4 (15 December 1895).

1013. [YL *1002].
—— 4 (15 January 1896).

1014. [YL *1003].
—— 4 (15 September 1896).

1015. [YL *1004].
—— 5 (15 September 1897).

1016. [YL 1005].
The Irish Times (Dublin). Review of *The Lemon Tree* by Margot Ruddock, ed. W. B. Yeats, [14 June 1937: 5].

1017. [YL 1006].
Jacob, Sir Lionel. "Architecture | Hindu and Mogul | Combining East and West," *The Times*, 17 Nov. 1921: xiv.

1018. [YL 1007].
James [I], King of Scotland. *The Kingis Quair*. Ed. Robert Steele. Designed by Charles Ricketts. London: The Vale Press, 1903.

1019. [*YL* *1008].
James, William. *Human Immortality*. 2nd ed. Boston: Houghton, Mifflin, 1899.

1020. [*YL* *1009].
Another copy. 4th ed. Westminster: Archibald Constable, 1899. Signed: WBY

1021. [*YL* *1010].
———. *Pragmatism*. London: Longmans, Green, 1910.

1022. [*YL* 1011].
Jammes, Francis. *Clairières dans le ciel, 1902–1906*. Paris: Mercure de France, 1916.

1023. [*YL* 1012].
———. *Le deuil des primevères, 1898–1900*. Paris: Mercure de France, 1917.

1024. [*YL* 1013].
———. *Le roman du lièvre*. Paris: Mercure de France, 1918.

1025. [*YL* 1014].
———. *Le triomphe de la vie, 1900–1901*. Paris: Mercure de France, [1902?].

1026. [*YL* 1015].
Japanese Drama and the Shochiku Dramatic Company. Tokyo: Tokyo Printing, n.d.

1027. [*YL* 1016].
John, Ivor B[ertram]. *The Mabinogion*. Popular Studies in Mythology, Romance, and Folklore, no. 11. London: David Nutt, 1901.

1028. [*YL* 1017].
John of the Cross, Saint. *The Dark Night of the Soul*. 4th rev. ed. London: Thomas Baker, 1916.

1029. [*YL* 1018].
Johnson, Lionel. *The Art of Thomas Hardy*. With bibliography by John Lane. London: Elkin Mathews and John Lane, 1894. Bp: WBY

1030. [*YL* *1019].
———. *Ireland, with Other Poems*. London: Elkin Mathews, 1897.

1031. [*YL* *1020].
——. *Poems*. London: Elkin Mathews, 1895.

1032. [*YL* *1021].
——. *Poetical Works*. London: Elkin Mathews, 1915.

1033. [*YL* 1022].
——. *Post Liminium: Essays and Critical Papers*. Ed. Thomas Whittemore. London: Elkin Mathews, 1911. Bp: WBY

1034. [*YL* 1023].
——. *Three Poems*. [Ed. Vincent Starrett]. Ysleta, Texas: Edwin B. Hill, 1928.

1035. [*YL* 1024].
Johnston, Edward. *Writing and Illuminating, and Lettering*. London: John Hogg, 1915.

1036. [*YL* 1025]. [NLI 40,568/112; 18 sheets; envelope 1175].
Johnston, G[eorge]. A[lexander]. *The Development of Berkeley's Philosophy*. London: Macmillan, 1923. Bp: WBY

1037. [*YL* 1026].
Jones, Ernest. *Essays in Applied Psycho-analysis*. London: The International Psycho-analytical Press, 1923.

1038. [*YL* 1027]. [NLI 40,568/113; vol. 1, 9 sheets; envelope 1150].
Jones, W[illiam]. Tudor. *Contemporary Thought of Germany*. 2 vols. London: Williams and Norgate, 1930. Signed: WBY

1039. [*YL* 1028].
Jonson, Ben. *Ben Jonson*. Ed. Brinsley Nicholson. 3 vols. The Mermaid Series. London: T. Fisher Unwin, [1893–95].

1040. [*YL* 1029]. [Envelope inserted, addressed to Frank O'Connor with notes on back, possibly by WBY].
——. *Ben Jonson*. Ed. C. H. Herford and Percy Simpson. 5 vols. Oxford: Clarendon Press, 1925–37. Bp: WBY

1041. [*YL* *1030].
——. *Every Man in His Humour*. Ed. W. Macneile Dixon. The Temple Dramatists. London: J. M. Dent, 1903.

1042. [*YL* 1031].
Another ed. Ed. Percy Simpson. Oxford: Clarendon Press, 1919.

1043. [*YL* *1032].
———. *Masques and Entertainments.* Ed. Henry Morley. London: George Routledge, 1890.

1044. [*YL* *1033]. [See Chapman, *YA* 6 (1988): 234–45].
———. *The Works of Ben Jonson.* Ed. Lt. Col. Francis Cunningham. 3 vols. London: Chatto and Windus, [1910–12]. Signed: George Hyde Lees.

1045. [*YL* 1034].
Joseph, H[orace]. W[illiam]. B[rindley]. *The Labour Theory of Value in Karl Marx.* London: Oxford University Press, 1923.

1046. [*YL* 1035].
[Josephson, Ernst]. *Ernst Josephson: 60 reproduktioner i tontryck efter fotografier af originalen.* [Monograph on the Swedish artist]. Sma Konstböcker, no. 14. Lund: Gleerupska Universitets-Bokhandeln, [1910?]. [Illustrated].

1047. [*YL* 1036].
The Journal of the Alchemical Society (London) 1 (May 1913).

1048. [*YL* 1037].
——— 2 (October 1913).

1049. [*YL* 1038].
——— 2 (April 1914).

1050. [*YL* 1039].
Jouve, P[ierre]. J[ean]. *Présences (poèmes).* First series. Paris: George Crès, 1912.

1051. [*YL* 1040].
Joyce, James. *Anna Livia Plurabelle.* New York: Crosby Gaige, 1928.

1052. [*YL* *1041].
———. *Dubliners.* London: Grant Richards, 1914.

1052a. [*YL* 1041a].
Another copy.

1053. [*YL* *1042].
———. *Exiles.* London: Grant Richards, 1918.

x   [*YL* 1043]. [NLI missing this copy].
———. *Pomes Penyeach.* Paris: Shakespeare and Company, 1927.

x   [*YL* 1043a]. [NLI missing this copy].
   Another copy.

1054.   [*YL* *1044].
   ——. *A Portrait of the Artist as a Young Man*. London: The Egoist, 1916. Bp: WBY

1055.   [*YL* 1045].
   ——. *Two Tales of Shem and Shaun*. London: Faber and Faber, 1932.

1056.   [*YL* 1046].
   ——. *Ulysses*. Paris: Shakespeare and Company, 1922.

1057.   [*YL* *1047]. [NLI 40,568/114; 2 sheets; envelope 1558]. [Though reported in *YL*, did not come to NLI with a horoscope, unidentied birth date of 22 Jan. 1897].
   Jubainville, H[enri]. D'Arbois de. *Le cycle mythologique irlandais et la mythologie celtique*. Paris: Ernest Thorin, 1884.

1058.   [*YL* *1048]. [NLI 40,568/115; 8 sheets; envelope 1557].
   ——. *Introduction à l'étude de la littérature celtique*. Paris: Ernest Thorin, 1883.

1059.   [*YL* *1049]. [NLI 40,568/116; vol. 1, 13 sheets; envelope 985].
   Julian the Emperor. *The Works of the Emperor Julian*. Trans. Wilmer Cave Wright. 3 vols. Loeb Classical Library. London: William Heinemann, 1913.

1060.   [*YL* *1050]. [NLI 40,568/117; 12 sheets; envelope 1305].
   Jung, C[arl]. G[ustav]. *Collected Papers on Analytical Psychology*. Trans. Constance E. Long. London: Baillière, Tindall and Cox, 1916.

1061.   [*YL* *1051].
   Kabir. *One Hundred Poems of Kabir*. Trans. Rabindranath Tagore assisted by Evelyn Underhill. London: The India Society, 1914.

1061A. [*YL* 1051A].
   Another ed. London: Macmillan, 1915.

1062.   [*YL* 1052]. [NLI 40,568/118; 10 sheets; envelope 1200].
   Kant, Immanuel. *Kant's Critical Philosophy for English Readers*. 3rd ed. Vol. 2: *The Prolegomena*. Trans. J. P. Mahaffy and J. H. Bernard. London: Macmillan, 1915. Bp: WBY

1063. [YL *1053].

———. *Kant's Critique of Aesthetic Judgement.* Trans. James Creed Meredith. Oxford: Clarendon Press, 1911. Bp: WBY

1064. [YL 1054].

Keats, John. *The Complete Works of John Keats.* Ed. H. Buxton Forman. 5 vols. Glasgow: Gowars and Gray, 1901. [Lacks vols. 1–3]. Vols. 4–5: *Letters, 1814–1820.*

1065. [YL *1055].

———. *The Poems of John Keats.* Ed. Sidney Colvin. 2 vols. London: Chatto and Windus, 1920. Bp: WBY

1066. [YL *1056].

———. *The Poetical Works of John Keats.* Ed. William T. Arnold. London: Kegan Paul, Trench, 1888. Bp: WBY

1067. [YL 1057].

Keith, A[rthur]. Berriedale. *Buddhist Philosophy in India and Ceylon.* Oxford: Clarendon Press, 1923.

1068. [YL 1058].

———. *The Religion and Philosophy of the Veda and Upanishads.* Harvard Oriental Series, vols. 31 and 32. Cambridge: Harvard University Press, 1925.

1069. [YL 1059].

Kelleher, D[aniel]. L[awrence]. *A Poet Passes.* London: Ernest Benn, 1927.

1070. [YL 1060].

Kennedy, James. *Poems, Lyrical and Descriptive.* Melbourne and Sydney: Lothian Publishing, 1936.

1071. [YL 1061].

Khunrath, Henricus. *Amphitheatrum sapientiae aeternae solius verae, Christiano-Kabalisticum, divino-magicum, nec non physico-chymicum, tertriunum, catholicon....*[Ed. E. Wolfart]. Hanoviae: Guilielmus Antonius, 1609. Signed: Georgie Hyde Lees | 1913

1072. [YL 1062].

King, Henry. *The Poems of Bishop Henry King.* Ed. John Sparrow. London: The Nonesuch Press, 1925.

1073.   [YL *1063].
King, Richard Ashe. *Swift in Ireland*. The New Irish Library. London: T. Fisher Unwin, 1895.

1074.   [YL *1064]. [NLI 40,568/119; 7 sheets; envelope 1306].
Kingsford, Anna (Bonus). *The Credo of Christendom and Other Addresses and Essays on Esoteric Christianity*. With some letters by Edward Maitland. Ed. Samuel Hopgood Hart. London: John W. Watkins, 1916.

1075.   [YL 1065].
Kingston, William H[enry]. G[iles]. *Roger Willoughby, or The Times of Benbow: A Tale of the Sea and Land*. London: James Nisbet, 1881.

1076.   [YL 1066].
[Kingsway Theatre (London) Program]. *The Dynasts* by Thomas Hardy. 25 November 1914.

1077.   [YL 1067]. [NLI 40,568/120; 10 sheets; envelope 1495].
Kirby, William and William Spence. *An Introduction to Entomology, or Elements of the Natural History of Insects*. People's ed. London: Longmans, Green, 1873. Signed: WBY

1078.   [YL *1068]. [NLI 40,568/121; 29 sheets; envelope 1307].
Kirk, Robert. *The Secret Commonwealth of Elves, Fauns, and Fairies*. London: David Nutt, 1893. Bp: WBY

1079.   [YL 1069].
Ki Tsurayuki. *The Tosa Diary*. Trans. William N. Porter. London: Henry Frowde, 1912.

1080.   [YL 1070].
Knight, G[eorge]. Wilson. *Myth and Miracle: An Essay on the Mystic Symbolism of Shakespeare*. London: Edward J. Burrow, [1929].

1081.   [YL 1071].
Komusashinokami Minamoto no Moronao. [Biography of a Japanese court official]. [Lacks publication details].

1082.   [YL 1072].
Kosor, Josip. *People of the Universe: Four Serbo-Croatian Plays*. London: Hendersons, 1917.

1083.   [*YL* 1073].
Kramer, Henry and James Sprenger. *Malleus maleficarum*. Trans. the Rev. Montague Sommers. [London]: John Rodker, 1928. Bp: WBY

1084.   [*YL* *1074].
Krans, Horatio Sheafe. *William Butler Yeats and the Irish Literary Revival*. Contemporary Men of Letters Series. New York: McClure, Phillips, 1904.

1085.   [*YL* 1075].
Krishnamurti, M. *Love Sonnets and Other Poems*. Oxford: Shakespeare Head Press, 1937.

1086.   [*YL* 1076].
Kurata, Hyakuzo. *Shunkan*. Trans. Kan-ichi Ando. Tokyo: Kenkyusha, 1925.

1087.   [*YL* *1077]. [NLI 40,568/122; 4 sheets; envelope 1675].
Lalor, James Fintan. *The Writings of James Fintan Lalor*. Introduction by John O'Leary. The Shamrock Library. Dublin: T. G. O'Donoghue, 1895.

1088.   [*YL* 1078].
Lamb Charles. *The Last Essays of Elia*. The Temple Classics. London: J. M. Dent, 1897. Bp: Elizabeth Corbet Yeats

1089.   [*YL* 1079].
———. *Tales from Shakespeare*. Designed for the use of young persons. 2 vols. 4th ed. London: M. J. Godwin, 1822. Bp: William Hay

1090.   [*YL* 1080]. [NLI 40,568/123; 4 sheets; envelope 447].
Landor, Walter Savage. *Imaginary Conversations*. The Camelot Classics. London: Walter Scott, 1886. Signed: W B Yeats | 1886

1091.   [*YL* *1081]. [NLI 40,568/124/1-6; 50, 35, 57, 48, 36, 34 sheets from vols. 1-6, respectively; envelope 445/1-6].
Another ed. Ed. Charles G. Crump. 6 vols. London: J. M. Dent, 1909. Bp: WBY

1092.   [*YL* *1082]. [NLI 40,568/125/1-2; vols. 1-2, 50 and 34 sheets; envelope 445/1-2].
———. *The Longer Prose Works of Walter Savage Landor*. Ed. Charles G. Crump. 2 vols. London: J. M. Dent, 1911. Bp: WBY

1093.   [*YL* *1083]. [NLI 40,568/126/1–2; vols. 1–2, 21 and 12 sheets; envelope 444].

———. *Poems, Dialogues in Verse, and Epigrams*. Ed. Charles G. Crump. 2 vols. London: J. M. Dent, 1909. Bp: WBY

1094.   [*YL* *1084].

———. *Selections from the Writings of Walter Savage Landor*. Ed. Sidney Colvin. London: Macmillan, 1913. Bp: WBY

1095.   [*YL* *1085]. [NLI 40,568/127; 13 sheets; envelope 1309].

Lang, Andrew. *The Making of Religion*. 2nd ed. London: Longmans, Green, 1900. Signed: W B Yeats | Nov. | 1900

1096.   [*YL* *1086].

Larminie, William. *Fand and Other Poems*. Dublin: Hodges, Figgis, 1892. Signed: Jos. P. Quinn

1097.   [*YL* 1087].

[Larsson, Carl]. *Carl Larsson: 60 reproduktioner i tontryck efter fotografier af originalen*. [Monograph on the Swedish artist]. Sma Konstböcker, no. 4. Lund; Gleerupska Universitets-Bokhandeln, [1907?]. [Illustrated].

1098.   [*YL* 1088].

Laski, Harold J[oseph]. *Communism*. Home University Library. London: Williams and Norgate, 1927.

1099.   [*YL* 1089].

Last, Hugh. "Dr. H. R. Hall." Offprint from *The Journal of Egyptian Archaeology* 17 (1931): 111–16.

1100.   [*YL* 1090].

Lavery, Emmet. *The First Legion: A Drama of the Society of Jesus*. New York: Samuel French, 1934. Signed: L. Robinson | N.Y. 1935.

1101.   [*YL* 1091]. [NLI 40,568/128; copy of letter inserted from Law to WBY (4 July 1926); 3 sheets; envelope 1310]. [Though reported in *YL*, did not come to NLI with said letter from Law].

Law, William. *The Spirit of Love in Dialogues*. London: Griffith Farran, [1893].

1102.   [*YL* 1092].

Lawrence, Brother [Laurent, de la Resurrection]. *The Practice of the Presence of God*. The best rule of a holy life, being conversations and letters of Brother Lawrence. Authentic ed. London: Epworth Press, [1933].

1103.   [*YL* 1093].
Lawrence, D[avid]. H[erbert]. *The Collected Poems*. London: Martin Secker, 1933.

1104.   [*YL* 1094].
Lawrence, T[homas]. E[dward]. *Seven Pillars of Wisdom*. London: Jonathan Cape, [1935?].

1105.   [*YL* *1095].
Lawrence, W[illiam]. J[ohn]. *The Elizabethan Playhouse and Other Studies*. Stratford: Shakespeare Head Press, 1912.

1106.   [*YL* *1096].
——. Second series. Stratford: Shakespeare Head Press, 1913.

1107.   [*YL* 1097].
Ledrede, Richard de, Bishop of Ossory. *A Contemporary Narrative of the Proceedings against Dame Alice Kyteler*. Ed. Thomas Wright. London: The Camden Society, 1843.

1108.   [*YL* *1098].
Le Fanu, Joseph Sheridan. *The Poems*. Ed. Alfred Perceval Graves. London: Downey, 1896.

1109.   [*YL* 1099].
[Leinster, Edward Fitzgerald, 7th Duke of]. *Catalogue of Important Pictures by Old Masters sold by the order of the trustees of His Grace The Duke of Leinster…by Messrs. Christie, Manson, and Woods, at their Great Rooms 8 King Street, St. James Square, London, on Friday May 14, 1926*. [Illustrated].

1110.   [*YL* 1100].
The Leisure Hour (London), part 448 (April 1889).

1111.   [*YL* 1101].
Lempriere, J[ohn]. *A Classical Dictionary*. London: George Routledge, [1888]. Signed: W B Yeats | January 1898

1112.   [*YL* 1102].
   Lenin, V[ladimir]. I[lich]. *Materialism and Empirio Criticism*. Trans. David Kvitko and Sidney Hook. London: Martin Lawrence, [1927]. Signed: WBY

1113.   [*YL* *1103]. [NLI 40,568/129; 54 sheets; envelope 143].
   [Leo, Alan]. *A Thousand and One Notable Nativities*. Alan Leo's Astrological Manuals, no. 11. London: Modern Astrology Office, 1911. Bp: GY

1114.   [*YL* 1104]. [NLI 40,568/130; 38 sheets; envelope 141].
   ——. *Astrology for All*. Part 2. Calculations and Ephemeris. London: Modern Astrology, 1904. Bp: GY

1115.   [*YL* 1105].
   ——. *How to Judge a Nativity*. London: Modern Astrology, 1912. Bp: GY

1116.   [*YL* *1106].
   Leo, John. *A Geographical Historie of Africa*. Trans. and collected by John Pory. Londini: Impensis G. Bishop, 1600. Bp: WBY

1117.   [*YL* *1107].
   Lesage, Alain René. *The Adventures of Gil Blas of Santillana*. Trans. Henri van Laun. 4 vols. London: Gibbings, 1896.

1118.   [*YL* *1108].
   Levi, Eliphaz. *The Magical Ritual of the Sanctum Regnum Interpreted by the Tarot Trumps*. Trans. and ed. W. Wynn Westcott. London: George Redway, 1896.

1119.   [*YL* *1109].
   ——. *Transcendental Magic*. Its doctrine and ritual. Trans. Arthur Edward Waite. London: George Redway, 1896. Bp: WBY

1120.   [*YL* 1110].
   Lewes, George Henry. *The Life of Goethe*. 2nd ed. London: George Routledge, [1864].

1121.   [*YL* 1111].
   Lewis, C[ecil]. Day. *Collected Poems, 1929–1933*. London: Hogarth Press, 1935.

1122. [YL 1112].
——. *From Feathers to Iron*. London: Hogarth Press, 1931.

1123. [YL 1113].
——. *A Hope for Poetry*. Oxford: Basil Blackwell, 1935.

1124. [YL 1114].
——. *A Time to Dance and Other Poems*. London: Hogarth Press, 1935.

1125. [YL 1115].
Lewis, M[atthew]. G[regory]. *The Monk: A Romance*. 3 vols. 3rd ed. London: J. Bell, 1797. Bp: Edward Ricketts

1126. [YL 1116].
Lewis, Wyndham. *The Apes of God*. London: Arthur Press, 1930.

1127. [YL 1117].
——. *The Art of Being Ruled*. London: Chatto and Windus, 1926.

1128. [YL 1118].
——. *The Caliph's Design*. Architects! Where is your Vortex? London: The Egoist, 1919.

1129. [YL 1119].
——. *The Childermass*. Section I. London: Chatto and Windus, 1928. Bp: WBY

1130. [YL 1120].
——. *Count Your Dead: They Are Alive! Or a New War in the Making*. London: Lovat Dickson, 1937.

1131. [YL 1121].
——. *The Diabolical Principle and The Dithyrambic Spectator*. London: Chatto and Windus, 1931.

1132. [YL 1122].
——. *Hitler*. London: Chatto and Windus, 1931.

1133. [YL 1123].
——. *The Lion and the Fox: The Role of the Hero in the Plays of Shakespeare*. London: Grant Richards, 1927.

1134. [YL 1124].
——. *One-Way Song: A Series of Four Poems*. London: Faber and Faber, 1933.

1135.   [YL 1125].
——. *Paleface. The Philosophy of the 'Melting Pot.'* London: Chatto and Windus, 1929.

1136.   [YL 1126]. [NLI 40,568/131; 29 sheets; envelope 458].
——. *Time and Western Man.* London: Chatto and Windus, 1927. Signed: WBY

1137.   [YL 1127].
Lhote, André. *Georges Seurat.* Rome: Éditions de Valori Plastici, 1922. [Illustrated].

1138.   [YL 1128].
Life and Letters (London) 1 (Sept. 1928).

1139.   [YL 1129].
——. 10 (April 1934).

1140.   [YL 1130].
——. 11 (Nov. 1934).

1141.   [YL 1131].
Life and Letters To-Day 13 (Winter Quarter, 1935–36).

1142.   [YL *1132].
Light: Journal of Psychical, Occult, and Mystical Research (London) 35 (30 Oct. 1915–25 Dec. 1915).

1143.   [YL *1133].
——. 36 (1 Jan. 1916–24 June 1916).

1144.   [YL 1134].
[Liljefors, Bruno]. *Bruno Liljefors: 60 reproduktioner i tontryck efter fotografier af originalen.* [Monograph on the Swedish artist]. Sma Konstböcker, no. 5. Lund: Gleerupska Universitets-Bokhandeln, 1908. [Illustrated].

1145.   [YL 1135].
Limebeer, Ena. *To a Proud Phantom: Poems.* Richmond: Hogarth Press, 1923.

1146.   [YL 1136].
Lindsay, Jack. *Helen Comes of Age: Three Plays.* London: Fanfrolico Press, 1927.

1147.   [*YL* 1137].
——. *Marino Faliero: A Verse Play*. London: Fanfrolico Press, 1927.

1148.   [*YL* 1138].
Lindsay, Norman and Jack Lindsay. *A Homage to Sappho: Poems*. London: Fanfrolico Press, 1928.

1149.   [*YL* 1139].
Lindsay, Vachel. *General William Booth Enters into Heaven and Other Poems*. New York: Macmillan, 1921.

1150.   [*YL* 1140].
Li-Po. *The Works of Li-Po the Chinese Poet*. Trans. Shigeyoshi Obata. London and Toronto: J. M. Dent, 1923.

1151.   [Not listed in *YL* and assigned NLI Number 3025].
A List of Books Published by the Dun Emer Press and the Cuala Press founded in Nineteen Hundred and Three by Elizabeth Corbet Yeats. N.p.: n.p., 1943. [Extensively annotated].

1152.   [*YL* 1141].
The Listener (London) 16 (14 Oct. 1936).

1152a.   [*YL* 1141a].
Another copy.

1153.   [*YL* 1142].
Litchfield, Frederick. *Illustrated History of Furniture*. From the earliest to the present time. 4th ed. London and New York: Truslove, Hanson, and Comba, 1899.

1154.   [*YL* 1143].
The Little Review (New York) 8 (Spring, 1922).

1155.   [Not listed in *YL* and assigned NLI Number 3026].
*A Living Theatre. The Gordon Craig School. The Arena Goldoni. The Mask. Setting Forth the Aims and Objects of the Movement and Showing by Many Illustrations the City of Florence the Aren*a. Florence, Italy, 1913.

1156.   [*YL* 1144].
Lomax, John A[very]. *Cowboy Songs and Other Frontier Ballads*. New York: Sturgis and Walton, 1916.

Figure 5. Frontispiece and title page of 1157. Cesare Lombroso, *After Death—What?* (1909)

1157.   [*YL* 1145]. [NLI 40,568/132; 81 sheets; envelope 1313].
Lombroso, Cesare. *After Death—What? Spiritistic Phenomena and Their Interpretation*. Trans. William Sloane Kennedy. London: T. Fisher Unwin, 1909. Signed: WBY

1158.   [*YL* 1146].
The London Mercury 10 (Sept. 1924).

1159.   [*YL* 1147].
—— 16 (May 1927).

1160.   [*YL* 1148].
—— 16 (Aug. 1927).

1161.   [*YL* 1149].
—— 30 (July 1934).

1162.   [*YL* 1150].
—— 31 (Dec. 1934).

1162a.   [*YL* 1150a].
Another copy.

1163. [*YL* 1151].
—— 37 (April 1938).

1163a. [*YL* 1151a].
Another copy.

1164. [*YL* 1152].
—— 38 (May 1938).

1165. [*YL* 1153].
—— 39 (March 1939).

1165a-b. [*YL* 1153a-b].
Two more copies.

1166. [*YL* 1154].
Londonderry, The Marchioness of. *The Land of the Living Heart*. Privately printed, 1936.

1167. [*YL* 1155].
Long, Haniel. *Interlinear to Cabeza de Vaca: His Relation of the Journey from Florida to the Pacific, 1528–1536*. Sante Fe: Writers' Editions, 1936.

1168. [*YL* 1156].
Longford, The Earl of. *Yahoo: A Tragedy in Three Acts*. Dublin: Hodges, Figgis, [1934].

1169. [*YL* *1157].
[Louvre]. *Les chefs d'oeuvre du musée du Louvre*. Paris: Les Grand Magasins du Louvre, [1900?].

1170. [*YL* *1158].
Lucas, St. John. *The Oxford Book of French Verse. XIII–XIX Centuries*. New York: Oxford University Press, [1907]. Bp: WBY

1171. [*YL* 1159].
Luce, A[rthur]. A[ston], *Berkeley and Malebranche: A Study in the Origins of Berkeley's Thought*. London: Oxford University Press, 1934.

1172. [*YL* 1160].
——. "Berkeley's *Commonplace Book*—Its Date, Purpose, Structure, and Marginal Signs." Offprint from *Hermathena* 22 (1932): 99–132.

1173.   [*YL* 1161].
Lucian. *True History*. Trans. Francis Hickes. Illustrated by Aubrey Beardsley and Others. London: A. H. Bullen, 1902.

1174.   [*YL* 1162].
Lucretius, Carus (Titus). *Titi Lucretii cari de rerum natura libri sex*. Londini: Jacobi Tonson, 1712.

1174A.   [*YL* 1162A].
Another ed. Trans. H. A. J. Munro. 2 vols. 2nd ed. rev. Cambridge: Deighton Bell, 1866.

1175.   [*YL* 1163].
Lutoslawski, W[incenty]. *Pre-Existence and Reincarnation*. London: George Allen, 1928. Bp: WBY

1176.   [*YL* *1164].
Lyrics from the Chinese. Adapted [from J. Legge's translation of the Shih Ching] by Helen Waddell. London: Constable, 1913.

1177.   [*YL* *1165].
Lytton, Edward Bulwer, Lord. *The Dramatic Works*. Comprising *The Duchess de la Vallière, Richelieu, The Lady of Lyons, Money, Not so Bad as We Seem*. New ed. London: George Routledge, [187?]. Signed: Jessop Browne | Xmas 1870

1178.   [*YL* *1166]. [NLI 40,568/133; 12 sheets; envelope 1318].
The Mabinogion, from the Welsh of the Llyfr Coh O Hergest (The Red Book of Hergest) in the library of Jesus College, Oxford. Trans. Lady Charlotte Guest. London: Bernard Quaritch, 1877.

1179.   [*YL* 1167].
Macardle, Dorothy. *The Irish Republic: A Documented Chronicle of the Anglo-Irish Conflict and the Partitioning of Ireland, with a Detailed Account of the Period 1916–1923*. Preface by Eamon de Valera. London: Victor Gollancz, 1937. [With map].

1180.   [*YL* 1168].
McCartan, Patrick. *With de Valera in America*. New York: Brentano, 1932.

1181.   [*YL* 1169].
McCarthy, Justin, ed.-in-chief. *Irish Literature*. 10 vols. Philadelphia: John D. Morris, 1904.

1182. [*YL* 1170].
Mac Cathmhaoil, Seosamh (Joseph Campbell). *The Rush-Light: Poems*. Dublin: Maunsel, 1906.

1183. [*YL* 1171].
McCrae, Hugh. *Satyrs and Sunlight: Collected Poetry*. Illustrated and decorated by Norman Lindsay. London: Fanfrolico Press, 1928.

1184. [*YL* 1172].
M'Diarmid, Hugh. *A Drunk Man Looks at the Thistle*. Edinburgh and London: William Blackwood, 1926.

1185. [*YL* 1173].
——. *Sangschaw*. Edinburgh and London: William Blackwood, 1925.

1186. [*YL* 1174].
——. *Second Hymn to Lenin and Other Poems*. London: Stanley Nott, 1935.

1187. [*YL* 1175].
——. *Selected Poems*. London: Macmillan, 1934.

1188. [*YL* 1176].
——. *Stony Limits and Other Poems*. London: Victor Gollancz, 1934.

1189. [*YL* 1177].
——. *To Circumjack Cencrastus or The Curly Snake*. Edinburgh and London: William Blackwood, 1930.

1190. [*YL* 1178].
[M'Diarmid, Hugh]. *Speaking for Scotland: Tributes Concerning Hugh M'Diarmid*. [N.p.: n.p., 1936].

1191. [*YL* *1179].
MacDonagh, Michael. *Bishop Doyle, "J. K. L." A biographical and historical study*. The New Irish Library. Ed. Sir Charles Gavan Duffy. London: T. Fisher Unwin, 1896.

1192. [*YL* *1180]. [NLI 40,568/134; 27 sheets; envelope 1580]. [See Chapman, *YA* 6 (1988): 234–45].
MacDonagh, Thomas. *Literature in Ireland*. Studies Irish and Anglo-Irish. Dublin: Talbot Press, 1916. Bp: WBY

1193. [*YL* *1181].
——. *Lyrical Poems*. Dublin: Irish Review, 1913. Bp: WBY

1194.   [YL *1182]. [NLI 40,568/135; 9 sheets; envelope 266]. [See Chapman, YA 6 (1988): 234–45].
——. *Thomas Campion and the Art of English Poetry*. Dublin: Hodges, Figgis, 1913. By: WBY

1195.   [YL *1183].
Macdonald, J[ames]. *National Defence: A Study of Militarism*. London: George Allen and Unwin, 1917.

1196.   [YL *1184]. [NLI 40,568/136; 9 sheets; envelope 1315].
McDougall, William. *Body and Mind: A History and a Defense of Animism*. 2nd ed. London: Methuen, 1913.

1197.   [YL 1185].
——. *The Group Mind: A Sketch of the Principles of Collective Psychology with Some Attempt to Apply them to the Interpretation of National Life and Character*. Cambridge: University Press, 1920. Bp: WBY

1198.   [YL 1186].
——. *National Welfare and National Decay*. London: Methuen, 1921. Signed: GY

1199.   [YL 1187].
M'Gee, Thomas D'Arcy. *A Memoir of the Life and Conquests of Art MacMurrough, King of Leinster, from A.D. 1377 to A.D. 1417*. 2nd ed. Dublin: James Duffy, [1886].

1200.   [YL 1188].
McGreevy, Thomas. *Poems*. London: William Heinemann, 1934.

1200a.   [YL 1188a].
Another copy.

1201.   [YL 1189].
——. *Richard Aldington, An Englishman*. The Dolphin Books. London: Chatto and Windus, 1931.

1202.   [Not listed in *YL* and assigned NLI number 3027].
Another copy.

1203.   [YL 1190].
——. *Thomas Stearns Eliot: A Study*. The Dolphin Books. London: Chatto and Windus, 1931.

1204.   [*YL* 1191].
Machiavelli. *The Prince*. Trans. Luigi Ricci. The World's Classics, vol. 43. London: Grant Richards, 1903.

1205.   [*YL* 1192].
Mackay, Eric. *Love Letters of a Violinist and Other Poems*. London: Walter Scott, 1886. Signed: W. B. Yeats | Dublin | 1887

1206.   [*YL* *1193].
Macleod, Fiona (William Sharp). *From the Hills of Dream: Mountain Songs and Island Runes*. Edinburgh: Patrick Geddes, [1896].

1206A.   [*YL* *1193A].
Another ed. Portland, Maine: Thomas B. Mosher, 1901.

1207.   [*YL* *1194].
——. *The House of Usna: A Drama*. Portland, Maine: Thomas B. Mosher, 1903.

1208.   [*YL* *1195].
——. *The Immortal Hour: A Drama*. Edinburgh and London: T. N. Foulis, 1908.

1209.   [*YL* *1196].
——. *Under the Dark Star* [and *The Kingdom of Silence* and *Chant d'amour*]. N.p.: Privately printed, n.d.

1210.   [*YL* 1197].
Mac Mic Cuinn na M-Bocht, Moelmuiri. *Fled Bricrend, the Feast of Bricriu. An early Gaelic saga, etc.* Ed. George Henderson. Irish Texts Society, vol. 2. London: Published for the Irish Texts Society by David Nutt, 1899.

1211.   [*YL* 1198].
MacMillan, Dougald and Howard Mumford Jones, eds. *Plays of the Restoration and Eighteenth Century as they were acted at the Theatres-Royal....*London: George Allen and Unwin, 1931.

1212.   [*YL* 1199].
MacNeice, Louis. *Poems*. London: Faber and Faber, 1935.

1212a.   [*YL* 1199a].
Another copy.

1212b.   [*YL* 1199b].
Another copy.

1213.   [*YL* 1200].
McTaggart, John McTaggart Ellis. *A Commentary on Hegel's Logic.* Cambridge: University Press, 1910.

1213a.   [*YL* 1200a].
Another copy.

1214.   [*YL* 1201]. [NLI 40,568/139; 8 sheets; envelope 1317].
———. *Human Immortality and Pre-Existence.* London: Edward Arnold, 1916.

1215.   [*YL* 1202]. [NLI 40,568/137; vol. 1, 23 sheets; envelope 1205].
———. *The Nature of Existence.* 2 vols. Cambridge: University Press, 1921. Bp: WBY

1216.   [*YL* 1203]. [NLI 40,568/138; 39 sheets; envelope 1204].
———. *Studies in Hegelian Cosmology.* Cambridge: University Press, 1918.

1217.   [*YL* 1204].
———. *Studies in the Hegelian Dialectic.* 2nd ed. Cambridge: University Press, 1922.

1218.   [*YL* 1205].
Madeleva, Sister M[ary]. *The Happy Christmas Wind and Other Poems.* Paterson, NJ: St. Anthony Guild Press, 1936.

1219.   [*YL* 1206].
———. *Penelope and Other Poems.* New York and London: D. Appleton, 1927.

1220.   [*YL* 1207].
———. *A Question of Lovers and Other Poems.* Patterson, NJ: St. Anthony Guild Press, 1936.

1221.   [*YL* 1208].
Maeterlinck, Maurice. *Ruysbroeck and the Mystics.* With selections from Ruysbroeck. Trans. Jane T. Stoddart. London: Hodder and Stoughton, 1894.

1222. [*YL* 1209].
Mahaffy, John Pentland. With the collaboration of Arthur Gilman. *Alexander's Empire*. London: T. Fisher Unwin, 1920.

1223. [*YL* 1210].
Mairet, Philippe. *Aristocracy and the Meaning of Class Rule: An Essay upon Aristocracy Past and Future*. London: C. W. Daniel, 1931.

1224. [*YL* *1211].
Maitland, Francis. *Poems*. London: Elkin Mathews, 1917.

1225. [*YL* 1212].
Mallarmé, Stéphane. *Poems*. Trans. Roger Fry. London: Chatto and Windus, 1936.

1226. [*YL* 1213].
Malone, Andrew E. *The Irish Drama*. London: Constable, 1929.

1227. [*YL* 1214].
Malory, Sir Thomas. *The birth, life and acts of King Arthur: of his noble Knights of the Round Table, their marvellous enquests and adventures, the achieving of the San Greal and in the end le morte d'Arthur, with the dolourous death and departing out of this world of them all*. [Le Morte d'Arthur]. Designs by Aubrey Beardsley. 2 vols. London: J. M. Dent, 1893. [Illustrated].

1228. [*YL* 1215].
Mannin, Ethel. *Dryad*. London: Jarrolds, 1933.

1229. [*YL* *1216].
Manning, Frederic. *Poems*. London: John Murray, 1910.

1230. [*YL* 1217].
Manning-Sanders, Ruth. *Martha Wish-You-Ill*. London: Hogarth Press, 1926.

1231. [*YL* *1218].
Mantzius, Karl. *A History of Theatrical Art in Ancient and Modern Times*. Trans. Louise von Cossell [and C. Archer]. 6 vols. London: Duckworth, 1903–1921.

1232. [*YL* 1219].
[Map]. *Bacon's Motoring and Cycling Road Map*. Stratford-on-Avon District. Stratford-on-Avon: A. J. Stanley, n.d.

1233.   [*YL* 1220].
[Map]. *Bartholomew's Quarter Inch Map of Ireland.* Killarney and Cork. Edinburgh and London: John Bartholomew, n.d.

1234.   [*YL* 1221].
[Maps]. *Cambridge Medieval History. Maps.* 8 vols. Cambridge: Cambridge University Press, 1911–36.

1235.   [*YL* 1222].
[Map]. *Ireland,* by Sidney Hall. London: Longman, Rees, Orme, Browne and Green, 1830.

1236.   [*YL* 1223].
[Maps]. *London Street Guide.* With 4 maps. An entirely new ed. including L. C. C. changes of street names. London: Geographia, n.d.

1237.   [*YL* *1224].
[Maps]. *Maps of Old London.* Ed. G. E. Mitton. London: Adam and Charles Black, 1908.

1238.   [*YL* 1225].
[Map]. *Nuova Pianta de Verona.* Firenze: Stabilimento Grafico Cartographico, n.d.

1239.   [*YL* 1226].
[Map]. *Ordnance Survey Map of Kenmare River and District.* Coloured ed. Sheets 191 and 198. Southampton: Ordnance Survey Office, n.d.

1240.   [*YL* 1227].
Mardrus, Dr. J[oseph]. C[harles]. *The Queen of Sheba.* Trans. E. Powys Mather. London: Casanova Society, [1924].

1241.   [*YL* *1228].
Margaret [D'Angoulemne], Queen Consort of Henry II, King of Navarre. *The Heptameron: Tales.* [Trans. W. M. Thomson]. Unexpurgated ed. London: [Temple, 1896].

1242.   [*YL* *1229].
Marillier, H[enry]. C[urrie]. *Dante Gabriel Rossetti: An Illustrated Memorial of His Art and Life.* London: George Bell, 1899. xxiii, [1], 270 pp. Bp: WBY

1243. [*YL* *1230].
The Marionette (Florence) 1 (Nov. 1918).

1244. [*YL* 1231].
Maritain, Jacques. *An Introduction to Philosophy*. Trans. E. I. Watkin. London: Sheed and Ward, 1932.

1245. [*YL* *1232].
——. *Three Reformers: Luther—Descartes—Rousseau*. London: Sheed and Ward, 1928. Bp: WBY

1246. [*YL* 1233].
Marivaux [Carlet de Chamblain de Marivaux, Pierre]. *Theatre choisi de Marivaux*. [Ed. F. De Marescot and D. Jouaust?]. 2 vols. Paris: Librairie des bibliophiles, [1881].

1247. [*YL* 1234].
Marlowe, Christopher. *Doctor Faustus*. Ed. John Masefield. Decorated by Charles Ricketts. London: Ballantyne Press, 1903. Bp: WBY

1248. [*YL* 1235].
Marpicati, Arturo. *The Achievements of Fascism*. [N.p.: n.p., 1930s?].

1249. [*YL* 1236].
Marriott, Ernest. "Jack B. Yeats, Pictorial and Dramatic Artist." Reprint from the *Manchester Quarterly*, no. 119. Manchester: For the Manchester Literary Club by Sherratt and Hughes, 1911.

1249a. [*YL* 1236a].
Another copy.

1250. [*YL* *1237].
[Marsh, Edward Howard, ed.]. *Georgian Poetry, 1913–1915*. London: Poetry Bookshop, 1915. Bp: WBY

1251. [*YL* *1238].
Marston, John. *The Works of John Marston*. Ed. A. H. Bullen. 3 vols. London: John C. Nimmo, 1887.

1252. [*YL* 1239].
Martyn, Oliver [H. O. White]. *The Man They Couldn't Hang*. A Morrow Mystery. New York: William Morrow, 1933. Signed: WBY

1253. [*YL* *1240].
Masefield, John. *Ballads*. London: Elkin Mathews, 1903.

1253A.   [*YL* 1240A].
2nd ed., rev. and enlarged. 1910.

1254.   [*YL* *1241].
———. *Ballads and Poems.* London: Elkin Mathews, 1919.

1255.   [*YL* 1242].
———. *The Collected Poems.* London: William Heinemann, 1935.

1256.   [*YL* 1243].
———. *The Daffodil Fields.* London; William Heinemann, 1918. Signed: Katharine B. Scott

1257.   [*YL* 1244].
———. *The Dream.* Illustrated by Judith Masefield. [Oxford]: Printed by Slatter and Rose, [1922?].

1258.   [*YL* *1245].
———. *The Everlasting Mercy.* London: Sidgwick and Jackson, 1911.

1259.   [*YL* *1246].
———. *The Faithful. A Tragedy in Three Acts.* London William Heinemann, 1915.

1260.   [*YL* 1247].
———. *Gallipoli.* London: William Heinemann, 1917.

1261.   [*YL* 1248].
———. *Good Friday. A Play in Verse.* London: William Heinemann, 1917.

1262.   [*YL* 1249].
———. *The Hawbucks.* London: William Heinemann, 1929.

1263.   [*YL* 1250].
———. *Lollingdon Downs and Other Poems.* London: William Heinemann, 1919.

1264.   [*YL* 1251].
———. *A Mainsail Haul.* Frontispiece by Jack Yeats. London: Elkin Mathews, 1905.

1265.   [*YL* 1252].
———. *Midsummer Night and Other Tales in Verse.* London: William Heinemann, 1928.

1266.   [*YL* 1253].
——. *On the Spanish Main, or Some English Forays on the Isthmus of Darien, with a Description of the Buccaneers.*...London: Methuen, 1906.

1267.   [*YL* *1254].
——. *Philip the King and Other Poems.* London: William Heinemann, 1914.

1268.   [*YL* 1255].
——. *Reynard the Fox or The Ghost of Heath Run.* London: William Heinemann, 1920.

1269.   [*YL* 1256].
——. *A Tarpaulin Muster.* London: Grant Richards, 1907.

1270.   [*YL* *1257].
——. *The Tragedy of Nan and Other Plays.* London: Grant Richards, 1909.

1271.   [*YL* *1258].
——. *The Tragedy of Pompey the Great.* London: Sidgwick and Jackson, 1910.

1272.   [*YL* 1259].
——. *The Wanderer of Liverpool.* London: William Heinemann, 1930. Signed: John Masefield

1273.   [*YL* *1260].
——. *The Widow in the Bye Street.* London: Sidgwick and Jackson, 1912.

1274.   [*YL* *1261]. [Though reported in *YL*, did not come to NLI with letter of presentation from Masefield to WBY].
——. *William Shakespeare.* New York: Henry Holt; London: Williams and Norgate, 1911.

1274a.   [*YL* 1261a].
Another printing, [1925]

1275.   [*YL* *1262].
——, ed. *An English Prose Miscellany.* London: Methuen, 1907.

1276.   [*YL* *1263].
——, ed. *A Sailor's Garland.* London: Methuen, 1906.

1277. [*YL* *1264].
—— and Constance Masefield, eds. *Lyrists of the Restoration*. From Sir Edward Sherburne to William Congreve. London: E. Grant Richards, 1905.

1278. [*YL* *1265].
The Mask: A Quarterly Journal of the Art of the Theatre (Florence) 2 (Oct. 1909–Apr. 1910).

1279. [*YL* *1266].
—— 3 (July 1910–Apr. 1911).

1280. [*YL* *1267].
—— 3 (Oct. 1910).

1280a. [*YL* *1267a].
Another copy.

1281. [*YL* *1268].
—— 4 (July 1911–Apr. 1912).

1282. [*YL* *1269].
—— 5 (July 1912–Apr. 1913).

1283. [*YL* *1270].
—— 6 (Oct. 1913–Apr. 1914).

1284. [*YL* *1271].
—— 7 (May 1915).

1285. [*YL* 1272].
—— 8 (May 1918).

1286. [*YL* 1273].
—— 8 (Nov. 1918).

1287. [*YL* 1274].
—— 8.11 [1919?].

1288. [*YL* 1275].
—— 11 (4 Oct. 1925).

1289. [*YL* 1276].
—— 12 (1 Jan. 1926).

1290. [*YL* 1277].
—— 12 (3 July 1926).

1291.   [*YL* 1278].
—— 12 (4 Oct. 1926).

1292.   [*YL* 1279].
—— 12 (Oct.–Dec. 1927).

1293.   [*YL* 1280].
—— 14. (Apr.–June 1928.)

1294.   [*YL* 1281].
—— 14 (July–Sept. 1928).

1295.   [*YL* 1282].
—— 14 (Oct.–Dec. 1928).

1296.   [*YL* 1283].
—— 15 (Apr.–June 1929).

1297.   [*YL* 1284].
—— 15 (July–Sept. 1929).

1298.   [*YL* 1285].
—— 15 (Oct.–Dec. 1929.)

1299.   [*YL* *1286].
[Massinger, Philip]. *Philip Massinger*. Ed. Arthur Symons. 2 vols. The Mermaid Series. London: T. Fisher, Unwin, [1887–89].

1300.   [*YL* *1287].
Masters, Edgar Lee. *Spoon River Anthology*. London: T. Werner Laurie, 1915. Bp: WBY

1301.   [*YL* 1288].
Mathers, E[dward]. Powys. *Red Wise*. Waltham Saint Lawrence: Golden Cockerell Press, 1926.

1302.   [*YL* 1289].
——, trans. *Black Marigolds: Being a Rendering into English of the "Panchasika of Chauras."* Oxford: Basil Blackwell, [1919].

1303.   [*YL* *1290].
——, trans. *Coloured Stars: Versions of Fifty Asiatic Love Poems*. Oxford: Basil Blackwell, 1919.

1304. [*YL* 1291].
——, trans. *The Garden of Bright Waters: One Hundred and Twenty Asiatic Love Poems*. Oxford: Basil Blackwell, 1920.

1305. [*YL* 1292]. [NLI 40,568/140; 45 sheets; envelope 135].
Mathers, S. L[iddell]. MacGregor, trans. *The Kabbalah Unveiled* [Kabbala Denudata], *Containing the Following Books of the Zohar: 1. The Book of Concealed Mystery. 2. The Greater Holy Assembly. 3. The Lesser Holy Assembly; Translated from the Latin Version of Knorr von Rosenroth, and Collated with the Original Chaldee and Hebrew Text*. London: George Redway, 1887. Signed: Georgie Hyde Lees. | February, 1914

1305a. [*YL* *1292a*].
Another copy. Bp: WBY

1306. [*YL* 1293]. [NLI 40,568/141; 5 sheets; envelope 1321].
——, ed. *The Key of Solomon the King (Clavicula Salomonis): Now First Translated and Edited from Ancient MSS. in the British Museum*. London: Kegan Paul, Trench, Trübner, 1909. [Illustrated].

1307. [*YL* 1294].
Maupassant, Guy de. *Bel-ami*. Illustrated by Berdinand Bac. Engravings by G. Lemoine. Les Oeuvres Complètes Illustrées. Paris: Société d'éditions littéraires et artistiques, 1903. [Illustrated].

1308. [*YL* 1295].
Maurois, Andre. *Voltaire*. Trans. Hamish Miles. London: Thomas Nelson, 1938.

1309. [*YL* *1296].
Mayne, Rutherford. *The Troth: A Play in One Act*. Dublin: Maunsel, 1909.

1310. [*YL* *1297].
Mazzini, Joseph. *Essays: Selected from the Writings, Literary, Political, and Religious, of Joseph Mazzini*. Ed. William Clarke. The Camelot Series. London: Walter Scott, 1887. Signed: W B Yeats. | Dublin | December | 1887

1311.   [*YL* 1298]. [NLI 40,568/142; 4 sheets; envelope 1322].
Mead, G[eorge]. R[obert]. S[tow]. "The Spirit-Body: An Excursion into Alexandrian Psycho-Physiology." Offprint from *The Quest* (London) [1 (Apr. 1910)]: 472–88.

x   [*YL* 1299]. [NLI 40,568/143; 7 sheets; envelope 1322]. [NLI missing this copy].
——. "The Augoeides or Radiant Body." Offprint from *The Quest* [1 (July 1910)]: 705–24.

1312.   [Not listed in *YL* and assigned NLI number 3028]. [See Chapman, *YA* 8 (1991): 202, for a short descriptive account of Yeats's reading notes]. [NLI 40,568/144; 12 sheets; envelope 1322A].
——. *Orpheus*. London: Theosophical Publishing Society, 1896.

1313.   [*YL* 1300]. [Though reported in *YL*, did not come to NLI with pencil drawing, unidentified].
[Medici Prints]. *Catalogue of the Medici Prints and Other Colour Reproductions*. London: The Medici Society, [1935].

1314.   [*YL* *1301].
The Medium and Daybreak: A Weekly Journal Devoted to the History, Phenomena, Philosophy, and Teachings of Spiritualism (London) 2 (13 Jan. 1871–29 Dec.1871).

1315.   [*YL* *1302].
—— 3 (5 Jan. 1872–27 Dec. 1872).

1316.   [*YL* *1303].
—— 4 (3 Jan. 1873–26 Dec. 1873).

1317.   [*YL* 1304].
Meinhold, William. *Sidonia the Sorceress: The Supposed Destroyer of the Whole Reigning Ducal House of Pomerania*. 2 vols. London: Simms and M'Intyre, 1849.

1317A.   [*YL* 1304A].
——. Another ed. Trans. Lady Wilde. 2 vols. London: Reeves and Turner, 1894. Bp: Anne Butler Yeats | 1934

1318. [*YL* 1305]. [NLI 40,568/145/1-2; vols. 1-2, 6 and 8 sheets; envelope 1325].

Mercier, Cardinal [Désiré Félicien]. *A Manual of Modern Scholastic Philosophy*. Trans. T. L. Parker and S. A. Parker. 2nd ed. 2 vols. London: Kegan Paul, Trench, Trubner, 1921.

1319. [*YL* 1306].

Meredith, George. *Chillianwallah*. Jamaica, Queensborough, New York: Printed at the Marion Press, 1909.

1320. [*YL* *1307].

——. *Evan Harrington: A Novel*. London: Constable, 1909. [Illustrated]. Signed: W B Yeats | June 25 | 1910

1321. [*YL* *1308].

The Merry Devil of Edmonton: A Comedy. Ed. Hugh Walker. Temple Dramatists. London: J. M. Dent, 1897.

1322. [*YL* 1309].

[Méryon, Charles]. *Old Paris: Twenty Etchings*. With an essay on the etcher by Philip Gilbert Hamerton. Liverpool: Henry Young, 1914. [Illustrated].

1323. [*YL* *1310]. [NLI 40,568/146/1-2; vols. 1-2, 27 and 28 sheets; envelope 1569].

Meyer, Kuno, ed and trans. *The Voyage of Bran Son of Febal to the Land of the Living: An Old Irish Saga*. With an essay upon the Irish vision of the happy otherworld and the Celtic doctrine of rebirth by Alfred Nutt. With appendices "The Transformations of Tuan Mac Cairill" and "The Dinnschenchas of Mag Slecht." 2 vols. London: David Nutt, 1895-97. Bp: Lady Gregory

1324. [*YL* 1311].

Meyerstein, E[dward]. H[arry]. W[illiam]. *Selected Poems*. London: Macmillan, 1935.

1325. [*YL* *1312].

Meynell, Everard. *The Life of Francis Thompson*. London: Burns and Oates, 1913.

1326.   [YL 1313].
Michelangelo. *The Sonnets of Michael Angelo Buonarroti.* Trans. John Addington Symonds. 3rd ed. London: John Murray, 1912. Bp: Louise Alexander Billstein

1327.   [YL 1314].
Milbanke, Ralph, Earl of Lovelace. *Astarte: A Fragment of Truth Concerning George Gordon Byron.* London: Chiswick Press, 1905. [With facsimiles]. Bp: WBY

1328.   [YL 1315].
Millay, Edna St. Vincent. *The Buck in the Snow and Other Poems.* London: Harper, 1928.

1329.   [YL 1316].
——. *Fatal Interview: Sonnets.* London: Hamish Hamilton, [193?].

1330.   [YL 1317].
——. *Poems.* London: Martin Secker, 1931.

1331.   [YL 1318].
——. *Wine from These Grapes.* London: Hamish Hamilton, 1934.

1332.   [YL 1319].
Milton, John. *Early Poems.* [ed. Charles Sturt?]. Decorations by Charles Ricketts. London: [Vale Press, 1896].

1333.   [YL 1320].
——. *On the Morning of Christ's Nativity.* Illustrated by William Blake. Cambridge: University Press, 1923.

1334.   [YL 1321].
——. *Paradise Lost.* Illustrated by William Blake. Liverpool: Liverpool Booksellers, 1906. Bp: WBY

1335.   [YL 1322].
——. *Paradise Regained. Sampson Agonistes and Other Poems.* Ed. W. H. D. Rouse. The Temple Classics. London: J. M. Dent, 1899.

1336.   [YL 1323]. [NLI 40,568/147; 15 sheets; envelope 1076].
Mirsky, D[mitri]. S[vyatopolk]. *Lenin.* Makers of the Modern Age. London: Holme Press, 1931.

1337.   [YL 1324].
Mitchel, John. *An Apology for the British Government in Ireland.* Dublin: O'Donoghue, 1905.

1338.   [YL 1325].
[Mitchell, Susan, ed.]. *Secret Springs of Dublin Song.* London: Fisher Unwin; Dublin: Talbot Press, 1918.

1339.   [YL 1326].
Mitsuru, Yamamiya, ed. and trans. *Benisuzume* [an anthology of Modern poetry in English translated into Japanese]. [Kyoto: Naigai-shuppan, 1926].

1340.   [YL 1327].
Moberly, C[harlotte]. Anne E[lizabeth]. and Eleanor F[rances]. Jourdain. *An Adventure.* 4th ed. London: Faber and Faber, 1931. [With maps].

1341.   [YL 1328].
[Modern British Painters]. *An Exhibition of Paintings by Eight Modern British Painters, July 2nd–July 26, 1930.* [Catalog]. Arthur Tooth, 155 New Bond Street, [London].

1342.   [YL *1329].
Molière. *The Dramatic Works.* Trans. Charles Heron Wall. 3 vols. London: George Bell, 1901.

1343.   [YL 1330].
———. *The Kiltartan Molière.* Trans. Lady Gregory. Dublin: Maunsel, 1910.

1344.   [YL 1331].
———. *Oeuvres Complètes de Molière.* Avec des remarques nouvelles par Félix Lemaistre précédée de la vie de Molière par Voltaire. Nouvelle edition. 3 vols. Paris: Garnier Frères, [19??].

1345.   [YL *1332].
Molinos, Michael de. *The Spiritual Guide Which Disentangles the Soul.* Ed. Kathleen Lyttleton. 2nd ed. London: Methuen, 1911. Signed: W. B. Yeats | Sept 1913

1345a.   [YL 1332a]. [NLI 40,568/148; 18 sheets; envelope 130].
Another copy? [Title p. and pp. through 48 lacking]. [London]: Methuen, [1911?]. Signed: Georgie Hyde Lees | August, 1913

1346. [*YL* 1333].
Molmenti, Pompeo. *Venezia*. 3rd ed. Bergamo: Istituto Italiano d'Arti Grafiche, 1907. [Illustrated].

1347. [*YL* 1334].
Monck, [Walter] Nugent. *The Interlude of Holly and Ivy, Made... from Fifteenth Century Sources*. Norwich: Saint William Press, 1913.

1348. [*YL* 1335].
——. *Narcissus: A Water Frolic in One Act*. Written and produced by Nugent Monck at Blickling Park. By the author, n.d.

1349. [*YL* 1336].
—— and Martin Kinder. *Aucassin and Nicolette*. Norwich: Saint William Press, 1913.

1350. [*YL* *1337].
Monro, Harold. *Children of Love*. London: Poetry Bookshop, 1919.

1351. [*YL* 1338].
——. *The Collected Poems*. Ed. Alida Monro. Biographical sketch by F. S. Flint. Critical note by T. S. Eliot. London: Cobden-Sanderson, 1933.

1352. [*YL* 1339].
——. *Real Property*. London: Poetry Bookshop, 1922.

1353. [*YL* *1340].
——. *Strange Meetings*. London: Poetry Bookshop, 1917.

1354. [*YL* 1341].
——. *The Winter Solstice*. Illustrated by David Jones. The Ariel Poems, no. 13. London: Faber and Gwyer, [1928?]. [Illustrated].

1355. [*YL* 1342].
Montagu, Lady Mary Wortley. *The Travel Letters*. Ed. A. W. Lawrence. London: Jonathan Cape, 1930. Signed: WBY

1356. [*YL* 1343].
Montaigne. *Essays of Montaigne*. 4 vols. Ed. William Carew Hazlitt. Trans. Charles Cotton. New ed. London: Reeves and Turner, 1902. 4 vols.

1357.   [*YL* 1344].
——. *Love and Marriage: Being Montaigne's Essay "Sur des vers de Virgil."* Trans. Constance Vera Norman. Illustrated by Bruno Bramanti. Florence: Printed by the Tipografia Giuntina, [1930?]. [Illustrated].

1358.   [*YL* *1345].
Montfaucon de Villars, Nicolas de. *Comte de Gabalis.* London: William Rider, [1913]. Bp: WBY

1359.   [*YL* 1346].
Moore, Francis. *Vox stellarum, or A Loyal Almanack for the Year of Human Redemption 1835.*...London: Printed for C. Baldwin by George Greenhill, [1834?].

1360.   [*YL* 1347].
——. A further no. for 1921. London: Cassell, [1920?].

1361.   [*YL* 1348]. [NLI 40,568/149; copy of inserted letter from Herbert Vincent Reade to GY (5 Dec. 1924); 2 sheets; envelope 23]. [Though reported in *YL*, did not come to NLI with Reade's letter].
Moore, George. *Avowals.* London: William Heinemann, 1924.

1362.   [*YL* *1349].
——. *The Bending of the Bough: A Comedy in Five Acts.* London: T. Fisher Unwin, 1900.

1363.   [*YL* 1350].
——. *The Works of George Moore.* Vol. 11: *The Brook Kerith: A Syrian story.* London: William Heinemann, 1933.

1364.   [*YL* 1351].
——. *Elizabeth Cooper: A Comedy in Three Acts.* Dublin and London: Maunsel, 1913.

1365.   [*YL* *1352]. [NLI 40,568/150; 22 sheets; envelope 1682].
——. *Evelyn Innes.* London: T. Fisher Unwin, 1898.

1366.   [*YL* 1353].
——. *Hail and Farewell! Ave.* London: William Heinemann, 1911.

1367.   [*YL* 1354].
——. *The Works of George Moore.* Vol. 9: *Hail and Farewell! Salve.* London: William Heinemann, 1933.

1368.   [YL 1355].
——. *The Works of George Moore*. Vol. 10: *Hail and Farewell! Vale*. London: William Heinemann, 1933.

1369.   [YL 1356].
——. "Morality in Literature." [*Westminster Gazette*, 24 June 1898].

1370.   [YL 1357].
——, ed. *Pure Poetry: An Anthology*. London: Nonesuch Press, 1924.

1371.   [YL *1358].
Moore, T[homas]. Sturge. *Absalom: A Chronicle Play in Three Acts*. London: Unicorn Press, 1903.

1372.   [YL *1359].
——. *Aphrodite against Artemis: A Tragedy*. London: Unicorn Press, 1901.

x   [YL 1360]. [NLI missing this copy].
——. *Armour for Aphrodite*. London: Grant Richards and Humphrey Toulmin, 1929.

1373.   [YL *1361].
——. *Art and Life*. London: Methuen, 1910.

1374.   [YL *1362].
——. *Danae, Aforetime, and Blind Thamyris: Poems*. London: Grant Richards, 1920.

1375.   [YL *1363].
——. *Hark to These Three: Talk about Style*. London: Elkin Mathews, 1915.

1376.   [YL 1364].
——. *Judas*. London: Grant Richards, 1923.

1377.   [YL *1365].
——. *The Little School*. London: Grant Richards, 1917.

1378.   [YL *1366].
——. *Mariamne*. London: Duckworth, 1911.

1379.   [YL *1367].
——. *Pan's Prophecy*. London: Duckworth, 1904.

1380.   [YL *1368].
——. *Poems: Collected in One Volume*. London: Duckworth, 1906. Bp: WBY

1381.   [YL 1369]. [NLI 40,568/151; vol. 2, 4 sheets; envelope 531].
——. *The Poems*. Collected ed. 4 vols. London: Macmillan, 1931.

1382.   [YL *1370].
——. *The Powers of the Air*. London: Grant Richards, 1920.

1383.   [YL *1371].
——. *The Sea Is Kind*. London: Grant Richards, 1914. Bp: WBY

1384.   [YL 1372].
——. *Selected Poems*. London: Macmillan, 1934.

1385.   [YL 1373].
——. *A Sicilian Idyll and Judith: A Conflict*. London: Duckworth, 1911.

1386.   [YL *1374].
——. *Theseus, Medea and Lyrics*. London: Duckworth, 1904.

1387.   [YL *1375].
——. *Tragic Mothers*. [Three verse plays: *Medea, Niobe, Tyrfing*]. London: Grant Richards, 1920.

1388.   [YL 1376].
——. *T. Sturge Moore*. Modern Woodcutters, no. 3. London: Little Art Rooms, 1921. [Illustrated].

1389.   [YL 1377]. [NLI 40,568/152; 54 sheets; envelope 1327]. [See Chapman, *YA* 6 (1988): 234–45].
More, Dr. Henry. *A Collection of Several Philosophical Writings*. [Contains *An Antidote against Atheism*; *A Brief Discourse of the Nature, Causes, Kinds and Cure of Enthusiasm*; *Epistulae quator ad Renatum Descartes*; *The Immortality of the Soul*; *Conjectura Cabalistica*]. Second ed. London: William Morden, 1662. Bp: WBY

1390.   [YL 1378]. [NLI 40,568/153; 12 sheets; envelope 1328].
——. *The Immortality of the Soul, So Farre Forth As It Is Demonstrable from the Knowledge of Nature and the Light of Reason*. London: William Morden, 1659. Bp: WBY

1391. [YL 1379].
——. *Philosophical Poems of Henry Moore, Comprising Psychozoia and Minor Poems*. Ed. Geoffrey Bullough. Manchester: Manchester University Press, 1931. Signed: WBY

1392. [YL 1380]. [See Chapman, *YA* 6 (1988): 234–45].
——. *The Theological Works*. London: Joseph Downing. 1708. Bp: WBY

1393. [YL 1381].
More, Sir Thomas. *Utopia*. Ed. Robert Steele. Trans. Ralph Robinson. London: Chatto and Windus, 1908.

1394. [YL *1382].
More Ancient Carols. The Shakespeare Head Press Booklets, no. 5. Stratford-on-Avon: Shakespeare Head Press, 1906.

1395. [YL 1383].
Morgan, A[rthur]. E[ustace]. *Tendencies of Modern English Drama*. London: Constable, 1924.

1396. [YL *1384].
Morley, Henry. *The Life of Henry Cornelius Agrippa von Nettesheim, Doctor and Knight, Commonly Known As a Magician*. 2 vols. London: Chapman and Hall, 1856. Bp: WBY

1397. [YL 1385].
Morrell, Ottoline. *A Farewell Message*. [Memorial booklet]. Written in her journal on Feb. 1, 1936. [Lacks publication details].

1398. [YL *1386].
Morris, H[erbert]. N[ewall]. *Flaxman, Blake, Coleridge and Other Men of Genius Influenced by Swedenborg: Together with Flaxman's Allegory of the "Knight of the Blazing Cross."* London: New-Church Press, 1915.

1399. [YL 1387].
Morris, William. *Art and the Beauty of the Earth*. London: Chiswick Press, 1899.

1400. [YL 1388].
——. *Art and Its Producers and the Arts and Crafts of Today: Two Addresses Delivered before the National Association for the Advancement of Art*. London: Chiswick Press, 1901.

1401.　　[*YL* 1389].
———. *The Collected Works.* 24 vols. London: Longmans, Green, 1910–15.

1402.　　[*YL* 1390].
———. *The Defence of Guenevere and Other Poems.* Ed. Robert Steele. London: De la More Press, 1904.

1403.　　[*YL* 1391].
———. *News from Nowhere.* Large paper ed. London: Reeves and Turner, 1891.

1404.　　[*YL* 1392].
———. *Some Hints on Pattern Designing.* London: Chiswick Press, 1899.

1405.　　[*YL* 1393].
———. *Useless Work Versus Useless Toil.* Socialist Platform, no. 2. London: Socialist League Office, 1886.

1406.　　[*YL* 1394].
———. *The Well at the World's End: A Tale.* 2 vols. London: Longmans, Green, 1896.

1407.　　[*YL* 1395].
Morris, William and Eiríkr Magnússon, trans. *The Saga Library.* 6 vols. London: Bernard Quaritch, 1891–1905.

1408.　　[*YL* *1396].
———. *Volsunga Saga: The Story of the Volsungs and Niblungs, with Certain Songs from the Elder Edda.* Ed. H. Halliday Sparling. London: Walter Scott, 1888. Signed: W B Yeats | September 6 | 1888 | London

1409.　　[*YL* 1397]. [NLI 40,568/154; 3 sheets; envelope 1232].
[Moses, William Stanton] M. A., Oxon. *Spirit-Identity and Higher Aspects of Spiritualism.* London: London Spiritualist Alliance, 1908.

1410.　　[*YL* 1398]. [NLI 40,568/155; 9 sheets; envelope 288].
Muirhead, John H[enry]. *Coleridge as Philosopher.* London: George Allen and Unwin, 1930.

1411.　　[*YL* 1399]. [NLI 40,568/156; 20 sheets; envelope 1148].
———, ed. *Contemporary British Philosophy: Personal Statements.* First series. London: George Allen and Unwin, 1924. [Illustrated].

1412. [YL 1400]. [NLI 40,568/157; 21 sheets; envelope 1148].
——, ed. *Contemporary British Philosophy: Personal Statements.* Second series. London: George Allen and Unwin, 1925.

1413. [YL 1401].
Murasaki, Lady. *Blue Trousers: Being the Fourth Part of "The Tale of Genji."* Trans. Arthur Waley. London: George Allen and Unwin, 1928.

1414. [YL 1402].
——. *The Sacred Tree: Being the Second Part of "The Tale of Genji."* Trans. Arthur Waley. London:George Allen and Unwin, 1926. Bp: GY

1415. [YL 1403].
——. *The Tale of Genji.* Trans. Arthur Waley. London: George Allen and Unwin, 1925. Bp: GY

1416. [YL 1404].
——. *A Wreath of Cloud: Being the Third Part of "The Tale of Genji."* Trans. Arthur Waley. London: George Allen and Unwin, 1927. Bp: GY

1417. [YL *1405].
Murdoch, Walter, ed. *The Oxford Book of Australasian Verse.* London: Oxford University Press, 1918.

1418. [YL *1406].
Murray, A[lexander]. S[tuart]. *A History of Greek Sculpture from the Earliest Times Down to the Age of Pheidias.* London: John Murray, 1880.

1419. [YL 1407].
Murray, Margaret Alice. *The Witch-Cult in Western Europe: A Study in Anthropology.* Oxford: Clarendon Press, 1921. Bp: WBY

1420. [YL 1408].
——. Letter to the Editor. *The Times,* 25 Jan. [1932, p. 13].

1421. [YL *1409].
Murray, T[homas]. C[ornelius]. *Spring and Other Plays.* Dublin: Talbot Press, 1917.

1422. [YL *1410].
Musset, Alfred de. *Comedies.* Trans. S. L. Gwynn. The Camelot Classics. London: Walter Scott, [1890].

1422a. [YL 1410a].
Another copy.

1423.   [*YL* 1411].
Mussolini, Benito. *The Political and Social Doctrine of Fascism.* Trans. Jane Soames. London: Hogarth Press, 1933.

1424.   [*YL* *1412].
Mylne, Rev. R[obert]. S[cott]. *The Cathedral Church of Bayeux and Other Historical Relics in Its Neighbourhood.* Bell's Handbook to Continental Churches. London: George Bell, 1904. [Illustrated].

1425.   [*YL* *1413]. [NLI 40,568/158; copy of letter from Naidu to WBY (26 Oct. 1912); 4 sheets; envelope 993A].
Naidu, Sarojini. *The Bird of Time: Songs of Life, Death and the Spring.* London: William Heinemann, 1912.

1426.   [*YL* *1414].
——. *The Broken Wing: Songs of Love, Death and Destiny, 1915–1916.* London: William Heinemann, 1917.

1427.   [*YL* *1415].
——. *The Golden Threshold.* Introduction by Arthur Symons. London: William Heinemann, 1905.

1428.   [*YL* 1416].
Nares, Robert. *A Glossary of Words, Phrases, Names and Allusions in the Works of English Authors, Particularly of Shakespeare and His Contemporaries.* New ed. Additions by J. O. Halliwall and Thomas Wright. London: George Routledge, 1905.

1429.   [*YL* 1417].
Nandikesvara. *The Mirror of Gesture: Being the Abhinaya Darpana of Nandikesvara.* Trans. Ananda Coomaraswamy and Gopala Kristnayya Duggirala. Cambridge: Harvard University Press, 1917. [Illustrated]. Signed: WBY

1430.   [*YL* 1418].
The Nation (New York) 146 (12 March 1938).

1430a–b.   [*YL* 1418a–b].
Two more copies.

1431.   [*YL* 1419].
The National Observer, 24 December 1892, pp. 12(?), 33 only.

WORKS IN THE COLLECTION   149

1432.   [*YL* 1420].
——, 27 May 1893, pp. 41–43 only.

x   [*YL* 1421]. [NLI missing this copy].
[National Theatre Company Program]. *Irish Plays*, by the National Theatre Company, from the Abbey Theatre, Dublin. King's Theatre, Glasgow. 4 June [1906] for six nights.

x   [*YL* 1421a–d]. [NLI missing all four copies].
Four other copies.

x   [*YL* 1422]. [NLI missing this copy].
——. *Irish Plays*. Theatre Royal, Cardiff. Summer 1906. Bp: Elizabeth Corbet Yeats.

1433.   [*YL* 1423].
National Theatre Society. *Rules of the National Theatre Society, Limited*. Dublin: Cahill, [1903].

1433a–b.   [*YL* 1423a–b].
Two more copies.

1434.   [*YL* *1424].
Nero and Other Plays. Ed. Herbert P. Horne, Havelock Ellis, Arthur Symons, and A. Wilson Verity. The Mermaid Series. Unexpurgated large paper ed. London: Vizetelly, 1888.

1434A.   [*YL* *1424A].
Small paper ed. London: T. Fisher Unwin, [1904].

1435.   [*YL* 1425].
Nettleship, John T[rivett]. *Robert Browning: Essays and Thoughts*. London: Elkin Mathews, 1890. Signed: J.T. Nettleship

1436.   [*YL* 1426].
Nevinson, Henry W[ood]. *The Plea of Pan*. London: John Murray, 1901.

1437.   [*YL* 1427].
Newman, John Henry, Cardinal. *The Dream of Gerontius*. London: Burns Oates and Washbourne, [1911].

1438.   [*YL* 1428]. [Photograph, unidentified portrait, inserted (Wykeham Studios Ltd.)].
Newson, Ranald. *Dud Planet*. London: New Temple Press, 1934.

1439.   [YL 1429].
——. *New Poems*. London: New Temple Press, 1931.

1440.   [YL 1430]. [Though reported in *YL*, did not come to NLI with a letter from the author stating his wish to meet WBY].
——. *This Rough Magic*. London: New Temple Press, 1934.

1441.   [YL 1431].
Newton, Sir Isaac. *The Chronology of Ancient Kingdoms Amended: To Which is Prefix'd, A Short Chronicle from the First Memory of Things in Europe, to the Conquest of Persia by Alexander the Great*. London: Printed for J. Tonson, J. Osborn, and T. Longman, 1728.

1442.   [YL *1432].
Nichols, Robert. *Ardours and Endurances: Also, a Faun's Holiday and Poems and Phantasies*. London: Chatto and Windus, 1917.

1443.   [YL 1433].
——. *Aurelia and Other Poems*. London: Chatto and Windus, 1920.

1444.   [YL 1434].
——. *The Budded Branch*. Westminster: Beaumont Press, 1918.

1445.   [YL *1435].
——. *Invocations: War Poems and Others*. London: Elkin Mathews, 1915.

1445a. [Not listed in *YL* and assigned NLI number 3029].
Another copy. Flyleaf: "Homage a Madame | Vandervelde | 1916 | Robert Nichols."

1445b. [Not listed in *YL* and assigned NLI number 3029a].
Another copy.

1446.   [YL 1436].
——. *Robert Nichols*. The Augustan Books of Poetry. London: Ernest Benn, [1932].

1447.   [YL *1437].
Nietzsche, Friedrich. *The Complete Works of Friedrich Nietzsche*. Ed. Oscar Levy. Vol. 1: *The Birth of Tragedy, or Hellenism and Pessimism*. Trans. William A. Haussmann. Edinburgh and London: T. N. Foulis, 1909. [Vols. have been renumbered for collected ed.]

1448.   [*YL* *1438]. [NLI 40,568/159; 10 sheets; envelope 1213].
———. Vol. 4: *Thoughts out of Season: Part One*. [Includes *David Strauss, the Confessor and the Writer* and *Richard Wagner in Bayreuth*]. Trans. Anthony M. Ludovici. Edinburgh and London: T. N. Foulis, 1909.

1449.   [*YL* *1439].
———. Vol. 5: *Thoughts out of Season: Part Two*. [Includes *The Use and Abuse of History* and *Schopenhauer as Educator*]. Trans. Adrian Collins. Edinburgh and London: T. N. Foulis, 1909.

1450.   [*YL* *1440].
———. Vol. 14: *The Will to Power: Part One*. Trans. Anthony M. Ludovici. Edinburgh and London: T. N. Foulis, 1909.

1451.   [*YL* *1441].
———. Vol. 15: *The Will to Power: Part Two*. Trans. Anthony M. Ludovici. Edinburgh and London: T. N. Foulis, 1910.

1452.   [*YL* *1442]. [NLI 40,568/160; 12 sheets; envelope 1214].
———. *Nietzsche in Outline and Aphorism*. Ed. A. R. Orage. Edinburgh and London: T. N. Foulis, 1907.

1453.   [*YL* *1443]. [NLI 40,568/161; 6 sheets; envelope 1210].
———. *The Works of Friedrich Nietzsche*. Ed. Alexander Tille. Vol. 1: *A Genealogy of Morals. Poems*. Trans. William A. Haussmann and John Gray. London: T. Fisher Unwin, 1899. Signed: WBY

1454.   [*YL* *1444]. [NLI 40,568/162; 6 sheets; envelope 1208].
———. Vol. 3: *The Case of Wagner. Nietzsche Contra Wagner. The Twilight of the Idols*. Trans. Thomas Common. London: T. Fisher Unwin, 1899. Signed: WBY

1455.   [*YL* *1445]. [NLI 40,568/163; 5 sheets; envelope 1209].
———. Vol. 4: *The Dawn of Day*. Trans. Johanna Volz. London: T. Fisher Unwin, 1903.

1456.   [*YL* 1446].
Nieuwe rotterdamsche courant, 20 Aug. 1929

1457.   [*YL* 1447].
Nippon toh [Japanese Sword]. Osaka: T. Nagahara for the Society for Distributing Gwassan's Sword, [1931]. [Illustrated].

1458. [YL 1448].
Noel, Roden. *Poems of the Hon. Roden Noel.* Ed. Robert Buchanan. London: Walter Scott, [1884?].

1459. [YL 1449].
Nogaka-komen shū [Collection of Old Noh Masks]. Catalog. Published on occasion of the special exhibition at Onshi Kyoto Museum, Kyoto, 1933. Kyoto: Onshi Kyoto Hakubutsukan, 1933.

1460. [YL 1450].
Noguchi, Yone. *Hiroshige.* New York: Orientalia, 1921. [Illustrated].

1461. [YL 1451].
——. *Japanese Hokkus.* Boston: Four Seas Company, 1920.

1462. [YL *1452].
——. *The Pilgrimage.* New York: Mitchell Kennerley, 1912; London: Elkin Mathews, 1912.

1463. [YL 1453].
——. *Seen and Unseen, or Monologues of a Homeless Snail.* New ed. New York: Orientalia, 1920.

1464. [YL 1454].
——. *The Spirit of Japanese Art.* London: John Murray, 1915.

1465. [YL *1455].
——. *Through the Torii.* London: Elkin Mathews, 1914.

1466. [YL 1456].
——. *The Ukiyoye Primitives.* Tokyo: By the author, 1933. [Illustrated]. Signed: Yone Noguchi.

1467. [YL 1457].
Norman, A. O. [Harry Felix?]. "George Russell." Offprint from *Year Book of Agricultural Co-Operation* [1936]: 11–27.

1468. [YL 1458].
[Norstedt, P. A. and Söner]. *I anledning av P. A. Norstedt & Söner 100-årsjubileum den 1 December 1923.* Stockholm: P. A. Norstedt, 1923. [Illustrated].

1469. [YL 1459].
Notzing, Baron von Schrenck. *Phenomena of Materialisation: A Contribution to the Investigation of Mediumistic Teleplastics.* Trans. E.

E. Fournier d'Albe. London: Kegan Paul, Trench, Trubner, 1920. [Illustrated]. Bp: WBY

1470. [*YL* 1460].
Novalis [Friedrich von Hardenberg]. *The Disciples at Saïs and Other Fragments*. Trans. F. V. M. T. and U[na]. C. B[irchi]. London: Methuen, 1903.

1471. [*YL* *1461].
Noyes, Alfred. *The Loom of Years*. London: Grant Richards, 1902.

1472. [*YL* *1462]. [NLI 40,568/164; 58 sheets; envelope 1474B].
Noyes, Ella. *The Story of Ferrara*. Illustrated by Dora Noyes. London: J. M. Dent, 1904. [Illustrated].

1473. [*YL* 1463].
Nuovo dizionario tascabile: italiano-inglese e inglese-italiano. Compiled by Prof. Jane Pulford. Milan: Bietti, [1939?].

1474. [*YL* 1464].
The Nutbrown Maid. The Shakespeare Head Press Booklets, no. 4. Stratford-on-Avon: Shakespeare Head Press, 1906.

1475. [*YL* 1465].
Nutt, Alfred. *Celtic and Mediaeval Romance*. Popular Studies in Mythology, Romance and Folklore, no. 1. London: David Nutt, 1899.

1475a. [*YL* 1465a].
Another copy, mostly uncut.

1476. [*YL* 1466].
———. *Cuchulainn, the Irish Achilles*. Popular Studies in Mythology, Romance and Folklore, no. 8. London: David Nutt, 1900.

1476a. [*YL* 1466a].
Another copy.

1477. [*YL* 1467].
———. *The Legends of the Holy Grail*. Popular Studies in Mythology, Romance and Folklore, no. 14. London: David Nutt, 1902.

1478. [*YL* *1468].
O'Brien, R[ichard]. Barry. *The Life of Charles Stewart Parnell, 1846–1891*. 2 vols. London: Smith, Elder, 1898. Bp: Greene's Library Dublin, 1843–1912.

1479. [*YL* 1469].
O'Byrne, Dermot. *A Dublin Ballad and Other Poems*. Poetry Booklets, no. 2. Dublin: The Candle Press, 1918.

1479a. [*YL* 1469a].
Another copy.

1480. [*YL* 1470].
O'Casey, Sean. *The Plough and the Stars*. London: Macmillan, 1927.

1481. [*YL* 1471].
——. *The Silver Tassie*. London: Macmillan, 1928. Signed: GY

1481a. [*YL* 1471a].
Another copy. Signed: J.W. Wilhem's [?]

1482. [*YL* 1472].
——. *Two Plays: Juno and the Paycock. The Shadow of a Gunman.* London: Macmillan, 1925.

1482a. [*YL* 1472a].
Another copy. Signed: "GY | 1925."

1483. [Not listed in *YL* and assigned NLI number 3030].
O'Connell, J. B. *The Financial Administration of Saorstát Éireann*. Dublin: Browne & Nolan, n.d. Flyleaf inscribed by the author to WBY, Dec. 1934.

1484. [*YL* 1473].
O'Connor, Frank. *The Big Fellow: A Life of Michael Collins*. London: Thomas Nelson, 1937.

1485. [*YL* 1474].
——. *Guests of the Nation*. London: Macmillan, 1931.

1486. [*YL* 1475].
——. *The Saint and Mary Kate*. London: Macmillan, 1932.

1487. [*YL* 1476].
——. *Three Old Brothers and Other Poems*. London: Thomas Nelson, 1936.

1487a–b. [*YL* 1476a–b].
Two more copies, paper covers.

x   [YL 1477]. [NLI missing this copy, in the possession of Senator Michael Yeats].

O'Curry, Eugene. *Lectures on the Manuscript Materials of Ancient Irish History*. Delivered at the Catholic University of Ireland, during the sessions of 1855 and 1856. Dublin: William A. Hinch, 1872. [Illustrated]. Bp: WBY

x   [YL *1478]. [NLI missing this 3-vol. set].

———. *On the Manners and Customs of the Ancient Irish: A Series of Lectures*. Ed. W. K. Sullivan. 3 vols. London: Williams and Norgate, 1873. Bp: WBY

1488.   [YL 1479].

O'Donnell, F[rank?]. Hugh. *Souls for Gold! Pseudo-Celtic Drama in Dublin*. London: By the author[?], 1899.

1489.   [YL 1480].

O'Donnell, Peadar. *Salud! An Irishman in Spain*. London: Methuen, 1937. Signed: George Yeats | May 1937

1490.   [YL 1481].

———. *Wrack: A Play*. London: Jonathan Cape, 1933.

1491.   [YL *1482]. [NLI 40,568/165; 16 sheets; envelope 1605].

O'Donoghue, David J[ames]. *The Life of William Carleton: Being his Autobiography and Letters and an Account of His Life and Writings from the Point at Which the Autobiography Breaks Off*. 2 vols. London: Downey, 1896.

1492.   [YL 1483].

———. *The Life and Writings of James Clarence Mangan*. Edinburgh: Patrick Geddes, 1897.

1493.   [YL 1484].

———. *The Poets of Ireland: A Biographical Dictionary with Bibliographical Particulars*. 3 parts. London: By the author, 1892. Signed: WBY

1494.   [YL 1485].

O'Faoláin, Seán. "The Spurious Fenian Tale," offprint from *Folk-Lore: Transactions of the Folk-Lore Society; A Quarterly Review* 41 (June 1930): 154–68.

1495. [YL 1486].
Ó Faracháin, Roibeárd [Robert Farren]. *Thronging Feet*. London: Sheed and Ward, 1936.

1496. [YL 1487].
O'Flaherty, Liam. *The Informer*. London: Jonathan Cape, 1925. Signed: GY

1497. [YL 1488].
———. *Mr. Gilhooley*. London: Jonathan Cape, 1926.

1498. [YL 1489].
———. *Red Barbara and Other Stories: The Mountain Tavern, Prey, The Oar*. New York: Crosby Gaige, 1928. Signed: Liam O'Flaherty

1499. [YL *1490].
O'Grady, Standish. *The Coming of Cuculain: A Romance of the Heroic Age of Ireland*. London: Methuen, 1894.

1500. [YL *1491].
———. *Finn and His Companions*. Illustrated by J. B. Yeats. The Children's Library. London: T. Fisher Unwin, 1892. [Illustrated].

1501. [YL 1492].
———. *Red Hugh's Captivity: A Picture of Ireland, Social and Political, in the Reign of Queen Elizabeth*. London: Ward and Downey, 1889. Signed: W B Yeats | March 25th | 1889

1502. [YL 1493].
———. *The Story of Ireland*. London: Methuen, 1894. Bp: Lily Yeats

1503. [YL 1494].
O'Hegarty, P[atrick]. S[arsfield]. *Sinn Fein: An Illumination*. Dublin and London: Maunsel, 1919.

1504. [YL 1495].
[Old Vic and Sadler's Wells]. *Annual Reports for Season 1935–36 of the Old Vic and Sadler's Wells with Balance Sheet and Accounts of Both Foundations. For the year ending 30th June, 1936*. London: Williams and Strahan, [1936?].

1505. [YL *1496]. [NLI 40,568/166; 60 sheets; envelope 1332].
Oliphant, Laurence. *Scientific Religion or Higher Possibilities of Life and Practice through the Operation of Natural Forces*. Edinburgh and

London: For the author by William Blackwood, 1888. Bp: Coventry Patmore

1506.   [*YL* 1497].
O'Malley, Ernie. *On Another Man's Wound*. Dublin: At the Sign of the Three Candles, 1936. Signed: Ernie O Malley

1507.   [*YL* 1498].
Omar Khayyam. *Fifty Rubaiyat of Omar Khayyam*. Paraphrased from literal translations by Richard Le Gallienne. Wausau, Wisc.: The Philosopher Press, 1901. Signed: Richard Le Gallienne [at limitation]

1508.   [*YL* *1499].
———. *Rubáiyát of Omar Khayyám*. Trans. Edward Fitzgerald. London: Macmillan, 1899.

1509.   [*YL* 1500].
———. *Les Rubáiyat d'Omar Khayyám*. Traduits en vers français d'après la version anglaise d'Edward Fitzgerald. Extrait du *Correspondant*. Paris: Imprimerie Louis de Soye, 1932.

1510.   [*YL* 1501].
O'Neill, Eugene. *Days without End*. New York: Random House, 1934. Bp: WBY. Signed: WBY

1511.   [*YL* 1502].
———. *The Great God Brown. The Fountain. The Dreamy Kid. Before Breakfast*. London: Jonathan Cape, 1926.

1512.   [*YL* 1503].
———. *The Moon of the Caribbees and Six Other Plays of the Sea*. London: Jonathan Cape, 1923.

1513.   [*YL* 1504].
———. *A Play, Strange Interlude*. New York: Boni and Liveright, 1928.

1514.   [*YL* 1505]. [NLI 40,568/167; 17 sheets; envelope 1707].
O'Neill, Joseph. *Land under England*. London: Victor Gollancz, 1935.

1515.   [*YL* 1506].
O'Neill, Mary Devenport. *Prometheus and Other Poems*. London: Jonathan Cape, 1929.

1516. [*YL* *1507]. [Though reported in *YL*, printed slip "With the Publisher's Compliments" is missing].
O'Neill, Moira. *Songs of the Glens of Antrim*. Edinburgh and London: William Blackwood, 1900.

1517. [*YL* *1508].
Orage, A[lfred]. R[ichard]. *The Dionysian Spirit of the Age*. London and Edinburgh: T. N. Foulis, 1906.

1518. [*YL* 1509].
O'Rahilly, Egan. *The Poems*. Ed. Rev. Patrick S. Dinneen. The Irish Texts Society, vol. 3. London: The Irish Texts Society, 1900.

1519. [*YL* 1510]. [NLI 40,568/168; 6 sheets; envelope 1423].
Orion's Prophetic Guide, Weather Almanac, and Ephemeris for the Year 1882. London: Simpkin, Marshall, [1881?].

1520. [*YL* 1511].
Another number, for 1887.

1521. [*YL* 1512].
O'Rourke, Horace T[ennyson]. and the Dublin Civic Survey Committee. *The Dublin Civic Survey*. Publications of the Civics Institute of Ireland, vol. 2. London: Hodder and Stoughton, 1925.

1522. [*YL* 1513].
Osborne, Dorothy. *Letters to Sir William Temple, 1652–54*. Ed. Edward Abbott Parry. London and Manchester: Sherratt and Hughes, 1903.

1523. [*YL* 1514].
O'Sheel, Shaemas. *The Blossomy Bough*. New York: Franklin Press, 1911.

1524. [*YL* 1515]. [Though reported in *YL*, did not come to NLI with calling card with the author's name and address].
Oshima, Shōtarō. *Shishū: Hakkon Sōbi* [The Twilight Rose: Poems]. Tokyo: Taibun Sha. B., [1928?].

1525. [*YL* 1516].
———. "Some Notes on William Blake and Macpherson's 'Ossian.'" Reprint from *The Studies in English Literature* (Japan) 10 (October 1930).

1526.   [YL 1517].
——. *Uiriamu batora Jeitsu kenkyu* [W. B. Yeats: A Study]. Tokyo: Taibunsha, 1927.

1527.   [YL 1518].
——. *W. B. Yeats*. Tokyo: Kenkyusha, 1934.

1528.   [YL 1519].
Ossendowski, Ferdinand. *Beasts, Men and Gods*. London: Edward Arnold, 1923.

1529.   [YL 1520].
Osty, Eugene. *Supernormal Faculties in Man*. Trans. Stanley de Brath. London: Methuen, 1923.

1530.   [YL *1521]. [NLI 40,568/169; 3 sheets; envelope 1710].
O'Sullivan, Seumas. *Poems*. Dublin: Maunsel, 1912. Bp: WBY

1531.   [YL 1522].
O'Sullivan, Vincent. *A Dissertation upon Second Fiddles*. London: Grant Richards, 1902.

1532.   [YL 1523].
Otto, Rudolf. *The Idea of the Holy*. Trans. John W. Harvey. 4th imp., rev., with additions. London: Oxford University Press, 1926.

1533.   [YL 1524].
Owlett, F[rederick]. C[harles]. "The Eulogy of Marlow." An essay reprinted from *The Poetry Review* (London) 26 (Jan.–Feb. 1935).

1534.   [YL 1525].
Page, H. A. [Alexander Hay Japp] *Thoreau, His Life and Aims: A Study*. London: Chatto and Windus, 1878. Signed: E. Blackburne | 1878.

1535.   [YL 1526]. [Wade 295].
The Pageant. Ed. C. Hazelwood Shannon and J. W. Gleeson White. London: Henry, 1896.

x   [YL 1526a]. [NLI missing this copy].
Another copy.

1536.   [YL 1527].
Palmer, Herbert Edward. *The Collected Poems*. London: Ernest Benn, 1933.

1537.   [*YL* 1528]. [Though reported in *YL*, did not come to NLI with a letter of presentation, 9 March 1919].
——. *Two Fishers and Other Poems*. London: Elkin Mathews, 1918.

1538.   [*YL* 1529].
——. *Two Foemen and Other Poems*. London: Elkin Mathews, 1920.

1539.   [*YL* 1530]. [NLI 40,568/170; 6 sheets; envelope 589].
——. *Two Minstrels. The Wolf Knight: His Book. The Wolf Minstrel: Caedomon's Book*. London: Elkin Mathews, 1921.

1540.   [*YL* 1531].
——. *The Vampire and Other Poems and Rimes of a Pilgrim's Progress*. London: J. M. Dent, 1936.

1541.   [*YL* 1532].
Panchatantra and Hitopadesa Stories. Trans. A. S. Panchapakesa Ayyar. Great Short Stories of India. Bombay: D. B. Taraporevala, 1931.

1542.   [Not listed in *YL* and assigned NLI number 3031].
The Parables from the Gospels with Ten Original Woodcuts Designed and Engraved on the Wood by Charles Ricketts. N.p.: n.p., 1903. Inscribed on flyleaf: "To my friend Yeats on the occasion | of his marriage | T. Sturge Moore."

1543.   [*YL* 1533]. [NLI 40,568/171; 3 sheets; envelope 1335].
Paracelsus. *The Hermetic and Alchemical Writings of Aureolus Philippus Theophrastus Bombast, of Hohenheim, called Paracelsus the Great*. Ed. and trans. Arthur Edward Waite. 2 vols. London: James Elliott, 1894. Bps.: WBY

1544.   [*YL* 1534].
Partridge, John. *Merlinus liberatus: Being an Almanack for the Year...1802*. London: Company of Stationers, [1801?].

1545.   [*YL* 1535]. [Wade 286].
Patanjali, Bhagwān Shree. *Aphorisms of Yoga*. Trans. Shree Purohit Swāmi. Introduction by WBY. London: Faber and Faber, 1938.

1545a-b.   [*YL* 1535a-b].
Two more copies.

1546.   [Not listed in *YL* and assigned NLI number 3032].
Another copy.

WORKS IN THE COLLECTION 161

1547.   [*YL* 1536]. [NLI 40,568/172; 6 sheets; envelope 1025].
———. *The Yoga-System of Patanjali, or The Ancient Hindu Doctrine of Concentration of Mind.* Trans. James Haughton Woods. Harvard Oriental Series, vol. 17. Cambridge: Harvard University Press, 1927.

1548.   [*YL* 1537].
Pater, Walter. *Marius the Epicurean.* 2 vols. London: Macmillan, 1902.

1549.   [*YL* 1538]. [NLI 40,568/173; 20 sheets; envelope 1160].
———. *Plato and Platonism.* London: Macmillan, 1893.

1550.   [*YL* 1539].
———. *The Renaissance: Studies in Art and Poetry.* London: Macmillan, 1935.

1551.   [*YL* *1540].
Patmore, Coventry. *Poems.* 2 vols. London: George Bell, 1906. Bp: WBY

1552.   [*YL* *1541].
———. *Principle in Art.* Uniform ed. London: George Bell, 1907. Bp: WBY

1553.   [*YL* *1542].
———. *Religio poetae.* New ed. London: George Bell, 1898.

1554.   [*YL* *1543].
[Patrick, Saint]. *The Remains of St. Patrick, Apostle of Ireland: The Confession and Epistle to Coroticus.* Trans. Sir Samuel Ferguson. Dublin: Sealy, Bryers and Walker, 1888.

1555.   [*YL* 1544].
Paul V, Pope. *Rituale romanum Pauli V.* 11th ed. Rome: Friderici Pustet, 1912.

1556.   [*YL* 1545]. [NLI 40,568/174; 9 sheets; envelope 982].
Pausanias. *Description of Greece.* Trans. W. H. S. Jones. 6 vols. Loeb Classical Library. London: William Heinemann, 1918.

1557.   [*YL* 1546].
Pauw, Cornelius de. *Philosophical Dissertations on the Egyptians and Chinese.* Trans. Capt. J. Thomson. 2 vols. London: T. Chapman, 1795.

1558. [YL 1547].
Peacock, T[homas]. Love. *Nightmare Abbey.* Ed. Richard Garnett. London: J. M. Dent, 1891. Bp: Lady Gregory

1559. [YL 1548].
Pearce, Alfred J[ohn]. *The Text-Book of Astrology.* Vol. 1: *Genethialogy.* London: Cousins, [1879]. Bp: WBY

1560. [YL *1549]. [NLI 40,568/175; 4 sheets; envelope 1712].
Pearse, Padraic H[enry]. *Collected Works of Padraic H. Pearse: Plays, Stories, Poems.* Dublin and London: Maunsel, 1917. Bp: WBY

1561. [YL 1550].
Pearse, Salem. *The Coelestial Diary, or an Ephemeris for the Year...1759.* 41st impression. London: The Company of Stationers, [1758?].

1562. [YL 1551].
Péguy, Charles. *Le mystère de la charité de Jeanne d'Arc.* Sixième cahier, cahier pour le jour de Noël et pour le jour des rois de la onzième série. Paris: Cahiers de la quinzaine, [1910?].

1563. [YL 1552].
——. *Oeuvres complètes de Charles Péguy, 1873–1914.* 15 vols. Paris: Éditions de la Nouvelle Revue Française, [1916–34].

1564. [YL *1553].
Penny, A[nne]. J[udith]. *Studies in Jacob Böhme.* London: John M. Watkins, 1912. [Illustrated]. Bp: WBY

1565. [YL 1554].
People's National Theatre Magazine (London) 2 (Oct. 1935).

1566. [YL 1555].
Percival, Milton O[swin]. *William Blake's Circle of Destiny.* New York: Columbia University Press, 1938.

1567. [YL *1556].
Percy, Thomas, ed. *Reliques of Ancient English Poetry.* Re-edited by Henry B. Wheatley. 3 vols. London: Swan Sonnenschein, 1889. Bp: WBY

1568.   [YL 1557].
Persian Art: An Illustrated Souvenir of the Exhibition of Persian Art at Burlington House, London, 1931. 2nd ed. [London]: Printed for the executive committee of the exhibition, [1931]. [Illustrated].

1569.   [YL *1558].
Petrarch. *The Sonnets, Triumphs, and Other Poems of Petrarch*. Trans. various hands. London: George Bell, 1904.

1570.   [YL 1559].
Petrie, W[illiam]. M[athew]. *The Revolutions of Civilisation*. 3rd ed. London and New York: Harper, 1922.

1570a.   [YL 1559a].
Another copy.

1571.   [YL 1560].
Petronius. *The Satyricon of T. Petronius Arbiter*. Trans. Burnaby. The Abbey Classics. London: Simpkin, Marshall, Hamilton, Kent, [1923?].

1572.   [YL 1561].
——. *The Works of Petronius Arbiter*. Biographical sketch by Monsieur St. Evremont. ["To which is added some other of the Roman poets, viz., Catullus, Tibullus, and Propertius," along with translations of Pindar, Anacreon, and Sappho]. Poem on Telemachus by the Duke of Devonshire. Essay by John Duke of Buckingham. Trans. "various hands." 4th ed. London: Printed for Sam. Briscoe, 1713.

1573.   [YL *1562].
Petrovitch, Woislav M[aximus]. *Hero Tales and Legends of the Serbians*. London: G. Harrap, 1914. Bp: WBY

1574.   [YL 1563].
Philalethes, Eugenius [pseud., Thomas Vaughan]. *Euphrates or the Waters of the East, 1655*. With a commentary by S. S. D. D. [pseud., Florence Farr Emery]. Collectanea Hermetica. Ed. W. Wynn Westcott. Vol. 7. London: Theosophical Publishing Society, 1896.

1575.   [YL 1564]. [NLI 40,568/176; copy of ms. poem (line 1: "Astrea's holy child"); 4 sheets; envelope 187].
[Phillimore, Cecily]. *Paul: The Christian*. London: Hodder and Stoughton, 1930.

1576.   [*YL* *1565].
Philpotts, Eden. *The Secret Woman*. London: Duckworth, 1912.

1577.   [*YL* 1566].
The Phoenix Libraries. Prospectus of the Irish Library. [Dublin?]: Phoenix Publishing, n.d.

1578.   [*YL* 1567]. [NLI 40,568/177; 8 sheets; envelope 137].
Pico Della Mirandola, Giovanni. *Le sette sposizioni del S. Giovanni Pico De La Mirandola, intitolate Heptaplo, sopra i sei giorni del Genesi*. Tradotte in lingua Toscana da M. Antonio Buonagrazia. Pescia: Lorenzo Torrentino, 1555. Signed: Georgie Hyde Lees. | 1914.

1579.   [*YL* 1568].
Piccoli, Raffaello. *Italian Humanities: An Inaugural Lecture*. Cambridge: University Press, 1929.

1580.   [*YL* 1569].
The Picture of Dublin, or Stranger's Guide to the Irish Metropolis. With a brief description of the surrounding country and of its geology. New ed. Dublin: William Curry, 1843. [With maps and illustrations].

1581.   [*YL* 1570].
Pirandello, Luigi. *All'uscita, mistero profano*: Il dovere del medico, un atto; La Morsa; L'uomo dal fiore in bocca, dialogo. Firenze: F. Bemporad, 1926.

1582.   [*YL* 1571].
——. *L'amica delle mogli*. Commedia in tre atti. Firenze: R. Bemporad, 1927.

1583.   [Not listed in *YL* and assigned NLI number 3033].
——. *Come Prima Meglio di Prima*. Florence: R. Bemporad & Figlio, 1923.

1584.   [*YL* 1572].
——. *Come prima meglio di prima: Commedia in tre atti*. Firenze: R. Bemporad, 1929.

1585.   [*YL* 1573].
——. *Come tu mi vuoi: Tre atti*. Milano: Mondadori, 1930.

1586. [YL 1574].
———. *Diana e la tuda: Tragedia in tre atti*. 2nd ed. Firenze: R. Bemporad, 1926.

1587. [YL 1575].
———. *Il giuco delle parti in tre atti; Ma non è una cosa seria: Commedia in tre atti*. Milano: Fratelli Treves, 1919. Signed: GY

1588. [YL 1576].
———. *L'imbecille; Lumie di Sicilia; Cecè; La patente: Commedie in un atto*. Firenze: R. Bemporad, 1926.

1589. [YL 1577].
———. *Novelle per uno anno*. Vol. 6: *In silenzio*. Firenze: R. Bemporad, 1923.

1590. [YL 1578].
———. *Tutto per bene: Commedia in tre atti*. 2nd ed. Firenze: R. Bemporad, 1925.

1591. [YL 1579].
———. *L'uomo, la bestia e la virtù: Apologo in tre atti*. Firenze: R. Bemporad, 1922.

1592. [YL 1580].
———. Another printing, 1925.

1593. [YL 1581].
———. *Vestire gli ignudi: Commedia in tre atti*. 3rd ed. Firenze: R. Bemporad, 1927.

1594. [YL 1582].
———. *La vita che ti diedi: Tragedia in tre atti*. Firenze: R. Bemporad, 1924.

1595. [YL *1583].
Pitt, Ruth J. *The Tragedy of the Norse Gods*. London: T. Fisher Unwin, 1893.

1596. [YL 1584].
Pius X, Pope. *On Social Reform*. Catholic Social Guild Pamphlets, no. 4. London: Catholic Truth Society, 1910.

1597. [YL *1585].

Plarr, Victor. *Ernest Dowson, 1888–1897: Reminiscences, Unpublished Letters and Marginalia.* Bibliography compiled by H. Guy Harrison. London: Elkin Mathews, 1914. Bp: WBY

1598. [YL 1586]. [NLI 40,568/178; vols. 1 and 5, 35 and 2 sheets; envelope 1156].

Plato. *The Dialogues.* Trans. B. Jowett. 5 vols. 2nd ed. Oxford: Clarendon Press, 1875.

1599. [YL *1587].

——. *The Republic.* Trans. John Llewelyn Davies and David James Vaughan. New ed. London: Macmillan, 1885.

1599A. [YL 1587A].

——. Another ed. Trans. Benjamin Jowett. 3rd ed. Oxford: Clarendon Press, 1908.

1600. [YL *1588].

Plautus. *Five of His Plays.* Trans. Sir Robert Allison. London: Arthur L. Humphreys, 1914. Bp: WBY

1601. [YL 1589]. [NLI 40,568/179; 2 sheets; envelope 125A].

Plotinus. *Plotinus.* Trans. Stephen Mackenna. Vol. 1: *The Ethical Treatises* being the treatises of the first Ennead with Porphyry's life of Plotinus, and the Preller-Ritter extracts forming a conspectus of the Plotinian system. London: P. L. Warner for the Medici Society, 1917. Bp: GY

1602. [YL 1590].

——. Vol. 2: *Psychic and Physical Treatises,* comprising the second and third Enneads. London: P. L. Warner, 1921.

1603. [YL 1591].

——. Vol. 3: *On the Nature of the Soul,* being the fourth Ennead. London: Medici Society, 1924.

1604. [YL 1592].

——. Vol. 4: *The Divine Mind,* being the treatises of the Fifth Ennead. London: P. L. Warner for the Medici Society, 1926.

1605.   [YL 1593].
——. Vol. 5: *On the One and the Good*, being the treatises of the sixth Ennead. Trans. S. M. and B. S. Page. London: P. L. Warner for the Medici Society, 1930.

1606.   [YL *1594].
——. *Plotinus on the Beautiful*. Being the sixth treatise of the First Ennead. Trans. Stephen MacKenna. Stratford-on-Avon: Shakespeare Head Press, 1908.

1607.   [YL 1595]. [NLI 40,568/180; 15 sheets; envelope 126].
——. *Select Works of Plotinus*. With extracts from the Treatise of Synesius On Providence. With the substance of Porphyry's life of Plotinus. Trans. Thomas Taylor. London: By the author, 1817. Signed: Georgie Hyde Lees | 1914

1607A.   [YL 1595A]. [NLI 40,568/181; 11 sheets; envelope 127].
——. Another edition. Ed. G. R. S. Mead. London: George Bell, 1895. Signed: Georgie Hyde Lees | July, 1913

1608.   [YL *1596]. [NLI 40,568/182; 10 sheets; envelope 1403].
Plunket, Emmeline M[ary]. *Ancient Calendars and Constellations*. London: John Murray, 1903.

1609.   [YL 1597].
Plutarch. *The Lives of the Noble Grecians and Romanes* [sic], compared together by that grave learned philosopher and historiographer, Plutarke of Chaeronea. Translated into French by James Amyot and into English by Thomas North. 8 vols. Stratford-upon-Avon: Basil Blackwell for the Shakespeare Head Press, 1928.

1610.   [YL *1598].
——. *Morals*. Vol. 1: *Ethical Essays*. Trans. Arthur Richard Shilleto. Bohn's Classical Library. London: George Bell, 1908.

1611.   [YL *1599]. [NLI 40,568/183; 4 sheets; envelope 983].
——. Vol. 2: *Theosophical Essays*. Trans. C. W. King. Bohn's Classical Library. London: George Bell, 1908.

1611a.   [YL 1599a].
Another copy.

1612.   [*YL* *1600*].
Poe, Edgar Allan. *The Raven. The Pit and the Pendulum.* Illustrated by William Thomas Horton. London: Leonard Smithers, 1899. [Illustrated].

1613.   [*YL* *1601*].
Poël, William. "Shakespeare's Jew and Marlowe's Christians." Reprint from *The Westminster Review* [Jan. 1909].

1614.   [*YL* 1602]. [Wade 289].
Poems and Ballads of Young Ireland. Dublin: M. H. Gill, 1888. Bp: Lily Yeats.

1615.   [*YL* 1603].
Poetry: A Magazine of Verse (Chicago) 3 (Jan. 1914).

1616.   [*YL* 1604].
—— 37 (Feb. 1931).

1617.   [*YL* 1605].
—— 45 (Dec. 1934).

1617a. [*YL* 1605a–c]. [NLI missing two copies].
Three more copies, of which one remains.

1618.   [*YL* 1606].
—— 45 (March 1935).

1618a. [*YL* 1606a].
Another copy.

1619.   [*YL* 1607].
—— 49 (Oct. 1936).

x   [*YL* 1608]. [NLI missing this copy].
—— 49 (Nov. 1936). Reprint, pp. 85–93 only, "Harriet Monroe, 1860–1936" by M. D. Z. Inserted in *YL* 1609.

1620.   [*YL* 1609].
—— 49 (Dec. 1936).

1621.   [*YL* 1610].
—— 49 (Jan. 1937).

1622.   [*YL* *1611*].
Porphyry. *Porphyry the Philosopher to His Wife Marcella.* Trans. Alice Zimmern. London: George Redway, 1896.

1623.   [*YL* 1612].
Potocki, Geoffrey, Count de Montalk. *Snobbery with Violence. A Poet in Gaol.* The Here and Now Pamphlets, no. 10. London: Wishart, 1932.

1624.   [*YL* *1613*].
Pound, Ezra. *Canzoni.* London: Elkin Mathews, 1911.

1625.   [*YL* *1614*].
——. *Cathay.* Translations…for the most part from the Chinese of Rihaku from the notes of the late Ernest Fenollosa.…London: Elkin Mathews, 1915.

1626.   [*YL* 1615].
——. *Dialogues of Fontenelle.* London: The Egoist, 1917.

1627.   [*YL* 1616].
——. *A Draft of XVI Cantos.* Paris: Three Mountains Press, 1925. Bp: GY

1628.   [*YL* 1617].
——. *A Draft of the Cantos 17–27.* London: John Rodker, 1928. Bp: GY

1629.   [*YL* 1618].
——. *A Draft of XXX Cantos.* London: Faber and Faber, 1933.

1630.   [*YL* *1619*].
——. *Exultations.* London: Elkin Mathews, 1909.

1630a.   [*YL* *1619a*]. [NLI 40,568/184; copy of insert and transcription by GY of Dante's "Guido, vorrei che tu e Lap ed io"; 6 sheets; envelope 30]. [Though reported in *YL*, did not come to NLI with said transcription].

Another copy. Signed: George Hyde-Lees | Xmas 09

1631.   [*YL* 1620].
——. *Gaudier-Brzeska: a Memoir.* London: John Lane, 1916. Signed: GY

1632. [*YL* 1621].
———. *Homage to Sextus Propertius*. London: Faber and Faber, 1934.

1633. [*YL* 1622].
———. *Indiscretions, or Une revue de deux mondes*. Paris: Three Mountains Press, 1923. Signed: GY

1634. [*YL* *1623].
———. *Instigations*, together with an essay on the Chinese written character by Ernest Fenollosa. New York: Boni and Liveright, 1920.

1635. [*YL* *1624].
———. *Lustra*. [London: Elkin Mathews for the author, 1916]. Bp: WBY

1635a. [*YL* 1624a].
Another copy.

1636. [*YL* *1625].
———. *Lustra*, with earlier poems. New York: Alfred A. Knopf, 1917.

1637. [*YL* *1626].
———. *Pavannes and Divisions*. New York: Alfred A. Knopf, 1918. Signed: GY

1638. [*YL* *1627].
———. *Personae*. London: Elkin Mathews, 1909.

1639. [*YL* 1628].
———. *Personae*. The Collected Poems. Including Ripostes, Lustra, Homage to Sextus Propertius, H. S. Mauberley. New York: Boni and Liveright, 1926. Bp: WBY

1640. [*YL* 1629].
———. *A Quinzaine for This Yule: Being Selected from a Venetian Sketch-Book—"San Trovaso."* London: Elkin Mathews, 1908.

1640a. [*YL* 1629a].
Another copy.

1641. [*YL* *1630].
———. *Ripostes*. Whereto are appended the complete poetical works of T. E. Hulme. London: Stephen Swift, 1912.

1641a. [*YL* 1630a]. [NLI 40,568/185; 3 sheets; envelope 31].
Another copy.

1642.   [YL 1631].
———. *Social Credit: An Impact.* London: Stanley Nott, 1935.

1643.   [YL *1632].
———. *The Spirit of Romance.* London: J. M. Dent, [1910].

1644.   [YL 1633].
———. *Ta hio,* The Great Learning. Seattle: University of Washington Book Store, 1928.

1645.   [YL *1634].
———, ed. *Catholic Anthology, 1914–1915.* London: Elkin Mathews, 1915.

1645a.   [YL 1634a].
Another copy.

1646.   [YL *1635].
———, ed. *Des imagists: An Anthology.* London: Poetry Bookshop, 1914; New York: Albert and Charles Boni, 1914.

1647.   [YL 1636].
———, ed. *Profile,* an anthology collected in MCMXXXI. Milan: Privately printed for John Scheiwiller, 1932.

1648.   [YL *1637].
——— and Ernest Fenollosa. *'Noh' or Accomplishment.* A study of the classical stage of Japan. London: Macmillan, 1916.

1649.   [YL 1638].
Prescott, William H[ickling]. *History of the Reign of Philip the Second, King of Spain.* London: George Routledge, [1872?]. Bp: Eliz. C. Yeats

1650.   [YL 1639].
Pourtalès, Guy de. *Louis II de Bavière ou Hamlet-Roi.* Paris: Gallimard, 1928.

1651.   [YL 1640].
Prévost d'Exiles, Antoine François. *Manon lescaut.* Trans. D. C. Moylan. London: George Routledge, [1886?].

1652. [YL 1641].
Prior, James. *Memoir of the Life and Character of the Right Hon. Edmund Burke.* With specimens of his poetry and letters. London: Baldwin, Cradock, and Joy, 1824.

1653. [YL 1642].
Privat-Deschanel, Augustin. *Elementary Treatise on Natural Philosophy.* Trans. J. D. Everett. 4th ed. London: Blackie, 1878.

1654. [YL 1643]. [NLI 40,568/186; 12 sheets; envelope 1370].
Proceedings of the Society for Psychical Research (Glasgow) 28 (Dec. 1915).

1655. [YL 1644].
Prokosch, Frederic. *The Assassins.* London: Chatto and Windus, 1936.

1656. [YL 1645].
——. *The Black Hart.* New Haven, Conn.: By the author, 1931. Signed: Frederic Prokosch.

1657. [YL 1646].
——. *Three Deaths.* New Haven, Conn.: By the author, 1932. Signed: Frederic Prokosch

1658. [YL 1647].
——. *The Wolves.* New Haven, Conn.: By the author, 1933.

1659. [YL 1648].
Propertius and others. *Erotica.* The Elegies of Propertius, the Satyricon of Petronius Arbiter, and the Kisses of Johannes Secundus | the Love Epistles of Aristaenetus. Ed. Walter K. Kelly. Trans. R. Brinsley Sheridan and Mr. Halhed. Bohn's Classical Library. London: Henry G. Bohn, 1854.

1660. [YL 1649]. [NLI 40,568/187; 5 sheets; envelope 129].
Prophetia et alia. Venice: Bernardinum Benalium, 1516 LXXVIII. Signed: Georgie Hyde Lees | June 1915.

1661. [Not listed in *YL* and assigned NLI number 3034].
The Psalms of David. Newly Interpreted by John Henry Nash. San Francisco: John Henry Nash, 1929.

1662. [YL 1650].
Ptolemy. *The Tetrabiblos: or, Quadripartite of Ptolemy, being four books relative to the starry influences*. Translated from the copy of Leo Allatius by James Wilson. London: William Hughes, [1828]. Signed: Ralph Shirley

1663. [YL 1651].
[Puvis de Chavannes]. *Puvis de Chavannes*. Introduction by Arsène Alexandre. Newnes' Art Library. London: George Newnes, [1905].

1664. [YL 1652].
Quiller-Couch, Arthur Thomas, ed. *The Oxford Book of Ballads*. Oxford: Clarendon Press, 1927.

1664a. [YL 1652a].
Another copy, 1920 printing.

1665. [YL *1653].
——. *The Oxford Book of English Verse, 1250–1900*. Oxford: Clarendon Press, 1902. Signed: W B Yeats | Nov. 3, 1903

x [YL 1654]. [NLI missing this copy].
——. *The Oxford Book of English Verse, 1250–1918*. New ed. Oxford: Clarendon Press, 1939. Signed: George Yeats

1666. [YL 1655].
——. *The Oxford Book of Victorian Verse*. Oxford: Clarendon Press, 1912. Bp: WBY

1667. [YL 1656].
"Quinn" Catalogue of First Editions, no. 89, part 2. New York: Schulte's Book Store, 1926.

1667a. [Not listed in *YL* and assigned NLI number 3035].
Another copy.

1667b. [Not listed in *YL* and assigned NLI number 3035a].
Another copy.

1668. [YL 1657].
——. Part 3.

x   [*YL* 1658]. [NLI missing this copy].
[Quinn, John]. "How German Agents Get Their Funds," Letter to the editor of *The New York Times*, 6 Sept. 1917: 10. [Contained in envelope dated 6 Sept. 1917. See *YL* 1658a and 1659].

x   [*YL* 1658a]. [NLI missing this copy].
Reprint of *YL* 1658 but dated 5 Sept. 1917. [In envelope as above.]

x   [*YL* 1659]. [NLI missing this copy].
———. "Remarks of Mr. John Quinn at the Lafayette Monument, Union Square, New York, Sept. 6, 1917." [In envelope as above.]

x   [*YL* 1659a]. [NLI missing this copy].
Another copy.

1669.   [*YL* 1660].
[Quinn, John, ed.]. *Some Critical Appreciations of William Butler Yeats as Poet, Orator and Dramatist.* N.p.: n.p., [1903].

1669a. [Not listed in *YL* and assigned NLI number 3036].
Another copy.

1669b. [Not listed in *YL* and assigned NLI number 3036a].
Another copy.

1670.   [*YL* *1661].
Rabelais, Francis. *Five Books of the Lives, Heroic Deeds and Sayings of Gargantua and His Son Pantagruel.* Trans. Sir Thomas Urquhart of Cromarty and Peter Antony Motteux. 3 vols. London: A. H. Bullen, 1904.

1671.   [*YL* 1662].
Racine, Jean. *Athalie, tragédie.* Ed. Henri Maugis. Paris: Larousse, [1933].

1672.   [*YL* 1663]. [NLI 40,568/188; vols. 1–2, 21 and 3 sheets; envelope 1028A].
Radhakrishnan, S[arvepalli]. *Indian Philosophy.* 2 vols. London: George Allen and Unwin, 1923–27.

1673.   [*YL* 1664].
Raphael [Robert C. Smith]. *The Familiar Astrologer.* An Easy guide to fate, destiny, and foreknowledge, as well as to the secret and wonderful properties of nature. London: John Bennett, 1831.

1674.   [*YL* 1665]. [NLI 40,568/189/1; 4 sheets; envelope 1420].
——. *Raphael's Astronomical Ephemeris of the Planets*. Places for 1852. 2nd ed. London: By the author, 1896.

1675.   [*YL* 1666].
——. For 1859. London, 1911.

1676.   [*YL* 1667].
——. 1860. London, 1911.

1677.   [*YL* 1668]. [NLI 40,568/189/2; 5 sheets; envelope 1420].
——. 1865. London, 1911.

1677a–b. [*YL* 1668a–b]. [NLI 40,568/189/3; "a" copy: 5 sheets; envelope 1420]. [NLI 40,568/189/4; "b" copy: 6 sheets; envelope 1420].
Two more copies.

1678.   [*YL* 1669]. [NLI 40,568/189/5; 3 sheets; envelope 1420].
——. 1866. London, 1896.

1679.   [*YL* 1670]. [NLI 40,568/189/6; 5 sheets; envelope 1420].
——. 1867. London, 1896.

1680.   [*YL* 1671]. [NLI 40,568/189/7; 4 sheets; envelope 1420].
——. 1869. London, 1896.

1681.   [*YL* 1672]. [NLI 40,568/189/8; 9 sheets; envelope 1420].
——. 1870. London, 1896.

1682.   [*YL* 1673]. [NLI 40,568/189/9; 7 sheets; envelope 1420A].
——. 1875. London, 1896.

1683.   [*YL* 1674]. [NLI 40,568/189/10; 4 sheets; envelope 1420A].
——. 1876. London, 1896.

1684.   [*YL* 1675]. [NLI 40,568/189/11; 4 sheets; envelope 1420A].
——. 1881. London, [188?].

1685.   [*YL* 1676]. [NLI 40,568/189/12; 4 sheets; envelope 1420A].
——. Another ed. London, 1900.

1686.   [*YL* 1677]. [NLI 40,568/189/13; 4 sheets; envelope 1420A].
——. 1884. London, 1900.

1687.   [*YL* 1678]. [NLI 40,568/189/14; 9 sheets; envelope 1420A].
——. 1885. London, 1911.

1688.   [*YL* 1679]. [NLI 40,568/189/15; 6 sheets; envelope 1420A].
——. 1886. London, 1911.

1688a–b. [*YL* 1679a–b]. [NLI 40,568/189/16; "a" copy: 3 sheets; envelope 1420A]. [NLI 40,568/189/17; "b" copy: 6 sheets; envelope 1420A].
Two more copies. Another ed. London, 1925.

1689.   [*YL* 1680]. [NLI 40,568/189/18; 2 sheets; envelope 1420A].
——. 1890. London, 1912.

x   [*YL* 1681]. [NLI 40,568/189/19; 6 sheets; envelope 1420B]. [NLI missing this copy].
——. 1891. London, 189?.

1690.   [*YL* 1681a].
Another copy.

1691.   [*YL* 1682]. [NLI 40,568/189/20; 1909, 1927: 9, 3, 3, 4 sheets; envelope 1420B].
——. 1892. London, 1909.

1691a.   [*YL* 1682a].
Another copy.

1691b–c. [*YL* 1682b–c].
Two more copies. Another ed. London, 1927.

1692.   [*YL* 1683]. [NLI 40,568/189/21; 6, 4 sheets; envelope 1420B].
——. 1893. London, 1906.

1692a.   [*YL* 1683a].
Another copy.

1693.   [*YL* 1684]. [NLI 40,568/189/22; 4 sheets; envelope 1420B].
——. 1894. London, 1912.

1694.   [*YL* 1685]. [NLI 40,568/189/23; 2 sheets; envelope 1420B].
——. 1896. London, 189[7?].

1695.   [*YL* 1686]. [NLI 40,568/189/24; 4 sheets; envelope 1420B].
——. 1897. London, 189[7?].

1696.   [Not listed in *YL* and assigned NLI number 3037].
Another copy.

1697.   [*YL* 1687]. [NLI 40,568/189/25; 4 sheets; envelope 1420B].
——. 1898. London, 189[9?].

1698.   [*YL* 1688]. [NLI 40,568/189/26; 1 sheet; envelope 1420B].
——. 1899. London, 1899.

1699.   [*YL* 1689]. [NLI 40,568/189/27; 2 sheets; envelope 1420B].
——. 1900. London, 1900.

1700.   [*YL* 1690]. [NLI 40,568/189/28; 5 sheets; envelope 1420C].
——. 1901. London, 1901.

1701.   [*YL* 1691]. [NLI 40,568/189/29; 4 sheets; envelope 1420C].
——. 1902. London, 1902.

1702.   [Not listed in *YL* and assigned NLI number 3038].
——. 1903–1910. Bound volume.

1703.   [*YL* 1692]. [NLI 40,568/189/30; 3 sheets; envelope 1420C].
——. 1904. London, 1904.

1704.   [*YL* 1693]. [NLI 40,568/189/31; 5 sheets; envelope 1420C].
——. 1906. London, 1906.

1705.   [*YL* 1694]. [NLI 40,568/189/32; 6 sheets; envelope 1420C].
——. 1907. London, 1907.

1705a.   [*YL* 1694a].
Another copy.

1706.   [*YL* 1695]. [NLI 40,568/189/33; 8 sheets; envelope 1420C].
——. 1909. London, 1909.

1707.   [*YL* 1696]. [NLI 40,568/189/34; 6 sheets; envelope 1420C].
——. 1910. London, 1910.

1708.   [*YL* 1697]. [NLI 40,568/189/35; 11 sheets; envelope 1420D].
——. 1911. London, 1911.

1709.   [*YL* 1698]. [NLI 40,568/189/36; 9 sheets; envelope 1420D].
——. 1912. London, 1912.

1709a.   [*YL* 1698a].
Another copy.

1710.   [*YL* 1699]. [NLI 40,568/189/37; 9 sheets; envelope 1420D].
——. 1913. London, 1913.

1710a.   [*YL* 1699a].
Another copy.

1711.   [*YL* 1700]. [NLI 40,568/189/38; 9 sheets; envelope 1420D].
——. 1914. London, 1914.

1711a.   [*YL* 1700a].
Another copy.

1712.   [*YL* 1701]. [NLI 40,568/189/39; 9 sheets; envelope 1420D].
——. 1915. London, 1915.

1712a.   [*YL* 1701a].
Another copy.

1713.   [*YL* 1702].
——. 1916. London, 1916.

1714.   [*YL* 1703]. [NLI 40,568/189/40; 4 sheets; envelope 1420E].
——. 1917. London, 1917.

1715.   [*YL* 1704]. [NLI 40,568/189/41; 17 sheets; envelope 1420E]. [Though reported in *YL*, did not come to NLI with a slip: "Sept 28th 1854. Waterford"].
——. 1918. London, 1918.

1716.   [*YL* 1705]. [NLI 40,568/189/42; also copies "a"–"c": 19, 2, 9, and 7 sheets; envelope 1420E].
——. 1919. London, 1919.

1716a–c. [*YL* 1705a–c].
Three more copies; unmarked.

1717.   [*YL* 1706]. [NLI 40,568/189/43; also "a" copy: 16, 18 sheets; envelope 1420E].
——. 1920. London, 1920.

1717a.   [*YL* 1706a].
Another copy.

1718.   [*YL* 1707]. [NLI 40,568/189/44; also "a" copy: 15, 15 sheets; envelope 1420E].
——. 1921. London, 1921.

1718a–b. [*YL* 1707a–b].
Two more copies, one unmarked.

1719.   [*YL* 1708]. [NLI 40,568/189/45; 3 sheets; envelope 1420E].
——. 1922. London, 1922.

1720.   [*YL* 1709]. [NLI 40,568/189/46; 9 sheets; envelope 1420E].
——. 1923. London, 1923.

1720a.   [*YL* 1709a].
Another copy.

1721.   [*YL* 1710]. [NLI 40,568/189/47; 10 sheets; envelope 1420F].
——. 1924. London, 1924.

1722.   [*YL* 1711]. [NLI 40,568/189/48; 9 sheets; envelope 1420F].
——. 1925. London, 1925.

1723.   [*YL* 1712]. [NLI 40,568/189/49; 12 sheets; envelope 1420F].
——. 1929. London, 1929.

1724.   [*YL* 1713]. [NLI 40,568/189/50; 8 sheets; envelope 1420F].
——. 1930. London, 1930.

1725.   [*YL* 1714]. [NLI 40,568/189/51; 13 sheets; envelope 1420F].
——. 1931. London, 1931.

1725a.   [*YL* 1714a].
Another copy.

1726.   [*YL* 1715].
——. 1932. London, 1932.

1727.   [*YL* 1716].
——. 1933. London, 1933.

1727a.   [*YL* 1716a].
Another copy.

1728.   [*YL* 1717]. [NLI 40,568/189/52; also "a" copy: 4, 6 sheets; envelope 1420G].
——. 1934. London, 1934.

1728a.   [*YL* 1717a].
Another copy.

1729.   [*YL* 1718]. [NLI 40,568/189/53; 3 sheets; envelope 1420G].
——. 1935. London, 1935.

1730.   [*YL* 1719].
——. 1937. London, 1937.

1730a.   [*YL* 1719a].
Another copy.

1731.   [*YL* 1720].
——. 1938. London, 1938.

1731a.   [*YL* 1720a].
Another copy.

1732.   [Not listed in *YL* and assigned NLI number 3039].
——. 1939. London, 1939.

1733.   [Not listed in *YL* and assigned NLI number 3040].
——. 1940. London, 1940.

1734.   [Not listed in *YL* and assigned NLI number 3041].
——. 1942. London, 1942.

1735.   [*YL* 1721]. [NLI 40,568/190; 18 sheets; envelope 1418].
——. Bound vol. 1861–70. London, 1896.

1736.   [*YL* 1722]. [NLI 40,568/191; 20 sheets; envelope 1419].
——. Bound vol. 1871–80. London, 1882.

1737.   [*YL* 1723].
——. *Raphael's Horary Astrology, by which every question relating to the future may be answered*. London: Foulsham, 1906. pp. Bp: GY

1738.   [*YL* 1724].
——. *Raphael's Prophetic Almanac, or the prophetic messenger and weather guide for 1904*. London: W. Foulsham, [1903?]. Unpag.

1739.   [*YL* 1725]. [NLI 40,568/192; 8 sheets; envelope 1424A].
——. Another number for 1916.

1740.   [*YL* 1726].
Ravenna. Roma: Istitutio geografico visceglia, n.d. Signed: GY

1741.   [*YL* 1727].
Raymond, Jean Paul [Charles Ricketts]. *Beyond the Threshold*. Translated and illustrated by Charles Ricketts. Plaistow: Curwen Press, 1929. [Illustrated].

1742.   [*YL* 1728].
Read, Herbert. *Poems, 1914–1934*. London: Faber and Faber, 1935.

1743.   [YL 1729].
———. *Poetry and Anarchism*. London: Faber and Faber, 1938.

1744.   [YL 1730].
Reade, Winwood. *The Martyrdom of Man*. London: Watts, 1924.

1745.   [YL *1731].
Redesdale, Lord [Algernon B. F. Mitford]. *Tales of Old Japan*. London: Macmillan, 1908. [Illustrated].

1746.   [YL *1732].
Redford, George. *A Manual of Ancient Sculpture: Egyptian—Assyrian—Greek—Roman; With...Illustrations, a Map of Ancient Greece, and a Chronological List of Ancient Sculptors and Their Works*. 2nd ed., enlarged. London: Sampson Low, Marston, Searle, and Rivington, 1886. [Illustrated]. Bp.: WBY

1747.   [YL *1733].
Reid, Forrest. *W. B. Yeats: A Critical Study*. London: Martin Secker, 1915. Bp: WBY

1748.   [YL *1734].
Reinach, S[alomon]. *Apollo: An Illustrated Manual of the History of Art throughout the Ages*. Trans. Florence Simmonds. New ed. London: William Heinemann, 1907.

1749.   [YL *1735]. [NLI 40,568/193; 15 sheets; envelope 1559].
Renan, Ernest. *The Poetry of the Celtic Races*. Trans. William G. Hutchison. London: Walter Scott, [1896].

1750.   [YL 1736].
Renier, G[ustaaf]. J[ohannes]. *Oscar Wilde*. Short Biographies, no. 19. London: Thomas Nelson, 1938.

1751.   [YL 1737].
Restoration Plays from Dryden to Farquhar. Introduction by Edmund Gosse. London and Toronto: J. M. Dent, 1925.

1752.   [YL 1738].
Revue anglo-americaine (Paris) 1 (Oct. 1929).

1753.   [*YL* *1739*].
Reynolds, John Hamilton. *The Fancy*. [Prefatory memoir by John Masefield]. Illustrated by Jack Yeats. London: Elkin Mathews, [1905]. [Illustrated].

1754.   [*YL* *1740*].
Rhys, Ernest. *Welsh Ballads*. London: David Nutt, [1898]. Signed: WBY

1755.   [*YL* *1741*].
Rhys, John. *Lectures on the Origin and Growth of Religion as Illustrated by Celtic Heathendom*. 2nd ed. The Hibbert Lectures. London: Williams and Norgate, 1892. Bp: WBY

1756.   [*YL* *1742*].
Richardson, Samuel. *The History of Sir Charles Grandison Bart*. 7 vols. London: Chapman and Hall, 1902. Bp: Lady Gregory

1757.   [*YL* 1743].
Richet, Charles. *Thirty Years of Psychical Research: A Treatise on Metaphysics*. Trans. Stanley DeBrath. London: W. Collins, 1923.

1758.   [*YL* *1744*].
Richter, Helene. *William Blake*. Strassburg: Heitz und Mundel, 1906. [Illustrated].

1759.   [*YL* 1745].
[Ricketts, Charles]. *A Bibliography of the Books Issued by Hacon and Ricketts*. London: Ballantyne Press, 1904.

1760.   [*YL* 1746].
——. *Charles Ricketts R. A.* Introduction by T. Sturge Moore. London: Cassell, 1933. [Illustrated].

1761.   [*YL* *1747*].
——. *Pages on Art*. London: Constable, 1913. Bp: WBY

1762.   [*YL* *1748*].
——. *Titian*. London: Methuen, 1910. [Illustrated].

1763.   [*YL* 1749].
——. *Unrecorded Histories*. With six designs by the author. London: Martin Secker, 1933. [Short stories; illustrated].

1764.   [*YL* 1750].
Riding, Laura. *Collected Poems*. London: Cassell, 1938.

1765.   [*YL* 1751].
———. *Poems: A Joking Word*. London: Jonathan Cape, 1930.

1766.   [Not listed in *YL* and assigned NLI number 3042].
Rivoallan, A. *Littérature irlandaise contemporaine*. Paris: Librairie Hachette, 1939.

1767.   [*YL* 1752].
Robertson, Eric S[utherland]. *The Children of the Poets: An Anthology*. London: Walter Scott, 1886.

1768.   [*YL* 1753].
Robertson, John M[ackinnon]. *Pagan Christs: Studies in Comparative Hierology*. 2nd ed., revised and expanded. London: Watts, 1911. Signed: WBY

1769.   [*YL* 1754].
Robinson, Edwin Arlington. *Nicodemus: A Book of Poems*. New York: Macmillan, 1932.

1770.   [*YL* 1755].
———. *Sonnets, 1889–1927*. New York: Crosby Gaige, 1928. Signed: E.A. Robinson

1771.   [*YL* 1756].
Robinson, Forbes. *Coptic Apocryphal Gospels: Translations Together with the Texts of Some of Them*. Texts and Studies: Contributions to Biblical and Patristic Literature, vol. 4, no. 2. Cambridge: University Press, 1896.

1772.   [*YL* 1757].
Robinson, Lennox. *The Big House: Four Scenes in Its Life*. London: Macmillan, 1928.

1773.   [*YL* 1758].
———. *Bryan Cooper*. London: Constable, 1931.

1774.   [*YL* 1759].
———. *Crabbed Youth and Age: A Little Comedy*. London and New York: G. P. Putnam's, 1924.

1775.   [YL 1760].
——. *The Dreamers: A Play in Three Acts*. London and Dublin: Maunsel, 1915.

1776.   [YL 1761].
——. *Eight Short Stories*. Dublin: Talbot Press, [1920]; London: T. Fisher Unwin, [1920].

1776a.   [YL 1761a].
Another copy.

1777.   [YL 1762].
——. *Ever the Twain: A Comedy in Three Acts*. London: Macmillan, 1930.

1778.   [YL 1763].
——. *The Far-Off Hills: A Comedy in Three Acts*. London: Chatto and Windus, 1931.

1779.   [YL 1764].
——. *Give a Dog—: A Play in Three Acts*. London: Macmillan, 1928.

1780.   [YL 1765].
——. *More Plays*. London: Macmillan, 1935.

x   [YL 1766]. [NLI missing this copy].
——. *Patriots: A Play*. Dublin and London: Maunsel, 1912.

1781.   [YL 1767].
——. *Plays*. [*The Round Table. Crabbed Youth and Age. Portrait. The White Blackbird. The Big House. Give a Dog—*]. London: Macmillan, 1928.

1782.   [YL 1768].
——. *The Round Table: A Comic Tragedy*. London and New York: G. P. Putnam's, 1924.

1783.   [YL 1769].
——. *The White Blackbird. Portrait*. [*Plays*]. Dublin and Cork: Talbot Press, [1926].

1784.   [YL 1770].
——, ed. *A Golden Treasury of Irish Verse*. London: Macmillan, 1925.

1784a.   [YL 1770a].
Another copy. Signed: GY | 1925

1785. [YL 1771].
Robinson, Stanford F[rederick]. H[udson]. *Celtic Illuminative Art in the Gospel Books of Durrow, Lindisfarne, and Kells.* Dublin: Hodges, Figgis, 1908. [Illustrated].

1786. [YL 1772].
Robson, Vivian E[rwood]. *The Fixed Stars and Constellations in Astrology.* London: Cecil Palmer, 1923.

1787. [YL 1773].
——. *A Student's Text-Book of Astrology.* London: Cecil Palmer, 1922.

1788. [YL *1774]. [NLI 40,568/194; 1 sheet; envelope 1345].
Rochas, Albert de. *Les états profonds de l'hypnose.* 5th ed. Paris: Bibliothèque Chacornac, 1904. [Bound with:] *Les états superficiels de l'hypnose.* 5th ed. Paris: Chamuel, 1897.

1789. [YL *1775]. [NLI 40,568/195; 19 sheets; envelope 1346].
——. *L'extériorisation de la motricité: Recueil d'expériences et d'observations.* 4th ed. Paris: Bibliothèque Chacornac, 1906.

1790. [YL *1776]. [NLI 40,568/196; 44 sheets; envelope 1348].
——. *L'extériorisation de la sensibilité.* Étude expérimentale et historique. 6th ed. Paris: Bibliothèque Chacornac, 1909. [Illustrated].

1791. [Not listed in *YL*]. [NLI 40,568/197; 20 sheets; envelope number not given].
——. *Les frontières de la science.* 2e série. Paris: Librairie des sciences psychologiques, 1904.

1792. [YL *1777].
——. *La science des philosophes et l'art des thaumaturges dans l'antiquité.* 2nd ed. Paris: Dorbon-Ainé, [1912].

1793. [YL *1778].
Rodker, John. *Poems.* Whitechapel: By the author, [1914].

1794. [YL 1779].
Rolfe, Fr. [Frederick, Baron Corvo]. *Hadrian the Seventh.* The Phoenix Library. London: Chatto and Windus, 1929.

1795. [YL *1780].
Rolland, Romain. *The People's Theater.* Trans. Barrett H. Clark. New York: Henry Holt, 1918.

1796.   [YL 1781].
———. *Prophets of the New India*. Trans. E. F. Malcolm-Smith. London: Cassell, 1930. Bp: WBY

1797.   [YL 1782].
The Roman Missal, in Latin and English for Every Day in the Year. Ed. an Irish bishop. [With supplements for Ireland and other English speaking-countries]. Dublin: M. H. Gill, [1938].

1798.   [YL *1783].
Ronsard, P[ierre]. de. *Poesies choisies*. Paris: Bibliothèque Charpentier, [1873]. Bp: WBY

1799.   [YL 1784].
Roosval, Johnny et al., eds. *Stockholms stadshus vid dess invigning midsommarafton 1923*. 3 vols. Stockholm: Aktiebolaget Gunnar Tisells Tekniska Förlag, 1923. [Illustrated].

1800.   [YL 1785].
Rose, William and G[ertrude]. Craig Houston, eds. *Rainer Maria Rilke: Aspects of His Mind and Poetry*. London: Sidgwick and Jackson, 1938.

1801.   [YL 1786].
[Rosen, Georg Von]. *G. Von Rosen*. Sma Konstböcker, no. 9. Lund: Gleerupska Universitets-Bokhandeln, [1910?].

1802.   [YL 1787].
Rosenberg, Adolf. *A. Von Werner*. Bielefeld und Leipzig: Velhagen und Klasing, 1900.[Illustrated].

1803.   [YL *1788].
Rossetti, Christina. *Poems*. Ed. William M. Rossetti. London: Macmillan, 1905.

1804.   [YL *1789].
Rossetti, Dante Gabriel. *The Collected Works*. Ed. William M. Rossetti. 2 vols. London: Ellis and Elvey, 1897. Bps.: WBY

1805.   [YL 1790].
———. *The House of Life: Sonnets and Songs*. Illustrated by Phoebe Anna Traquair. Edinburgh: William J. Hay, 1904. [Illustrated]. Bp: WBY

1806.   [*YL* 1791].
——. *Letters of Dante Gabriel Rossetti to William Allingram, 1854–1870*. Ed. George Birkbeck Hill. London: T. Fisher Unwin, 1897.

1807.   [*YL* 1792].
Rossi, M[ario]. M[anlio]. *Viaggio in Irlanda*. Milano: Doxa Editrice, 1932. Signed: Mario M. Rossi

1808.   [*YL* 1793].
—— and Joseph M[aunsell]. Hone. *Swift, or The Egotist*. London: Victor Gollancz, 1934.

1809.   [Not listed in *YL* and assigned NLI number 3043].
Roth, William M. *A Catalogue of English and American First Editions of William Butler Yeats*. Maine: New Haven, 1939. Inscribed by Roth to GY.

1809a. [Not listed in *YL* and assigned NLI number 3043a].
Another copy. Annotated and with a typed letter inserted from Louise Terrien to Sean O'Faolain and a handwritten note from O'Faolain to GY.

1809b. [Not listed in *YL* and assigned NLI number 3043b].
Another copy. Some pencil markings.

1809c. [Not listed in *YL* and assigned NLI number 3043c].
Another copy. Some corrections and markings. Flyleaf: "George Yeats."

1809d. [Not listed in *YL* and assigned NLI number 3043d].
Another copy.

1810.   [*YL* 1794].
Rowley, Richard. *City Songs and Others*. Dublin and London: Maunsel, 1918.

1811.   [*YL* 1795]. [Wade 284].
Ruddock, Margot. *The Lemon Tree*. [Ed. W. B. Yeats]. With an intro. by W. B. Yeats. London: J. M. Dent, 1937.

1812.   [Not listed in *YL* and assigned NLI number 3044].
Rules of the Irish Academy of Letters. Dublin: Cahill, 12 Sept. 1932.

1813.   [*YL* 1796].
Russell, Archibald G[eorge]. B[lomefield]. *The Engravings of William Blake*. London: Grant Richards, 1912. [Illustrated].

1814.   [*YL* 1797]. [NLI 40,568/198; 5 sheets; envelope 1227].
Russell, Bertrand. *The ABC of Relativity*. London: Kegan Paul, Trench, Trubner, 1925.

1815.   [*YL* 1798]. [NLI 40,568/199; 59 sheets; envelope 1146].
——. *An Outline of Philosophy*. London: George Allen and Unwin, 1927.

1816.   [*YL* 1799]. [NLI 40,568/200; 2 sheets; envelope 1727]. [Though reported in *YL*, did not come to NLI with letter from T. Sturge Moore to WBY].
Russell, George [AE, pseud.]. *The Candle of Vision*. London: Macmillan, 1918.

1817.   [*YL* *1800]. [NLI 40,568/201; 5 sheets; envelope 1722].
——. *Collected Poems*. London: Macmillan, 1913. Bp: WBY

1818.   [*YL* 1801].
——. *Collected Poems*. London: Macmillan, 1926.

1819.   [*YL* *1802].
——. *The Divine Vision and Other Poems*. London: Macmillan, 1904.

1820.   [*YL* *1803]. [NLI 40,568/202; 33 sheets; envelope 1725].
——. *The Earth Breath and Other Poems*. New York and London: John Lane, the Bodley Head, 1897. Signed: WBY

1821.   [*YL* 1804].
——. *The Inner and Outer Ireland*. Reprinted from *Pearson's Magazine* (New York, NY). Dublin: Talbot Press, 1921. Signed: George Russell

1821A.   [*YL* 1804A].
Another ed. London: T. Fisher Unwin, 1921.

1822.   [*YL* 1805].
——. *The Interpreters*. London: Macmillan, 1922.

1823.   [*YL* 1806].
——. *Ireland, Past and Future*. [A paper read to the Sociological Society on 21st February, 1922]. [Lacks publication details].

1824. [*YL* *1807].
——. *The Mask of Apollo and Other Stories*. Dublin: Whaley, [1904].

1825. [*YL* *1808].
——. *The National Being: Some Thoughts on an Irish Polity*. Dublin and London: Maunsel, 1916. Bp: WBY

1826. [*YL* 1809].
——. Review of *Reveries over Childhood and Youth* (1916), by W. B. Yeats. [*New Ireland*, 16 Dec. 1916: 88–89].

1827. [*YL* 1810].
——. *Salutation: A Poem on the Irish Rebellion of 1916*. London: Privately printed by Clement Shorter, 1917.

1828. [*YL* 1811].
——. *Selected Poems*. London: Macmillan, 1935.

1829. [*YL* 1812]. [NLI 40,568/203; 4 sheets; envelope 1730].
——. *Song and Its Fountains*. London: Macmillan, 1932.

1830. [*YL* 1813].
——. *Thoughts for a Convention: Memorandum on the State of Ireland*. Dublin and London: Maunsel, 1917.

1831. [*YL* 1814].
——. *To the Fellows of the Theosophical Society*. March 20th, 1894. Dublin: Irish Theosophist Press, [1894].

1832. [*YL* 1815].
——. *Vale and Other Poems*. London: Macmillan, 1931.

1833. [*YL* 1816].
——. *Verses for Friends*. Dublin: By the author, 1932.

1834. [*YL* *1817].
——, ed. *New Songs: A Lyric Selection…from Poems by Padraic Colum, Eva Gore-Booth, Thomas Keohler, Alice Milligan, Susan Mitchell, Seumas O'Sullivan, George Roberts, and Ella Young*. Dublin: O'Donoghue, 1904.

1834A. [*YL* 1817A].
Another ed. 2nd ed., 1904.

1835. [YL *1818].
Ryan, W[illiam]. P[atrick]. *The Irish Literary Revival: Its History, Pioneers and Possibilities*. London: Ward and Downey, [1894]. Signed: W B Yeats | Coole 1899

1836. [YL 1819].
The Saga of the Faroe Islanders. Trans. Muriel A. C. Press. London: J. M. Dent, 1934.

1837. [YL 1820].
Sainte-Beuve, Charles Augustin. *The Essays of Saint-Beuve*. Ed. William Sharp. 3 vols. London: Gibbings, 1901.

1838. [YL 1821].
Salkeld, Blanaid. *The Engine Is Left Running*. With cover and four pictures by Cecil ffrench Salkeld. Dublin: Gayfield Press, 1937. Signed: Blanaid Salkeld and Cecil ffrench Salkeld

1839. [YL 1822]. [Wade 227].
Samhain, ed. W. B. Yeats, 1 (Oct. 1901).

1840. [YL 1823]. [Wade 228].
—— 2 (Oct. 1902).

1841. [YL 1824]. [Wade 229].
—— 3 (Oct. 1903).

1842. [YL 1825]. [Wade 230].
—— 4 (Dec. 1904). Signed: Lily Yeats

1843. [YL 1826]. [Wade 237].
—— 6 (Dec. 1906).

1843a–b. [YL 1826a–b].
Two more copies.

1843c. [YL 1826c].
Another copy.

1844. [YL 1827]. [NLI 40,578; an inserted copy—TS. with MS. corrections by WBY of his "Samhain 1908. First Principles"; 13 numbered sheets]. [Though reported in *YL*, did not come to NLI with said 13-page TS.].
——. Bound vol., complete.

1845.   [YL 1828].
Sanctis, Francesco de. *History of Italian Literature*. Trans. Joan Redfern. 2 vols. London: Oxford University Press, [1932]. Bp: WBY

1846.   [YL 1829].
Sandars, Mary F[rances]. *Honoré de Balzac: His Life and Writings*. London: John Murray, 1904.

1847.   [YL 1830].
Santayana, George. *Winds of Doctrine: Studies in Contemporary Opinion*. London: J. M. Dent, 1913; New York: Charles Scribner's Sons, 1913.

x   [YL 1831]. [NLI missing this copy].
Santesson, C[arl]. G[ustaf]. *Les Prix Nobel en 1938*. Stockholm: P. A. Norstedt, [1938?].

1848.   [YL 1832].
Sa'di. *Gulistan or Flower-Garden*. Translated with an essay by James Ross. With a note on the translator by Charles Sayle. The Camelot Series. London: Walter Scott, [1890].

x   [YL 1833]. [NLI missing this copy].
An Saorstat [The Free State], no. 8 (19 Aug. 1922). War Special. [Tribute to Arthur Griffith].

x   [YL 1834]. [NLI missing this copy].
———. (30 Aug. 1922). Michael Collins Memorial Number.

1849.   [YL *1835].
Sappho. *Memoir*. Trans. Henry Thornton Wharton. 3rd ed. London: John Lane, 1895.

1850.   [YL *1836].
———. *The Poems*. Trans. John Myers O'Hara. Chicago: By the author, 1907. Signed: John Myers O'Hara

1851.   [YL 1837].
Sardou, V[ictorien]., L. Illica and G. Giacosa. *Tosca*. [Libretto]. Trans. W. Beatty-Kingston. London: G. Ricordi, 1900.

1852.   [YL 1838]. [NLI 40,568/204; 21 sheets; envelope 123].
Sarolea, Charles. *Impressions of Soviet Russia*. London: Eveleigh Nash and Grayson, 1924. Signed: GY, Nov. 1924

1853.   [YL 1839].
———. *Letters on Polish Affairs.* With an introduction by G. K. Chesterton. Edinburgh: Oliver and Boyd, 1922.

1854.   [YL 1840].
Sackville-West, V[ita]. *Collected Poems.* 2 vols. London: Hogarth Press, 1933.

1855.   [YL 1841]. [NLI 40,568/205; 2 sheets; envelope 647].
Sassoon, Siegfried. *The Heart's Journey.* London: William Heinemann, 1935.

1856.   [YL 1842]. [Though reported in *YL*, did not come to NLI with a note from Sassoon dated 31 March (1925?)].
———. *Lingual Exercises for Advanced Vocabularians.* Cambridge: Privately printed at the University Press, 1925. Signed: Siegfried Sassoon. Signed: WBY

1857.   [YL 1843].
———. *Memoirs of an Infantry Officer.* London: Faber and Faber, 1930.

1858.   [YL 1844].
———. *Satirical Poems.* London: William Heinemann, 1933.

1859.   [YL 1845].
———. *To My Mother.* Drawings by Stephen Tennant. The Ariel Poems, no. 14. London: Faber and Gwyer, [1928]. [Illustrated].

1860.   [YL 1846]. [NLI 40,568/206; 17 sheets; envelope 1908A].
Saurat, Denis. *Blake and Modern Thought.* London: Constable, 1929.

1861.   [YL 1847]. [NLI 40,568/207; 13 sheets; envelope 523].
———. *Milton: Man and Thinker.* London: Jonathan Cape, [1925].

1862.   [YL 1848]. [NLI 40,568/208; 10 sheets; envelope 2012/1].
———. *The Savoy* 1 (Jan.–Aug. 1896). Bp: WBY

1863.   [YL 1849]. [NLI 40,568/209; 6 sheets; envelope 2012/2].
——— 2 (Sept.–Dec. 1896). Bp: WBY

1864.   [YL 1850].
Sayler, Oliver M[artin]., ed. *Max Reinhardt and His Theatre.* Trans. Mariele S. Dudernatsch and others. New York: Brentano's, 1924. [Illustrated]. Signed: GY

1865.   [*YL* 1851].

Scherer, Valentin. *Dürer: Des Meisters Gemälde Kupferstiche und Holzschnitte in 473 Abbildungen*. Stuttgart: Deutsche Verlags-Anstalt, 1908. [Illustrated].

1866.   [*YL* 1852].

Schmidt, Peter M. D. *The Conquest of Old Age: Methods to Effect Rejuvenation and to Increase Functional Activity*. Trans. Eden and Cedar Paul. London: George Routledge, 1931. [Illustrated].

1867.   [*YL* 1853]. [NLI 40,568/210; 9 sheets; envelope 1043].

Schneider, Hermann. *The History of World Civilization*. Trans. Margaret M. Green. 2 vols. London: George Routledge, 1931. Bp: WBY

1868.   [*YL* 1854].

Schnitzler, Arthur. *Professor Bernhardi: A Comedy*. Trans. Hetty Landstone. London: Faber and Gwyer, 1927. Signed: Lennox Robinson | 1927

1869.   [*YL* *1855].

Schopenhauer, Arthur. *The Art of Controversy and Other Posthumous Papers*. Selected and translated by T. Bailey Saunders. London: Swan Sonnenschein, 1896; New York: Macmillan, 1896.

1870.   [*YL* *1856].

——. *The Wisdom of Life: Being the First Part of* Aphorismen zur Lebensweisheit. Trans. T. Bailey Saunders. London: Swan Sonnenschein, 1891.

1871.   [*YL* *1857]. [NLI 40,568/211; 3 sheets; envelope 135].

Scot, Reginald. *The Discoverie of Witchcraft*. A reprint of the first ed. published in 1584. Ed. Brinsley Nicholson. London: Elliott Stock, 1886. Bp: WBY

1872.   [*YL* 1858].

Scott, Geoffrey. *A Box of Paints*. With drawings by Albert Rutherston. London: At the Office of the Bookman's Journal, 1923. [Illustrated].

1873.   [*YL* 1859].

Scott, Sir Walter. *Ivanhoe*. Edinburgh: Adam and Charles Black, 1871.

1874.   [*YL* 1860].

——. *Letters on Demonology and Witchcraft, Addressed to J. G. Lockhart, Esq.* London: John Murray, 1830. Bp: R. H. Robertson. Signed: George Hyde-Lees, 1914

1874A.   [*YL* *1860A].

Another ed. 4th ed. Morley's Universal Library. London: George Routledge, 1899.

1875.   [*YL* 1861].

Scripture Topography: Being Some Account of Places Mentioned in Holy Scripture, Given Principally in Extracts from the Works of Travellers; Palestine. 4th ed. London: The Society for Promoting Christian Knowledge, 1852.

1876.   [*YL* 1862].

Seignobos, Charles. *History of Mediaeval Civilization, and of Modern to the End of the Seventeenth Century.* London: T. Fisher Unwin, 1908.

1877.   [*YL* 1863]. [NLI 40,568/212; 17 sheets; envelope 1042].

Sei Shonagon. *The Pillow-Book of Sei Shonagon.* Trans. Arthur Waley. London: George Allen and Unwin, 1928.

1878.   [*YL* *1864].

Selden, John. *De dis Syris syntagmata II: adversaria nempe de numinibus commentitiis in veteri instrumento memoratis: accedunt fere quae sunt reliqua Syrorum, prisca porro Arabum, Aegyptiorum, Persarum, Afrorum, Europaeorum item theologia, subinde illustratur.* Revised edition. Lugduni: Ex Officina Bonaventurae & Abrahami Elsevir, 1629. Signed: E Libris Comitis Guilford

1879.   [*YL* 1865].

Sensier, Alfred. *Jean-François Millet: Peasant and Painter.* Trans. Helena de Kay. London: Macmillan, 1881. Bp: Lily Yeats; Bp: Anne Yeats. Signed: Anne B. Yeats, 1934

1880.   [*YL* 1866].

Sepharial [pseud., Walter Gorn Old]. *Directional Astrology: To Which is Added a Discussion of Problematic Points and a Complete Set of Tables Necessary for the Calculation of Arcs of Direction.* London: William Rider, 1915. [Illustrated]. Bp: GY

1881.   [*YL* 1867].

———. *Eclipses, Astronomically and Astrologically Considered and Explained*. London: W. Foulsham, [1915]. Bp: GY

1882.   [*YL* 1868].

———. *Primary Directions Made Easy*. London: W. Foulsham, [1917]. Bp: GY

1883.   [*YL* 1869]. [NLI 40,568/213; 32 sheets; envelope 148].

———. *The Science of Foreknowledge*. London: W. Foulsham, 1918. [Illustrated].

1884.   [*YL* 1870]. [NLI 40,568/214; 8 sheets; envelope 131].

Sepher yetzirah: The Book of Formation, with the Fifty Gates of Intelligence and the Thirty-Two Paths of Wisdom. Trans. W. Wynn Westcott. London: J. M. Watkins, 1911. Signed: Georgie Hyde Lees | April 1914

1885.   [*YL* *1871].

Shakespear, Olivia. *The Devotees: A Novel*. London: William Heinemann, 1904.

1886.   [*YL* 1872].

———. *The False Laurel: A Tale*. London: Osgood, McIlvaine, 1896.

1887.   [*YL* 1873].

———. *The Journey of High Honour: A Novel*. London: Osgood, McIlvaine, 1895.

1888.   [*YL* 1874].

———. *Love on a Mortal Lease: A Novel*. London: Osgood, McIlvaine, 1894.

1889.   [*YL* 1875].

Shakespeare, William. *The Complete Works*. Ed. W. J. Craig. London: Oxford University Press, 1935.

1890.   [*YL* *1876].

———. *A Lover's Complaint and* The Phoenix and Turtle. The Shakespeare Head Press Booklets, no. 6. Stratford-on-Avon: Shakespeare Head Press, 1906.

1891.   [*YL* 1877].

———. *Othello, the Moor of Venice*. Ed. C[harles]. H[arold]. Herford. The Warwick Shakespeare. London and Glasgow: Blackie, [1893?].

1892. [YL *1878].
——. *Shakespeare's Songs.* The Shakespeare Head Press Booklets, no. 3. Stratford-on-Avon: Shakespeare Head Press, 1906.

1893. [YL 1879].
——. *The Sonnets.* Ed. Edward Dowden. The Parchment Library. London: C. Kegan Paul, 1881.

1894. [YL *1880].
——. *The Winter's Tale.* An acting edition prepared with a preface by Granville Barker. With costume designs by Albert Rothenstein. London: William Heinemann, 1912. [Illustrated].

1895. [YL *1881].
——. *The Works.* 10 vols. Stratford-on-Avon: Shakespeare Head Press, 1904–1907. Bp: WBY

1896. [YL 1882].
The Shanachie 1 (Spring 1906).

1896a. [YL 1882a].
Another copy.

1897. [YL 1883].
—— 1 (Winter 1906)]. Includes works by AE, John Butler Yeats, and Jack Yeats.

1898. [YL 1884].
—— 2 (March 1907). Includes work by John Butler Yeats and Synge. Inside back cover, ink: 80 Rath [?] | 31 Upper S. Columba's Rd. | Drumcondra [possibly WBY's]

1899. [YL 1885].
—— 2 (Summer 1907).

1900. [YL 1886].
—— 2 (Autumn 1907).

1901. [YL *1887].
Sharp, Elizabeth, ed. *Lyra Celtica: An Anthology of Representative Celtic Poetry.* With an intro. by William Sharp. The Celtic Library. Edinburgh: Patrick Geddes, 1896.

1902.   [*YL* *1888].
Sharp, William. *Madge O' the Pool: The Gypsy Christ and Other Tales*. Westminster: Archibald Constable, 1896.

1903.   [*YL* 1889].
Shaw, George Bernard. *The Adventures of the Black Girl in Her Search for God*. London: Constable, 1932.

1903a.   [*YL* 1889a].
Another copy.

1904.   [*YL* 1890].
——. *Androcles and the Lion*. The Dramatic Works of Bernard Shaw, no. 23. London: Constable, 1927.

1905.   [*YL* 1891].
——. *Caesar and Cleopatra: A History*. The Dramatic Works of Bernard Shaw, no. 9. London: Constable, 1923. Signed: GY | 1926

1906.   [*YL* 1892].
——. *Heartbreak House, Great Catherine, and Playlets of the War*. London: Constable, 1926.

1907.   [*YL* 1893].
——. *The Intelligent Woman's Guide to Socialism and Capitalism*. London: Constable, 1928. Bp: GY

1908.   [*YL* 1894].
——. *The Irrational Knot*. London: Constable, 1914

1909.   [*YL* 1895].
——. *Overruled, and The Dark Lady of the Sonnets*. The Dramatic Works of Bernard Shaw, nos. 20 and 24. London: Constable, 1921.

1910.   [*YL* 1896].
——. *Pygmalion*. The Dramatic Works of Bernard Shaw, no. 25. London: Constable, 1928.

1911.   [*YL* 1897].
——. *Saint Joan*. London: Constable, 1924.

1912.   [*YL* *1898].
——. *The Sanity of Art: An Exposure of the Current Nonsense about Artists Being Degenerate*. London: New Age Press, 1908.

1913.   [*YL* 1899].
———. *Too True to Be Good, Village Wooing, and on the Rocks: Three Plays*. London: Constable, 1934. Signed: WBY

1914.   [*YL* 1900].
———. *Translations and Tomfooleries*. London: Constable, 1926.

1915.   [*YL* 1901].
———. *Widowers' Houses: A Play*. The Dramatic Works of Bernard Shaw, no. 1. London: Constable, 1924.

1916.   [*YL* 1902]. [NLI 40,568/215; 24 sheets; envelope 673].
Shelley, Percy Bysshe. *Essays and Letters*. Ed. Ernest Rhys. The Camelot Classics. London: Walter Scott, 1886. Signed: WBY. Bp: Lily Yeats

1917.   [*YL* 1903].
———. *The Lyrical Poems and Translations*. Ed. C. H. Herford. London: Chatto and Windus, 1918.

1918.   [*YL* 1904].
———. *The Lyrics and Minor Poems*. With a prefatory notice by Joseph Skipsey. The Canterbury Poets. London: Walter Scott, 1885. Signed: WBY, 1886.

1919.   [*YL* *1905]. [NLI 40,568/216; vols. 1–2: 13 and 5 sheets; envelope 669/1–2].
———. *The Poems of Percy Bysshe Shelley*. Ed. C. D. Locock. 2 vols. London: Methuen, 1911. Bp: WBY

1920.   [*YL* 1906].
———. *The Poetical Works of Percy Bysshe Shelley*. [London: C. Daly, 1836?].

1921.   [*YL* 1907]. [NLI 40,568/217; vols. 1–3: 41, 51, 49 sheets; envelope 666].
———. *The Poetical Works of Percy Bysshe Shelley*. Ed. Mrs. Shelley. 3 vols. London: Edward Moxon, 1847. Bp: Robert Corbet. Vols. 2 and 3, Bp: Lily Yeats

1922.   [*YL* *1908]. [NLI 40,568/218; 31 sheets; envelope 667].
———. *The Poetical Works of Percy Bysshe Shelley*. Ed. William B. Scott. Excelsior Series. London: George Routledge, [1880].

1923.   [*YL* *1909]. [NLI 40,568/219; 16 sheets; envelope 48].
———. *Prometheus Unbound: A Lyrical Drama in Four Acts*. Ed. G. Lowes Dickinson. The Temple Dramatists Series. London: J. M. Dent, 1898.

1924.   [*YL* 1910].
———. *Shelley*. Edited and printed by T. J. Cobden-Sanderson. [Hammersmith]: The Doves Press, [1914?]. Bp: WBY

1925.   [*YL* 1911].
Sherard, Robert Harborough. *André Gide's Wicked Lies about the Late Mr. Oscar Wilde in Algiers in January, 1895 as Translated from the French and Broadcast by Dr. G. J. Renier*. Calvi (Corsica), France: Vindex Publishing, 1933.

1926.   [*YL* 1912].
Sibly, Ebenezer. *A [Complete] Illustration of [the Celestial Science of] Astrology [or the Art of Foretelling Future Events and Contingencies by the Aspects Positions, and Influences of the Heavenly Bodies]*. [London: Printed for Green and Co., 1784–88]. Bp: John F. Cooper

1927.   [*YL* *1913].
Sidgwick, Frank, ed. *Popular Ballads of the Olden Time*. First series: *Ballads of Romance and Chivalry*. London: A. H. Bullen, 1903. [With maps].

1928.   [*YL* *1914].
———. *Popular Ballads of the Olden Time*. Third series: *Ballads of Scottish Tradition and Romance*. London: A. H. Bullen, 1906.

1929.   [*YL* *1915].
———. *Popular Ballads of the Olden Time*. Fourth series: *Ballads of Robin Hood and Other Outlaws*. London: Sidgwick and Jackson, 1912. [With maps].

1930.   [*YL* 1916].
Sidney Sir Philip. *Astrophel and Stella*. Ed. Mona Wilson. London: Nonesuch Press, 1931.

1931.   [*YL* *1917]. [NLI 40,568/220; 1 sheet; envelope 679].
———. *The Poems*. Ed. John Drinkwater. The Muses' Library. London: George Routledge, [1910].

1932. [*YL* *1918*].
Sigerson, Dora [Mrs. Clement Shorter]. *Ballads and Poems*. London: James Bowden, 1899.

1933. [*YL* *1919*].
———. *The Fairy Changeling and Other Poems*. London and New York: John Lane, 1898.

1934. [*YL* *1920*].
———. *Love of Ireland: Poems and Ballads*. Dublin and London: Maunsel, 1916.

1935. [*YL* *1921*].
Sigerson, George, trans. *Bards of the Gael and Gall: Examples of the Poetic Literature of Erinn*. London: T. Fisher Unwin, 1897. Signed: WBY | June, 1897

1936. [*YL* 1922].
Simmonite, W[illiam]. J[oseph]. *Horary Astrology: The Key to Scientific Prediction, Being the Prognostic Astronomer*. New ed., with additions by John Story. London: W. Foulsham, [1896]. Bp: GY

1937. [*YL* 1923].
Sinn Fein Rebellion Handbook: A Complete and Connected Narrative of the Rising, with Detailed Accounts of the Fighting at All Points in Dublin and in the Country. 2nd ed. Dublin: Compiled by the Weekly Irish Times, [1916]. Signed: Lily Yeats | Dundrum

1938. [*YL* 1924].
Sitwell, Edith. *Alexander Pope*. London: Faber and Faber, 1930.

1939. [*YL* 1925].
———. *Aspects of Modern Poetry*. London: Duckworth, 1934.

1940. [*YL* 1926]. [NLI 40,568/221; 14 sheets; envelope 683].
———. *The Collected Poems*. London: Duckworth, 1930.

1941. [*YL* 1927].
———. *Epithalamium*. Christmas 1931. London: Duckworth, [1931].

1942. [*YL* 1928].
———. *Five Poems*. London: Duckworth, 1928. Signed: Edith Sitwell

1943. [*YL* 1929].
———. *Five Variations on a Theme*. London: Duckworth, 1933.

1944. [*YL* 1930].
——. *Gold Coast Customs*. London: Duckworth, 1929. Bp: WBY

1945. [*YL* 1931].
——. *Rustic Elegies*. London: Duckworth, 1927.

1946. [*YL* 1932].
——, ed. *The Pleasures of Poetry: A Critical Anthology*. First series: *Milton and the Augustan Age*. London: Duckworth, 1930.

1947. [*YL* 1933].
——, Osbert Sitwell, and Sacheverell Sitwell. *Poor Young People*. With drawings by Albert Rothenstein. London: Fleuron, 1925. [Illustrated].

1948. [*YL* 1934].
Sitwell, Osbert. *Winters of Content: More Discursions of Travel, Art, and Life*. London: Duckworth, 1932. [Illustrated].

1949. [*YL* 1935].
——, Edith Sitwell, and Sacheverell Sitwell. *Trio: Dissertations on Some Aspects of National Genius*. London: Macmillan, 1938. Signed: GY

1950. [*YL* 1936]. [NLI 40,568/222; 2 sheets; envelope 698].
Sitwell, Sacheverell. *Canons of Giant Art: Twenty Torsos in Heroic Landscapes*. London: Faber and Faber, 1933.

1951. [*YL* 1937].
——. *Collected Poems*. London: Duckworth, 1936.

1952. [*YL* 1938].
——. *Doctor Donne and Gargantua: The First Six Cantos*. London: Duckworth, 1930.

1953. [*YL* 1939].
——. *The Gothick North: A Study of Mediaeval Life, Art, and Thought*. 3 vols. London: Duckworth, 1929–30.

1954. [*YL* 1940].
——. *The Hundred and One Harlequins*. The New Readers Library. London: Duckworth, 1929.

1955. [*YL* 1941].
——. *The People's Palace*. Oxford: B. H. Blackwell, 1918.

1956.   [YL 1942].
———. *The Thirteenth Caesar and Other Poems*. London: Grant Richards, 1924. Signed: Gwin [?] Russell

1956a.   [YL 1942a].
Another copy. London: Duckworth, 1927.

1957.   [YL 1943].
———. *Two Poems, Ten Songs*. London: Duckworth, 1929. Signed: Sacheverell Sitwell

1958.   [YL 1944].
———. *La vie parisienne: A Tribute to Offenbach*. London: Faber and Faber, 1937.

1959.   [YL *1945].
Skeat, Walter. *The Chaucer Canon*. Oxford: Clarendon Press, 1900.

1960.   [YL *1946].
Skipsey, Joseph. *Songs and Lyrics*. London: Walter Scott, 1892. Signed: J.S.

1961.   [YL 1947].
Slater, Montagu. *Easter: 1916*. [A play]. London: Lawrence and Wishart, 1936.

1962.   [YL 1948].
Smart, John Semple. *Shakespeare, Truth and Tradition*. London: Edward Arnold, 1929.

1963.   [YL 1949].
Smith, G[rafton]. Elliot. *The Evolution of the Dragon*. Manchester: University Press, 1919.

1964.   [YL 1950].
Smith, Janet Adam, ed. *Poems of Tomorrow: An Anthology of Contemporary Verse, Chosen from* The Listener. London: Chatto and Windus, 1935.

1965.   [YL 1951].
Smith, William. *A Smaller Dictionary of Greek and Roman Antiquities*. 11th ed. London: John Murray, 1880. [Illustrated].

1966.   [YL 1952].
Smith, W[alter]. Whately. *A Theory of the Mechanism of Survival: The Fourth Dimension and Its Applications.* London: Kegan Paul, Trench, Trubner, 1920.

1967.   [YL 1953].
Smollett, Tobias [George]. *The Adventures of Ferdinand Count Fathom.* London: Waverley Book Company, [189?]. Signed: W. Sullivan

1968.   [YL *1954].
——. *The Adventures of Roderick Random.* London: George Routledge, [189?].

1968a.   [YL *1954a].
Another printing. London: Waverley, [189?].

1969.   [YL 1955].
——. *The Adventures of Sir Launcelot Greaves and the History and Adventures of an Atom.* London: Waverley, [189?]. Signed: W. Sullivan

1970.   [YL 1956].
——. *The Expedition of Humphry Clinker.* London: Waverley, [189?]. Signed: W. Sullivan

1971.   [YL 1957].
——. *The Soldiers' Song Book: Stirring Spirited Songs of the Soldiers Who Fought for the Honour and the Freedom of Ireland in Every Generation.* Dublin: Irish Book Bureau, [1938].

1972.   [YL 1958].
Solovyoff, Vladimir. *The Justification of the Good: An Essay on Moral Philosophy.* Trans. Nathalie A. Duddington. London: Constable, 1918.

1973.   [YL 1959].
Sophocles. *Antigone: A New Redaction in the American Language.* Trans. Shaemas O'Sheel. Brooklyn: By the author, 1931.

1974.   [YL 1960].
——. *The Oedipus at Colonus.* Translated from the text of Jebb by Edward P. Coleridge. London: George Bell, 1892.

1975.　[Not listed in *YL* and assigned NLI number 3045]. [See Chapman, *YA* 8 (1991): 202].
———. *Oedipus, King of Thebes*. Trans. Gilbert Murray. London: George Allen & Sons, 1911.

1976.　[*YL* 1961].
———. *Oedipus Tyrannus*. Trans. Roscoe Mongan. Kelly's Keys to the Classics, vol. 41. London: James Cornish, [1865].

1977.　[*YL* 1962]. [NLI 40,568/223&224; 51 sheets; envelope 966].
———. *The Oedipus Tyrannus*. As performed at Cambridge, Nov. 22–26, 1887. Translated in prose by R. C. Jebb with a translation of the Songs of the Chorus in verse adapted to the music of C. Villiers Stanford by A. W. Verall. Cambridge: Cambridge University Press, 1887.

1978.　[*YL* 1963]. [NLI 40,568/225; 20 sheets; envelope 963].
———. *The Seven Plays in English Verse*. Trans. Lewis Campbell. New ed., rev. World's Classics, vol. 116. London: Oxford University Press, 1906.

1979.　[*YL* 1964]. [NLI 40,568/226; 2 sheets; envelope 964].
———. *Sophocle*. Tome I: *Ajax, Antigone, Oedipe-Roi, Electre*. Trans. Paul Masqueray. Paris: Société d'Édition "Les Belles Lettres," 1922.

1980.　[*YL* 1965].
———. *Sophocle*. Tome II: *Les Trachiniennes, Philoctete, Oedipe à Colone, Les Limiers*. Trans. Paul Masqueray. Paris: Société d'Édition "Les Belles Lettres," 1924.

1981.　[*YL* 1966].
The Southern Review 4 (Summer 1938).

1982.　[*YL* *1967]. [Wade 290].
Sparling, H[enry]. Halliday, ed. *Irish Minstrelsy: Being a Selection of Irish Songs, Lyrics, and Ballads*. London: Walter Scott, 1888.

1983.　[*YL* 1968].
The Spectator 2 (2 June 1711–13 Sept. 1711).

1984.　[*YL* 1969].
The Spectator (London) No. 5,405 (Jan. 1932).

1985.　[*YL* 1970].
——— No. 5,415 (9 April 1932).

1986.   [*YL* 1971].
——— No. 5,547 (19 Oct. 1934).

x   [*YL* 1972]. [NLI missing this copy].
——— No. 5,656 (20 Nov. 1936). Literary Supplement.

1987.   [*YL* 1973].
Spender, Stephen. *Poems*. London: Faber and Faber, 1933.

1988.   [*YL* 1974].
———. *Vienna*. London: Faber and Faber, 1934.

1989.   [*YL* 1975]. [NLI 40,568/227; vol. 1: 45 sheets; envelope 1083].
Spengler, Oswald. *The Decline of the West: Form and Actuality*. Trans. Charles Francis Atkinson. 2 vols. London: George Allen and Unwin, [1926-69].

1989A.   [*YL* 1975A]. [NLI 40,568/228; vol. 2: 96 sheets; envelope 1083].
———. Vol. 2 Bp: WBY

1990.   [*YL* 1976].
Spenser, Edmund. *The Poems of Spenser*. Ed. Roden Noel. London: Walter Scott, 1886. Signed: WBY

1991.   [*YL* 1977]. [Wade 235].
———. *Poems of Spenser*. Ed. W. B. Yeats. Edinburgh: T. C. and E. C. Jack, 1906.

1992.   [*YL* 1978]. [NLI 40,568/229; vols. 1-5: 20, 111, 26, 38, and 46 sheets; envelope 713/1-5]. [See Chapman, *YA* 6 (1988): 234-45].
———. *The Works of Edmund Spenser*. Ed. J[ohn]. Payne Collier. 5 vols. London: Bell and Daldy, 1862. Bp: WBY

1992A.   [*YL* 1978A].
———. Vol. 2.

1992B.   [*YL* 1978B].
———.Vol. 3.

1992C.   [*YL* 1978C].
———.Vol. 4.

1992D.   [*YL* 1978D].
———. Vol. 5.

1993. [YL 1979].
Spoelberch de Lovenjoul, Charles. *Histoire des oeuvres de Balzac*. 2nd ed. Paris: Calmann Lévy, 1886.

1994. [YL *1980].
Squire, J[ohn]. C[ollings]. *The Birds and Other Poems*. London: Martin Secker, 1919.

1995. [YL *1981].
——. *The Lily of Malud and Other Poems*. London: Martin Secker, 1917.

1996. [YL *1982].
——. *Twelve Poems*. Decorations by A. Spare. London: Morland Press, 1916.

1997. [YL 1983]. [NLI 40,568/230; 4 sheets; envelope 1085].
Stalin, Joseph. *The October Revolution: A Collection of Articles and Speeches*. New York: International Publishers, 1934.

x   [YL 1984]. [NLI missing this copy].
The Star (London), 10 March 1794.

1998. [YL 1985].
Stead, William Force. *Festival in Tuscany and Other Poems*. London: Richard Cobden-Sanderson, 1927.

1999. [YL 1986].
——. *The House on the Wold and Other Poems*. London: Cobden-Sanderson, 1930.

1999a. [YL 1986a].
Another copy.

2000. [YL 1987].
——. *Lyrics*. Oxford: By the author, 1922.

2001. [YL 1988].
——. *The Sweet Miracle and Other Poems*. London: Richard Cobden-Sanderson, 1922.

2002. [YL 1989].
——. *Uriel: A Hymn in Praise of Divine Immanence*. London: Cobden-Sanderson, 1933.

2003.   [*YL* 1990].
———. *Verd antique: Poems*. Oxford: Basil Blackwell, 1920.

2004.   [*YL* 1991].
———. *Wayfaring: Songs and Elegies*. London: Richard Cobden-Sanderson, 1924.

2005.   [*YL* *1992].
Stenbock, Count Stanislaus Eric. *The Shadow of Death: A Collection of Poems, Songs, and Sonnets*. London: Leadenhall Press, 1893.

2006.   [*YL* 1993].
Stendhal. *The Abbess of Castro and Other Tales*. Trans. C. K. Moncrieff. London: Chatto and Windus, 1926.

2007.   [*YL* 1994].
———. *The Charterhouse of Parma*. Trans. C. K. Moncrieff. 2 vols. London: Chatto and Windus, 1926.

2008.   [*YL* 1995].
———. *Scarlet and Black*. Trans. C. K. Moncrieff. 2 vols. London: Chatto and Windus, 1927.

2009.   [*YL* 1996].
Stephen, Leslie. *Swift*. English Men of Letters. London: Macmillan, 1927. Signed: WBY

2010.   [*YL* 1997].
Stephens, James. *Collected Poems*. London: Macmillan, 1931.

2011.   [*YL* *1998].
———. *The Crock of Gold*. London: Macmillan, 1913. Signed: George Hyde-Lees | May 1914

2012.   [*YL* 1999].
———. *Deirdre*. London: Macmillan, 1923.

2013.   [*YL* *2000].
———. *The Demi-Gods*. London: Macmillan, 1914.

2014.   [*YL* 2001].
———. *Etched in Moonlight*. London: Macmillan, 1928.

2015.   [*YL* *2002]. [NLI 40,568/231; 6 sheets; envelope 1762].
———. *The Hill of Vision*. Dublin: Maunsel, 1912.

2016.   [*YL* 2003].
——. *Kings and the Moon*. London: Macmillan, 1938. Signed: GY | 1938

2017.   [*YL* *2004]. [NLI 40,568/232; 2 sheets; envelope 1764].
——. *Reincarnations*. London: Macmillan, 1918.

2017a. [*YL* 2004a].
Another copy.

2018.   [*YL* *2005].
——. *Songs from the Clay*. London: Macmillan, 1915.

2019.   [*YL* 2006].
——. *Strict Joy*. London: Macmillan, 1931.

2020.   [*YL* *2007].
Sterne, Laurence. *The Life and Opinions of Tristram Shandy, Gentleman, and A Sentimental Journey through France and Italy*. 2 vols. London: Macmillan, 1900.

2021.   [*YL* 2008].
Stevens, Wallace. *Owl's Clover*. New York: Alcestis Press, [1936]. Signed: Wallace Stevens

2022.   [*YL* 2009].
Stokes, Margaret. *Early Christian Art in Ireland: Handbook and Guide to the Irish Antiquities Collection in the National Museum of Science and Art, Dublin*. Revised by G[eorge]. N[oble]. Count Plunkett. Dublin: His Majesty's Stationery Office, 1911.

2023.   [*YL* *2010].
Stone, Walter George Boswell. *Shakespeare's Holinshed: The Chronicle and the Historical Plays Compared*. 2nd ed. London: Chatto and Windus, 1907.

2024.   [*YL* 2011].
Story, John, ed. *The Daily Guide, with Simmonite's Prognostications on Revolutions or Solar Figures, Showing the Daily Events Likely to Occur Throughout the Natal Year of Any Person's Horoscope; Also, the Approximate Longitudes of the Planets' Places from 1889 to 1900, with Additions and Emendations....*New ed. London: Foulsham, 1891.

2025. [YL 2012].
Strachey, Lytton. *Elizabeth and Essex*. London: Chatto and Windus, 1928. Signed: Lytton Strachey

2026. [YL 2013].
———. *Queen Victoria*. London: Chatto and Windus, 1921.

2027. [YL 2014].
Strong, Archibald. *Three Studies in Shelley and an Essay on Nature in Wordsworth and Meredith*. London: Oxford University Press, 1921.

2028. [YL 2015].
Strong, Mrs. Arthur [Eugenie (Sellers)]. *Apotheosis and After Life: Three Lectures on Certain Phases of Art and Religion in the Roman Empire*. London: Constable, 1915. Signed: George Hyde-Lees | 1916

2029. [YL 2016].
Strong, L[eonard]. A[lfred]. G[eorge]. *At Glenan Cross: A Sequence*. Christmas 1928. Oxford: Basil Blackwell, 1928.

2030. [YL 2017].
———. *Difficult Love*. Oxford: Basil Blackwell, 1927.

2031. [YL 2018].
———. *Dublin Days*. Oxford: Basil Blackwell, 1921.

2032. [YL 2019].
———. *A Letter to W. B. Yeats*. Hogarth Letters, no. 6. London: Hogarth Press, 1932.

2033. [YL 2020].
———. *The Lowery Road*. Adventures All, n.s., no. 1. Oxford: Basil Blackwell, 1923.

2034. [YL 2021].
———. *The Minstrel Boy: A Portrait of Tom Moore*. London: Hodder and Stoughton, 1937. [Illustrated].

2035. [YL 2022].
———. *Northern Light*. London: Victor Gollancz, 1930.

2036. [YL 2023].
———. *Selected Poems*. London: Hamish Hamilton, 1931.

x [YL 2024]. [NLI missing this copy].
———. *Seven Verses*. Christmas, 1925. [Lacks publication details].

2037. [*YL* 2025].
———. *Twice Four*. Christmas, 1921. [Lacks publication details].

2038. [*YL* 2026].
Strzygowski, Josef. *Origin of Christian Church Art: New Facts and Principles of Research…to Which is Added a Chapter on Christian Art in Britain*. Trans. O. M. Dalton and H. J. Braunholtz. Oxford: Clarendon Press, 1923. [Illustrated]. Bp: WBY

2039. [*YL* 2027].
——— and others. *The Influences of Indian Art*. London: India Society, 1925.

2040. [*YL* 2028].
Stuart, H. [Francis]. *We Have Kept the Faith: Poems*. Dublin: Oak Leaf Press, 1923.

2040a–c. [*YL* 2028a–c].
Three more copies.

2041. [*YL* 2029].
Sturm, Frank Pearce. *Eternal Helen*. Cover and decorations by T. Sturge Moore. Oxford: Basil Blackwell, 1921. [Illustrated].

2042. [*YL* 2030]. [NLI 40,568/233; copy of letter from Sturm to WBY (5 June 1906); 3 sheets; envelope 1372]. [Though reported in *YL*, did not come to NLI with said holograph letter from Sturm].
———. *Umbrae silentes*. London: Theosophical Publishing House, 1918.

2043. [*YL* 2031].
Suckling, Sir John. *The Poems*. Ed. John Gray. Decorated by Charles Ricketts. London: Hacon and Ricketts, 1896. Bp: WBY

2044. [*YL* 2032].
Sutherland, A[lexander]. C[harles]. *Dramatic Elocution and Action*. With appendixes on the influence of mysticism on dramatic expression. London: W. H. and L. Collingridge, 1908.

2045. [*YL* 2033]. [NLI 40,568/234; 21 sheets; envelope 1033].
Suzuki, Daisetz Teitaro. *Essays in Zen Buddhism*. First series. London: Luzac, 1927.

2046.   [*YL* 2034]. [NLI 40,568/235; 10 sheets; envelope 1034].
——. *Zen Buddhism and Its Influence on Japanese Culture*. The Ataka Buddhist Library, no. 9. Kyoto: Eastern Buddhist Society, 1938.

2047.   [*YL* 2035]. [NLI 40,567/9; 4 sheets; Wade 281].
Swami, Shri Purohit. *An Indian Monk: His Life and Adventures*. Intro. by W. B. Yeats. London: Macmillan, 1932.

2047a.   [*YL* 2035a]. [NLI 40,567/10; 2 sheets; Wade 281].
Another copy.

2048.   [*YL* 2036]. [NLI 40,568/236; 43 sheets; envelope 1361]. [See Chapman, *YA* 15 (2002): 288–312].
Swedenborg, Emanuel. *Angelic Wisdom Concerning the Divine Love and Concerning the Divine Wisdom*. Trans. J. J. Garth Wilkinson and Rudolph L. Tafel. London: Swedenborg Society, 1883.

Figure 6. Front cover of 2048. Emanuel Swedenborg, *Angelic Wisdom Concerning the Divine Love and Concerning the Divine Wisdom* (1883)

2049.   [*YL* 2037]. [NLI 40,568/237; 34 sheets; envelope 1364]. [See Chapman, *YA* 15 (2002): 288–312].

——. *Arcana Coelestia: The Heavenly Arcana Contained in the Holy Scripture, or Word of the Lord Unfolded in an Exposition of Genesis and Exodus*. 13 vols. London: Swedenborg Society, 1891. Vol. 1 only (trans. John Clowes).

2050.   [*YL* 2038]. [See Chapman, *YA* 15 (2002): 288–312].

——. *The Delights of Wisdom Relating to Conjugial Love, after Which Follows the Pleasures of Insanity Relating to Scortatory Love*. Trans. A. H. Searle. London: Swedenborg Society, 1891.

2051.   [*YL* 2039]. [NLI 40,568/238; vol. 1: 32 sheets; envelope 1359]. [See Chapman, *YA* 15 (2002): 288–312].

——. *The Principia or the First Principles of Natural Things, to Which Are Added the Minor Principia and Summary of the Principia*. Trans. James R. Rendell and Isaiah Tansley. 2 vols. London: Swedenborg Society, 1912.

2051A.   [*YL* 2039A]. [NLI 40,568/239; vol. 2: 25 sheets; envelope 1359]. [See Chapman, *YA* 15 (2002): 288–312].

——. Vol. 2.

2052.   [*YL* 2040]. [NLI 40,568/240; vol. 1: 17 sheets; envelope 1360]. [See Chapman, *YA* 15 (2002): 288–312].

——. *The Spiritual Diary: Being the Record during Twenty Years of His Supernatural Experience*. Trans. George Bush and Rev. John H. Smithson. 5 vols. London: James Speirs, 1883–1902. Bp: WBY

2052A.   [*YL* 2040A]. [NLI 40,568/241; vol. 2: 17 sheets; envelope 1360]. [See Chapman, *YA* 15 (2002): 288–312].

——. *The Spiritual Diary*. Vol. 2 [continued from above].

2052B.   [*YL* 2040B]. [NLI 40,568/242; vol. 3: 13 sheets; envelope 1360]. [See Chapman, *YA* 15 (2002): 288–312].

——. *Spiritual Diary*. Vol. 3 [continued from above].

2052C.   [*YL* 2040C]. [See Chapman, *YA* 15 (2002): 288–312].

——. *Spiritual Diary*. Vol. 4 [continued from above].

2052D.   [*YL* 2040D]. [NLI 40,568/243; vol. 5: 4 sheets; envelope 1360]. [See Chapman, *YA* 15 (2002): 288–312].

——. *Spiritual Diary*. Vol. 5 [continued from above].

2053.   [*YL* 2041].
Swift, Jonathan. *Gulliver's Travels*. The text of the first ed. edited by Harold Williams. London: First Edition Club, 1926.

2054.   [*YL* 2042].
——. *Gulliver's Travels and Selected Writings in Prose and Verse*. Ed. John Hayward. London: Nonesuch Press, 1934.

2055.   [*YL* 2043].
——. *The Works of the Rev. Dr. Jonathan Swift, Dean of St. Patrick's, Dublin*. Ed. Thomas Sheridan. New ed. 17 vols. London: Printed for W. Strahan, B. Collins and others, 1784. Bp: WBY

2056.   [*YL* *2044].
Swinburne, Algernon Charles. *The Duke of Gandia*. London: Chatto and Windus, 1908.

2057.   [*YL* *2045].
——. *Poems and Ballads*. London: John Camden Hotten, 1871.

2058.   [*YL* *2046].
——. Second series. 4th ed. London: Chatto and Windus, 1884. Signed: Georgie Hyde Lees | October 1910

2059.   [*YL* *2047].
——. *Song of Italy*. London: John Camden Hotten, 1867. Signed: Georgie Hyde Lees | October 5, 1910

2060.   [*YL* *2048].
——. *A Study of Victor Hugo*. London: Chatto and Windus, 1886. Signed: H.T. Tucker | August 1886

2061.   [*YL* *2049].
Symonds, John Addington. *Ben Jonson*. English Worthies. London: Longmans, Green, 1888.

2062.   [*YL* *2050].
——. *A Short History of the Renaissance in Italy*. Ed. Alfred Pearson. London: Smith, Elder, 1893.

2063.   [Not listed in *YL* and assigned NLI number 3046; inserted was note on psychic Anna Louisa Karschen].
Symons, A[lphonse]. J[ames]. A[lbert]. *A Bibliography of the First Editions of Books by William Butler Yeats*. London: The First Edition

Club, 1924. Contains notes. Flyleaf: "George Yeats | June 1924 | Not to be taken away."

2063a. [Not listed in *YL* and assigned NLI number 3046a].
Another copy.

2064.   [*YL* 2051].
——. *The Quest for Corvo: An Experiment in Biography*. London: Cassell, 1934.

2065.   [*YL* *2052].
Symons, Arthur. *Amoris victima*. London: Leonard Smithers, 1897.

2066.   [*YL* *2053].
——. *A Book of Twenty Songs*. London: J. M. Dent, 1905.

2067.   [*YL* *2054].
——. *Cities*. London: J. M. Dent, 1903.

2068.   [*YL* *2055].
——. *The Fool of the World and Other Poems*. London: William Heinemann, 1906.

2069.   [*YL* *2056].
——. *Images of Good and Evil*. London: William Heinemann, 1899.

2070.   [*YL* *2057].
——. *Knave of Hearts: 1894–1908*. London: William Heinemann, 1913.

2071.   [*YL* *2058]. [NLI 40,568/244; 1 sheet; envelope 755].
——. *London: A Book of Aspects*. London: Privately printed for Edmund D. Brooks, 1909.

2072.   [*YL* *2059].
——. *London Nights*. 2nd ed. London: Leonard Smithers, 1897.

2073.   [*YL* *2060].
——. *Plays, Acting, and Music*. London: Duckworth, 1903.

2074.   [*YL* *2061].
——. *Poems*. 2 vols. London: William Heinemann, 1902.

2075.   [*YL* *2062].
——. *The Romantic Movement in English Poetry*. London: Archibald Constable, 1909.

2076.   [YL *2063].
——. *Silhouettes*. London: Elkin Mathews and John Lane, 1892.

2077.   [YL *2064].
——. *Silhouettes*. 2nd ed. London: Leonard Smithers, 1896.

2078.   [YL *2065].
——. *Spiritual Adventures*. London: Archibald Constable, 1905.

2079.   [YL 2066].
——. *Studies in Prose and Verse*. London: J. M. Dent, [1904].

2080.   [YL *2067].
——. *Studies in Two Literatures*. London: Leonard Smithers, 1897.

2081.   [YL *2068].
——. *The Symbolist Movement in Literature*. London: William Heinemann, 1899.

2082.   [YL *2069].
——. *The Toy Cart: A Play in Five Acts*. Dublin and London: Maunsel, 1919.

2083.   [YL *2070].
——. *William Blake*. London: Archibald Constable, 1907.

2084.   [YL *2071].
Synge, John M[illington]. *The Aran Islands*. Illustrated by Jack B. Yeats. Large paper ed. Dublin: Maunsel, 1907. [Illustrated]. Sigs.: J.M. Synge, Jack B. Yeats

2085.   [YL 2072].
——. *The Aran Islands*. Small paper ed. Bp: Lily Yeats.

2086.   [YL *2073]. [NLI 40,568/245; 7 sheets; envelope 1793].
——. *Deirdre of the Sorrows*. Dublin: Maunsel, 1911.

2087.   [YL *2074].
——. *The Playboy of the Western World*. Dublin: Maunsel, 1907.

2087a. [YL 2074a].
Another copy.

2088.   [Not listed in *YL* and assigned NLI number 3047].
——. *Poems and Translations*. New York: Printed for J. Quinn, 1909. [Printed by the Cuala Press?]

2089.   [*YL* *2075]. [NLI 40,567/11; 14 sheets; Wade 262].
——. *The Well of the Saints*. With an introduction by WBY. Plays for an Irish Theatre, vol. 4. London: A. H. Bullen, 1905.

2090.   [Not listed in *YL* and assigned NLI number 3048].
Another copy.

2091.   [*YL* *2076]. [NLI 40,568/246; vol. 2: 16 sheets; envelope 1790].
——. *The Works of John M. Synge*. 4 vols. Dublin: Maunsel, 1910. Bp: WBY

2092.   [*YL* 2077].
Tagore, Rabindranath. *Creative Unity*. London: Macmillan, 1922.

2093.   [*YL* *2078].
——. *The Crescent Moon*. Translated by the author. London: Macmillan, 1913.

2094.   [*YL* 2079].
——. *The Curse at Farewell*. Trans. Edward Thompson. London: George G. Harrap, 1924.

2095.   [*YL* *2080].
——. *The Cycle of Spring*. London: Macmillan, 1917.

2096.   [*YL* *2081].
——. *Fruit-Gathering*. London: Macmillan, 1916.

2097.   [*YL* 2082].
——. *The Fugitive*. London: Macmillan, 1921.

2098.   [*YL* *2083].
——. *The Gardener*. Translated by the author. [Ed. W. B. Yeats and T. Sturge Moore]. London: Macmillan, 1913.

x   [*YL* *2084]. [NLI missing this copy; Wade 263].
——. *Gitanjali (Song Offerings)*. Translated by the author. [Edited and] with an introduction by W. B. Yeats. London: India Society, 1912. Bp: Lady Gregory.

2099.   [*YL* 2084a].
Another copy.

2100.   [YL 2085].
——. *Glimpses of Bengal: Selected from the Letters of Sir Rabindranath Tagore, 1885 to 1895*. London: Macmillan, 1921.

2101.   [YL 2086].
——. *Gora*. London: Macmillan, 1925.

2102.   [YL *2087].
——. *The Home and the World*. Trans. Surendranath Tagore and revised by the author. London: Macmillan, 1919.

2103.   [YL *2088].
——. *The King of the Dark Chamber*. Translated by the author. London: Macmillan, 1914. Signed: GHY | July, 1914

2104.   [YL *2089].
——. *Lover's Gift and Crossing*. London: Macmillan, 1918.

2105.   [YL *2090].
——. *Mashi and Other Stories*. Translated by various writers. London: Macmillan, 1918.

2106.   [YL *2091].
——. *My Reminiscences*. London: Macmillan, 1917.

2107.   [YL *2092].
——. *Nationalism*. London: Macmillan, 1917.

2108.   [YL *2093].
——. *The Parrot's Training*. Translated by the author. Illustrated by Abanindra Nath Tagore. Calcutta and Simla: Thacker, Spink, 1918. [Illustrated].

2109.   [YL *2094].
——. *Personality: Lectures Delivered in America*. London: Macmillan, 1917.

2110.   [YL 2095].
——. "The Philosophy of our People." Reprint from *The Modern Review* (Calcutta). Presidential address at the Indian Philosophical Congress, n.d.

2111.   [YL 2096].

——. *Phalguni (The Cycle of Spring): A Musical Play*. Performed in aid of the distressed at Bankura, Jan. 1916. [Lacks publication details]. Signed: WBY

2112.   [YL *2097]. [Wade 268].

——. *The Post Office*. Trans. Devabrata Mukerjea. Preface by W. B. Yeats. London: Macmillan, 1914.

2113.   [YL *2098].

——. *Sacrifice and Other Plays*. London: Macmillan, 1917.

2114.   [YL *2099]. [NLI 40,568/247; copy of letter from Tagore to WBY (2 Sept. 1912); 2 sheets; envelope 994]. [Though reported in YL, did not come to NLI with said letter of presentation from Tagore].

——. *Sadhana: The Realisation of Life*. London: Macmillan, 1913. Bp: WBY

2115.   [YL *2100].

——. *Stray Birds*. New York: Macmillan, 1916.

2115A.   [YL 2100A].

Another ed. London: Macmillan, 1917.

2116.   [YL 2101].

Taki, Sei-ichi and others. *The Year Book of Japanese Art, 1929–30*. Tokyo: National Committee on Intellectual Cooperation of the League of Nations Association of Japan, 1930. [Illustrated].

[YL *2102; erroneously listed without attributing author, since moved; see Chaucer, Geoffrey].

2117.   [YL 2103].

The Tale of King Florus and the Fair Jehane. Trans. William Morris. Portland, Maine: Thomas B. Mosher, 1898.

2118.   [YL 2104].

Talmage, James. *The Articles of Faith: A Series of Lectures on the Principal Doctrines of The Church of Jesus Christ of Latter-day Saints*. 10th ed. Salt Lake City, Utah: The Deseret News, 1917.

2119.   [YL *2105].

Tantra of the Great Liberation (Mahanirvana tantra). Trans. with commentary by Arthur Avalon. London: Luzac, 1913.

2120.   [*YL* *2106].
Tasso, Torquato. *Godfrey of Bulloigne, or The Recovery of Jerusalem.* Trans. Edward Fairfax. London: Printed for H. Herringman, 1687.

2121.   [*YL* 2107]. [NLI 40,568/248; 6 sheets; envelope 1158].
Taylor, A[lfred]. E[dward]. *A Commentary on Plato's "Timaeus."* Oxford: Clarendon Press, 1928.

2122.   [*YL* 2108].
——. *Philosophical Studies.* London: Macmillan, 1934.

2123.   [*YL* 2109]. [NLI 40,568/249; 6 sheets; envelope 1162].
——. *Plato: The Man and His Work.* London: Methuen, 1926.

2124.   [*YL* 2110].
——. *Platonism and Its Influence.* London: George G. Harrap, [1925].

2125.   [*YL* 2111].
Taylor, G[eorge]. R[obert]. Stirling. *An Historical Guide to London.* London: J. M. Dent, 1911. [Illustrated].

2126.   [*YL* *2112].
Taylor, J[ohn]. F[rancis]. *Owen Roe O'Neill.* London: T. Fisher Unwin, 1896.

2126a.   [*YL* *2112a].
Another copy. [Paper covers].

2127.   [*YL* 2113].
De telegraaf (Amsterdam), 24 August 1929.

2128.   [*YL* 2114]. [NLI 40,567/12; 11 sheets; Wade 252].
The Ten Principal Upanishads. Trans. Shree Purohit Swami and W. B. Yeats. Preface by W. B. Yeats. London: Faber and Faber, 1937.

2128a.   [*YL* 2114a].
Another copy.

2128A.   [*YL* 2114A]. [Wade 253].
Another ed. New York: Macmillan, 1937.

2128Aa.   [*YL* 2114Aa].
Another copy.

2129.   [*YL* 2115]. [NLI 40,568/250/1–2; 2 and 3 sheets; envelope 757]. [See Chapman, *YA* 6 (1988): 234–45].
Tennyson, Alfred. *The Works of Alfred Tennyson*. Cabinet Edition. Vol. 3: *Locksley Hall and Other Poems*. London: Henry S. King, 1874.

2130.   [*YL* 2116].
Teresa of Jesus, St. *The Book of the Foundations…with the Visitation of Nunneries, the Rule and Constitutions*. Trans. David Lewis. New, rev. ed. London: Thomas Baker, 1913.

2131.   [*YL* 2117].
——. *The Interior Castle, or The Mansions*. Trans. the Benedictines of Stanbrook. Revised and annotated by the Very Rev. Prior [Benedict] Zimmerman. 3rd ed. London: Thomas Baker, 1921.

2132.   [*YL* 2118]. [NLI 40,568/251&252; 5 and 4 sheets; envelopes 1353 and 1355].
——. *The Life of St. Teresa of Jesus of the Order of Our Lady of Carmel*. Ed. [Prior] Benedict Zimmerman. Trans. David Lewis. 5th ed. London: Thomas Baker, 1924.

2133.   [*YL* 2119]. [NLI 40,568/253; 7 sheets; envelope 1354].
——. *St Teresa of Jesus of the Order of Our Lady of Carmel: Embracing the Life, Relations, Maxims and Foundations Written by the Saint; Also a History of St. Teresa's Journeys and Foundations, with a Map and Illustrations* Ed. John J. Burke. New York: Columbus Press, 1911. [Illustrated]. Bp: WBY

2134.   [*YL* 2120].
——. *Minor Works of St. Teresa: Conceptions of the Love of God, Exclamations, Maxims and Poems of Saint Teresa of Jesus*. Trans. the Benedictines of Stanbrook. Rev. with notes and intro. by [Prior] Benedict Zimmerman. London: Thomas Baker, 1913.

2135.   [*YL* 2121].
The Theatre of the Greeks. [Ed. John William Donaldson]. 3rd ed. Cambridge: J. and J. J. Deighton etc., 1830. Bp: The Right Honble W. H. Gregory, K.C.M.G. | Coole Park, Gort, Ireland

2136.   [*YL* 2122]. [NLI 40,568/254; 165 sheets; envelope 1022].
The Thirteen Principal Upanishads. Trans. Robert Ernest Hume. With a list of recurrent and parallel passages by George C. O. Haas. London: Oxford University Press, 1931.

2137.   [*YL* *2123].
Thirty Songs from the Panjab and Kashmir. Recorded by Ratan Devi [Mrs. A. K. Coomaraswamy]. Trans. Ananda K. Coomaraswamy. With a foreword by Rabindranath Tagore. London: Old Bourne Press, 1913.

2138.   [*YL* 2124].
Thomas, Dylan. *Twenty-Five Poems*. London: J. M. Dent, 1936.

2139.   [*YL* 2125].
Thomas, G. Bevan. *The Banshee*. [Holograph ms].

2140.   [*YL* 2126].
Thomas, Edward. *Edward Thomas*. The Augustan Books of Modern Poetry. London: Ernest Benn, [1926].

2141.   [*YL* *2127].
Thompson, Francis. *The Collected Poetry of Francis Thompson*. Royal octavo ed. London: Hodder and Stoughton, 1913. [Illustrated]. Bp: WBY

2142.   [*YL* *2128].
——. *New Poems*. Westminster: Archibald Constable, 1897. Signed: John Butler Yeats

2142a.   [*YL* 2128a].
Another copy.

2143.   [*YL* *2129].
——. *Poems*. London: Elkin Mathews and John Lane, 1894.

2144.   [*YL* 2130].
——. *The Poems of Francis Thompson*. [Ed. Wilfrid Meynell]. London: Oxford University Press, 1937.

2145.   [*YL* *2131].
——. *Shelley*. London: Burns and Oates, 1909.

2146.   [*YL* *2132]. [NLI 40,568/255; vols. 1–2: 3 and 4 sheets; envelope 750/1–2].
——. *The Works*. 3 vols. London: Burns and Oates, 1913. Bp: WBY

2146a.   [*YL* 2132a].
Another copy, Vol. 1 only.

2147.   [YL 2133]. [NLI 40,568/256; 10 sheets; envelope 766].
Thoreau, Henry David. *Walden*. With an introductory note by Will H. Dircks. London: Walter Scott, 1886. Signed: WBY | April 2nd 1886

2148.   [YL 2134].
Thorndike, Lynn. *A History of Magic and Experimental Science During the First Thirteen Centuries of Our Era*. 2 vols. London: Macmillan, 1923.

2149.   [YL *2135].
Three Chester Whitsun Plays. With an intro. and notes by Joseph C. Bridge. Chester: Phillipson and Golder, 1906.

2150.   [YL 2136].
The Times (London). "Blackfriars Theatre," 21 Nov. 1921: 5.

2151.   [YL 2137].
———. "Changing Russia | The Bourgeois Proletariat | Capitalism Again," 2 Dec. 1921: [10].

2152.   [YL 2138].
———. "The Globe Theatre," [28 Oct. 1921: 8].

2153.   [YL 2139].
———. "Jewish World Plot | An Exposure | The Source of the Protocols," [16 Aug. 1921]: 9.

2154.   [YL 2140].
———. "The Protocol Forgery | Use in Russian Politics," [16 Aug. 1921]: 9.

x   [YL 2141]. [NLI missing this copy; inserted in YL 1972, also missing].
———. Review of *The Oxford Book of Modern Verse* edited by WBY, 20 Nov. 1936: 10.

2155.   [YL 2142].
———. "Shakespeare and Blackfriars," 17 Nov. 1921: 5.

2156.   [YL 2143].
———. "The Theatre in Japan: III. The Art of the Doll," [18 Dec. 1919]: 10

2157.   [YL 2144].
———. "The Theatre in Japan: IV. The Tokyo Stage," [2 Jan. 1920]: 8.

2158.   [*YL* 2145].
———. *Landscape and Letters*. A series of twenty pictures from *The Times*. [London: Times Publishing, 1933]. 20 plates loose in a folder.

2159.   [*YL* 2146].
The Times Literary Supplement. "Recent Philosophy | The School of Husserl," Recent German Literature Number, 18 Apr. [1929: xv–xvi].

2160.   [*YL* 2147].
———. Review of *Ardours and Endurances* by Robert Nichols, 12 July 1917: 330.

2161.   [*YL* 2148].
———. Review of *Mount Everest* by Sven Hedin, [21 June 1923: 422].

x   [*YL* 2149]. [NLI missing this copy; inserted in *YL* 1972, also missing].
———. Review of *The Oxford Book of Modern Verse* edited by WBY, 21 Nov. 1936: 957.

2162.   [*YL* 2150].
———. Review of *W. B. Yeats: A Critical Study* by Forrest Reid, [30 Sept. 1915: 331].

2163.   [*YL* 2151].
Titis, Placidus de. *Primum mobile: With Theses to the Theory, and Canons for Practice; Wherein Is Demonstrated, from Astronomical and Philosophical Principles, the Nature and Extent of Celestial Influx upon the Mental Faculties and Corporeal Affections of Man; Containing the Most Rational and Best Approved Modes of Direction,…Exemplified in Thirty Remarkable Nativities of the Most Eminent Men in Europe, According to the Principles of the Author, Laid Down in His "Celestial Philosophy."* Trans. with notes by John Cooper. London: Davis and Dickson, [1814 or 1815].

2164.   [*YL* 2152].
To-Day (London) 1 (June 1917).

2165.   [*YL* 2153].
Todhunter, John. *Forest Songs and Other Poems*. London: Kegan Paul, Trench, 1881. Bp: Lily Yeats

2166. [YL 2154].
Toller, Ernst. *Masses and Man: A Fragment of the Social Revolution of the Twentieth Century*. Trans. Vera Mendel. London: Nonesuch Press, 1924.

2167. [YL 2155].
[Toorop, Jan]. *De kruiswegstaties van Jan Toorop in de St. Bernulfuskerk to Oosterbeek*. Hague: Koninklijke Kunstzaal Kleykamp, [1921?].

2168. [Not listed in YL and assigned NLI number 3049].
The Touchstone 6. New York: Mary Fanton Roberts, October 1919. Inscribed on front cover: "To Jack from Lilly, Oct. 1920." [Contains article by J. B. Yeats on WBY on p. 10].

2169. [YL 2156]. [NLI 40,568/257; 28 sheets; envelope 1087].
Towner, R[utherford]. H[amilton]. *The Philosophy of Civilization*. 2 vols. New York and London: G. P. Putnam's, 1923. Sigs.: Oliver St. J. Gogarty

2170. [YL 2157].
Toynbee, Arnold J[oseph]. *A Study of History*. 3 vols. 2nd ed. London: Oxford University Press, 1935.

2171. [YL 2158].
[*Traité sommaire d'astrologie scientifique*]. [189?]. [Lacks publication data]. [Imperfect copy, pp. 113–72 only. Includes "Représentation du ciel de nativité," "Interprétation du ciel de nativité," "Pèriodes d'influences" and "Recueil d'exemples célèbres."].

2172. [YL 2159]. [NLI 40,568/258; 7 sheets; envelope 1410].
Trent, A. G. [Richard Garnett]. *The Soul and the Stars*. Reprinted from *The University Magazine*, March, 1880. Revised and extended by the author. Halifax, Yorkshire: Occult Book Co., 1893.

2172a–b. [YL 2159a–b].
Two more copies, one bound.

2173. [Not in YL]. [NLI 40,579; 2 sheets].
Turner, G. W. "The Cuala Industries." *Lady's Pictorial*, 2 Sept. 1916: 301–302.

2174.   [YL 2160].
Turner, W[alter]. J[ames]. *Blow for Balloons: Being the First Hemisphere of the History of Henry Airbubble.* London: J. M. Dent, 1935.

2175.   [YL 2161].
——. *The Dark Fire.* London: Sidgwick and Jackson, 1918.

2176.   [YL 2162].
——. *The Duchess of Popocatapetl.* London: J. M. Dent, 1939.

2177.   [YL 2163].
——. *Henry Airbubble, or In Search of a Circumference to His Breath: Being the Second Hemisphere of the History of Henry Airbubble.* London: J. M. Dent, 1936. Signed: GY

2178.   [YL 2164].
——. *In Time Like Glass.* London: Sidgwick and Jackson, 1921. Signed: WBY

2179.   [YL 2165].
——. *Jack and Jill.* London: J. M. Dent, 1934. Signed: WBY

2180.   [YL 2166].
——. *Landscape of Cytherea: Record of a Journey into a Strange Country.* London: Chatto and Windus, 1923.

2181.   [YL 2167].
——. *New Poems.* London: Chatto and Windus, 1928.

2182.   [YL 2168].
——. *Paris and Helen.* London: Sidgwick and Jackson, 1921.

2183.   [YL 2169].
——. *Pursuit of Psyche.* London: Wishart, 1931.

2184.   [YL 2170].
——. *The Seven Days of the Sun: A Dramatic Poem.* London: Chatto and Windus, 1925.

2184a.   [YL 2170a].
Another copy.

2185.   [YL 2171].
——. *Songs and Incantations.* London: J. M. Dent, 1936.

2186. [YL 2172].
——. *W. J. Turner*. The Augustan Books of Poetry. London: Ernest Benn, [1926].

2187. [YL *2173].
Tylor, Edward B[urnett]. *Primitive Culture: Researches into the Development of Mythology, Philosophy, Religion, Language, Art and Custom*. 2 vols. London: John Murray, 1873.

2188. [YL *2174].
Tynan, Katharine. *The Flower of Peace: A Collection of Devotional Poetry*. London: Burns and Oates, 1914.

2189. [YL 2175].
——. *A Little Book for John O'Mahony's Friends*. Portland, Maine: Thomas B. Mosher, 1909.

2190. [YL 2176]. [NLI 40,568/259; 26 sheets; envelope 1799].
——. *Poems*. London: Lawrence and Bullen, 1901.

2191. [YL 2177]. [NLI 40,568/260; copy of letter from Katharine Tynan Hinkson to WBY (1 Oct. 1927); 2 sheets; envelope 1797]. [Though reported in *YL*, did not come to NLI with said holograph letter from Hinkson].
——. *Twilight Songs*. Oxford: Basil Blackwell, 1927.

2192. [YL 2178]. [NLI 40,568/261; 82 sheets; envelope 1375].
Tyrrell, G[eorge]. N[ugent]. M[erle]. *Science and Psychical Phenomena*. London: Methuen, 1938.

2193. [YL 2179].
Uddgren, Gustaf. *Strindberg the Man*. Trans. Axel Johan Uppvall. Boston: Four Seas, 1920.

2194. [YL 2180].
Ukiyo-e taikashusei (Ukiyo-e Masters). 18 vols. Tokyo: Taihokaku, 1930–31. Vol. 7: *Buncho Ippitsusai*. [Japanese text].

2195. [YL 2181].
Ulad: A Literary and Critical Magazine (Belfast) 1 (Feb. 1905).

2195a. [YL 2181a].
Another copy. Bp: E.C. Yeats

2196. [YL 2182].
Unamuno, Miguel de. *The Tragic Sense of Life in Men and in Peoples.* Trans. J. E. Crawford Flitch. London: Macmillan, 1921.

2197. [YL 2183].
Ure, P[ercy]. N[eville]. *The Greek Renaissance.* London: Methuen, 1921.

2198. [Not listed in *YL* and assigned NLI number 3050].
[The Vale Press]. [Publicity leaflet]: "The Vale Chelsea SW | The Second Number of the *Dial* will appear early in February 1892." Chelsea [London]: Vale Press, n.d.

2199. [YL 2184].
Valéry, Paul. *Charmes.* Paris: Gallimard, 1926.

2200. [YL 2185].
———. *Eupalinos, ou L'architecte: précédé de l'âme et la danse.* Paris: Gallimard, 1924.

2201. [YL 2186].
———. *Le serpent.* With English translation by Mark Wardle. Intro. by T. S. Eliot. London: Published for the *Criterion* by R. Cobden-Sanderson, 1924.

2202. [YL 2187].
———. *Variété.* Paris: Gallimard, 1924.

2203. [YL 2188].
———. *Variety.* Trans. Malcolm Cowley. New York: Harcourt, Brace, 1927.

2204. [YL *2189].
VanBrugh, John. *Sir John VanBrugh.* Ed. A. E. H. Swaen. The Mermaid Series. London: T. Fisher Unwin, [1896].

2205. [YL 2190].
Vasari, Giorgio. *Lives of Seventy of the Most Eminent Painters, Sculptors and Architects.* Ed. and annotated by E. H. and E. W. Blashfield and A. A. Hopkins. 4 vols. London: George Bell, 1897. Vols. 2, 3, and 4 are signed: E. Reginald Taylor | May 19th 1902

2206.   [YL 2191]. [NLI 40,568/262; 16 sheets; envelope 1229].
Vasiliev, A[leksandr]. V[asil'evich]. *Space, Time, Motion: An Historical Introduction to the General Theory of Relativity*. Trans. H. M. Lucas and C. P. Sanger. Intro. by Bertrand Russell. London: Chatto and Windus, 1924. Bp: WBY

2207.   [YL *2192].
Vaughan, Henry. *The Works*. Ed. Leonard Cyril Martin. 2 vols. Oxford: Clarendon Press, 1914. Bp: WBY

2208.   [YL 2193].
Vaughan, Robert Alfred. *Hours with the Mystics: A Contribution to the History of Religious Opinion*. 2 vols. in one. 7th ed. London: Gibbings, 1895. Bp: WBY

2209.   [YL *2194].
Verhaeren, Émile. *The Dawn (Les aubes)*. Trans. Arthur Symons. London: Duckworth, 1898.

2210.   [YL 2195].
———. *The Plays of Émile Verhaeren: The Dawn; The Cloister; Philip II; Helen of Sparta*. Trans. Arthur Symons, Osman Edwards, F. S. Flint, and Jethro Bithell. London: Constable, 1916.

2211.   [YL 2196].
Verona: La citta di Giulietta. Verona: ENTE Provinciale per il turismo, n.d. [Guidebook].

2212.   [YL 2197].
Vesme, Caesar de. *A History of Spiritualism*. Vol. 1: *Primitive Man*. Trans. Stanley de Brath. London: Rider, 1931.

2213.   [YL *2198].
Vidyapati: Bangiya padabali; Songs of the Love of Radha and Krishna. With illustrations from Indian paintings. Trans. Ananda Coomaraswamy and Arun Sen. London: Old Bourne Press, 1915. [Illustrated].

2214.   [YL *2199].
Vielé-Griffin, Francis. *Sapho*. Paris: Bibliothèque de l'Occident, 1911.

2215.   [YL 2200].
Villiers de l'Isle Adam, Comte. *Axël*. Paris: Maison Quantin, 1890.

2216. [*YL* 2201]. [Wade 275].
———. *Axel*. Trans. H. P. R. Finberg. Preface by W. B. Yeats. Illustrated by T. Sturge Moore. London: Jarrolds, 1925. Signed: H.P.R. Finberg Bp: WBY.

2217. [*YL* 2202].
Virgil. *An English Version of the Eclogues of Virgil*. Trans. Samuel Palmer. Illustrated by Samuel Palmer. London: Seeley, 1883. [Illustrated].

2218. [*YL* 2203].
———. *The Works*. Trans. C. Davidson. New ed., rev. with additional notes by Theodore Alois Buckley. Bohn's Classical Library. London: George Bell, 1875.

2219. [*YL* 2204]. [Though reported in *YL*, did not come to NLI with slip "With the Editor's Compliments"].
Visva-Bharati Quarterly (Calcutta), n.s., 2 (Feb.–April 1937).

2220. [*YL* 2205].
Volpe, Gioacchino. *History of the Fascist Movement*. Roma: Soc. An. Poligrafica Italiana, [1934].

2221. [*YL* 2206].
Voltaire. *La Henriade: Poëme*. Londres: Whittaker, 1835.

2222. [*YL* 2207].
———. *The History of Candide*. Abbey Classics, vol. 7. London: Chapman and Dodd, [1922].

2223. [*YL* 2208].
———. *Le siècle de Louis XIV*. 2 vols. Paris: Garnier Frères, [1922?].

2224. [Not listed in *YL* and assigned NLI number 3051]. [Inserted in front a sheet with titles of books and prices].
Wade, Allan. *A Bibliography of the Writings of William Butler Yeats*. Stratford-on-Avon: The Shakespeare Head Press, 1908.

2225. [Not listed in *YL*]. [NLI 40,577/1–4; copies inserted of the follow poems by W. B. Yeats: (1) "Mourn—And Then Onward!" from *United Ireland* 10 Oct. 1891, 1 sheet TS.; (2–3) "Meditations Upon Death" dated at end "February 4. 1929," 2 sheets TS. carbons; (4)

"Cracked Mary and the Dancers," TS. with MS. corrections and underscorings, 1 sheet].

——. *A Bibliography of the Writings of W. B. Yeats.* London: Rupert Hart-Davis, 1951. [One of two copies].

2226.   [YL *2209].

Wagner, Richard. *Prose Works.* Trans. William Ashton Ellis. Vol. 8: *Posthumous* [etc.]. London: Kegan Paul, Trench, Trubner, 1899.

2227.   [YL *2210].

Waite, Arthur Edward. *Lives of Alchemystical Philosophers.* With a bibliography of alchemy and hermetic philosophy. London: George Redway, [1888]. Bp: WBY

2228.   [YL *2211]. [NLI 40,568/263; 73 sheets; envelope 1382].

——. *The Real History of the Rosicrucians: Founded on Their Own Manifestoes, and on Facts and Documents Collected from the Writings of Initiated Brethren.* London: George Redway, 1887. Bp: WBY

2229.   [YL 2212].

——, ed. *Elfin Music: An Anthology of English Fairy Poetry.* London: Walter Scott, 1888. Signed: WBY | August 4, 1888

2230.   [YL 2213]. [NLI 40,568/264; 41 sheets; envelope 151].

Waite, Herbert T. *Compendium of Natal Astrology and Universal Ephemeris.* London: Kegan Paul, Trench, Trubner, [1917]. Bp: GY

2231.   [YL *2214].

[Wakeman, William Fredrick]. *Wakeman's Handbook of Irish Antiquities.* Ed. John Cooke. 3rd ed. Dublin: Hodges, Figgis, 1903.

2232.   [YL 2215].

Waley, Arthur. *An Introduction to the Study of Chinese Painting.* London: Ernest Benn, 1923. [Illustrated]. Bp: WBY

2233.   [YL 2216].

——. *A Hundred and Seventy Chinese Poems.* London: Constable, 1920.

2234.   [YL 2217].

——. *The Nò Plays of Japan.* With letters by Oswald Sickert. London: George Allen and Unwin, 1921. Bp: WBY

2235. [*YL* 2218].

——, trans. *The Temple and Other Poems*. With an intro. essay on early Chinese poetry, and an appendix on the development of different metrical forms. London: George Allen and Unwin, 1925. Bp: WBY

2236. [*YL* 2219].

[Walker, Sir Emery]. *Sir Emery Walker: Born 2nd April 1851, Died 22nd July 1933*. [Memorial with obituary notices.] [London]: Privately printed, [1933].

2237. [*YL* 2220]. [NLI 40,568/265; 31 sheets; envelope 1193].

Wallace, William. *Prolegomena to the Study of Hegel's Philosophy and Especially of His Logic*. 2nd ed., rev. and augmented. Oxford: Clarendon Press, 1894.

2238. [*YL* 2221].

Walpole, Horace. *The Letters of Horace Walpole, Earl of Orford*. Ed. Peter Cunningham. 9 vols. London: Bickers, 1877. Signed: GY

2239. [*YL* 2222].

Walton, Izaak. *The Lives of Dr. John Donne, Sir Henry Wotton, Mr. Richard Hooker, Mr. George Herbert, and Dr. Robert Sanderson*. New ed. London: Henry Washbourne, 1840. Bp: WBY. Signed: C. Bowles.

2240. [*YL* 2223].

—— and Charles Cotton. *The Compleat Angler*. Ed. Richard Le Gallienne. Illustrated by Edmund H. New. London and New York: John Lane, 1897. [Illustrated].

2241. [*YL* 2224].

Ward, Adolphus William. *Sir Henry Wotton: A Biographical Sketch*. Westminster: Archibald Constable, 1898. Bp: WBY

[*YL* 2225 has been moved to "Acton, Lord [John Emerich Edward Dalberg]"].

2242. [*YL* *2226].

Ward, Richard. *The Life of the Learned and Pious Dr. Henry More, Late Fellow of Christ's College in Cambridge, to Which are Annexed Divers Philosophical Poems and Hymns*. Ed. M. F. Howard. London: Theosophical Publishing Society, 1911.

2243.   [YL 2227]. [NLI 40,568/266; 34 sheets; envelope 1363]. [See Chapman, *YA* 15 (2002): 288–312].
   Warren, Samuel. *A Compendium of the Theological Writings of Emanuel Swedenborg*. London: Swedenborg Society, 1909.

2244.   [YL 2228].
   Webster, John and Cyril Tourneur. *Webster and Tourneur*. [Includes *The White Devil*, *The Duchess of Malfi*, *The Atheist's Tragedy*, *The Revenger's Tragedy*]. The Mermaid Series. [Ed. John Addington Symons]. Unexpurgated ed. London: Vizetelly, 1888. Signed: WBY | Oct. 9, 1888.

2245.   [YL *2229].
   Webster, Nesta H[elen]. *The French Revolution: A Study in Democracy*. London: Constable, 1919. Bp: WBY

2245A.   [YL 2229A].
   ——. *World Revolution: The Plot Against Civilization*. London: Constable, 1921.

2246.   [YL 2230].
   Webster's New International Dictionary of the English Language. Completely rev. General ed. London: G. Bell, 1924.

2247.   [YL *2231].
   Weekes, Charles. *Reflections and Refractions*. London: T. Fisher Unwin, 1893.

x   [YL 2232]. [NLI missing this copy].
   Weekly Sun Literary Supplement (London), 1 Dec. 1895.

2250.   [YL 2233].
   Weichardt, C[arl]. *Le palais de Tibére et autre èdifices romains de Capri*. Traduit par J. A. Simon. Paris: Schleicher Frères, [1902?].

2251.   [YL 2234].
   Weird Tales: Scottish. London and Edinburgh: William Paterson, [1888]. Signed: WBY | Jan. 16, 1889

2252.   [YL 2235]. [NLI 40,568/267; 26 sheets; envelope 794/2].
   Wellesley, Dorothy. *Poems of Ten Years, 1924–1934*. London: Macmillan, 1934.

2252a.   [*YL* 2235a]. [NLI 40,568/268; 51 sheets; envelope 794/3].
Another copy.

2252b.   [*YL* 2235b]. [NLI 40,568/269; 42 sheets; envelope 794/1].
Another copy.

2252c.   [*YL* 2235c]. [NLI 40,568/270; 4 sheets; envelope 794/4].
Another copy.

2253.   [*YL* 2236]. [Wade 283].
——. *Selections from the Poems of Dorothy Wellesley*. [Ed. and] intro. W. B. Yeats. Illustrated by Sir William Rothenstein. London: Macmillan, 1936. [Illustrated].

2253a.   [*YL* 2236a].
Another copy.

2253b.   [*YL* 2236b].
Another copy.

2254.   [*YL* 2237].
——. *Sir George Goldie: Founder of Nigeria; A Memoir*. London: Macmillan, 1934.

2255.   [*YL* 2238].
Wells, Warre B[radley]. *An Irish Apologia: Some Thoughts on Anglo-Irish Relations and the War*. Dublin and London: Maunsel, 1917. Signed: Lily Yeats

2256.   [*YL* *2241].
Wentz, Walter Yeeling Evans. *The Fairy-Faith in Celtic Countries: Its Psychical Origin and nature*. Ph.D. dissertation. Université de Rennes, 1909.

2257.   [Not listed in *YL* and assigned NLI number 3052; inscribed by author to Lady Gregory, 17 Oct. 1909].
Another copy.

2258.   [*YL* 2242]. [NLI 40,568/271; 7 sheets; envelope 1268B].
——. *The Fairy-faith in Celtic Countries*. London: Oxford University Press, 1911. Bp: WBY

2259.   [YL 2243]. [NLI 40,568/272; 35 sheets; envelope 1029A].

——. *The Tibetan Book of the Dead, or The After-Death Experiences on the Bardo Plane, According to Lama Kazi-Samdup's English Rendering.* London: Oxford University Press, 1927.

2260.   [YL *2244].

Weston, Jessie L[aidlay]. *King Arthur and His Knights: A Survey of Arthurian Romance.* Popular Studies in Mythology, Romance and Folklore, no. 4. London: David Nutt, 1899.

2261.   [YL *2245].

——. *The Romance Cycle of Charlemagne.* Popular Studies in Mythology, Romance and Folklore, no. 10. London: David Nutt, 1901.

2262.   [YL *2246].

——. *Wheels: An Anthology of Verse.* [Ed. Edith Sitwell]. Oxford: Basil Blackwell, 1916.

2263.   [YL 2247].

[Whistler, James Abbott McNeill]. *Oils, Water Colors, Pastels, and Drawings: An Exhibition at the Galleries of M. Knoedler, 556 Fifth Ave., Commencing April 2nd, 1914.*

2264.   [YL 2248].

Whistler, Laurence. *The Emperor Heart.* Decorated by Rex Whistler. London: William Heinemann, 1936.

2265.   [YL 2249].

——. *Four Walls.* London: William Heinemann, 1934.

2266.   [YL 2250].

White, Robert. *The Coelestial Atlas, or A New Ephemeris for the Year of Our Lord 1795.* 46th impression. London: Printed for the Company of Stationers, [1795?].

2267.   [YL 2251].
——. 1797.

2268.   [YL 2252].
——. 1798.

2269.   [YL 2253].
——. 1799.

2270.   [*YL* 2254].
——. 1800.

2271.   [*YL* 2255].
——. 1830.

2272.   [*YL* 2256].
——. 1800–11. Bound vol.

2273.   [*YL* 2257].
——. 1812–24. Bound vol.

2274.   [*YL* 2258]. [NLI 40,568/273; 100 sheets; envelope 1229].
Whitehead, Alfred North. *Science and the Modern World*. Lowell Lectures, 1925. Cambridge: University Press, 1926. Signed: WBY

2275.   [*YL* *2259].
Whitman, Walt. *The Book of Heavenly Death*. Compiled from *Leaves of Grass* by Horace Traubel. Portland, Maine: Thomas B. Mosher, 1905.

2276.   [*YL* 2260]. [NLI 40,568/274; 31 sheets; envelope 799].
——. *Poems*. Ed. William Michael Rossetti. London: John Camden Hotten, 1868. Signed: JB Yeats - Nov. 1869

2277.   [*YL* 2261].
——. *Specimen Days in America*. Rev. by the author. Camelot Series. London: Walter Scott, 1887. Signed: WBY | 3 Blenheim Road | Bedford Park

2278.   [*YL* *2262].
Wicksteed, Joseph H[artley]. *Blake's Vision of the Book of Job*. London: J. M. Dent, 1910. [Illustrated].

2279.   [*YL* *2263].
Wiel, Alethea. *The Story of Verona*. Illustrated by Nelly Erichsen and Helen M. James. London: J. M. Dent, 1904. [With illustrations, map].

2280.   [*YL* 2264].
Wijdeveld, H[enricus]. Th[eodorus]. *An International Guild: A Project*. Santpoort, Holland: C. A. Mees, 1931. [Illustrated].

2281.   [*YL* 2265]. [NLI 40,568/275; 54 sheets; envelope 1564].
Wilde, Jane Francesca Speranza, Lady. *Ancient Cures, Charms, and Usages of Ireland: Contributions to Irish Lore*. London: Ward and Downey, 1890.

2282. [*YL* *2266].
——. *Ancient Legends, Mystic Charms, and Superstitions of Ireland.* With a chapter on "The Ancient Race of Ireland" by Sir William Wilde. 2 vols. London: Ward and Downey, 1887–88.

2283. [*YL* 2267].
Wilde, Oscar. *De profundis.* London: Methuen, 1905.

2284. [*YL* 2268].
——. *Intentions.* Leipzig: Heinemann and Balestier, 1891.

2285. [*YL* 2269].
——. *Resurgam: Unpublished Letters.* London: Privately printed by Clement Shorter for distribution among his friends, 1917. Signed: Clement Shorter

2286. [*YL* 2270].
——. *The Rise of Historical Criticism.* Hartford, CT: Privately printed by Sherwood Press, 1905.

2287. [*YL* 2271]. [NLI 40,568/276; 37 sheets; envelope 1801].
——. *Salome: A Tragedy in One Act.* London: John Lane, 1906.

2288. [*YL* 2272].
——. *Sebastian Melmoth.* London: Arthur L. Humphreys, 1904.

2289. [*YL* 2273].
—— and J. A. McNeill Whistler. *Wilde v. Whistler: Being an Acrimonious Correspondence on Art between Oscar Wilde and James A. McNeill Whistler.* London: Privately printed, 1906.

2290. [*YL* 2274].
Wilenski, R[eginald]. H[oward]. *A Miniature History of European Art.* London: Oxford University Press, 1930. [Illustrated]. Signed: WBY

2291. [*YL* 2275].
——. *The Modern Movement in Art.* London: Faber and Gwyer, 1927. Bp: WBY

2292. [*YL* 2276].
Wilhelm, Theodor and Gerhard Graefe. *German Education Today.* 2nd ed. Berlin: Terramare Office, 1937.

2293. [YL 2277].
[Wilhelmson, Carl]. *Carl Wilhelmson: 60 reproduktioner i tontryck efter fotografier af originalen.* [Monograph on the Swedish artist]. Sma Konstböcker, no. 19. Lund: Gleerupska Universitets-Bokhandeln, [1915?]. [Illustrated].

2294. [YL 2278].
W[ilkinson]., J[ames]. J[ohn]. G[arth]. *Improvisations from the Spirit.* London: W. White, 1857. Signed: WBY, Oct. 1916.

2295. [YL 2279].
William Butler Yeats, Aetat. 70. Reprint from *The Irish Times*, 13 June 1935.

2296. [YL 2279a-d].
Four more copies.

2297. [YL 2280].
Williams, Harold. *Dean Swift's Library: With a Facsimile of the Original Sale Catalogue and Some Account of Two Manuscript Lists of His Books.* Cambridge: University Press, 1932.

2298. [YL *2281].
Williams, Rose Sickler and others. *Chinese, Corean, and Japanese Potteries: Descriptive Catalog of a Loan Exhibition at M. Knoedler Galleries, New York, 2-21 March 1914.* New York: Japan Society, 1914. Bp: WBY

2299. [YL 2282].
Wilson, Andrew. *Leaves from a Naturalist's Notebook.* London: Chatto and Windus, 1882. Signed: WBY

2300. [YL 2283].
Wilson, Harriette. *Harriette Wilson's Memoirs of Herself and Others.* London: Peter Davies, 1929.

2301. [YL 2284].
Wilson, James. *A Complete Dictionary of Astrology.* London: William Hughes, 1819. [Illustrated].

2302. [YL 2285].
Wilson, Mona. *The Life of William Blake.* London: Nonesuch Press, 1927.

2303. [*YL* 2286]. [NLI 40,568/277; copy of letter from Wilson to WBY (17 Dec. 1937); 2 sheets; envelope 803A].

Wilson, R[obert]. N[oble]. D[enison]. *The Holy Wells of Orris and Other Poems*. London: John Lane, 1927.

2304. [Not listed in *YL* and assigned NLI number 3053]. [See Chapman, *YA* 8 (1991): 202].

Wilson, Robin. *Equinox*. London: Thomas Nelson & Sons, 1937. [Presentation copy to WBY from Wilson, Christmas 1937, once accompanied by letter].

2305. [*YL* 2239, out of order].

Windingen (Antwerp) No. 1 (1927). [Features photographs of works by Hildo Krop, designer of masks for *The Only Jealousy of Emer*].

2306. [*YL* 2240, out of order].

—— No. 1 (1929)

2307. [*YL* 2287].

Wolfe, Humbert. *Humbert Wolfe*. The Augustan Books of Modern Poetry. First series. London: Ernest Benn, [1926].

2308. [*YL* 2288].

——. *Troy*. Illustrated by Charles Ricketts. The Ariel Poems, no. 12. London: Faber and Gwyer, [1928]. [Illustrated].

2309. [*YL* 2289].

Wollstonecraft, Mary. *Letters to Imlay*. London: C. Kegan Paul, 1879.

2310. [*YL* 2290].

Wood, Charles Erskine Scott. *Circe: A Drama with a Prologue*. Portland, Oregon: By the author, 1919.

2311. [*YL* *2291].

Worcester, John. *Physiological Correspondences*. Boston: Massachusetts New-Church Union, 1895. Bp: WBY

2312. [*YL* *2292]. [NLI 40,568/278/1–5; vols. 1, 2, 5, 6, 7: 4, 6, 3, 12, and 53 sheets; envelope 807].

Wordsworth, William. *The Poetical Works of William Wordsworth*. Ed. Edward Dowden. Aldine Edition of the British Poets. 7 vols. London: George Bell, 1892. Bp: WBY [in all vols.]

2313.   [YL *2293].
——. *The Prelude or Growth of a Poet's Mind*. [Ed. G. C. Moore Smith]. The Temple Classics. London: J. M. Dent, 1896. Signed: WBY | May 1897.

2314.   [YL *2294].
——. *Wordsworth's Guide to the Lakes*. Ed. Ernest De Selincourt. 5th ed. London: Henry Frowde, 1906. Bp: WBY

2315.   [YL 2295].
The Wren Boys. Dublin: Cuala Press, [1920].

2316.   [YL 2296].
Wright, Thomas. *The Life of Daniel Defoe*. London: Cassell, 1894.

2317.   [YL 2297].
——. *The Life of William Blake*. 2 vols. Olney, Buckinghamshire: Thomas Wright, 1929. Bp: WBY

2318.   [YL *2298].
Wycherley, William. *William Wycherley*. Ed. W. C. Ward. The Mermaid Series. London: T. Fisher Unwin, [190?].

2318a.   [YL *2298a].
Another copy.

2319.   [YL 2299].
Wylie, Elinor. *Black Armour: A Book of Poems*. London: Martin Secker, 1927.

2320.   [YL 2300].
——. *Nets to Catch the Wind*. London: Alfred A. Knopf, 1928.

2321.   [YL 2301].
——. *Trivial Breath*. New York and London: Alfred A. Knopf, 1928.

2322.   [YL 2302].
Wynne, Frances. *Whisper!* London: Kegan Paul, Trench, Trubner, 1890.

2323.   [YL 2303].
The Yale Review 27 (Spring 1938). Signed: GY.

2324.   [Not listed in *YL* and assigned NLI number 3054].
The Yale Review 29 (Dec. 1940).

2325. [YL 2304].
Yashiro, Yukio. *Sandro Botticelli*. 3 vols. London and Boston: The Medici Society, 1925.

2326. [YL 2305].
Yeats, Jack B[utler]. *The Amaranthers*. London: William Heinemann, 1936.

2327. [YL 2306].
——. *Apparitions: Three Plays; "Apparitions," "The Old Sea Road," "Rattle."* Illustrated by the author. London: Jonathan Cape, 1933. [Illustrated].

2328. [YL *2307].
——. *Life in the West of Ireland*. Illustrated by the author. Dublin and London: Maunsel, 1912. [Illustrated].

2329. [YL 2308].
——. *Sailing Sailing Swiftly*. London: Putnam, 1933.

2330. [YL 2309].
——. *Sligo*. London: Wishart, 1930.

2330a. [YL 2309a].
Another copy.

2331. [YL 2310].
——. *The Treasure of the Garden*. Illustrated by the author. London: Elkin Mathews, [1902].

2332. [YL 2311].
Yeats, John Butler. *Essays Irish and American*. Dublin: Talbot Press, 1918. Bp: Lily Yeats

x   [YL 2312]. [NLI missing this copy].
——. "On the Stones." *The Manchester Guardian*, 28 Jan. 1905: 7.

x   [YL 2313]. [NLI missing this copy].
[Yeats, Susan Mary]. *The Order for the Burial of the Dead*. London: For W. G. Barratt, n.d.

2333. [YL 2314].
Yeats, W[illiam]. B[utler]. *[At] the Hawk's Well*. [Program]. Concert in aid of the Social Institute's Union, at 8 Chesterfield Gardens, W. By

kind permission of Lord and Lady Islington. Under the patronage of Her Majesty Queen Alexandra. [4 April 1916].

[*YL* 2315–2315e moved to 2470–2470e].

2334.   [*YL* 2316]. [NLI 40,567/14; 34 sheets; Wade 151].
———. *Autobiographies*. London: Macmillan, 1926.

2334a.   [*YL* 2316a]. [NLI 40,567/15; 14 sheets; Wade 151].
Another copy.

2335.   [*YL* 2317]. [Wade 198].
———. *The Autobiography*. New York: Macmillan, 1938.

2336.   [Not listed in *YL* and assigned NLI number 3055].
———. *Blæsten Mellem Sivene. Digte og Skuespil af W. B. Yeats*. Copenhagen: P. Haase & Sons Forlag, 1924.

2337.   [*YL* 2318]. [Wade 62].
———. *Cathleen Ni Houlihan*. London: A. H. Bullen, 1906.

2338.   [*YL* 2319]. [Wade 63].
———. *Cathleen Ni Houlihan*. London: Bullen, 1909.

x   [*YL* 2319a–b]. [NLI missing both copies].
Two more copies.

2339.   [*YL* 2320]. [NLI 40,567/16; 4 sheets; Wade 8].
———. *The Celtic Twilight*. London: Lawrence Bullen, 1893.

2339a.   [*YL* 2320a].
Another copy. Signed: "WBY."

2339b.   [*YL* 2320b].
Another copy. Signed: "WBY, 5 May 1925."

2339c.   [*YL* 2320c].
Another copy. Bp: Lily Yeats.

2340.   [Not listed in *YL* and assigned NLI number 3056; Wade 38].
———. *The Celtic Twilight*. London: A. H. Bullen, 1902. Signed: "George Hyde Lee. 1913."

2341.   [*YL* 2322]. [Wade 38].
———. *The Celtic Twilight*. London: A. H. Bullen, 1912 printing. Bp: GY. Signed: GY, Oct. 1913

2342.   [*YL* 2321]. [Wade 37].
———. *The Celtic Twilight*. Dublin: Maunsel, 1905.

2343.   [*YL* 2324, out of order]. [NLI 40,567/17; 2 sheets; Wade 177].
———. *The Collected Plays*. London: Macmillan, 1934.

2343a. [Not listed in *YL* and assigned NLI number 3057; inserted slip: "177 c.2 at pp. 24–25].
Another copy.

2343A.   [*YL* 2324A]. [Wade 178].
Another ed. New York: Macmillan, 1935. Signed: GY

2344.   [*YL* 2323, out of order]. [NLI 40,567/18; 127 sheets; Wade 172]. [Blue slip of paper inserted bearing notes]. [See Chapman, *YA* 9 (1992): 271–94].
———. *The Collected Poems*. London: Macmillan, 1933.

2344a.   [*YL* 2323a].
Another copy.

2344b.   [*YL* 2323b]. [NLI 40,567/19; 12 sheets; Wade 172]. [Fragment of a newspaper column inserted about Yeats's poetry].
Another copy. 1937 printing.

x   [*YL* 2323c]. [NLI 40,567/20; 11 sheets; Wade 211]. [NLI missing this copy].
Another copy. 1950 printing.

2344A.   [*YL* 2323A]. [Wade 171].
———. *The Collected Poems*. New York: Macmillan, 1933.

2345.   [*YL* 2325]. [NLI 40,567/21; 29 sheets; Wade 75]. [Though reported in *YL*, did not come to NLI with two unsigned drafts of a letter to T. Fisher Unwin, Oct. 14, 190(?)].
———. *Collected Works in Verse and Prose*. Vol. 1: *Poems Lyrical and Narrative*. Stratford: Shakespeare Head Press, 1908. Signed: GY.

2346.   [*YL* 2326]. [NLI 40,567/22; 34 sheets; Wade 76].
———. Vol. 2: *The King's Threshold, On Baile's Strand, Deirdre, Shadowy Waters*. Stratford: Shakespeare Head Press, 1908.

2346A.   [YL 2326A].

———. *The King's Threshold and Stories of Red Hanrahan.* [pp. 1–68 of Wade 76, vol. 2 of *The Collected Works* and pp. 195–262 of Wade 79, vol. 5 of *The Collected Works*. Uniquely bound together in one volume, in blue covers, quarter cloth.] Hand-lettered on spine by WBY, in ink: "Kings Threshold"

2347.   [YL 2327]. [NLI 40,567/23; 11 sheets; Wade 77].

———. Vol. 3: *The Countess Cathleen, The Land of Heart's Desire, The Unicorn from the Stars.* Stratford: Shakespeare Head Press, 1908. Bp: WBY.

2348.   [YL 2328]. [NLI 40,567/24; 10 sheets; Wade 78].

———. Vol. 4: *The Hour-Glass, Cathleen Ni Houlihan, The Golden Helmet, The Irish Dramatic Movement.* Stratford: Shakespeare Head Press, 1908.

2349.   [YL 2329]. [Wade 79].

———. Vol. 5: *The Celtic Twilight and the Stories of Red Hanrahan.* Stratford: Shakespeare Head Press, 1908.

2350.   [YL 2330]. [NLI 40,567/25; 7 sheets; Wade 80]. [Though reported in *YL*, did not come to NLI with holograph letter from Robert Bridges to WBY, 15 June 1897].

———. Vol. 6: *Ideas of Good and Evil.* Stratford: Shakespeare Head Press, 1908.

2351.   [YL 2331]. [Wade 81].

———. Vol. 7: *The Secret Rose. Rosa Alchemica. The Tables of the Law. The Adoration of the Magi. John Sherman and Dhoya.* Stratford: Shakespeare Head Press, 1908.

2352.   [YL 2332]. [NLI 40,567/26; 5 sheets; Wade 82].

———. Vol. 8: *Discoveries. Edmund Spenser. Poetry and Tradition. And Other Essays.* Stratford: Shakespeare Head Press, 1908.

2353.   [YL 2333]. [NLI 40,567/27; 37 sheets; Wade 27]. [See Chapman, *YA* 9 (1992): 271–94].

———. *The Countess Cathleen.* [Lacks publication details]. [Cover missing].

2354.   [YL 2334]. [NLI 40,567/28; 28 sheets; Wade 93].

———. *The Countess Cathleen.* London: T. Fisher Unwin, 1912.

2354a.   [*YL* 2334a].
Another copy. Signed: Lily Yeats

2354b.   [*YL* 2334b].
Another copy.

2354c.   [*YL* 2334c].
Another printing. 9th ed., 1916.

2354d.   [*YL* 2334d].
Another printing. 13th ed., 1922.

2355.   [*YL* 2335]. [Wade 95].
———. *The Countess Cathleen* [and *The Land of Heart's Desire*]. London: T. Fisher Unwin, 1924.

2355a.   [*YL* 2335a].
Another printing, 1925.

2355b.   [*YL* 2335b].
Another printing, 1929. Benn's Essex Library, No. 12.

2356.   [Not listed in *YL* and assigned NLI number 3058; bought by GY from Tom Kelley's bookshop, 1940; Wade 6].
———. *The Countess Kathleen and Various Legends and Lyrics*. London: F. Fisher Unwin, 1892. Flyleaf: "L. M. R. 6th Oct. 1892."

2357.   [*YL* 2336]. [NLI 40,567/29; 15 sheets; Wade 102].
———. *The Cutting of an Agate*. New York: Macmillan, 1912. Bp: WBY.

2358.   [*YL* 2337]. [Wade 126].
———. *The Cutting of an Agate*. London: Macmillan, 1919.

2358a.   [*YL* 2337a].
Another copy.

2359.   [*YL* 2338]. [NLI 40,567/30; 23 sheets; Wade 69].
———. *Deirdre*. London: A. H. Bullen, 1907.

2360.   [*YL* 2339]. [Wade 70].
———. *Alterations in "Deirdre."* [1908].

2361.   [*YL* 2340]. [NLI 40,567/31; 8 sheets; Wade 86].
———. *Deirdre*. Stratford: Shakespeare Head Press, 1911.

x   [*YL* 2340a]. [NLI missing this copy].
Another copy.

x   [*YL* 2340b]. [NLI missing this copy].
Another copy.

2362.   [*YL* 2341]. [Wade 186].
——. *Dramatis Personae 1896–1902. Estrangement. The Death of Synge. The Bounty of Sweden.* New York: Macmillan, 1936.

x   [*YL* 2341a]. [NLI missing this copy].
Another copy.

2363.   [*YL* 2342]. [Though reported in *YL*, did not come to NLI with loose bookplate with design by T. Sturge Moore with inscription; Wade 187].
——. *Dramatis Personae 1896–1902. Estrangement. The Death of Synge. The Bounty of Sweden.* London: Macmillan, 1936.

x   [*YL* 2342a]. [NLI missing this copy].
Another copy.

2364.   [*YL* 2343]. [NLI 40,567/32; 6 sheets; Wade 148].
——. *Early Poems and Stories.* London: Macmillan, 1925.

2365.   [*YL* 2344]. [NLI 40,567/33; 16 sheets; Wade 148].
——. *Early Poems and Stories.* New York: Macmillan, 1925.

2365a.   [*YL* 2344a]. [NLI 40,567/34; 5 sheets; Wade 148].
Another copy. Limited ed. in brown paper boards. Signed: WBY

2366.   [*YL* 2345]. [Wade 114].
——. *Eight Poems.* Transcribed by Edward Pay. London: Published by "Form" at the Morland Press, 1916.

2366a.   [*YL* 2345a].
Another copy. Signed: Lily Yeats, June 1916

2366b.   [*YL* 2345b].
Another copy.

x   [*YL* 2345c]. [NLI missing this copy].
Another copy.

2367.   [*YL* 2346]. [Wade, p. 373].
——. *Enhörningen Från Stjärnorna Drottningen* [*The Unicorn from the Stars* and *The Player Queen*]. Stockholm: P. A. Norstedt, 1924.

246   YEATS SHORT-TITLE CATALOG

2368.   [*YL* 2347]. [NLI 40,567/35; 37 sheets; Wade 141].
——. *Essays*. London: Macmillan, 1924.

2368a. [Not listed in *YL* and assigned NLI number 3061]. Another copy.

2369.   [*YL* 2348]. [NLI 40,567/36; 44 sheets; Wade 142].
——. *Essays*. New York: Macmillan, 1924.

2370.   [*YL* 2349]. [NLI 40,567/37; 6 sheets; Wade 129]. [Letter inserted from Noel Mac Mahon to GY, 2 Jan. 1956].
——. *Four Plays for Dancers*. London: Macmillan, 1921.

2371.   [*YL* 2350]. [NLI 40,567/38; 7 sheets; Wade 130].
——. *Four Plays for Dancers*. New York: Macmillan, 1921.

Figure 7. Front cover of 2371. W. B. Yeats, *Four Plays for Dancers* (1921; Wade 130)

2372.   [*YL* 2351]. [NLI 40,567/39; 8 sheets; Wade 182].
——. *A Full Moon in March*. London: Macmillan, 1935.

2373.   [*YL* 2352]. [Wade 74].
——. *The Golden Helmet*. New York: John Quinn, 1908.

2373a. [*YL* 2352a]. [NLI 40,567/40; 11 sheets; Wade 74].
Another copy.

2373b. [*YL* 2352b].
Another copy.

2374.   [*YL* 2353]. [Wade, p. 374].
——. *Gräfin Cathleen* [*The Countess Cathleen*]. Hellebrau: Jakob Hegner, 1925.

2375.   [Not listed in *YL*, nor in Wade, and assigned NLI number 3059].
——. *Die Gräfin Katlin* [*The Countess Cathleen*]. Frankfurt: S. Fischer, n.d.

2376.   [*YL* 2354]. [Wade 89].
——. *The Green Helmet*. Stratford: Shakespeare Head Press, 1911.

2376a. [*YL* 2354a].
Another copy.

x   [*YL* 2354b]. [NLI missing this copy].
Another copy.

x   [*YL* 2354c]. [NLI missing this copy].
Another copy.

2377.   [*YL* 2355]. [Wade 101].
——. *The Green Helmet and Other Poems*. New York and London: Macmillan, 1912.

2377a. [*YL* 2355a].
Another copy.

x   [*YL* 2355b]. [NLI missing this copy].
Another copy.

2378.   [*YL* 2356]. [Wade, p. 371].
——. *Grevinnan Cathleen* [*The Countess Cathleen*]. Trans. Teresia Euren. Stockholm: Thure Wahledows Förlag, 1923.

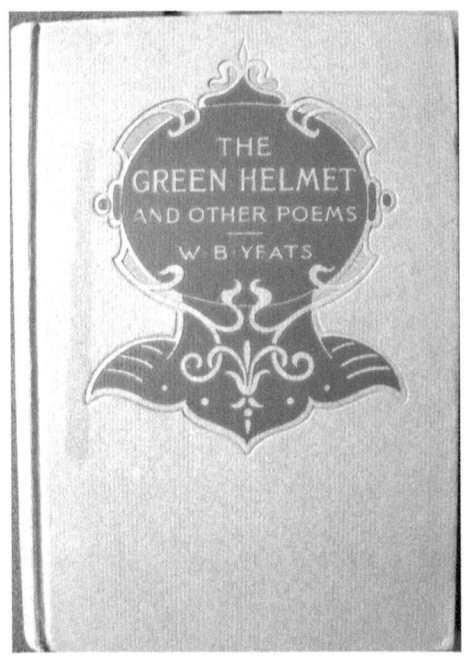

Figure 8. Front cover of 2377. W. B. Yeats, *The Green Helmet and Other Poems* (1912; Wade 101)

2379.   [*YL* 2357]. [NLI 40,567/41; 10 sheets; Wade 195].
——. *The Herne's Egg*. London: Macmillan, 1938.

2380.   [*YL* 2358]. [Wade 196].
——. *The Herne's Egg and Other Plays*. New York: Macmillan, 1938.

2380a.   [*YL* 2358a].
Another copy.

2380b.   [*YL* 2358b].
Another copy.

2381.   [*YL* 2359]. [Wade 51].
——. *The Hour-Glass*. London: William Heinemann, 1903.

2382.   [*YL* 2360]. [NLI 40,567/42; 3 sheets; Wade 52].
——. *The Hour-Glass*. New York: Macmillan, 1904.

2382a.   [*YL* 2360a].
Another copy. 1906 printing. Bp: Eliz. C. Yeats

2383.   [*YL* 2361]. [NLI 40,567/44; 7 sheets; Wade 67].
———. *The Hour-Glass*. London: A. H. Bullen, 1907.

2383a.   [*YL* 2361a].
Another copy.

2383b.   [*YL* 2361b].
Another copy.

2383c.   [*YL* 2361c].
Another copy.

x   [*YL* 2361d]. [NLI missing this copy].
Another copy.

x   [*YL* 2361e]. [NLI missing this copy].
Another copy.

x   [*YL* 2361f]. [NLI missing this copy].
Another copy.

2384.   [*YL* 2362]. [NLI 40,567/45; 27 sheets; Wade 53].
———. *The Hour-Glass. Cathleen Ni Houlihan. The Pot of Broth.* London: A. H. Bullen, 1904.

2384a.   [*YL* 2362a].
Another copy. Bp: Lily Yeats

x   [*YL* 2362b]. [NLI missing this copy].
Another copy.

2385.   [*YL* 2363]. [NLI 40,567/46; 8 sheets; Wade 54].
———. *The Hour-Glass. Cathleen Ni Houlihan. The Pot of Broth.* Dublin: Maunsel, 1905.

2386.   [*YL* 2364]. [Wade, p. 375].
———. *Hraběnka Cathleenová (1892–1912)* [*The Countess Cathleen*]. Vprazle: Nová Bibliotéka, 1929.

2387.   [Not listed in *YL* and assigned NLI number 3061].
Another copy.

2388.   [*YL* 2365]. [Wade 46].
———. *Ideas of Good and Evil*. London: A. H. Bullen, 1903.

2388a.   [*YL* 2365a].
Another copy. 2nd ed. Signed: WBY

x   [*YL* 2365b]. [NLI missing this copy].
Another copy. 2nd ed.

2389.   [*YL* 2366]. [Wade 47].
——. *Ideas of Good and Evil.* New York: Macmillan, 1903. Bp: Elizabeth Corbet Yeats. Signed: Mrs. Whidden Grahame

2390.   [*YL* 2367]. [Wade 48].
——. *Ideas of Good and Evil.* Dublin: Maunsel, 1905.

2391.   [*YL* 2368]. [Wade 50].
——. *In the Seven Woods.* New York: Macmillan, 1903.

2391a.   [*YL* 2368a].
Another copy.

2392.   [*YL* 2369]. [Wade 181].
——. *The Irish National Theatre.* Roma: Reale Accademia d'Italia, 1935.

x   [*YL* 2369a]. [NLI missing this copy].
Another copy.

x   [*YL* 2369b]. [NLI missing this copy].
Another copy.

x   [*YL* 2369c]. [NLI missing this copy].
Another copy.

x   [*YL* 2369d]. [NLI missing this copy].
Another copy.

2392a.   [*YL* 2369e].
Another copy, but format not described in Wade: Reale Accademia d'Italia | Classe Delle Lettere [long rule] | IV Convegno "Volta"—Tema: Il Teatro | Roma 8–14 Ottobre 1934—XII [short rule] | Relazioni [short rule] William Butler Yeats | *The Irish National Theatre* | Roma | Reale Accademia.

2393.   [*YL* 2370]. [NLI 40,567/47; 16 sheets; Wade 33].
——. *Is the Order of R. R. and A. C. to Remain a Magical Order?* N.p.: n.p., 1901.

2393a.   [*YL* 2370a].
Another copy.

x   [*YL* 2370b]. [NLI missing this copy].
Another copy.

2394.   [*YL* 2371]. [Wade 4].
——. *John Sherman and Dhoya*. 2nd ed. London: T. Fisher Unwin, 1891. Bp: Eliz. C. Yeats.

2395.   [*YL* 2372]. [Wade 179A].
——. *The King of the Great Clock Tower*. New York: Macmillan, 1935.

2396.   [*YL* 2373]. [Wade 90].
——. *The King's Threshold*. Stratford: Shakespeare Head Press, 1911.

2397.   [*YL* 2374]. [Wade 189].
——. *The King's Threshold*. London: Macmillan, 1937.

2397a.   [*YL* 2374a].
Another copy.

2397b.   [*YL* 2374b].
Another copy.

2397c.   [*YL* 2374c].
Another copy.

x   [*YL* 2374d]. [NLI missing this copy].
Another copy.

x   [*YL* 2374e]. [NLI missing this copy].
Another copy.

2398.   [Not listed in *YL* and assigned NLI number 3060; at pp. 84–85 a typed page has been inserted].
——. *Die Komödiantenkönigin* [*The Player Queen*]. Frankfurt: S. Fischer, 1922.

2399.   [*YL* 2375]. [Wade 143].
——. *The Lake Isle of Innisfree*. San Francisco: John Henry Nash, 1924.

x   [*YL* 2375a]. [NLI missing this copy].
Another copy.

x   [*YL* 2375b]. [NLI missing this copy].
Another copy.

x   [*YL* 2375c]. [NLI missing this copy].
   Another copy.

x   [*YL* 2375d]. [NLI missing this copy].
   Another copy.

x   [*YL* 2375e]. [NLI missing this copy].
   Another copy.

2400.   [*YL* 2376]. [Wade 11].
   ——. *The Land of Heart's Desire.* Chicago: Stone and Kimball, 1894.

2401.   [*YL* 2377]. [Wade 13].
   ——. *The Land of Heart's Desire.* Portland, Maine: Thomas Mosher, 1903.

2401a.   [*YL* 2377a].
   Another copy.

x   [*YL* 2377b]. [NLI missing this copy].
   Another copy.

x   [*YL* 2377c]. [NLI missing this copy].
   Another copy. 10th ed. March 1912.

2402.   [*YL* 2378]. [Wade 10].
   ——. *The Land of Heart's Desire.* London: T. Fisher Unwin, 1904.

2403.   [*YL* 2379]. [Wade 14].
   ——. *The Land of Heart's Desire.* New York: Dodd, Mead, 1909. Signed: WB Yeats | May 5 | 1925

2404.   [*YL* 2380]. [Wade 94].
   ——. *The Land of Heart's Desire.* 7th ed. London: T. Fisher Unwin, 1912.

2404a.   [*YL* 2380a].
   Another copy.

2404b.   [*YL* 2380b].
   Another copy. 10th impression, 1916.

x   [*YL* 2380c]. [NLI missing this copy].
   Another copy. 11th impression, 1919.

2404c.   [*YL* 2380d].
   Another copy. 23rd impression, 1925.

2405.   [*YL* 2381]. [NLI 40,567/48; 44 sheets; Wade 203].
———. *Last Poems*. London: Macmillan, 1940.

2405a.   [*YL* 2381a]. [NLI 40,567/49; 39 sheets; Wade 203].
Another copy. Bp: GY

2405b.   [*YL* 2381b]. [NLI 40,567/50; 8 sheets; Wade 203].
Another copy.

2405c.   [*YL* 2381c]. [NLI 40,567/51; 12 sheets; Wade 203].
Another copy. Bp: GY

2405d.   [*YL* 2381d]. [NLI 40,567/52; 6 sheets].
Another copy. Bp: Lily Yeats

2406.   [*YL* 2382]. [NLI 40,567/53; 15 sheets; Wade 134/1].
———. *Later Poems*. London: Macmillan, 1922.

2406a.   [*YL* 2382a].
Another copy.

2406b.   [*YL* 2382b]. [NLI 40,567/54; 44 sheets; Wade 134/2].
Another copy. Dec. 1922 reprinting.

2406c.   [*YL* 2382c].
Another copy. 1922 printing.

2406d.   [*YL* 2382d].
Another copy. March 1926 reprinting; in dustjacket.

2407.   [*YL* 2383]. [NLI 40,567/55; 40 sheets; Wade 135].
———. *Later Poems*. New York: Macmillan, 1924.

2407a.   [*YL* 2383a].
Another copy. Signed: WBY

2408.   [Not listed in *YL*]. [NLI 40,567/56; 8 sheets; Wade 325].
———. *Letters on Poetry from W. B. Yeats to Dorothy Wellesley*. Intro. Kathleen Raine. London and New York: Oxford University Press, 1964.

2409.   [*YL* 2384]. [Wade 173].
———. *Letters to the New Island*. Cambridge: Harvard University Press, 1934.

2410.   [Not listed in *YL* but assigned NLI number 4057; Wade 127]. [NLI 40,597; inserted notes for a collected edition of poems by WBY; 7 sheets; sheets 1–7 are numbered; printed slips pasted to sheets

1–6; MS revisions by WBY; holograph text on sheet 7 is signed "WBY" and dated "March 1921"]. [See Chapman, *YA* 6 (1988): 239–45, as this book and inserted notes, with copies of *Poems: Second Series*, *Responsibilities* (rev. 1917), and *The Wild Swans at Coole* made up copy text for *Later Poems* (1922), Wade 134].

———. *Michael Robartes and the Dancer*. Dundrum: The Cuala Press, 1920.

2411.   [*YL* 2385]. [Wade 188].
———. *Modern Poetry*. Broadcast National Lectures, no. 18 [delivered 11 Oct. 1936]. London: BBC, 1936.

2412.   [*YL* 2386]. [Wade 190].
———. *Nine One-Act Plays*. London: Macmillan, 1937.

2413.   [*YL* 2387]. [Wade 109].
———. *Nine Poems*. [New York:] Privately printed for John Quinn and his friends, 1914.

2414.   [*YL* 2388]. [Wade 122].
———. *Nine Poems*. London: Privately printed by Clement Shorter, 1918.

2415.   [*YL* 2389]. [NLI 40,567/57; 6 sheets; Wade 58].
———. *On Baile's Strand*. Dublin: Maunsel, 1905. Bp: Eliz. C. Yeats.

2416.   [*YL* 2390]. [Wade 68].
———. *On Baile's Strand*. London: A. H. Bullen, 1907. Signed: WBY.

x   [*YL* 2390a–f]. [NLI missing four copies].
Six more copies.

2417.   [*YL* 2391]. [Wade 202].
———. *On the Boiler*. Dublin: Cuala Press, 1939.

x   [*YL* 2391a–c]. [NLI missing two copies].
Three more copies.

2418.   [*YL* 2392]. [NLI 40,567/58; 7 sheets; Wade 120].
———. *Per amica silentia lunae*. London: Macmillan, 1918.

2418a.   [*YL* 2392a].
Another copy.

2418b.   [*YL* 2392b].
Another copy.

x   [*YL* 2392c–d]. [NLI missing one copy].
Two more copies.

2419.   [*YL* 2393]. [Wade 121].
——. *Per amica silentia lunae*. New York: Macmillan, 1918.

x   [*YL* 2393a–c]. [NLI missing two copies].
Three more copies.

2420.   [*YL* 2394]. [Wade 138].
——. *The Player Queen*. London: Macmillan, 1922.

2420a.   [*YL* 2394a].
Another copy.

2421.   [*YL* 2395]. [Wade 139].
——. *Plays and Controversies*. London: Macmillan, 1923.

2422.   [*YL* 2396]. [NLI 40,567/59; 17 sheets; Wade 140].
——. *Plays and Controversies*. New York: Macmillan, 1924.

2422a.   [*YL* 2396a].
Another copy.

2423.   [*YL* 2397]. [Wade 92].
——. *Plays for an Irish Theatre*. London and Stratford: A. H. Bullen, 1911.

2423a.   [*YL* 2397a]. [NLI 40,567/60; 45 sheets; Wade 92].
Another printing, 1913.

2423b.   [*YL* 2397b].
Another copy, 1913 printing. Signed: GHY, 1914

2424.   [*YL* 2398]. [Wade 136].
——. *Plays in Prose and Verse*. London: Macmillan, 1922.

2424a.   [*YL* 2398a].
Another copy.

x   [*YL* 2398b]. [NLI missing this copy].
Another copy. Dec. 1922 printing.

2425.   [*YL* 2399]. [Wade 137].
——. *Plays in Prose and Verse*. New York: Macmillan, [April] 1924.

2425a.   [*YL* 2399a].
Another, but of limited ed. of March 1924. Signed: WBY

2426.   [*YL* 2400]. [Wade 64].
——. *Poems, 1899–1905*. London: A. H. Bullen, 1906. Bp: Lily Yeats.

2426a.   [Not listed in *YL* and assigned NLI number 3065].
Another copy. Flyleaf: Bought by George Yeats | 1940.

2426b.   [Not listed in *YL*, but noted by NLI as an exact duplicate of 2427, above, yet not the same as 2427a].
Another copy.

2427.   [*YL* 2401]. [NLI 40,567/61; 37 sheets; Wade 83]. [See Chapman, *YA* 6 (1988): 234–45].
——. *Poems: Second Series*. London: A. H. Bullen, 1909.

2428.   [Not listed in *YL* and assigned NLI number 3063; bought by GY in Aug. 1939; many lines numbered in pencil by her].
——. *Poems*. London: T. Fisher Unwin, 1895. Flyleaf: From M. L. H. P. | Aug. 28, 1897.

2429.   [Not listed in *YL* and assigned NLI number 3064; Wade 18]. [See Chapman, *YA* 8 (1991): 202, noting, too, that the book was also signed "O. S." for Olivia Shakespear; a copy given GY by her mother].
——. *Poems*. London: T. Fisher Unwin, 1901. 3rd English edition, revised. Flyleaf: Nelly Hyde Lees | July 1902.

2430.   [*YL* 2402]. [NLI 40,567/62; 8 sheets; Wade 99].
——. *Poems*. London: T. Fisher Unwin, 1912.

2430a.   [*YL* 2402a].
Another copy.

2431.   [*YL* 2403]. [Wade 100].
——. *Poems*. London: T. Fisher Unwin, 1922. Signed: M Davies Webster.

2431a.   [*YL* 2403a]. [NLI 40,567/63; 28 sheets; Wade 100].
Another printing, 1923.

2432.   [Not listed in *YL* and assigned NLI number 3066]. [See Chapman, *YA* 8 (1991): 202].
Another printing, 1924. Flyleaf signed by WBY and dated "June 27 | 1925."

2433.   [*YL* 2404]. [Wade 154].
——. *Poems*. London: Ernest Benn, [1929].

2434.   [Not listed in *YL* and assigned NLI number 3067; Wade 184].
——. *Poems by William Butler Yeats*. Dublin: The Cuala Press, 1935. On back flyleaf: Poems by William Butler Yeats; Thirty copies printed privately for Eleanor Lady Yarrow, by The Cuala Press, 133 Lower Baggot Street, Dublin, Ireland.

2435.   [Not listed in *YL* and assigned NLI number 3068. Wade 209 (vol. 1) and Wade 210 (vol. 2)].
——. *The Poems of W. B. Yeats*. 2 vols. London: Macmillan, 1949. Flyleaf of vol. 1: This is No. 352 of an Edition limited to 375 copies, signed by the Author, of which 350 are for sale. Signed: W. B. Yeats. [In slipcase].

2436.   [*YL* 2405]. [Wade 107].
——. *Poems Written in Discouragement, 1912–1913*. Dundrum: Cuala Press, 1913.

2437.   [*YL* 2406]. [Wade 65].
——. *The Poetical Works of William B. Yeats*. Vol. 1: *Lyrical Poems*. London: Macmillan, 1906. Bp: Lily Yeats

2438.   [*YL* 2407]. [Though reported in *YL*, did not come to NLI with 4 loose pages promoting novels by a number of writers; Wade 71].
——. Vol. 2: *Dramatical Poems*. New York: Macmillan, 1907. Bp: Lily Yeats. Signed: Lily Yeats

2438a.   [*YL* 2407a].
Another copy. Bp: Lily Yeats. Signed: Lily Yeats

2439.   [*YL* 2408]. [Wade 98].
——. *The Poetical Works of William B. Yeats*. Rev. ed. Vol. 2: *Dramatic Poems*. New York: Macmillan, 1914. Bp: WBY

2440.   [*YL* 2409]. [Wade 60].
——. *The Pot of Broth*. London: A. H. Bullen, 1905.

2441.   [*YL* 2410]. [Wade 61].
——. *The Pot of Broth*. 2nd theatre ed. London: A. H. Bullen, 1911.

x   [*YL* 2410a–f]. [NLI missing four copies].
Six more copies.

2442.   [*YL* 2411]. [Wade 144].
———. *Les Prix Nobel en 1923. The Irish Dramatic Movement.* Stockholm: P. A. Norstedt, 1924.

x   [*YL* 2411a–c]. [NLI missing one copy].
Three more copies.

2443.   [*YL* 2412]. [NLI 40,567/64; 11 sheets; Wade 115]. [See Chapman, *YA* 6 (1988): 234–45].
———. *Responsibilities and Other Poems.* London: Macmillan, 1916. Bp: WBY.

[*YL* 2412a moved to 2445].

x   [*YL* 2412b]. [NLI missing this copy]. [See Chapman, *YA* 6 (1988): 234–45].
Another copy.

2444.   [*YL* 2412a]. [NLI 40,567/65; 15 sheets; Wade 115]. [See Chapman, *YA* 6 (1988): 234–45].
Another ed., 1917. [Revised].

2444a.   [*YL* 2412c]. [NLI 40,567/66; 12 sheets; Wade 115; see Chapman, *YA* 6 (1988)]. [See Chapman, *YA* 6 (1988): 234–45].
Another copy.

2444b.   [*YL* 2412d]. [NLI 40,567/67; 4 sheets; Wade 115; see Chapman, *YA* 6 (1988): 243]. [Though reported in *YL*, did not come to NLI with a holograph letter from Sean O'Casey to WBY (25 Feb. 1935); a draft letter of a poem in ink on letterhead; GY's holograph copies of "'Ephemera' | 1899 Version," "'The Meditation of the Old Fisherman' | 1899 Version"; and "'A Song of the Rosy-Cross' from The Bookman, Oct 1895." A note was found as follows: "Enclosures in file 115. No. 5 | Xerox this AY"].
Another copy.

2445.   [*YL* 2413]. [Wade 116]. [See Chapman, *YA* 6 (1988): 234–45].
———. *Responsibilities and Other Poems.* New York: Macmillan, 1916.

x [*YL* 2413a]. [NLI missing this copy]. [See Chapman, *YA* 6 (1988): 234–45].
Another copy.

2446. [*YL* 2414]. [Wade 112].
———. *Reveries Over Childhood and Youth*. New York: Macmillan, 1916.

2447. [*YL* 2415]. [Wade 113].
———. *Reveries Over Childhood and Youth*. London: Macmillan, 1916. Bp: WBY.

2447a. [*YL* 2415a].
Another copy. Second printing, 1917.

2448. [*YL* 2416]. [Wade 21].
———. *The Secret Rose*. London: Lawrence and Bullen, 1897. Bp: Lily Yeats. Signed: Lily Yeats | May 25 | '97

2449. [*YL* 2417]. [NLI 40,567/68; 21 sheets; Wade 128]. [See Chapman, *YA* 6 (1988): 234–45].
———. *Selected Poems*. New York: Macmillan, 1921.

2449a. [*YL* 2417a]. [NLI 40,567/69; 9 sheets; Wade 128].
Another copy.

2449b. [*YL* 2417b].
Another copy.

2449c. [*YL* 2417c].
Another copy.

2450. [*YL* 2418]. [Wade 165].
———. *Selected Poems, Lyrical and Narrative*. London: Macmillan, 1929.

2451. [*YL* 2419]. [Wade 103]. [See Chapman, *YA* 6 (1988): 234–45].
———. *A Selection from the Poetry of W. B. Yeats*. Leipzig: Bernhard Tauchnitz, 1913. Bp: WBY

2452. [*YL* 2420]. [Wade 30].
———. *The Shadowy Waters*. London: Hodder and Stoughton, 1900.

2452a. [*YL* 2420a].
Another copy.

2452b.   [*YL* 2420b].
   Another, incomplete copy.

2453.   [*YL* 2421]. [NLI 40,567/70; 8 sheets; Wade 66].
   ——. *The Shadowy Waters*. London: A. H. Bullen, 1907.

x   [*YL* 2421a–i]. [NLI missing four copies].
   Nine more copies, of which five remain.

2454.   [*YL* 2422]. [Wade 180].
   ——. *The Singing Head and the Lady*. Bryn Mawr: Privately printed by Frederic Prokosch, 1934. ["A" inscribed on rice-paper label].

2454a–b.   [*YL* 2422a–b].
   Two more copies, inscribed with "d" and "e" on rice-paper labels.

2454c–d.   [*YL* 2422c–d].
   Two more copies, inscribed with "III" and "IV" on Dresden labels.

x   [*YL* 2422e–g]. [NLI missing two copies, "3" and "6" on Oland].
   Three more copies, inscribed with "2," "3," and "6" on Oland labels, of which one copy remains.

2455.   [*YL* 2423]. [NLI 40,567/71; 2 sheets; Wade 160].
   ——. *Sophocles' King Oedipus*. London: Macmillan, 1928.

2455a.   [*YL* 2423a].
   Another copy. Bp: Lily Yeats

2455b.   [*YL* 2423b].
   Another copy.

2455c.   [*YL* 2423c–e]. [NLI missing two copies].
   Three more copies, of which one remains.

2456.   [*YL* 2424]. [Wade 193].
   ——. *A Speech and Two Poems*. Dublin: For the Author at the Three Candles, 1937.

2456a.   [*YL* 2424a].
   Another copy.

2456b.   [*YL* 2424b]. [Though reported in *YL*, did not come to NLI with loose bookplate designed by T. Sturge Moore, signed by WBY].
   Another copy.

2456c.   [*YL* 2424c].
Another copy.

2457.   [*YL* 2425]. [Wade 104].
———. *Stories of Red Hanrahan. The Secret Rose. Rosa Alchemica.* London: A. H. Bullen, 1913.

2458.   [*YL* 2426]. [NLI 40,567/72; 10 sheets; Wade 105].
———. *Stories of Red Hanrahan. The Secret Rose. Rosa Alchemica.* New York: Macmillan, 1914. Bp: WBY

2458a.   [*YL* 2426a].
Another copy.

x   [*YL* 2426b]. [NLI missing this copy].
Another copy.

x   [*YL* 2427]. [NLI missing this copy; Wade 157].
———. *Stories of Red Hanrahan and the Secret Rose.* London: Macmillan, 1927.

2459.   [*YL* 2427a].
Another copy.

2460.   [*YL* 2428]. [Wade 24].
———. *The Tables of the Law. The Adoration of the Magi.* London: Privately Printed, 1897. Bp: Lily Yeats.

2461.   [Not listed in *YL* and assigned NLI number 3069; inserted paper inscribed, possibly by GY: "P. S. O'H[egarty], who was the young man?"; Wade 26].
———. *The Tables of the Law and The Adoration of the Magi.* London: Elkin Mathews, 1904.

2461a.   [Not listed in *YL* and assigned NLI number 3069a].
Another copy.

2462.   [*YL* 2429]. [Wade 166].
———. *Three Things.* The Ariel Poems, no. 18. London: Faber and Faber, 1929.

2462a–c.   [*YL* 2429a–e]. [NLI missing two copies].
Five more copies, of which three remain.

2463.   [*YL* 2430]. [Wade 158].
———. *The Tower.* London: Macmillan, 1928.

x   [*YL* 2430a]. [NLI missing this copy].
Another copy.

x   [*YL* 2430b]. [NLI missing this copy].
Another copy.

2463a.   [*YL* 2430c].
Another copy. March 1928 printing.

2463b.   [*YL* 2430d]. [NLI 40,567/73; 10 sheets; Wade 158].
Another copy. March 1928 printing.

2463c.   [*YL* 2430e]. [NLI 40,567/74; 5 sheets; Wade 158].
Another copy. March 1928 printing.

2463d.   [*YL* 2430f]. [NLI 40,567/75; 5 sheets; Wade 158].
Another copy. March 1928 printing.

2464.   [*YL* 2431]. [Wade, p. 369].
———. *Tragedie Irlandesi*. Milano: Studio Editoriale Lombardo, 1914.

2464a–b. [*YL* 2431a–b].
Two more copies.

2465.   [*YL* 2432]. [Wade 133].
———. *The Trembling of the Veil*. London: Privately Printed, 1922.

2465a.   [*YL* 2432a]. [NLI 40,567/76; 20 sheets; Wade 133].
Another copy.

x   [*YL* 2433]. [NLI missing this copy; evidently an unmarked copy in dust jacket; Wade 149].
———. *A Vision*. London: Privately Printed, 1925. Signed: WBY.

2466.   [*YL* 2433a]. [NLI 40,567/77; 16 sheets; Wade 149].
Another copy. Bp: GY

2466a.   [*YL* 2433b]. [NLI 40,567/78; 3 sheets; Wade 149].
Another copy.

2466b.   [*YL* 2433c]. [NLI 40,567/79; 92 sheets; Wade 149].
Another copy.

2467.   [*YL* 2434]. [NLI 40,567/80; 31 sheets; Wade 191]. [NLI 40,567/81; copy of letter not cited in *YL*, from F. P. Sturm to WBY (22 Nov. 1937); 1 sheet].
———. *A Vision*. London: Macmillan, 1937.

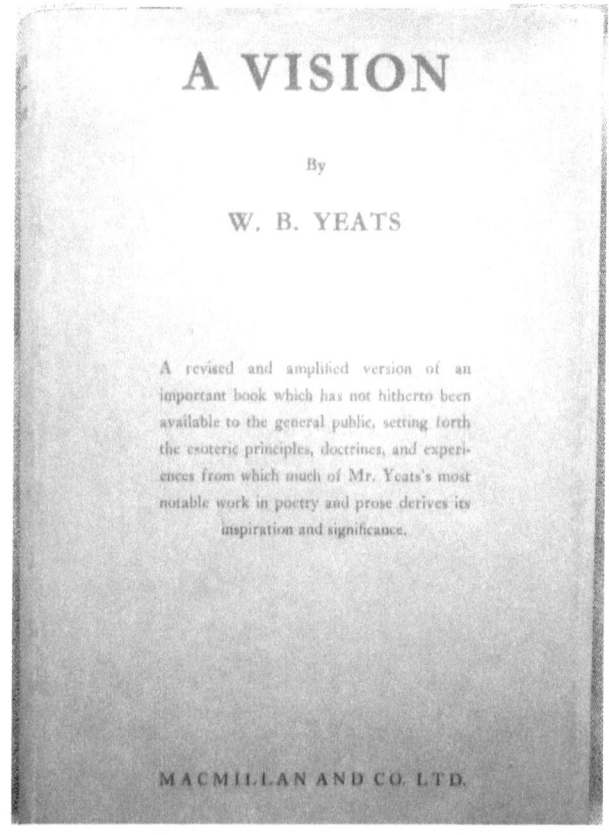

Figure 9. Front cover of 2467. W. B. Yeats, *A Vision* (1937; Wade 191)

2468.   [*YL* 2435]. [NLI 40,567/82; 19 sheets; Wade 192].
———. *A Vision*. New York: Macmillan, 1938. Signed: GY.

2469.   [*YL* 2436]. [Wade 2].
———. *The Wanderings of Oisin and Other Poems*. London: Kegan Paul, 1889.

2470.   [*YL* 2315]. [NLI 40,567/13; 7 sheets; Wade 155].
———. *W. B. Yeats*. The Augustan Books of English Poetry. Second series, no. 4. London: Ernest Benn, 1927.

2470a.   [*YL* 2315a].
Another copy.

2470b.   [*YL* 2315b].
Another copy.

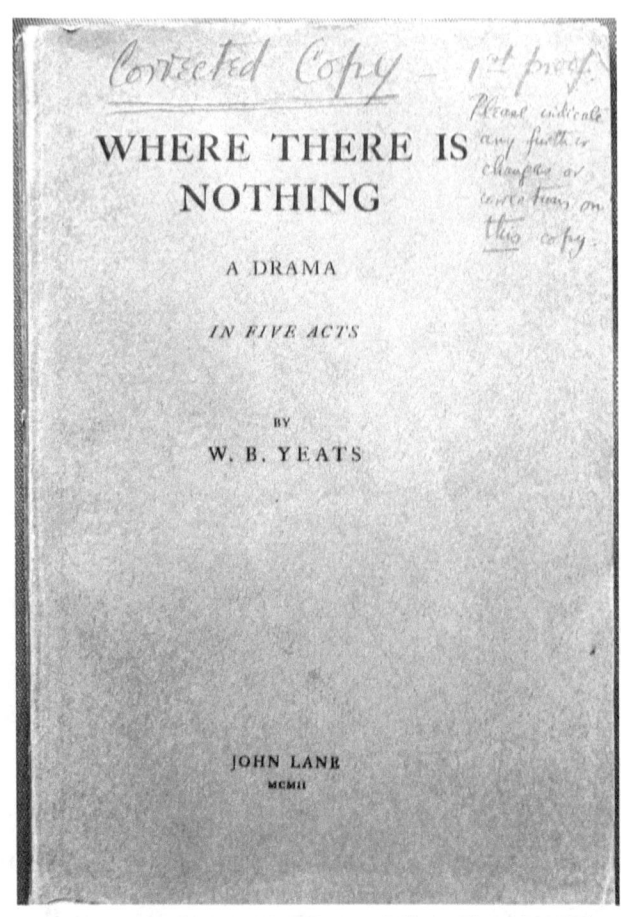

Figure 10. Front cover of 2473. W. B. Yeats, *Where There Is Nothing* (1902; Wade 42)

2470c.   [*YL* 2315c].
   Another copy.

2470d–e. [*YL* 2315d–e].
   Two more copies.

2471.   [*YL* 2437]. [Wade 175].
   ——. *Wheels and Butterflies*. London: Macmillan, 1934.

2471a.   [*YL* 2437a]. [Macmillan order card inserted].
   Another copy.

x   [*YL* 2437b]. [NLI missing this copy].
Another copy.

2472.   [*YL* 2438]. [Wade 176].
———. *Wheels and Butterflies*. New York: Macmillan, 1935.

2473.   [*YL* 2439]. [NLI 40,567/83; 53 sheets; Wade 42].
———. *Where There Is Nothing*. New York: John Lane, 1902.

2474.   [*YL* 2440]. [Wade 43].
———. *Where There Is Nothing*. [New York]: Privately printed for John Quinn, 1902. Signed: WBY

2475.   [*YL* 2441]. [Wade 44].
———. *Where There Is Nothing*. London: A. H. Bullen, 1903. Bp: Lily Yeats

2475a.   [*YL* 2441a].
Another copy.

2476.   [*YL* 2442]. [Wade 45].
———. *Where There Is Nothing*. New York: Macmillan, 1903. Bp: Elizabeth C. Yeats

2476a.   [*YL* 2442a].
Another copy. Large paper ed. No limitation notice.

x   [*YL* 2443]. [NLI missing this copy].
———. *Where There Is Nothing*. [Theatre Program]. The Stage Society. The Fifth Production (Fifth Season) at the Royal Court Theatre, Sloane Square. 26 June 1904.

2477.   [*YL* 2444]. [NLI 40,567/84; 5 sheets; Wade 124]. [See Chapman, *YA* 6 (1988): 234–45].
———. *The Wild Swans at Coole*. London: Macmillan, 1919.

2477a.   [*YL* 2444a]. [See Chapman, *YA* 6 (1988): 234–45].
Another copy.

2477b.   [*YL* 2444b]. [See Chapman, *YA* 6 (1988): 234–45].
Another copy.

2477c.   [*YL* 2444c]. [See Chapman, *YA* 6 (1988): 234–45].
Another copy.

2478. [*YL* 2445]. [Wade 27].
The Wind Among the Reeds. London: Elkin Mathews, 1899. Bp: Lily Yeats

2478a. [*YL* 2445a]. [Lacks the errata slip reported in Wade 27].
Another copy. 2nd ed.

2479. [*YL* 2446]. [NLI 40,567/85; 3 sheets; Wade 29].
———. *The Wind Among the Reeds.* 3rd ed. London: Elkin Mathews, 1900.

2479a. [*YL* 2446a]. [NLI 40,567/86; 2 sheets; Wade 29].
Another copy. Rebound. No advertising at end.

2479b. [*YL* 2446b].
Another copy. 4th ed., 1903. Bp: WBY

2479c. [*YL* 2446c]. [NLI 40,567/87; 9 sheets; Wade 29].
Another copy. 6th ed., 1911. Signed: George Hyde-Lees | May 1913

2480. [*YL* 2447]. [Wade 164].
———. *The Winding Stair.* New York: The Fountain Press, 1929. Signed: WBY

x [*YL* 2447a]. [NLI missing this copy].
Another copy.

2481. [*YL* 2448]. [Wade 169].
———. *The Winding Stair.* London: Macmillan, 1933. Bp: WBY.

2481a. [*YL* 2448a]. [Though reported in *YL*, did not come to NLI with holograph letter from Augustus John to WBY, 28 Feb. 1931].
Another copy.

2481b. [*YL* 2448b].
Another copy.

2481c. [*YL* 2448c].
Another copy.

2481d. [*YL* 2448d].
Another copy.

2482. [*YL* 2449]. [Wade 170].
———. *The Winding Stair.* New York: Macmillan, 1933.

2482a.   [*YL* 2449a].
   Another copy.

x   [*YL* 2449b–c]. [NLI missing both copies].
   Two other copies.

2483.   [*YL* 2450]. [NLI 40,567/88; 5 sheets; Wade 225].
   ——, ed. *A Book of Irish Verse*. 2nd rev. ed. London: Methuen, 1900.

2483a.   [*YL* 2450a]. [NLI 40,567/89; 3 sheets; Wade 225].
   Another copy. 3rd ed., Sept. 1911.

2484.   [*YL* 2451]. [NLI 40,567/90; 10 sheets; Wade 212].
   ——, ed. *Fairy and Folk Tales of the Irish Peasantry*. London: Walter Scott, 1888. Signed: WB Yeats | November | 1891.

2484a.   [*YL* 2451a]. [NLI 40,567/91; 6 sheets from this and the next copy (i.e., the a and b copies); Wade 212].
   Another copy. Bp: Lily Yeats.

2484b.   [*YL* 2451b]. [NLI 40,567/91; 6 sheets from the and the preceding copy (i.e., both the a and b copies); Wade 212].
   Another copy. Scott Library; smooth dark red cloth.

2485.   [*YL* 2452]. [Wade 216].
   ——, ed. *Irish Fairy Tales*. Illustrated by Jack B. Yeats. London: T. Fisher Unwin, 1892.

2485a.   [*YL* 2452a].
   Another copy. Second impression.

2485b.   [*YL* 2452b].
   Another copy. Second impression.

2486.   [*YL* 2453]. [NLI 40,567/92; 10 sheets; cf. Wade 223 and 224]. [Though reported in *YL*, did not come to NLI with a scrap from a newspaper dated 24 Feb. 1923].
   ——, ed. and intro. *Irish Fairy Tales*. Illustrated by James Torrance. London and Felling-on-Tyne: Walter Scott. New York: n.p., n.d. [Illustrated].

x   [*YL* 2454]. [NLI missing this copy; Wade 250].
   ——, ed. *The Oxford Book of Modern Verse*. Oxford: Clarendon Press, 1936. Signed: WBY

2487.   [YL 2454a].
Another copy.

x   [YL 2454b]. [NLI 40,567/93; 3 sheets; Wade 250]. [NLI missing this copy].
Another copy. Dec. 1936 reprinting.

2487a.   [YL 2454c].
Another copy. Dec. 1936 reprinting.

2487b-c.   [YL 2454d-e].
Two more copies. Dec. 1936 reprinting.

2488.   [YL 2455]. [Wade 215].
——, ed. *Representative Irish Tales*. 2 vols. New York and London: G. P. Putnam's, [1891].

2489.   [YL 2456].
[Yonge, Charlotte Mary]. *The Prince and the Pace: A Story of the Last Crusade*. New ed. London: Macmillan, 1873. Signed: WB Yeats | 14 Eustace Villas

2490.   [YL 2457].
[Yoshida, Kenko]. *The Miscellany of a Japanese Priest: Being a Translation of "Tsure-zure gusa."* Trans. William N. Porter. London: Humphrey Milford, 1914.

2491.   [YL 2458].
Zachrisson, Valdemar, ed. *Boktryckeri-Kalendar* 1902–1903 [Printing-office Almanac]. 9th and 10th year. Goteborg, Sweden: V. Zachrissons Boktryckeri, n.d.

2492.   [YL 2459].
Zadkielis Astronomical Ephemeris. Places for 1840. London: J. G. Berger, n.d. [Publishers vary ff.]

2493.   [YL 2460]. [NLI 40,568/279/1; inclusive of the years 1841, 1844–49: 28 sheets; envelope 1422].
——. 1841.

2494.   [YL 2461].
——. 1842.

2495.   [YL 2462].
——. 1843.

WORKS IN THE COLLECTION   269

2496.   [*YL* 2463]. [NLI 40,568/279/1; inclusive of the years 1841, 1844–49: 28 sheets; envelope 1422].
——. 1844.

2497.   [*YL* 2464]. [NLI 40,568/279/1; inclusive of the years 1841, 1844–49: 28 sheets; envelope 1422].
——. 1845.

2498.   [*YL* 2465]. [NLI 40,568/279/1; inclusive of the years 1841, 1844–49: 28 sheets; envelope 1422].
——. 1846.

2499.   [*YL* 2466]. [NLI 40,568/279/1; inclusive of the years 1841, 1844–49: 28 sheets; envelope 1422].
——. 1847.

2500.   [*YL* 2467]. [NLI 40,568/279/1; inclusive of the years 1841, 1844–49: 28 sheets; envelope 1422].
——. 1848.

2501.   [*YL* 2468]. [NLI 40,568/279/1; inclusive of the years 1841, 1844–49: 28 sheets; envelope 1422].
——. 1849.

2502.   [*YL* 2469].
——. 1850.

2503.   [*YL* 2470].
——. 1851.

2504.   [*YL* 2471].
——. 1852.

2505.   [*YL* 2472]. [NLI 40,568/279/2; 1 sheet; envelope 1422].
——. 1853.

2506.   [*YL* 2473].
——. 1854.

2507.   [*YL* 2474]. [NLI 40,568/279/3; 1 sheet; envelope 1422].
——. 1855.

2508.   [*YL* 2475].
——. 1856.

2509.   [*YL* 2476]. [NLI 40,568/279/4; 1 sheet; envelope 1422].
——. 1858.

2510.   [*YL* 2477].
——. 1879.

2511.   [*YL* 2478].
——. 1883.

2512.   [*YL* 2479].
——. 1884.

2513.   [*YL* 2480].
——. 1890.

x   [*YL* 2481]. [NLI missing this copy].
——. 1891.

2514.   [*YL* 2482].
——. 1895.

x   [*YL* 2483]. [NLI missing this copy].
——. 1896.

2515.   [Not listed in *YL* and assigned NLI number 3070]. [NLI 40,568/279/5; 5 sheets; envelope 1420C].
——. 1908.

2516.   [*YL* 2484].
——. 1914.

2517.   [*YL* 2485]. [NLI 40,568/279/6; 2 sheets; envelope 1422].
——. 1915.

2517a. [Not listed in *YL* and assigned NLI number 3071].
Another copy. Missing front and back covers.

2518.   [*YL* 2486]. [NLI 40,568/279/7; 20 sheets; envelope 1422].
——. 1916.

2519.   [*YL* 2487]. [NLI 40,568/279/8; with copies from the following two entries: 2, 6, and 11 sheets; envelope 1422].
——. 1917.

2519a.   [*YL* 2487a]. [See preceding entry].
Another copy.

2519b.   [Not listed in *YL* and assigned NLI number 3072]. [See two preceding entries].
Another copy.

2520.   [*YL* 2488]. [NLI 40,568/279/9; with another printed copy not in *YL*: 12 and 4 sheets; envelope 1422].
———. 1922.

2520a.   [Not listed in *YL* and assigned NLI number 3073]. [See preceding entry].
Another copy.

2521.   [*YL* 2489]. [NLI 40,568/279/10; 10 sheets; envelope 1422].
———. 1923.

2522.   [Not listed in *YL* and assigned NLI number 3074]. [See Chapman, *YA* 8 (1991): 202].
———. 1926.

2523.   [Not listed in *YL* and assigned NLI number 3075]. [See Chapman, *YA* 8 (1991): 202].
———. 1927.

2524.   [*YL* 2490]. [NLI 40,568/280; 34 sheets; envelope 1421].
———. Bound vol. 1881–90. London: Cousins, n.d.

2525.   [*YL* 2491].
Zola, Emile. *The Dreyfus Case. Four Letters to France.* London and New York: John Lane, 1898.

2526.   [*YL* 2492].
Zoroaster, the Magician. *The Chaldaean Oracles of Zoroaster.* Ed. Sapere Aude [pseud., W. Wynn Westcott]. Collectanea Hermetica, vol. 6. London: Theosophical Publishing Society, 1895.

Figure 11. A partial view of the poetry section of the library in 1997, in the home of Anne Yeats, "Avalon," Dalkey, Ireland

Appendices

On the W. B. Yeats Library in 1904

In 1989, I compiled, at the suggestion of *Yeats Annual* editor Warwick Gould, a list of books displayed in the now well-known photograph that first appeared in *The Tatler* (London) in 1904. See *YA* 8 (1991) 199–202 and plate 5, as well as Gould's "Editor's Note" in *YA* 5 (1987) xvii–xviii and frontispiece. In addition to my other studies

Figure 12. Yeats and his books, Woburn Buildings, London, from *The Tatler*, no. 157 (29 June 1904)

in the library at "Avalon," I was indebted to Anne Yeats, who was amused to watch as I ventured up and down the ladder in her study, comparing spines of books there with those of the small collection her father seems to have set out for public viewing in that photograph, so many years before, in the infancy of the library itself. Several wall ornaments, such as the death mask of Dante and Blake's engraving of "The Circle of the Corrupt Officials; the Devils Mauling Each Other" (for *Inferno*, Canto XII), had been identified by Gould, as well as the spine of one of WBY's recent acquisitions, the Reverend Arthur Devine's *A Manual of Mystical Theology* (1903), to which the poet's thumb seems to be gesturing in the photograph. After physically comparing books in the library in 1989 with those sixty-four books in the picture, and checking the 1920s card file for volumes evidently missing (such as 1.15–17, 1.20, 2.5–10, 2.14–15, 3.11, 3.18, and perhaps 3.19–20), I was able to offer a number of titles by relative shelf position (from top and left), thus:

1.1–5 Edmund Spenser, *The Works of Edmund Spenser*, ed. J. Payne Collier, 5 vols. (London: Bell and Daldy, 1862). A gift set from Lady Gregory, 1992–92D [*YL* 1976–78D].

1.8 A. Privat Deschanel, *Elementary Treatise on Natural Philosophy*, ed. and tr. J. D. Everett, 4th edn. (London: Blackie and Son, 1878). "NATURAL | PHILOSOPHY | — | DESCHANEL" on spine. See "Privat-Deschanel, Augustin" under 1653 [*YL* 1642].

1.10 Paul B. Du Chaillu, *The Viking Age: The Early History, Manners, and Customs of the Ancestors of the English-speaking Nations*, 2 vols. (London: John Murray, 1889). Bears distinctive anchor design on spine; only vol. I in the library. 596 [*YL* 584].

1.13 ?Aubrey Beardsley, *Under the Hill and Other Essays in Prose and Verse*, illus. by the author (London and New York: John Lane, 1904). Inscribed "J. Q. [John Quinn] to W. B. Y." 133 [*YL* 133].

1.14 ?Edgar Allen Poe, *The Raven [and] The Pit and the Pendulum*, illus. W. T. Horton (London: Leonard Smithers, 1899). Inscribed as a gift from Horton and dated "Saty. 22.7.99." 1612 [*YL* 1600].

1.20 Probably John Denham Parsons, *Our Sun-God; or Christianity before Christ* (London: published by the author, 1895). On label (?): "OUR | SUN- | GOD | PARSONS"; see *YA* 4 (1986) 287.

2.3–4 ?Walter Pater, *Marius the Epicurean*, 2 vols. (London: Macmillan, 1893). 1548 [*YL* 1537].

2.5–10 Apparently a 6-volume set no longer in the library, possibly the Walter W. Skeat edition of *The Complete Works of Geoffrey Chaucer*, 6 vols. (Oxford: Clarendon Press, 1894). See *YA* 4 (1986) 281; and *AVA* (Notes) 10; cf. 385, 387–88 [*YL* 376–78].

2.13 The Revd Arthur Devine, *A Manual of Mystical Theology* (London: R. & T. Washbourne, 1903). 531 [*YL* 520]. See "Editor's Note," *YA* 5 (1987) xviii.

2.14–15 2 vol. set no longer in the library, possibly the E. K. Chambers edition of *Poems of John Donne*, intro. George Saintsbury, 2 vols. (London Routledge, 1896). See *YA* 4 (1986) 282. Both vols. in photo bear the Routledge emblem.

2.16–17 Joseph Henry Green, *Spiritual Philosophy: Founded on the Teaching of the Late Samuel Taylor Coleridge*, ed. John Simon, 2 vols. (London and Cambridge: Macmillan, 1865). 786 [*YL* 775].

3.7–10 Four old books arranged as a set though of differing dates, etc., bound in leather with five spinal ribs. Five such books were dispersed in the library in 1989 in accordance with the subject arrangement then in effect. The damage of one makes its candidacy less likely than the others. The five books are

(i) Petronius, *The Works of Petronius Arbiter*, 4th edn. (London: Sam Briscoe, 1713). 1573 [*YL* 1561].
(ii) *The Spectator*, II (Dublin: G. Grierson and A. Ewing, 1753). 1983 [*YL* 1968].
(iii) [Torquato Tasso], *Godfrey of Bulloigne: or the Recovery of Jerusalem*, tr. Edward Fairfax (London: H. Herringman, 1687). 2120 [*YL* 2106].
(iv) Francis Hutchinson, *An Historical Essay Concerning Witchcraft* (London: R. Knaplock, 1720). 948 [*YL* 938]. Lower cover is torn off.
(v) [Anon.], *The Election*…(London: n.p., 1749); James Thomson [after Shakespeare], *Coriolanus* (Dublin: G. Grierson & A. Ewing, 1749); Thomas Otway, *The Cheats of Scapin* (Dublin: James Hoey, 1733); and P[aul] H[iffernan], *The Self-Enamour'd or the Ladies' Doctor* (Dublin: Augustus Long, 1750). All bound in a single volume. 622 [*YL* 608].

3.12 ?Dante Alighieri, *The Vision: or Hell, Purgatory, and Paradise of Dante Aligieri*, tr. H. F. Cary (London and New York: Frederick Warne, 1890). Signed and dated "October 1891." 487 [*YL* 476].

3.16 Although perhaps any one of several "Camelot Classics" in the library, the most probable candidate is Joseph Mazzini's *Essays: Selected from the Writings, Literary, Political, and Religious*, ed. William Clarke (London: Walter Scott, 1887). Signed and dated "December 1887." On label: "Camelot Series | — | ESSAYS | BY | MAZZINI." 1310 [*YL* 1297].

There was a part II to my Shorter Notes in *YA* 8 (201–202), entitled "Additional Books in the Library, 1989, and Other Problems," wherein books are listed that were overlooked in *YL* or, in the case of G. R. S. Mead's *Orpheus* (London: Theosophical Publishing Society, 1896), were returned to the library by Kathleen Raine in 1975, evidently missed on first pass by *YL*'s original team of compilers. As cited in the Introduction of this volume (above), irregularities of the kind were common after Anne Yeats's death in 2001, with Michael Yeats's 2002 Heritage

Donation of their parent's books to the National Library of Ireland. In the course of this gift, titles were either added beyond his sister's holdings or, in some cases, withheld as unexceptional duplicate copies selected for sale or perhaps kept because of some personal connection with the family. Even so, Yeats himself occasionally thinned books from his personal collection, as I have also indicated with examples in the Introduction. As the extension of a poet's working archive, the library's books were never static in number. However, neither can one say that the library failed to grow very substantially beyond the bounds of a single, charming picture taken in a bachelor's small room in the summer of 1904.

Related Collections and Online Resources

National Library of Ireland Resources (see http://purl.clemson.edu/yeats-special-collections)

    The National Library of Ireland (http://www.nli.ie/)
    Yeats Library: NLI Guide for Readers (http://www.nli.ie/pdfs/mss%20lists/Yeats%20Librarylistforpublic.pdf)
    Yeats Library: Supplemental Cuala Press Books (http://purl.clemson.edu/cuala-press-books)
    The Life and Works of William Butler Yeats Online Exhibition (http://www.nli.ie/yeats/)
    Occult Papers of W. B. Yeats (http://www.nli.ie/pdfs/mss%20lists/yeatsoccult.pdf)
    Yeats Collection, Mss. 30,001–31,122 (http://www.nli.ie/pdfs/mss%20lists/A16_Yeats.pdf)

Yeats in Special Collections, *International Yeats Studies* **website** (http://purl.clemson.edu/yeats-special-collections)

    W. B. Yeats Papers, Berg Collection, New York Public Library (http://archives.nypl.org/brg/19118)
    Boston College Collection of Yeats Family Papers, John J. Burns Library, Boston College (https://library.bc.edu/finding-aids/MS1986-054-finding-aid.pdf)
    Yeats-related publications, John J. Burns Library, Boston College (https://bc-primo.hosted.exlibrisgroup.com/primo-explore/search?query=lsr30,contains,leeming,OR&query=lsr30,contains,yeats,AND&tab=bcl_only&search_scope=bcl&sortby=rank&vid=bclib_new&lang=en_US&mode=advanced&offset=0)
    British Library Manuscripts Catalog (https://www.bl.uk/catalogues-and-collections)

Irish Literary Collections Portal, Emory University and Boston College (http://rose.library.emory.edu/collections/literature-poetry/irish-literary-collections-portal.html)

W. B. Yeats Papers, 1908–1934 (on microfilm), Houghton Library, Harvard University (http://oasis.lib.harvard.edu/)

W. B. Yeats Collection, Kenneth Spencer Research Library, University of Kansas (https://spencer.lib.ku.edu/collections/special-collections/irish)

Location Register of 20th-Century Manuscripts and Letters, University of Reading Library (https://www.reading.ac.uk/library/about-us/projects/lib-location-register.aspx)

W. B. Yeats Collection, Harry Ransom Humanities Research Center, University of Texas (https://norman.hrc.utexas.edu/fasearch/findingaid.cfm?eadid=00248)

Richard Ellmann Papers, Special Collections, McFarlin Library, University of Tulsa (https://utulsa.as.atlas-sys.com/repositories/2/resources/515)

William Butler Yeats Collection, Stony Brook University Libraries, SUNY-Stony Brook (https://www.stonybrook.edu/libspecial/collections/manuscripts/yeats/)

Index

NOTE: Apart from those items cited by O'Shea (*YL*) but presently missing at the NLI (as indicated by "x"), *numbers* appearing in this Index are the ones systematically assigned in this Catalog (i.e., in "Works in the Collection"). *They are not page numbers.* Missing items are indicated by *YL* number following an "x" (thus: "x1432"). All items, whether present or missing, are indexed by *author* and *subject*. Contiguous items are indicated in the usual manner, by hyphenated listings. For consistency, I follow the practice introduced by O'Shea in the use of lower-case letters for multiple copies of the same work (thus: "5a-f" or "x6a-g"] and capital letters to distinguish between editions (thus: "435, 435A").

A., Œ.   1
Abbey Theatre   2, x1432, 1565
  programs   3, 3a-d, 5, 5a-f, 6, x6, x6a-g, x7, x8
Abdul-Ali, Sijil   7
Abercrombie, Lascelles   8–10
Acorn, The   11
actors   48
Acton, Lord (John E. E. Dalberg)   12–13
Adam, C. G. M.   14
Adams, Henry   15–18
Adams, Morley   19
Aeschylus   21, 435, 435A
Africa   1116
afterlife   119, 678, 691, 708, 954, 1118, 1157, 1214
Agnelli, Guiseppe   22
Agrippa, Cornelius   23, 1396
Aksakoff, Alexandre   24
Aksakoff, Serghei   25–26
alchemy   7, 124–25, 1047, 1048, 1049, 1543, 2227
Aldington, Richard   27–28, 1201

Alexander the Great   1222
Alighieri, Dante see Dante
Aliotta, Antonio   30
Allingham, Hugh   31
Allingham, William   32–35, 1806
almanacs   1359, 1360, 1519, 1544, 2491
Alt, Phyllis Innocent   36
Altdorfer, Albrecht   37
Anderson, Maxwell   38
Anglo-French relations   127
Anglo-Irish relations   2255
Anglo-Irish War   1179
animism   1196
Annals of Psychical Science, The   39–45
anthropology   1963
antiquities, classical   1965, 2250
Apocrypha   46
Apuleius   47
Arabian Nights   258, 689
Archer, William   48
archeology   51, 292, 316, 361, 440, 472, 705, 838, 1099
architecture   440

Ardill, John Roche 49
Ariosto, Ludovico 738, 743
aristocracy 1223
Aristophanes 50
Armitage, Ella Sophia 51
Arnold, Matthew 52–55
Arrow, The 56–57, 57a, 58, 58a–d, 59
art 437, 677, 729, 745, 1748, 2187, 2290, 2291
  American 339
  Assyrian 1746
  British 1109, 1341
  Byzantine 472, 734
  Chinese 61, 194, 199, 201, 324, 2232, 2298
  Christian 2038
  Egyptian 292, 316, 360, 1746
  French 240–41, 300, 442, 735, 1137, 1169, 1663, 1879
  German 1802, 1865
  Greek 361, 828, 838, 1418, 1746
  Indian 291, 705, 868, 873, 2039
  Irish 240–41, 667, 968, 977, 978, 1785, 2022
  Italian 734, 1313, 1550, 1762, 2205, 2325
  Japanese 476, 730, 908, 1457, 1460, 1464, 1466, 2116, 2194, 2298
  Korean 2298
  Persian 1568
  Roman 1746, 2028
  Swedish 656, 1046, 1144, 1801, 2293
  see also modern art
  see also painting
art and morality 1912
Arthur, King 2260
Arts, The 60
Ashton, Leigh 61
astrology 14, 381, 466, 471, 669, 690, 784, 1113, 1114, 1115, 1559, 1662, 1673, 1786, 1787, 1880, 1881, 1882, 1883, 1926, 1936, 2163, 2171, 2172, 2301

astrological ephemera 1561, 1674–1739, 2024, 2230, 2266–73, 2492–2524
astronomy 874, 1883
Athenaeum 62
atlases 122
  of astronomy 874
  of classical geography 63
  of history 121, 13
  of literature 121
Auden, Wystan Hugh 64–67
Augustine, Saint 68
Austen, Jane 69
Author's and Writer's Who's Who 70
Australasian literature 1417
Aventinus, Johannes 71

Baedeker, Karl 72–73
Ball, Francis Elrington 74
ballads 597, 869, 1156, 1614, 1664, 1754, 1927, 1928, 1929, 1982
Ballantyne, Robert Michael 75
Balzac, Honoré de 76–112, 372, 1846, 1993
Baring-Gould, Sabine 113
Barker, Ernest 114
Barker, George 115–17
Barnes, James Strachey 118
Barrett, William F. 119
Barrington, Jonah 120
Bartholomew, John George 121–22
Barton, Dunbar Plunket 123
Basilius Valentinus 124–25
Basnage, Jacques 126
Bastide, Charles 127
Bate, Percy H. 128
Baudelaire, Charles 129–30
Baudouin, Charles 131
Bavarian Chronicle 71
Bayeux, Cathedral of 1424
Bayley, Harold 132
Beardsley, Aubrey 133
Beauclerk, Helen 134
Beaumont, Francis 135–37

Beaumont, John   138
Beckford, William   139-40
Bedell, William   141
Beedham, R. John   142
Beerbohm, Max   143-44
Bellini, Giovanni   145
Belloc, Hilaire   146-146a
Beltaine   147, 147a-b, 148, 148a, 149
Benavente, Jacinto   150
Benda, Julien   151
Benson, Edward Frederic   152
Benson, Stella   153
Berdyaev, Nicholas   154-55
Berger, Pierre   156
Bergson, Henri   157-58
Beritens, German   159
Berkeley, George   160, 160a, 161, 921, 1036, 1171, 1172
Bevan, Edwyn   162
Bhatâtachâaryya, Shiva Chandra Vidyârnava   163
Biagi, Guido   164
Bibelot, The   165-74, 174a-c, 175-77, 177a, 178-89
Bible, The, *see* Scriptures
Bickley, Francis   190
Billson, Charles J.   191
Binyon, Laurence   192, 192a, 193-201
biographical dictionaries
   see dictionaries—biographical
Bismarck, Otto von   323
Bisson, Juliette Alexandre   202
Bithell, Jethro   203
Bjørnson, Björnstjerne   204
Blake, William   44, 156, 196, 205-27, 227a, 228, 329, 474, 686, 736, 1398, 1525, 1566, 1758, 1813, 1860, 1862, 1863, 2083, 2278, 2302, 2317, 2491
Blum, Etta   229
Blunden, Edmund   230-33
Blunt, Wilfrid Scawen   234-35, 235a-d, 236
Boas, George   237
Boccaccio, Giovanni   238, 238a, 239

Bodkin, Thomas   240-41
Boehme, Jacob   242-47, 862, 1564
Bolton, Lyndon   248
Bond, Charles John   249
book design   1468, 1759, 2491
Book of Common Prayer, The   x249
Book of Irish Verse, A   1212
   ; reviews   62, 252
Book of the Rhymer's Club   257
Book of the Thousand Nights and One Night   258
Bookman, The   250-56, 256a
Borthwick, Norma   259-60
Bosanquet, Bernard   261
Bosis, Lauro de   262
Boswell, James   263
Botticelli, Sandro   2325
Bottomley, Gordon   264-67, 267a, 268-70
Boucicault, Dion   271
Boyd, Ernest Augustus   272
Boyle, William   273
Brabazon, Elizabeth Jane   274
Bradby, Godfrey Fox   275
Bradley, Francis Herbert   276
Bradley, John William   277
Brereton, Austin   278
Breton, Nicholas   279
Brewer, Robert Frederick   280
Bricriu, The Feast of   1210
Bridges, Robert   281-90
British Museum   291-93
Brodie-Innes, J. W.   294
Brodzky, Horace   295
Bronte, Charlotte   152
Brooke, Rupert   296, 566
Browne, Thomas   297-99
Brownell, William Crary   300
Browning, Elizabeth Barrett   301-303
Browning, Robert   304-306, 1435
Bruck, Arthur Moeller van den   307
Bryan's Dictionary of Painters and Engravers   308
Buddhism   2045, 2046

Buncho, Ippitsusai   2194
Bunting, Basil   309, 309a–d
Bunyan, John   310
Burdy, Samuel   311
Burghclere, Lady (Winifred Gardner)   312
Burke, Edmund   313–14, 1652
Burkitt, Francis Crawford   315
Burnet, John   316
Burney, Fanny   317
Burns, Robert   318, 880
Burton, Robert   319
Bury, John Bagnell et al.   320–22
Busch, Julius Hermann Moritz   323
Bushnell, Stephen Wooten   324
Butler, Samuel   325
Butt, Isaac   326
Butterfly Quarterly, The   327–28
Butterworth, Adeline M.   329
Bynner, Witter   330
Byron, George Gordon, Lord   331–34, 1327
Byron, Robert et al.   335
Byzantium   472, 734, 911

C., S. A. (Sophia Anne Cotton)   336
Cabala   126, 1305, 1358, 1389, 1884
   Christian   23, 513, 1071
Cabell, James Branch   337
Cabeza de Vaca   1167
Cafferata, Henry Taylor   338
Caffin, Charles Henry   339
Calvert, Edward   340
Calvert, Samuel   341
Campbell, John Gregerson   342–43
Campbell, Roy   344–45
Campion, Thomas   1194
Canfield, Curtis   346
Čapek, Karel   347–48
Capri   2250
Caran, d'Ache (Emmanuel Poiré)   349
Carleton, William   350–54, 1491
Carr, Herbert Wildon   355
Carrà, Carlo   356

Carroll, Lewis   357
Castiglione, Baldassare   358
castles   51, 987–94
catechisms   744
Catherine, Saint   939
Cattell, Raymond Bernard   361
Caulfield, James   362
Cavalcanti, Guido   363–65, 365a
Cecil, David   366
Cellini, Benvenuto   367
Celtic *see* Gaelic, Irish
Celtic Christmas, A
censorship   975
ceramics   368–70, 370a, 371
Cerfberr, Anatole   372
Chadwick, Hugh Brailsford   373
Chambers's Biographical Dictionary   374
Chambers's Cyclopaedia of English Literature   375
Chambers's English Dictionary   376
Chapman, George   377–79
Charpentier, John   380
Charlemagne, Cycle of   2261
Charubel (pseud.)   381
Chatelain, Heli   382
Chatterton, Thomas   383
Chattopadhyaya, Harindranath   384
Chaucer, Geoffrey   385–88, 1959
Chekhov, Anton   389–90
Cheney, Sheldon   391
Chettur, Govinda Krishna   392
children's books   75, 446, 511, 664, 689, 840, 1075, 1595
China   396, 937, 1528, 1557
Chinese art *see* art—Chinese
Chinese literature   1150, 1176, 1877, 2233, 2235
Choiseul-Meuse, Félicité   393
Christianity   489, 1074
Christophe, Jules   372
Church, Richard   394–95
Cibot, Pierre Martial   396
Cicero, Marcus Tullius   397

INDEX   285

Citizen's Manual, The   398
civilization   1570, 1867, 2169, 2170
Clark, Barrett Harper   401–402
Clarke, Austin   399–400
class   1223
Claudel, Paul   403–404
Clifton, Harry   405–406
Clodd, Edward   407
Cocteau, Jean   408
coinage   828, 871, 973
Coleridge, Mary Elizabeth   409
Coleridge, Samuel Taylor   380,
    410–13, 413A, 414–17, 786, 1398,
    1410
Coleridge, Sara   418
Collins, Clifton Wilbraham   419
Collins, Michael   x722, 1484, x1848
Collins Foreign Dictionaries.
    Italian   420
Colum, Padraic   421–23, 423A
Columban, The   424
Colvin, Sidney   425
Common Conditions   426
communism   1098, 1112, 1997
Concordance to [the Bible]   427
Congreve, William   428
Connolly, James Brendan   429–30
Conrad, Joseph   431–32
Convegno di Lettre   433
Coptic Gospels   1771
copyright   783
Corvo, Baron (Frederick William
    Rolfe)   2064
Copleston, Reginald Stephen   434, 434A
Coppard, Alfred Edgar   435
Cornford, Frances   436–37
Coryate, Thomas   438
Cotterill, Henry Bernard   439
Cotton, Charles   2240
Courier, The   x428
Cousens, Henry   440
Cousins, James Henry   441
Cousturier, Lucie   442
Craig, Edward Gordon   443–45

Crane, Walter   446
Crespi, Angelo   447
Criterion, The   448–50
Croce, Benedetto   356, 451–59
Croker, T. Crofton   584
Crookes, William   460
Crowley, Aleister   731
Cuala Industries   461, 1320
Cuala Press   462–63
Cuchulain   1476, 1499
Cudworth, Ralph   464–65
Cumont, Franz   466
Curcin, Milan   467
Curry, Samuel Silas   468–69
Curtin, Jeremiah   470

Däath, Henrich   471
Dalton, Ormonde Maddock   472
Daly, James   473
Damon, Samuel Foster   474
Dampier, William   475
Dan, Inō   476
Dante   458, 477–88, 626, 900
D'Annunzio, Gabriele   489
D'Arcy, Charles Frederick   490
Daryush, Elizabeth (Elizabeth
    Bridges)   491, 491a, 492–96
David, Villiers   497
Davidson, John   498
Davies, James   499
Davies, Oliver   500
Davies, William Henry   501–506
Davis, Bernard Eustace Cuthbert   507
Davis, Thomas   508–509, 509a, 598
Day, John   510
Day in a Child's Life, A   511
Day, Sri Mukul Chandra   532
De Blacam   512
Dee, John   513
defense, national   1195
Defoe, Daniel   2316
Dekker, Thomas   514–15
De la Mare, Walter   516–24
Delanne, Gabriel   525

Delphic Oracle   526
democracy   15
Dempsey, Thomas   526
Dennis, Jonas   527
De Quincey, Thomas   528
Derain, André   356
Descartes, René   1245
De Selincourt, Basil   X517
Deussen, Paul   529
de Valera, Eamon   1179, 1180
De Vere, Aubrey   530
Devine, Aurthur   531
Dial, The   533
dictionaries   376, 2246
   astrology   2301
   biographical   70, 374, 1493
   classical   1111, 1965
   foreign languages   420
   painting and engraving   308
Diogenes Läertius   534
Disraeli, Benjamin   535
Dobell, Sydney   536
Dodgson, Campbell   537
Dome, The   538–40
Donaghy, John Lyle   541
Donne, John   542–43, 2239
Donne, William Bodham   544, 544a
Donnelly, John   545
Doolittle, Hilda (H. D.)   546–47
Doro, Edward   548
Doughty, Charles Montagu   549–51
Douglas, Norman   552
Dowden, John   553
Dowson, Ernest   554–57, 1597
Doyle, Bishop   1191
drama   391, 401, 402, 443, 445, 468, 469, 622, 746, 773, x905, 927, 936, 941, 963, 1026, 1105, 1106, 1226, 1231, 1395, 1504, 1795, 1864, 2044, 2135, 2150, 2152, 2155, 2156, 2157
Drayton, Michael   558
Dream of Ravan, The   559
Dreyfus Affair   2525
Drinkwater, John   560–68, 568a

Drummond, William   569
Drummond of Hawthornden, William   570
Dryden, John   571, 571a, 572, 628
Dublin   10, 1521, 1580
Dublin Civic Survey Committee   1521
Dublin Figaro   573
Dublin Magazine, The   574–81
Dublin Municipal Gallery of Modern Art   582–83, 583a
Dublin University Magazine   584
Dublin University Review   584A, 585–88, 588a, 589, 589a, 590–91, 591a, 592–95
Du Chaillu, Paul Belloni   596
Duffy, Charles Gavan   597–99
Dunne, John William   600
Dunsany, Lord (Edward John Moreton Drax Plunkett)   601–603
Düntzer, Heinrich   604, 604A
Du Prel, Carl   605
Dürer, Albrecht   1865
Dutt, Romesh Chunder   607
Dutt, Toru   608

E., A. L. O. (Charlotte M. Tucker)   609
Easdale, Joan Adeney   610–11
Eastern Buddhist, The   612, 612a-l
Easter Rising   1937
Eastlake, Allan   613
Ecclesiastes   614
Eckartshausen, Karl von   615
Edda, The   671
Edel, Fritz   616
education   751
Eglinton, John (William Kirkpatrick Magee)   617–20, 620a
Egypt   1557
Egyptian antiquities   292, 316, 360, 841, 1099, 1746
Einstein, Albert   621
El Greco (Doménikos Theotokópoulos)   159
Eliot, John   623

INDEX 287

Eliot, T. S.   624–31, 631a, 632–39, 639a, 1203
Elizabeth I   2025
Elizabethan literature   426, 623, 1105, 1106, 1428
Ellis, Edwin John   640–41
Ellis, Frederick Startridge   642
emblems *see* Renaissance—emblems
Emmet, Robert   831
encyclicals   1596
Encyclopaedia Brittanica, The   643–44
encyclopedias of literature   375
encyclopedias of religion and ethics   864
Enemy, The   645–47
English history   362, 800, 824, 2025
English literature, general collections and treatments   742, 826, 1250, 1275, 1277, 1395, 1434, 1645, 1646, 1647, 1665, x1665, 1666, 1751, 1767, 1946, 1964, 2075, 2080, 2262
   translated into Japanese   1339
English Prayer Book, The   648
English Review, The   649
engraving   142
Ennemoser, Joseph   650
entomology   1077
Erasmian, The   651
Erdmann, Johann Eduard   652
Ernst, Otto   653
Essex, Earl of   2025
Esson, Luis   654
Estens, John Locke   655
Eugen, Napoleon Nicolaus   656
eugenics   249, 361, 657, 725, 1135, 1197, 1198
Euripides   544, 658–59, 659a, 660–62, 743
Evening World, The   x650
Everyman   663
evolution   872
Ewing, Juliana Horatia   664
Exile, The   665, 665a, 666
Exposition d'art irlandais   667, 667a

Exposition of the Malta Question   668
Eyre, Thomas Stephen   669

Fairfax, Edward   670
fairy lore   2256
fairy tales   393, 860, 1078, 2229
Faraday, Lucy Winifred   671
Farnell, Lewis Richard   672
Faroe Islands   1836
Farquhar, George   673
Farr, Florence   674–75, 675a–c, 675A, 676
fascism   29, 118, 616, 725, 1132, 1248, 1423, 2220, 2292
fate   878
Faure, Elie   677
Fechner, Theodor   678
Ferguson, Samuel   679–81
Ferrara   22, 737, 1472
Festive Songs of Christmas   682
Field, Michael   683–84
Fielding, Henry   685
Figgis, Darrell   686
Finnish literature   191
Fionn   342
Fischer, Eduard Wilhelm   687
Fisher, Herbert Albert Laurens   688
Five Favorite Tales from the Arabian Nights   689
Flambart, Paul   690
Flammarion, Camille   691
Flaubert, Gustave   692–95
Flaxman, John   1398
Flecker, James Elroy   696
Fletcher, John   135
Fletcher, Phineas   697
Flint, Frank Stewart   698
folk songs   699
folklore   709, 740
folktales   861
   Angolan   382
   English   860
   Irish   470, 811, 813, 821, 985, 2281, 2282

Scottish   343, 2251
Form   700
Formes   701
Forster, Edward Morgan   702
Forster, John   703
Fortescue, Winifred   704
Foucher, Alfred   705
Four Gospels, The   706
Franklin, Benjamin   707
Frazer, James George   708–16
Freeman, The   717, x704a, 718, x705a, 719, x706a, 720, x707a, 721, 721a–b, x708c
Freeman's Journal, The   722, x710, x711
French, Cecil   723, 723a, 724
French art *see* art—French
French literature   1170, 2080, 2117
Frercks, Rudolf   725
Frobenius, Leo   726
From the Upanishads   727
Il frontespizio   728
Fry, Roger   729
Fukui, Kikusaburo   730
Fuller, John Frederick Charles   731
furniture   1153

Gael, The   732–33
Gaelic American, The   x723
Gaelic literature   951, 952, 1192, 1210, 1323, x1487, 1518, 1749, 1755, 1935
Gaiety Theatre   x724
Galassi, Giuseppe   734
Galway   782
Gardner, Arthur   735
Gardner, Charles   736
Gardner, Edmund Garratt   737–38
Gardner, Frederick Leigh   739
Garnett, Lucy Mary   740
Garnett, Richard   741–42
Gascoigne, George   743
Gasparri, Peter Cardinal   744
Gaudier-Brzeska, Henry   295, 1631
Gaunt, William   745

Gayley, Charles Mills   746
Geeta, The   747, 747a–d, 748
Geley, Gustave   749
Gentile, Giovanni   750–52
geography   63, 972, 974, 979, 1116, 1875
Georgian poetry   1250
German education   2292
German history   307
German philosophy *see* philosophy—German
Gesta Romanorum   753
Ghose, Manmohan   754
Gibbon, Edward   755–56
Gibbon, Monk   757
Gide, André   758, 1925
Gill, Eric   759
Glanvil, Joseph   760
glossaries   1428
Goblet d'Alviella, Eugène Félicien Albert   761
Goddard, E. H.   762
Goddard, P. A.   762
Godolphin Foundation School   2415
Goethe, Johann Wolfgang von   604, 604A, 763, 1120
Gogarty, Oliver St. John   x722, 764–65, 765a–b, 766
Golden Dawn, The   294, 2393
Goldie, Sir George   2254
Goldsmith, Oliver   767
Gore-Booth, Eva   768
Gosse, Edmund   742, 769
Gowans, Adam Luke   770
Gower, John   771
Grail, The   905, 1477
Grandison, Sir Charles   1756
Grant, Francis James   772
Granville-Barker, Harley   773
Grattan, Henry   774–75
Graves, Robert   776–79
Gray, John   780
Great Britain   781–83
Greek art *see* art—Greek

INDEX   289

Greek civilization   2197
Greek literature   419, 434, 544, 740, 741, 1556, 2135
Greek philosophy and religion   316, 466, 672
Greek politics   114
Green, H. S.   784–85
Green, Joseph Henry   786
Greene, George Arthur   787
Green Sheaf, The   788, x777a, 789–90, x779a, 791–92, x781a, 793, x782a, 794–99
Greenwood, Alice Drayton   800
Gregory, Isabella Augusta   801–802, 802a, 803–809, 809a, 810, 810a, 811–20, x810, 821–23
Greville, Charles Cavendish Fulke   824
Grierson, Francis   825
Grierson, Herbert John   827
Griffith, Arthur   x722, 827, x1848
Grose, Sidney William   828
Gubernatis, Angelo de   829
Guedala, Philip   830
guidebooks   22, 36, 73, 1580, 1740, 2125
guilds   2280
Guiney, Louise Imogen   831
Gwynn, Stephen   832–33
Gypsy, The   834

Hackett, Francis   x825
Hadrian VII   1794
Hâfiz, Shirazi   835
haiku   1461
Haldane, Richard Burton   836
Halévy, Daniel   837
Hall, Harry Reginald   838, 1099
Hallam, Arthur Henry   839
Hamer, John   840
Hammer-Purgstall, Joseph   841
Hannay, James Ballantyne   842
Hardy, Thomas   843–58, 1029, 1076
Harrison, Henry   859

Hartland, Edwin Sidney   860–61
Hartmann, Franz   862–63
Hastings, James, et al.   864
Hauptmann, Gerhart   865–67
Havell, Ernest Binfield   868
Hayes, Edward   869
Hazlemere, Robert   870
Head, Barclay Vincent   871
Heard, Gerald   872
Heath, Lionel   873
Heath, Thomas   874
Heathcote, Henry   875
Hedin, Sven   876
Hegel, Georg Wilhelm Friedrich   459, x868, 877, 1213, 1216, 1217, 2237
Heitland, William Emerton   878
Henderson, Thomas Finlayson   879
Henley, William Ernest   172, 178, 880–85
heraldry   772
Herbert, Edward   886
Herbert, George   887–88, 2239
Hermes Trismegistus   889–92
hermeticism   397, 675A, 889, 890, 891, 892, 1543, 1574, 2227, 2526
Hermetic Students of the Golden Dawn   893
Herodotus   894
Herrick, Robert   895–98
Hesiod   499
Hessen, Boris   899
Hettinger, Franz   900
Heywood, Thomas   901, 901a
hieroglyphics   841
Higgins, Frederick Robert   x6, 902–903, 903a, 904, 904a
High History of the Holy Graal, The   905
Hiroshige   1460
History of the Theatre Royal, The   x897
history, philosophy of   1570, 1867, 1989, 2169, 2170
Hitler, Adolf   1132
Hofmannsthal, Hugo von   906

Hogg, Thomas Jefferson   907
Hokusai   908
Holberg, Ludvig   909
Holmes, Edmond   910
Holmes, William Gordon   911
Holinshed Chronicles   2023
Holt, Joseph   912
Holy Bible, The   913
Homer   53, 914–16
Hone, Joseph Maunsell   917, 917a, 918–21, 921a–b
Hone, Nathaniel   922
Hooker, Richard   2239
Hopkins, Gerard Manley   923–24
Hopper, Nora   925, 925a
Horne, Herbert Percy   926
Horrwitz, Ernest Philip   927
Horton, William Thomas   928–30
Housman, Alfred Edward   931–33
Houston, Gertrude Craig   1800
Howell, John Cyril   934
Hsiung, Shih I.   935
Hubbell, Jay Broadus   936
Huc, Père   937, 937a
Hueffer, Ford Madox   938
Hügel, Friedrich von   939
Hughes, Richard   940, 940A
Hughes, Samuel Carlyle   941, 941a
Hugo, Victor   942–44, 2060
Hulme, Thomas Ernest   945
Hume, David   946
humor   349
Hungary   827
Husserl, Edmund   2947, 159
Hutchinson, Francis   948
Hütteman, Gerta   949
Huxley, Aldous   950
Hyde, Douglas   722, 951–52
Hymns to the Goddess   953
hypnotism   131, 1788
Hyslop, James Hervey   954

Iamblichus   955
Ibsen, Henrik   956–60

idealism, philosophical   30
Ilin, M. (Il'ya Yakovlevich Marshak)   961
L'Illustation   962
illumination (books)   277, 293, 1035, 1785
immortality   1389, 1390
Inchbald, Elizabeth   963
Indian art and architecture   440, 705, 868, 873, 1017, 2039
Indian history and politics   1796
Indian literature   607, 927, 953, 1061, 1429, 1541, 2137, 2213, 2219
Indian philosophy and religion   163, 529, 532, 705, 727, 747, 1067, 1068, 1547, 1672, 2047, 2119, 2128, 2136
Inge, William Ralph   964–65
Ingoldsby, Thomas   966
Innisfree, Lake Isle of   2158
Ireland   968–72, 987–94, 1821, 1823, 1825, 2084, 2231
Ireland To-Day   967
Irish antiquities   2231
Irish art *see* art—Irish
Irish ethnography   970, 974, 974a
Irish government   398, 781, 782, 973, 973a–b, 974, 974a, 975–76, 976a, 977–81
Irish history   274, 917, 1199, 1937, 2126
Irish Industries   982
Irish Literary Theatre   983
Irish literature in English   55, 832, 951, 1181, 1192, 1338 1493, 1784, 1834, 1971, 1982
   dramatic movement   190, 272, 1226, 2195
Irish mythology   342, 803, 806, 1057, 1058, 1210, 1323, 1475, 1476, 1499, 1500, 1501, 1502
Irish National Theatre, The   984
Irish Pleasantry and Fun   985
Irish politics   398, 827, 1179, 1337, 1503, 1822, 2255

Irish Renaissance   1084, 1835
Irish Review, The   986
Irish scenes   987–94
Irish Statesman, The   995–97, 997a–b, 998–99, 999a, 1000–1008, 1008a–b, 1009–11, 1011a, 1012–15
Irish tales   31, 470, 679, 680, 801, 811, 813, 821, 985, 2281, 2282
   see also Irish mythology, folktales, folklore
Irish Times, The   1016
Irving, Henry   278
Isherwood, Christopher   67
Italian literature   737, 738
Italian politics   737
Italy   737, x1668
   guidebooks to   73, 1472

Jacob, Lionel   1017
James I, King of Scotland   1018
James, William   1019–21
Jammes, Francis   1022–25
Japanese art *see* art—Japanese
Japanese culture   2046
Japanese drama   1026, 2156, 2157
Japanese literature   1079, 1081, 1086, 1745
Japanese religion   2490
Japanese sword   1457
Jews   126, 2153, 2154, 2245A
John, Augustus   537, 1341
John, Ivor Bertram   1027
John of the Cross, Saint   1028
Johnson, Lionel   175, 1029–34
Johnston, Edward   1035
Johnston, George Alexander   1036
Jones, Ernest   1037
Jones, Howard Mumford   1211
Jones, William   1038
Jonson, Ben   1039–44, 2061
Joseph, Horace William Brindley   1045
Josephson, Ernst   1046
Josephus   126

Jourdain, Eleanor Frances   1340
Journal of the Alchemical Society   1047–49
Jouve, Pierre Jean   1050
Joyce, James   1051–52, 1052a, 1053, x1043, x1043a, 1054–56
Jubainville, Henri D'Arbois de   1057–58
Julian the Emperor   1059
Jung, Carl Gustav   1060

Kabir   1061, 1061A
Kant, Immanuel   1062–63
Keats John   1064–66
Keith, Arthur Berriedale   1067–68
Kelleher, Daniel Lawrence   1069
Kenmore District   1239
Kennedy, James   1070
Khunrath, Henricus   1071
Kinder, Martin   1349
King, Henry   1072
King, Richard Ashe   1073
Kingsford, Anna Bonus   1074
Kingston, William Henry Giles   1075
Kingsway Theatre   1076
Kirby, William   1077
Kirk, Robert   1078
Ki Tsurayuki   1079
Knight, George Wilson   1080
Komusashinokami Minamoto no Moronao   1081
Kosor, Josip   1082
Kramer, Henry   1083
Krans, Horatio Sheafe   1084
Krishnamurti, M.   1085
Krop, Hildo   1456, 2127, 2305
Kurata, Hyakuzo   1086
Kyteler, Dame Alice   1107

Lamb, Charles   1088–89
Landor, Walter Savage   426, 703, 1090–94
Lane, Hugh   240, 802, 807, 1164
Lang, Andrew   1095

Larminie, William   1096
Larsson, Carl   1097
Laski, Harold Joseph   198
Last, Hugh   1099
Latin, translations from   28, 47
Lavery, Emmet   1100
Law, William   1101
Lawrence, Brother   1102
Lawrence, David Herbert   1103
Lawrence, Thomas Edward   1104
Lawrence, William John   1105–1106
Ledrede, Richard de   1107
Le Fanu   1108
Leinster, Edward Fitzgerald   1109
Leisure Hour, The   1110
Lempriere, John   1111
Lenin, Vladimir   1112, 1336
Leo, Alan   1113–15
Leo, John   1116
Lesage, Alain René   1117
Levi, Eliphaz   1118–19
Lewes, George Henry   1120
Lewis, Cecil Day   1121–24
Lewis, Matthew Gregory   1125
Lewis, Wyndham   1126–36
Lhote, André   1137
life after death, *see* afterlife
Life and Letters   1138–40
Life and Letters To-Day   1141
Light   1142–43
Liljefors, Bruno   1144
Limebeer, Ena   1145
Lindsay, Jack   1146–48
Lindsay, Norman   1148
Lindsay, Vachel   1149
Li-Po   1150
List of Books Published by the Dun Emer and the Cuala Press   1151
Listener, The   1152, 1152a, 1964
Litchfield, Frederick   1153
Little Review, The   1154
liturgical manuals   336, 648, 934, 1555, 1797
Living Theatre, The   1155

Lomax, John Avery   1156
Lombroso, Cesare   1157
London   1236, 1237, 2125
London Mercury, The   1158–62, 1162a, 1163, 1163a, 1164–65, 1165a–b
Londonderry, The Marchioness of   1166
Long, Haniel   1167
Longford, The Earl of   1168
Louis II of Bavaria   1650
Louis XIV of France   2223
Louvre   1169
Lucas, St. John   1170
Luce, Arthur   1171–72
Lucian   1173
Lucretius, Carus   1174, 1174A
Luther, Martin   1245
Lutoslawski, Wincenty   1175
Lyrics from the Chinese   1176
Lytton, Edward Bulwer   1177

Mabinogion, The   1027, 1178
Macardle, Dorothy   1179
Mac Cathmhaoil, Seosamh (Joseph Campbell)
MacDonagh, Michael   1191
MacDonagh, Thomas   1192–94
Macdonald, James   1195
Machiavelli   1204
Mackay, Eric   1205
Macleod, Fiona (William Sharp)   1206, 1206A, 1207–1209
Mac Mic Cuinn na M-Bocht, Moelmuiri   1210
MacMillan, Dougald   1211
MacMurrough, Art, King of Leinster   1199
MacNeice, Louis   1212, 1212a–b
Macpherson, James   1525
Madeleva, Sister Mary   1218–20
Maeterlinck, Maurice   1221
magic   138, 650, 675A, 1119, 1396, 2148, 2526

Mahaffy, John Pentland   1222
Mairet, Philippe   1223
Maitland, Francis   1224
Malebranche, Nicolas   1171
Mallarmé, Stephané   1224
Malone, Andrew E.   1226
Malory, Thomas   1227
Malta   668
Mangan, James Clarence   1492
Mannin, Ethel   1228
Manning, Frederic   1229
Manning-Sanders, Ruth   1230
Mantzius, Karl   1231
maps   1232–39
marching songs   1971
Mardrus, Joseph Charles   1240
Margaret [D'Angoulemne]   1241
Marillier, Henry   1242
Marionette, The   1243
Maritain, Jacques   1244–45
Marivaux, Pierre   1246
Marlowe, Christopher   1247, 1613
Marpicati, Arturo   1248
Marriott, Ernest   1249, 1249a
Marsh, Edward Howard   1250
Marston, John   1251
Martyn, Oliver (H. O. White)   1252
Marx, Karl and Marxism   454, 1045, 1112
Masefield, Constance   1277
Masefield, John   1253, 1253A, 1254–74, 1274a, 1275–77
Mask, The   1278–80, 1280a, 1281–98
masks   1459, 2305
Massinger, Philip   1299
Masters, Edgar Lee   1300
mathematics   316, 1966
Mathers, Edward Powys   1301–1304
Mathers, S. Liddell MacGregor   1305, 1305a, 1306
Maunsel, Joseph   1808
Maupassant, Guy de   1307
Maurois, Andre   1308
Mayne, Rutherford   1309

Mazzini, Joseph   1310
McCartan, Patrick   1180
McCarthy, Justin   1181
McCrae, Hugh   1183
McDougall, William   1196–98
McGreevy, Thomas   1200, 1200a, 1201–1203
McTaggart, John McTaggart Ellis   1213, 1213a, 1214–17
M'Diarmid, Hugh   1184–90
M'Gee, Thomas Darcy   1199
Mead, George Robert Stow   1311, x1299, 1312
Medici Prints   1313
medieval literature   2149
Medium and Daybreak, The   1314–16
mediums *see* spiritualism
Meinhold, William   1317, 1317A
Mercier, Cardinal (Désiré Félicien)   1318
Meredith, George   1319–20, 2027
Merry Devil of Edmonton, The   1321
Méryon, Charles   1322
Mestrovic, Ivan   467
metaphysical poetry   826
Meyer, Kuno   1323
Meyerstein, Edward Harry William   1324
Meynell, Everard   1325
Michelangelo   1326
Middle Ages   18, 735, 1234, 1876, 1953
Middle English literature   386
Milbanke, Ralph   1327
militarism   1195
Millay, Edna St. Vincent   1328–31
Millet, Jean-François   1879
Milton, John   1332–35, 1861
miracles   1792
Mirsky, Dmitri Svyatopolk   1336
Mitchel, John   1337
Mitchel, Susan   1338
Mitsuru, Yamamiya   1339

Moberly, Charlotte Anne
  Elizabeth   1340
modern art   2291
Modern British Painters   1341
modern poetry   1939
Molière   1342–44
Molinos, Michael de   1345, 1345a
Molmenti, Pompeo   1346
Monck, Walter Nugent   1347–49
Monro, Harold   1350–54
Montagu, Mary Wortley   1355
Montaigne   1356–57
Montfaucon de Villars, Nicolas
  de   1358
Moore, Francis   1359–60
Moore, George   918, 1361–70
Moore, Thomas Sturge   1371–72,
  x1360, 1373–88
More, Henry   1389–92, 2242
More, Thomas   1393
More Ancient Carols   1394
Morgan, Arthur Eustace   1395
Morley, Henry   1396
Mormonism   2118
Morrell, Ottoline   1397
Morris, Herbert Newall   1398
Morris, William   168, 1399–1408
mosaics   734
Moses, William Stanton   1409
mountain climbing   876, 2161
Muirhead, John Henry   1410–12
Murasaki, Lady   1413–16
Murdock, Walter   1417
Murray, Alexander Stuart   1418
Murray, Margaret Alice   1419–20
Murray, Thomas Cornelius   1421
Musset, Alfred de   1422, 1422a
Mussolini, Benito   1423
Mylne, Robert Scott   1424
mysticism   531, 605, 825, 835, 939,
  1028, 1102, 1221, 1345, 2044, 2208
mythology   671, 861, 952, 1475, 1476,
  1477, 1963

Naidu, Sarojini   1425–27
Napoleon Bonaparte   113
Nandikesvara   1429
Nares, Robert   1428
Nation, The   1430, 1430a–b
National Gallery of Ireland   977, 978
National Observer, The   1431–32,
  x1421, x1421a–d, x1422
National Theatre Society   1433,
  1433a–b
natural history   770, 829, 969, 1077,
  2299
Nero and Other Plays   1434, 1434A
Nettleship, John Trivett   1435
Nevinson, Henry Wood   1436
Newman, John Henry, Cardinal   1437
Newson, Ranald   1438–40
Newton, Isaac   899, 1441
Nichols, Robert   1442–45, 1445a–b,
  1446, 2160
Nietzsche, Friedrich   837, 1447–55
Nieuwe rotterdamsche courant   1456
Nippon toh (Japanese Sword)   1457
Nobel Prize   x1847, 2442
Noel, Roden   1458
Nogaka-komen shu   1459
Noguchi, Yone   1460–66
Noh drama   1648, 2234
Noh masks   1459
Norman, A. O.   1467
Norman castles   51
Norstedt, P. A.   1468
Notzing, Baron von Schrenck   1469
Novalis (Friedrich von
  Hardenberg)   1470
Noyes, Alfred   1471
Noyes, Ella   1472
Nuovo dizionario tascabile   1473
Nutbrown Maid, The   1474
Nutt, Alfred   1475, 1475a, 1476,
  1476a, 1477

O'Brien, Richard Barry   1478
obscenity   401

O'Byrne, Dermot   1479, 1479a
O'Casey, Sean   1480–81, 1481a, 1482, 1482a
OConnell, J. B.   1483
O'Connor, Frank   1484–87, 1487a–b
occult   513, 655, 691, 739, 1074, 1142, 1143, 1311, x1311, 1789, 1790, 1792, 1874, 2163
occult philosophy   124, 125, 464, 1396
O'Curry, Eugene   x1477, x1478
O'Donnell, F. Hugh   1488
O'Donnell, Peadar   1489–90
O'Donoghue, David James   1491–93
O'Faoláin, Seán   1494
O Faracháin, Roibeárd (Robert Farren)   1495
O'Flaherty, Liam   1496–98
O'Grady, Standish   1499–1502
O'Hegarty, Patrick Sarsfield   1503
old age   1866
Old Vic and Sadler's wells   1504
Oliphant, Laurence   1505
O'Malley, Ernie   1506
Omar Khayyam   1507–1509
O'Neill, Eugene   1510–13
O'Neill, Joseph   1514
O'Neill, Mary Davenport   1515
O'Neill, Moira   1516
O'Neill, Owen Roe   2126
Orage, Alfred Richard   1517
O'Rahilly, Egan   1518
Oriental art   201
Orion's Prophetic Guide   1519–20
Ormonde, Duke of   312
O'Rourke, Horace Tennyson   1521
Osborne, Dorothy   1522
O'Sheel, Shaemas   1523
Oshima, Shōtāro   1524–27
Ossendowski, Ferdinand   1528
Osty, Eugene   1529
O'Sullivan, Seaumas   1530
O'Sullivan, Vincent   1531
Otto, Rudolf   1532
Owen, John   936

Owlett, Frederick Charles   1533
Oxford Book of Modern Verse, The   x528, 1621, x1986, x2154, x2161

Page, H. A. (Alexander Hay Japp)   1534
Pageant, The   1535, x1526a
painting   360, 745, 1109
  American   339
  British   1341
  dictionaries of   308
  French   442, 1137, 1663, 1879
  histories of   335
Palmer, Herbert Edward   1536–40
Panchatantra and Hitopadesa Stories   1541
Parables from the Gospels, The   1542
Paracelsus (Theophrastus von Hohenheim)   863, 1543
Paris   1322
Parnell, Charles Stewart   859, 1478
Partridge, John   1544
Patanjali, Bhagwan Shree   1545, 1545a–b, 1546–47
Pater, Walter   186–87, 1548–53
Patrick, Saint   49, 315, 1554
Paul, Saint   1575
Paul V, Pope   1555
Pausanias   1556
Pauw, Cornelius de   1557
Peacock, Thomas Love   1558
Pearce, Alfred John   1559
Pearse, Padraic Henry   1560
Pearse, Salem   1561
Péguy, Charles   1562–63
Penny, Anne Judith   1564
People's National Theatre Magazine   1565
Percival, Milton Oswin   1566
Percy, Thomas   1567
Persian Art   1568
Persian art *see* art—Persian
Petrarch   1569

Petrie, William Mathew   1570, 1570a
Petronius   1571–72
Petrovitch, Woislav Maximus   1573
Philalethes, Eugenius (Thomas
  Vaughan)   1574
Philip II of Spain   1649
Phillimore, Cecily   1575
philosophy   237, 1244, 1815, 2122,
  2187, 2274
  British   1411, 1412
  contemporary   261, 276, 447, 1038,
    1215, 1411, 1412, 2159
  German   1038, 2159
  Greek   316
  history of   652
  Italian   447
  moral   1972
  natural   1653
  scholastic   1318
Philpotts, Eden   1576
Phoenix Libraries, The   1577
Pico Della Mirandola   1578
Piccoli, Raffaello   1579
Picture of Dublin, The   1580
Pirandello, Luigi   1581–94
Pitt, Ruth J.   1595
Pius X, Pope   1596
Plarr, Victor   1597
Plato and platonism   965, 1549, 1598–
  99, 1599A, 2121, 2123, 2124, 2242
Plautus   1600
Plotinus   964, 1601–1607
Plunket, Emmeline Mary   1608
Plutarch   1609–11, 1611a
Poe, Edgar Allan   1612
Poël, William   1613
*Poems and Ballads of Young
  Ireland*   1614
Poetry   1615–17, 1617a, 1618, 1618a,
  1619, x1608, 1620–21
Poland   1853
Pomposa   22
Pope, Alexander   1938
Porphyry   1622

Potocki, Geoffrey   1623
Pound, Ezra   138, 365, 627, 1624–30,
  1630a, 1631–35, 1635a, 1636–40,
  1640a, 1641, 1641a, 1642–45, 1645a,
  1646–48
Pourtalès, Guy de   1650
pre-existence   1175, 2116
Pre-Raphaelites   128
Prescott, William Hickling   1649
Prévost d'Exiles, Antoine
  François   1651
primitive culture   2187
Prior, James   1652
Privat-Deschanel, Augustin   1653
*Proceedings of the Society for Psychical
  Research*   1654
Prokosch, Frederic   1655–58
Propertius et al.   1659
Prophetia et alia   1660
Protocol Forgery, The   2153, 2154,
  2245A
Provence   704
Psalms of David, The   1661
psychic phenomena   39, 1142, 1143,
  1757, 1966, 2192
psychoanalysis   1037
psychology   1060, 1197
Ptolemy   1662
Puvis de Chavannes   1663
Pythagoras   398

Quiller-Couch, Arthur Thomas   1664,
  1664a, 1665, x1654, 1666
*"Quinn" Catalogue of First
  Editions*   1667, 1667a–b, 1668,
Quinn, John   1669, 1669a–b

Rabelais, Francis   1670
Racine, Jean   1671
Radhakrishnan, Sarvepalli   1672
Raphael (Robert C. Smith   1673–77,
  1677a–b, 1678–88, 1688a–b, 1689,
  x1681, 1690–91, 1691a–c, 1692,
  1692a, 1693–1705, 1705a, 1706–1709,

INDEX   297

1709a, 1710, 1710a, 1711, 1711a,
  1712, 1712a, 1713–16, 1716a–c, 1717,
  1717a, 1718, 1718a–b, 1719–20,
  1720a, 1721–25, 1725a, 1726–27,
  1727a, 1728, 1728a, 1729–30, 1730a,
  1731, 1731a, 1732–39
Rapallo   36
Ravenna   734, 1740
Raymond, Jean Paul   1741
Read, Herbert   1742–43
Reade, Winwood   1744
Redesdale (Algernon B. F.
  Mitford)   1745
Redford, George   1746
Reid, Forrest   1747
Reinach, Salomon   1748
reincarnation   1175
Reinhardt, Max   1864
relativity   621, 1814, 2206
religion   1095, 1505, 1532, 1755, 1768, 2187
Renaissance   1550, 2062
  emblems   132
Renan, Ernest   1749
Renier, Gustaaf Johannes   1750
Restoration literature   1277, 1751, 1946
Revue anglo-americaine   1752
Reynolds, John Hamilton   1753
Rhys, Ernest   1754
Rhys, John   1755
Richardson, Samuel   1756
Richet, Charles   1757
Richter, Helene   1758
Ricketts, Charles   1759–63
Riding, Laura   1764–65
Rilke, Rainer Maria   1800
Rivoallan, A.   1766
Robertson, Eric Sutherland   1767
Robinson, John Mackinnon   1768
Robinson, Edwin Arlington   1769–70
Robinson, Forbes   1771
Robinson, Lennox   x6, 1772–76, 1776a, 1777–80, x1766, 1781–84, 1784a

Robinson, Stanford Frederick   1785
Robson, Vivian Erwood   1786–87
Rochas, Albert de   1788–92
Rodker, John   1793
Rolfe, Fr. (Frederick, Baron
  Corvo)   1794
Rolland, Romain   1795–96
romances   2260, 2261
Roman Missal, The   1797
Roman philosophy and religion   466, 842, 878, 2028
Romanticism   2075
Ronsard, Pierre de   1798
Roosval, Johnny et al.   1799
Rose, William   1800
Rosen, Georg Von   1801
Rosenberg, Adolf   1802
Rosicrucianism   739, 2228
Rossetti, Christina   1803
Rossetti, Dante Gabriel   165–66, 1242, 1804–1806
Rossi, Mario Manlio   1807–1808
Roth, William M.   1809, 1809a–d
Rousseau, Jean-Jacques   1245
Rowley, Richard   1810
Ruddock, Margot   728, 1115, 1811
*Rules of the Irish Academy of
  Letters*   1812
Russell, Archibald George
  Blomefield   1813
Russell, Bertrand   1814–15
Russell, George (Æ)   1467, 1816–21, 1821A, 1822–34, 1834A, 1835–43, 1843a–c, 1844, 1985
Ruysbroeck, John   1221

sagas   1407, 1408
sailing   75, 875
Sackville-West, Vita   1854
Sanctis, Francesco de   1845
Sandars, Mary Frances   1846
Sanderson, Robert   2239
Santayana, George   1847
Santesson, Carl Gustaf   x1831

Sa'di 1848
An Saorstat [The Free State] x1833, x1834
Sappho 1849–50
Sardou, Victorien et al. 1851
Sarolea, Charles 1852–53
Sassoon, Siegfried 1855–59
Saurat, Denis 1860–63
Sayler, Oliver Martin 1864
Scherer, Valentin 1865
Schmidt, Peter M. D. 1866
Schneider, Hermann 1867
Schnitzler, Arthur 1868
Schopenhauer, Arthur 1869–70
science, history of 899
Scot, Reginald 1871
Scott, Geoffrey 1872
Scott, Walter 1873–74, 1874A
Scottish literature 879, 2251
scriptures 427, 709, 913, 1771, 1875
sculpture 61, 1418, 1746
Seanad Éireann 980, 981
Sei Shonagon 1877
Seignobos, Charles 1876
Selden, John 1878
Sensier, Alfred 1879
Sepharial (Walter Gorn Old) 1880–83
Sepher Yetzirah 23, 1884
Serbian tales 1573
Seurat, Georges-Pierre 442, 1137
Shakespear, Olivia 676, 1885–88
Shakespeare, William 275, 622, 1080, 1089, 1105, 1106, 1274, 1428, 1474, 1613, 1889–95, 1962, 2023, 2152, 2155
  and Ireland 123
Shanachie, The 1896, 1896a, 1897–1900
Sharp, Elizabeth 1901
Sharp, William 1902
Shaw, George Bernard 1903–15
Shelley, Percy Bysshe 907, 1916–24, 2027

Sherard, Robert Harborough 1925
Shih Ching 1176
Sibly, Ebenezer 1926
Sidgwick, Frank 1927–29
Sidney, Philip 1930–31
Sidonia the Sorceress 1317
Sigerson, Dora (Mrs. Clement Shorter) 1932–34
Sigerson, George 1935
Simmonite, William Joseph 1936
Sinn Fein 1503, 1937
Sitwell, Edith 1938–47, 1949
Sitwell, Osbert 1947–49
Sitwell, Sacheverell 1947, 1949–56, 1956a, 1957–58
Skeat, Walter 1959
Skelton, Philip 311
skepticism 162
Skipsey, Joseph 1960
Slater, Montagu 1961
Smart, John Semple 1962
Smith, Grafton Elliot 1963
Smith, Janet Adam 1964
Smith, William 1965
Smith, W. Whately 1966
Smollett, Tobias George 1967–71
socialism 1907
Solovyoff, Vladimir 1972
songs 682, 1156, 1394, 1971, 1982, 2137
Sophocles 419, 1973–80
Southern Review, The 1981
Spanish history 1649
Sparling, Henry Halliday 1982
Spectator, The 1983–86, x1972
Spence, William 1077
Spender, Stephen 1987–88
Spengler, Oswald 688, 762, 1989, 1989A
Spenser, Edmund 507, 1990–92, 1992A–D
spiritualism 24, 119, 138, 202, 460, 513, 525, 527, 545, 650, 691, 760, 1157, 1314, 1315, 1316, 1340, 1409,

1469, 1529, 1654, 1741, 1757, 2212, 2294
Spoelberch de Lovenjoul, Charles 1993
Sprenger, James 1083
Squire, John Collings 1994–96
staging, including design 445, 2150, 2152, 2155, 2156, 2157
Stalin, Joseph 1997
Star, The x1984
Stead, William Force 1998–99, 1999a, 2000–2004
Steinach Operation 1866
Stenbock, Count Stanislaus Eric 2005
Stendhal 2006–08
Stephen, Leslie 2009
Stephens, James 2010–17, 2017a, 2018–19
Sterne, Laurence 2020
Stevens, Wallace 2021
Stockholm 1799
Stoicism 162
Stokes, Margaret 2022
Stone, Walter George Boswell
Story, John 2024
Strachey, Lytton 2025–26
Stratford-on-Avon 1232
Strindberg, August 2193
Strong, Archibald 2027
Strong, Mrs. Arthur (Eugenie [Sellers]) 2028
Strong, Leonard Alfred George 2029–36, x2024, 2037
Strzygowski, Josef 2038–39
Stuart, H. Francis 2040, 2040a–c
Sturm, Frank Pearce 2041–42
Suckling, John 2043
Sufism 835
superstitions 2282
Sutherland, Alexander Charles 2044
Suzuki, Daisetz Teitaro 2045–46
Swami, Shri Purohit 2047, 2047a
Swedenborg, Emanuel 1398, 2048–51, 2051A, 2052, 2052A–D, 2243

Swedenborgianism 2311
Swedish art and architecture 656, 104–106, 1097, 1144, 1468, 1799, 1801, 2293
Swift, Jonathan 74, 833, 1073, 1168, 1808, 2009, 2053–55, 2297
Swinburne, Algernon Charles 167, 184, 187, 2056–60
symbolism 474, 761, 1080, 2081
Symonds, John Aldington 2061–62
Symons, Alphonse James Albert 2063, 2063a, 2064
Symons, Arthur 171, 2065–83
Synge, John Millington 188–90, x834, 2084–87, 2087a, 2088–91
Syrian gods 1878

Tagore, Rabindranath 2092–98, x2084, 2099–2115, 2115A
Taki, Sei-ichi et al. 2116
Tale of King Florus and the Fair Jehane, The 2117
Talmage, James 2118
Tantra of the Great Liberation 2119
Tarot 1118
Tasso, Torquato 2120
Taylor, Alfred Edward 2121–24
Taylor, George Robert Sterling 2125
Taylor, John Francis 2126, 2126a
De telegraff 2127
Temple, Sir William 1522
Ten Principal Upanishads, The 2128, 2128a, 2128A
Tennyson, Alfred 2129
Teresa of Jesus, Saint 2130–34
theater *see* drama
Theatre of the Greeks, The 2135
Theognis 499
theosophy 955, 1118, 1119, 1306, 2242
Thirteen Principal Upanishads, The 2136
Thirty Songs from the Punjab and Kashmir 2137

Thomas, Dylan   2138
Thomas, G. Bevan   2139
Thomas, Edward   2140
Thompson, Francis   1325, 2141–42, 2142a, 2143–46, 2146a
Thoreau, Henry David   1534, 2147
Thorndike, Lynn   2148
Three Chester Whitsun Plays   2149
Tibet   876, 937, 2161
Tibetan religion   2259
time   600
Times, The   2150–54, x2141, 2156–58
Times Literary Supplement, The   2159–61, x2149, 2162
Titian (Tiziano Vecellio)   1762
Titis, Placidus de   2163
To-Day   2164
Todhunter, John   2165
Toller, Ernst   2166
Toorop, Jan   2167
Tosca (opera)   1851
Touchstone 6, The   2168
Tourneur, Cyril   2244
Towner, Rutherford Hamilton   2169
Toynbee, Arnold Joseph   2170
tragedy   2196
Traité sommaire d'astologie scientifique   2171
travel *see* guidebooks
Trent, A. G. (Richard Garnett)   2172, 2172a–b
Turner, G. W.   2173
Turner, Walter James   2174–84, 2184a, 2185–86
Tylor, Edward Burnett   2187
Tynan, Katharine   2188–91
typography   759
Tyrrell, George Nugent Merle   2192

Uddgren, Gustaf   2193
Ukiyo-e taikashusei   2194
Ukiyoye primitives   1466
Ulad   2195, 2195a
Ulster Literary Theatre   2195

Unamuno, Miguel de   2196
Ure, Percy Neville   2197
U.S.S.R. (Soviet Union)   758, 961, 1528, 1852, 1997, 2151
political philosophy of   155
utopian literature   613, 1393

Vale Press   1759
Valéry, Paul   2199–2203
VanBrugh, John   2204
Vasari, Giorgio   2205
Vasiliev, Aleksandr Vasilevich   2206
Vaughan, Henry   2207
Vaughan, Robert Alfred   2208
Verhaeren, Émile   2209–10
Venice   1346
Verona   1238, 2211, 2279
versification   280, 1194
Vesme, Caesar de   2212
Vico, Giambattista   456
Victoria (queen)   2026
Vidyapati   2213
Viélé-Griffin, Francis   2214
vikings   596
Villiers de l'Isle Adam, Comte   2215–16
Virgil   2217–18
Visva-Bharati Quarterly   2219
Volpe, Gioacchino   2220
Voltaire (François-Marie Arouet)   1308, 2221–23
von Werner, Anton   1802

Wade, Allan   2224–25
Wagner, Richard   1454, 2226
Waite, Arthur Edward   2227–29
Waite, Herbert T.   2230
Wakeman, William Frederick   2231
Waley, Arthur   2232–35
Walker, Emery   2236
Wallace, William   2237
Walpole, Horace   800, 2238
Walton, Izaak   2239–40
Ward, Adolphus William   2241

Ward, Richard   2242
Warren, Samuel   2243
Webster, John   2244
Webster, Nesta Helen   2245, 2245A
Weekes, Charles   2247
Weekly Sun Literary Supplement   x2232
Weichardt, Carl   2250
Weird Tales: Scottish   2251
Wellesley, Dorothy   2252, 2252a–c, 2253, 2253a–b, 2254
Wells, Warre Bradley   2255
Welsh literature   1754
Wentz, Walter Yeeling Evans   2256–59
Weston, Jessie Laidlay   2260–62
Whigs   800
Whistler, James Abbott McNeill   2263, 2289
Whistler, Laurence   2264–65
White, Robert   2266–73
Whitehead, Alfred North   2274
Whitman, Walt   2275–77
Who's Who, Literary   70
Wicksteed, Joseph Hartley   2278
Wiel, Alethea   2279
Wijdeveld, Henricus Theodorus   2280
Wilde, Jane Francesca Speranza   2281–82
Wilde, Oscar   1750, 1925, 2283–89
Wilenski, Reginald Howard   2290–91
Wilhelm, Theodor   2292
Wilhelmson, Carl   2293
Wilkinson, James John Garth   2294
William Butler Yeats, Aetat. 70   2295–96
Williams, Harold   2297
Williams, Rose Sickler et al.   2298
Wilson, Andrew   2299
Wilson, Harriette   2300
Wilson, James   2301
Wilson, Mona   2302
Wilson, Robert Noble   2303
Wilson, Robin   2304
Windingen   2305–2306

witchcraft   138, 670, 760, 948, 1107, 1317, 1419, 1871, 1874, 1874A
Wolfe, Humbert   2307–2308
Wollstonecraft, Mary   2309
women   830
Wood, Charles Erskine Scott   2310
Worcester, John   2311
Wordsworth, William   2027, 2312–14
Wotten, Henry   2239, 2241
Wren Boys, The   2315
Wright, Thomas   2316–17
Wycherley, William   2318, 2318a
Wylie, Elinor   2319–21
Wynne, Frances   2322

Yale Review, The   2323–24
Yashiro, Yukio   2325
Yeats, Jack B.   1249, 1249a, 1282, 1288, 2326, 2330, 2330a, 2331
Yeats, John Butler   922, 2332, x2312, x2313
Yeats, William Butler
   items about   x6, 203, 250, 920, 949, 1084, 1465, 1488, 1526, 1527, 1669, 1747, 1752, 1807, 2162, x2247, 2295, 2323
   items written or edited by   2333–34, 2334a, 2335–38, x2319a–b, 2339, 2339a–c, 2340–43, 2343a, 2343A, 2344, 2344a–b, x2323c, 2344A, 2345–46, 2346A, 2347–54, 2354a–d, 2355, 2355a–b, 2356–58, 2358a, 2359–61, x2340a–b, 2363, x2342a, 2364–65, 2365a, 2366, 2366a–b, x2345c, 2367–68, 2368a, 2369–73, 2373a–b, 2374–76, 2376a, x2354b–c, 2377, 2377a, x2355b, 2378–80, 2380a–b, 2381, 2382, 2382a, 2383, 2383a–c, x2361d–f, 2384, 2384a, x2362b, 2385–88, 2388a, x2365b, 2389–91, 2391a, 2392, x2369a–d, 2392a, 2393, 2393a, x2370b, 2394–97,

2397a–c, x2374d–e, 2398–99,
x2375a–e, 2400–2401, 2401a,
x2377b–c, 2402–2404, 2404a–c,
x2380c, 2405, 2405a–d, 2406,
2406a–d, 2407, 2407a, 2408–16,
x2390a–f, 2417, x2391a–c,
2418, 2418a–b, x2392c–d, 2419,
x2393a–c, 2420, 2420a, 2421–22,
2422a, 2423, 2423a–b, 2424,
2424a, x2398b, 2425, 2425a, 2426,
2426a–b, 2427–30, 2430a, 2431,
2431a, 2432–38, 2438a, 2439–41,
x2410a–f, 2442, x2411a–c,
2443, x2412b, 2444, 2444a–b,
2445, x2413a, 2446–47, 2447a,
2448–49, 2449a–c, 2450–52,
2452a–b, 2453, x2421a–I, 2454,
2454a–d, x2422e–g, 2455,
2455a–c, 2456, 2456a–c, 2457–58,
2458a, x2426b, x2427, 2459–61,
2461a, 2462a–c, 2463, x2430a–b,
2463a–d, 2464, 2464a–b, 2465,
2465a, x2433, 2466, 2466a–b,
2467–70, 2470a–e, 2471, 2471a,
x2437a, 2472–75, 2475a, 2476,
2476a, x2443, 2477, 2477a–c,
2478, 2478a, 2479, 2479a–c,
2480, x2447a, 2481, 2481a–d,
2482, 2482a, x2449b–c, 2483–84,
2484a–b, 2485, 2485a–b, 2486,
x2454, 2487, x2454b, 2487a–c,
2488
yoga 1545, 1547
Yonge, Charlotte Mary 2489
Yoshida, Kenko 2490
Young Ireland 599, 1614

Zachrisson, Valdemar 2491
Zadkielis Astronomical Ephemeris 2492–2513, x2481, 2514,
x2483, 2515–17, 2517a, 2518–19,
2519a–b, 2520, 2520a, 2521–24
Zola, Emile 2525
Zoroaster, the Magician 2526

www.ingramcontent.com/pod-product-compliance
Lightning Source LLC
Chambersburg PA
CBHW021346300426
44114CB00012B/1095